The Problem with Boys' Education

This book offers an illuminating analysis of the theories, politics, and realities of boys' education around the world—an insightful and often disturbing account of various educational systems' successes and failings in fostering intellectual and social growth in male students. Examining original research on the impact of implementing boys' education programs in schools, the book also discusses the role of male teachers in educating boys, strategies for aiding marginalized boys in the classroom, and the possibilities for gender reform in schools that begins at the level of pedagogy.

Complete with case studies of various classrooms, school districts, and governmental policy programs, the collected detailed essays provide a look into education's role in the development of masculinities, paying special attention to the ways in which these masculinities intersect with race, class, and sexuality to complicate the experience of boys within and outside of a classroom setting.

Wayne Martino is Professor of Education in the Faculty of Education at the University of Western Ontario, Canada. His research interests are in the field of gender equity, masculinities, and anti-oppressive education. He is currently working with Goli Rezai-Rashti on a research project funded by the SSHRC (Social Science Humanities Research Council of Canada) entitled, *The influence of male teachers in elementary schools*.

Michael Kehler is an Associate Professor currently teaching in the preservice and graduate education program at the University of Western Ontario. His research interests include the counter-hegemonic practices of high school young men, literacies, masculinities, and the ongoing negotiations involved for young men resisting heteronormativity.

Marcus B. Weaver-Hightower is an Assistant Professor of Educational Foundations and Research at the University of North Dakota (United States), where he teaches graduate courses in gender and education, action research, the sociology of education, and ethnographic research. He is a former Fulbright scholar to Australia, where he conducted a year-long study of the development and implementation of the first federal-level policy on the education of boys. His research interests include the politics of boys' education concerns, masculinity studies, literacy, qualitative and action research, and cultural studies.

The Problem with Boys' Education
Beyond the Backlash

Edited by Wayne Martino,
Michael Kehler, and
Marcus B. Weaver-Hightower

Routledge
Taylor & Francis Group

NEW YORK AND LONDON

First published 2009
by Routledge
270 Madison Ave, New York, NY 10016

Simultaneously published in the UK
by Routledge
2 Park Square, Milton Park, Abingdon, Oxon OX14 4RN

Routledge is an imprint of the Taylor & Francis Group, an informa business

© 2009 Taylor & Francis

Typeset in Sabon by
HWA Text and Data Management, London
Printed and bound in the United States of America on acid-free paper by
TBT Global

Library of Congress Cataloging in Publication Data
The problem with boys' education: beyond the backlash / edited by Wayne
    Martino, Michael Kehler, and Marcus Weaver-Hightower.
        p. cm.
    Includes bibliographical references and index.
    1. Boys–Education. 2. Sex differences in education. 3. Men–Identity.
    I. Martino, Wayne. II. Kehler, Michael. III. Weaver-Hightower, Marcus B.
    LC1390.P76 2009
    371.823´41–dc22   2008048437

ISBN10: 1-56023-682-5 (hbk)
ISBN10: 1-56023-683-3 (ebk)
ISBN10: 0-203-87771-3 (ebk)

ISBN13: 978-1-56023-682-5 (hbk)
ISBN13: 978-1-56023-683-2 (pbk)
ISBN13: 978-0-203-87771-5 (ebk)

Contents

Contributors

Rebecca Priegert Coulter is Professor and Director of Aboriginal Education in the Faculty of Education at The University of Western Ontario, Canada. Her research interests include the history of Canadian education; policy, power, and politics in education; and gender and education. She is co-editor, with Helen Harper, of *History is hers: Women educators in twentieth-century Ontario*.

Becky Francis is Professor of Education at Roehampton University, UK. Her expertise centers on the production of subjectivities in educational contexts, social identity and educational achievement, and feminist theory, and she has published widely in these areas. Her recent authored books include *Feminism and the schooling scandal* (Routledge, 2009), *Reassessing gender and achievement* (Routledge, 2005, both with Christine Skelton) and *Understanding minority ethnic achievement: Race, gender, class and 'success'* (Routledge, 2007, with Louise Archer). She has also co-edited several readers on theory and practice in gender and education, including the *Sage handbook of gender and education* (2006).

Carl E. James teaches in the Faculty of Education and in the graduate program in sociology at York University, UK. He takes an interdisciplinary approach to his work; however, his background in sociology informs his teaching and research and the insights he provides. A former youth worker, he teaches courses in urban education, adolescence, and foundations of education, among others and, in his research and publications, he explores issues of identity/identification in terms of race, ethnicity, gender, class, and citizenship/immigrant status; educational and occupational access and equity for marginalized youth; and the complementary and contradictory nature of sports in the schooling and educational attainments of racialized students. His publications include *Race in play: The socio-cultural worlds of student athletes* (2005); *Possibilities and limitations: Multicultural policies and programs in Canada* (2005); *Seeing ourselves: Exploring race, ethnicity and culture* (2003).

Michael Kehler is an Associate Professor in the Faculty of Education at The University of Western Ontario, Canada. His research interests include the counter-hegemonic practices of high school young men, literacies, and the intersection of masculinities, health, body image, and schooling. His research has been published in a range of journals, including *Journal of Curriculum Theorizing; Discourse: Studies in the Cultural Politics of Education; McGill Journal of Education; Educational Review; Taboo; Education and Society;* and *The International Journal of Inclusive Education.* He has contributed chapters in two books, *Masculinities and schooling: International practices and perspectives* (Althouse Press) and *Boys, girls and the myths of literacies and learning* (CSPI/Women's Press). He is currently working with Michael Atkinson and Kevin Wamsley on a project funded by the SSHRC (Social Science Humanities Research Council). This latest research examines why some adolescent boys are reluctant to participate in health and physical education.

Michael Kimmel is Professor of Sociology at SUNY Stony Brook, USA. Author or editor of more than twenty volumes, his books include *Changing men: New directions in research on men and masculinity* (1987); *Men confront pornography* (1990); *The politics of manhood* (1996); *The gender of desire* (2005); and *The history of men* (2005). His documentary history, *Against the tide: Pro-feminist men in the United States, 1776–1990* (Beacon, 1992), chronicled men who supported women's equality since the founding of the country. His recent work includes *Manhood in America: A cultural history* (Oxford, 2006, 10th anniversary edition) and *Guyland: The perilous world where boys become men* (HarperCollins, 2008), from which this chapter is adapted.

James R. King is a professor of Literacy Studies in the College of Education at the University of South Florida in Tampa, USA. His research is premised on queer theorizing about the reconceptualization of early childhood education and updating literacy with multimodal discourses. His publications include *Uncommon caring*, a book published in 1998, which addresses the significance of masculinities and sexuality in male elementary school teachers' lives. He has also published in a range of journals, including *Reading Research Quarterly; Journal of Literacy Research; Qualitative Studies in Education; Contemporary Ethnography; Journal of Adult and Adolescent Literacy; and Reading Research and Instruction,* and has chapters in several edited volumes.

Peter Kuriloff earned his doctorate in counseling psychology at Harvard and is a fellow of the American Psychological Association in School Psychology. He has taught at the Graduate School of Education (GSE) of the University of Pennsylvania since 1970 and twice chaired the Psychology in Education Division. He moved to the Foundations and Practices of Education Division in 1992. Besides teaching at the GSE, Dr. Kuriloff is the senior advisor on Group Effectiveness and Career Development in Wharton's Executive MBA program. His research interests include gender dynamics (masculinities, femininities, and school gender "offers") and their impact on the opportunities of children, and in general, the reinvention of schools as more inclusive, open, generous, and effective places for the children who inhabit them. In his capacity as research director of the Center for the Study of Boys' and Girls' Lives (www.csbgl.org), he fosters teacher-initiated research to discover and implement best educational practices for boys and girls.

Wayne Martino is Professor of Education in the Faculty of Education at The University of Western Ontario, Canada. His research interests are in the field of gender equity, masculinities, and anti-oppressive education. His books include *What about the boys?* (with Bob Meyenn, Open University Press); *Boys' stuff: Boys talking about what matters* (with Pallotta-Chiarolli, Allen & Unwin); *So what's a boy? Addressing issues of masculinity and schooling* (with Maria Pallotta-Chiarolli, Open University Press); *'Being normal is the only way to be': Adolescent perspectives on gender and school* (with Maria Pallotta-Chiarolli, University of New South Wales Press); and *Gendered outcasts and sexual outlaws: Sexual oppression and gender hierarchies in queer men's lives* (with Christopher Kendall, Haworth Press). His latest book (with Bob Lingard and Martin Mills) is *Boys and schooling: Beyond structural reform* (Palgrave). He is currently working with Goli Rezai-Rashti on a research project funded by the SSHRC (Social Science Humanities Research Council of Canada) entitled, "The influence of male teachers in elementary schools."

Lance T. McCready is Assistant Professor of Urban Education at the Ontario Institute for Studies in Education at the University of Toronto, Canada. He received his doctorate in Social and Cultural Studies with a Designated Emphasis in Women, Gender, and Sexuality Studies from the University of California, Berkeley. He teaches School and Society in the inner-city-focused cohort of the Secondary Initial Teacher Education program and a graduate course on intersectional perspectives in urban education for the new M.Ed. cohort in urban education. His research and writing focus on curricular and pedagogical issues in urban education, specifically "making space" for diverse masculinities in urban schools and the experiences of queer youth of color. A book-length manuscript in preparation looks at the ways gay and gender nonconforming black male students negotiate the sociopolitical environment of a racially segregated high school in Northern California.

Martin Mills is a Professor in the School of Education, The University of Queensland, Australia. He teaches and researches in the areas of gender and education and school reform and pedagogy. His recent books are *Challenging violence in schools: An issue of masculinities* (2001); *Leading learning: Making hope practical in schools* (2003); and *Teachers making a difference: Productive pedagogies, assessment and performance*. The latter two are co-authored. His 2006 book with Amanda Keddie is entitled *Teaching boys: Classroom practices that work*.

Anoop Nayak is Reader in Social and Cultural Geography at Newcastle University, UK. He research interests lie in the field of race and ethnic studies; masculinities and gender; and youth and cultural studies. He is author of the monograph *Race, place and globalization: Youth cultures in a changing world* (2003, Oxford: Berg) and a recent book with Mary Jane Kehily entitled *Gender, youth and culture: Young masculinities and femininities* (2008, Basingstoke: Palgrave).

Michael C. Reichert has specialized in work with children, families, and males in a clinical and consulting practice for the past 25 years. He created and served as director of an urban youth development program and currently serves as executive director of the Center for the Study of Boys' and Girls' Lives, a research collaborative composed of independent schools operating in partnership with the University of Pennsylvania. He has consulted with and conducted training for many organizations and schools and is currently on staff at The Haverford School outside of Philadelphia. Current research interests include the impact of gender curricula on boys' and girls' lives, strategies to mobilize schools as sites of gender possibility, and developmental trajectories toward violence. He has developed the Boys' and Girls' Audit as a methodology to help improve self-awareness.

Emma Renold is senior lecturer in Childhood Studies at the Cardiff School of Social Sciences, Cardiff University Wales, UK. She is co-editor of the international journal *Gender and Education* and convenor of the sexualities special interest group for the British Education Research Association. Working at the intersection of queer and feminist poststructuralist theory, her research has explored the gendering and sexualization of U.K. childhoods across diverse institutional sites and public spaces. These key areas are explored in her recent book, *Girls, boys and junior sexualities* (RoutledgeFalmer). Her next research project foregrounds space, bodies, femininity, and movement in a participative ethnography of girls' negotiations of their local outdoors.

Christine Skelton is Professor of Gender Equality in Education at the University of Birmingham, UK. Christine has published extensively in the field of gender and education with a particular interest in masculinities and primary schooling. Her recent publications include the co-authored book *Feminisms and the schooling scandal* (2009) and *Reassessing gender and achievement* (2005, both with Becky Francis) and the edited collection *Sage handbook of gender and education* (2006, with Becky Francis and Lisa Smulyan).

Brett Stoudt received his Ph.D. in Social-Personality Psychology at the Graduate Center of the City University of New York. He has worked with the Centre for the Study of Boys' and Girls' Lives (CSBGL) since 2003. He has consulted with a wide range of research enterprises in addition to CSBGL, including the Ruttenberg Cancer Center at Mt. Sinai Hospital, Global Rights, and the New York City Department of Health and Mental Hygiene. Recent publications include *The role of language in the investigation of privilege: Using participatory action research to discuss theory, develop methodology, and interrupt power.*

Marcus B. Weaver-Hightower is an Assistant Professor of Educational Foundations and Research at the University of North Dakota, USA, where he teaches graduate courses in gender and education, the sociology of education, and qualitative research. He is a former Fulbright scholar to Australia and the author of *The politics of policy in boys' education: Getting boys "Right"* (Palgrave). Previously, he taught high school English and coached girls' soccer in Goose Creek, South Carolina, United States. His research interests include the politics of boys' education, masculinity studies, literacy, qualitative research, and cultural studies.

Preface

In collecting essays for this book, our aim has been to solicit contributions that produce a deeper knowledge and understanding about boys' education, which takes readers beyond backlashes against recent gains for girls and, hence, a persistent recuperative masculinity politics on behalf of boys. Implicated in such a politics is what Deborah Britzman (1998) terms in her work as "the impulse to normalize" (p. 92). This impulse is most readily identifiable in the populist tendency to treat boys and girls as essentially different (though within each gender essentially the same) and, on this basis, advocate gender-based reform that is committed to reinforcing rather than challenging the limits of hegemonic masculinity (see Martino & Kehler, 2007). This has led to the familiar interventions to address the boy problem in schools which amount to advocating the following:

- A more "boy-friendly" curriculum, which is considered to be inclusive of boys' distinctive interests and learning needs
- More male teachers who, as a consequence of being male, are supposedly better equipped to relate to boys and to address their learning needs
- Single-sex classes where boys do not have to worry about girls and where teachers can more easily cater to boys' interests and learning styles

In Australia, Canada, the United Kingdom, and the United States, there is evidence that such approaches are being adopted in ways that are unreflective and which fail to address the complex dynamics of hierarchical masculinities in male teachers' and boys' lives in schools and how these interact with culture, the economy, and politics (see Weaver-Hightower, 2003).

What is needed, we believe, is a bringing together of the research-based literature about the politics of masculinities with that which is grounded in a sound knowledge about pedagogical reform. For example, Hayes and colleagues (2006), in drawing on the work of Linda Darling-Hammond (1997) and Newmann and associates (1996) about teacher threshold knowledges and authentic pedagogy, respectively, provide important insights into the conditions that are necessary for both building professional learning communities in schools and facilitating effective learning for all students. Such conditions entail the following:

1 *Intellectually quality*: This involves teachers developing higher-order thinking and problem-solving tasks that require students to think critically about the construction of knowledge. These tasks involve students' generalizing, generating hypotheses, and synthesizing and manipulating information to discover new meanings and understandings. These are accomplished within the context of substantive conversation involving sustained dialogue with peers and the teacher.

2 *Connectedness*: This involves developing a curriculum that connects with students' background knowledge and has purchase in their everyday lives outside of school. There is a focus on real-world problems, with the curriculum being connected to the larger social and cultural context in which students live. Hayes and colleagues (2006), however, raise an important concern about merely making a curriculum relevant to students and draw a distinction between "forms of connectedness that expose students to powerful cultural codes and those that limit their exposure" (p. 57).

3 *Supportive classroom environment*: This involves creating the conditions in which students feel safe to take risks in their learning and requires teachers to foster particular relationships with students that are based on mutual respect and an ethic of caring. Students are engaged academically and are encouraged to participate enthusiastically within a context in which the teacher communicates high expectations for all students. Explicit criteria about the nature and quality of student achievement and social interaction in the classroom are frequently detailed and contribute to giving students a clear direction in their learning while allowing for self-regulation and intellectual quality.

4 *Working with and valuing difference*: This involves avoiding 'the impulse to normalize' and, hence, providing students with knowledge about anti-oppressive ways of thinking or "non-dominant ways of being in terms of gender, ethnicity/race, sexualities" (Hayes et al., 2006, p. 68; see also Kumashiro, 2000). In this sense, it ensures that students' identities are acknowledged as a basis for building a community which values and acknowledges cultural and sexual diversity.

Hayes and her colleagues note that the above four dimensions need to be integrated to ensure that the conditions for a productive or authentic pedagogy are established for effective learning. This model of pedagogy provides a useful framework or lens for interrogating the limits of pedagogical reform within the context of boys' education across its various international iterations. As already indicated, there has been widespread support for single-sex classes for boys, for more male role models, and for implementing a supposedly *boy-friendly* curriculum designed to cater to boys' distinctive active or action-oriented learning styles (see House of Representatives Standing Committee, 2002; Ontario Ministry of Education, 2004; see Martino & Kehler, 2007; Mills, Martino, & Lingard, 2007; and Weaver-Hightower, 2008, for critiques of such government-sponsored initiatives). Such approaches to gender reform are often grounded in stereotyped or common-sense understandings about the way boys are, and these reforms are committed to normalizing and homogenizing boys rather than creating the intellectually demanding and socially supportive conditions that are necessary for working with and valuing differences among boys.

In light of these concerns about the necessity of building a research-based knowledge that attends to the politics of difference in boys' lives, as a basis for gender-based pedagogical reform in boys' education, the contributors to this book raise important questions about the complex and multi-layered dimensions of masculinity in boys' lives (see Davis, 2001; Kimmel, 2008; Martino & Pallotta-Chiarolli, 2003; McCready, 2004; Noguera, 2008; Pascoe, 2007; Price, 1999). They draw attention to the ways in which masculinities are constructed and reconstructed, invented and reinvented, managed and mismanaged. Many of the contributors provide further insight into the striking, and disturbingly powerful, influence of schooling in its capacity to both define and contribute to the problem of boys' masculinity in ways that are delimited by invoking a normalized, white, heterosexualized masculinity. In this sense, this collection provides further knowledge about and insight into the lives and experiences of marginalized boys whose voices have not often been heard within the context of debates about boys' education.

The first section of this book takes seriously the notion that, if we are to build threshold knowledges about boys and their educations, we must understand both the political and theoretical contexts of the work being done for boys as well as the many ways in which masculinities form, act, and interact in boys' lives and in the broader societies boys inhabit. All of the contributors to this volume touch on these to some degree, but the first four chapters take these contextual understandings as their explicit focus.

The first chapter, Marcus Weaver-Hightower's "Issues of boy's education in the United States," lays out the context of boys' education debates in the United States. This context he finds to be "diffuse, conservative, structurally and legally constrained, and localized." Understanding how this is so and why this makes the United States so different from other countries in the level to which boys' education debates have touched the general consciousness of educators, policymakers, and the public becomes the focus of the chapter. This takes Weaver-Hightower into the historical legacy of gender and education and the structural and cultural barriers to the growth of U.S. boys' education concerns. Along the way, though, he lays out the current condition of boys in the United States in terms of academics, social indicators, and cultural status. He also reviews major U.S. texts on boys and overviews the local interventions that have both followed and subverted some of the recuperativist trends of recent years. Finally, with a strong understanding that a context as complex as the United States is always changing, always in transition, he provides some compelling signs that boys' education concerns are in ascendancy in the United States.

In Chapter Two, Martin Mills, Becky Francis, and Christine Skelton's "Gender policies in Australia and the U.K.," the descriptions of these two diverse contexts provide some contrast to the U.S. situation, but they also—in their combination—show great similarities with the United States. As Mills and colleagues show, Australian policy on boys (which includes formal, national-level policy) presents boys as an "oppressed group," whereas in the United Kingdom boys are constructed in policy as "at-risk" or "problem boys." Just as in the first chapter, these authors turn to history and context to explain how Australia and the United Kingdom have taken divergent policy paths, including Australia's greater reliance on men's rights discourses and the United Kingdom's changing emphasis from "boys will be boys" to boys as rational economic actors within a wide-open field of choices. Still, though, they are careful also to show the larger, global dynamics that drive boys' education discourses in both places and elsewhere in the world, including neoliberal economic understandings of education's importance, backlashes against feminism and the gains of girls, and accountability means (or "comparability" in Australia) that focus almost exclusively on tests for measures of quality. In this chapter, too, we see a concern for movements toward boys' education on the ground, with critical analysis of national grant and professional development programs in Australia and a contrasting pulling away from programming for boys in the United Kingdom on the grounds that the boys are failing to take advantage of the opportunities being presented. Of great importance as well, finally, Mills, Francis, and Skelton see in these policy contexts a concomitant restructuring of social constructions of "the new girl" as overly advantaged.

The next two chapters turn the focus from policy and instead give insight into the various ways that masculinity is concretely constructed in the lives of boys in schools and in their interactions with peers and communities. Chapter Three, Michael Reichert, Peter Kuriloff, and Brett Stoudt's "What can we expect of boys?" once again turns our attention to the United States, and it provides a practice-based perspective behind the statistics about some boys' academic achievement and their antisocial and risk-taking behaviors. Echoing well-accepted arguments about the structuring of masculinity in schools (e.g., Connell, 1996; Haywood & Mac an Ghaill, 1996) and the powerful impact of the "hidden curriculum" (e.g., Jackson, 1968), these authors posit that schools' "man-making curricula" create antisocial and risk-taking behavior, for "boys' development of important character qualities, such as a commitment to justice, is undermined [in schools] by their certain exposure to an arduous, threatening and often punishing drill for becoming a man." In response, the authors suggest a new way of conceptualizing boys' "capacities" for justice and transformation. To wit, they describe an "ethnographic, participatory action research model" that allows schools to take stock of their own, contextually specific man-making curriculum while valuing the authentic voices of the boys they teach. Perhaps most importantly, Reichert and colleagues provide case studies of this approach in action and show, through a particularly striking anecdote of a conservative columnist's attacks on one school for questioning the masculinity regime on its campus, the challenges that lie ahead for those who go against the tide of recuperative masculinity politics.

Chapter Four, Rebecca Coulter's "'Why does she need me?' Young men, gender politics and personal practice," gives our first view of boys' education concerns in Canada. Though there is some policy specificity involved (a restrictive dating-age policy, for example), the boys in Coulter's study and the topics they discuss will sound familiar to most readers, regardless of context. These boys speak with remarkable candor about the pressures they face in fulfilling an acceptable male role, a role that often leaves them feeling as if they have a "split personality" divided between the unreal expectation and the real connected human. They also talk about their relationships with girls, inclusive of all their unvarnished feelings of competition, suspicion, sexual ambivalence, and protectiveness. Coulter, through the words of her participants, paints a crucial picture of boys as *not* uncritical victims of their socialization, *not* unreflective accomplices of a system that holds unfettered privileges for them. These boys, and so many like them, are instead variously insightful, resistant, complicit, and, yes, even sometimes unaware about the pressures and tensions they face in taking up their masculinities. These are truly crucial portraits to keep in mind when developing threshold knowledges about boys and masculinities in schools as well as in moving beyond conservative, recuperative notions of boys.

In his chapter, "Masculinity, racialization and schooling: The making of marginalized men," Carl James addresses the complex and multi-layered dimensions of African (or black) Canadian masculinities. Particularly powerful about his analysis is the attention he gives to how the heterosexual masculinities of black males are constructed and implicated in a process of racialization that then leads to their marginalization. His chapter raises important questions about the ways in which various forms of resistance are understood in an ongoing "process of manufacturing and utilizing the notion of race to structure and explain the cultural attitudes and behaviors of Black males." In this chapter and the ones that follow by Nayak, Kimmel, and Kehler, the authors provide a useful perspective from which to interrogate how schools participate in reinforcing the constructed oppositional identities of particular young men. James highlights the discriminatory process by which black male students are labeled as "at risk" or "underachievers" and furthers an argument, grounded in his research, to highlight how the institutional context of schooling is complicit in the solidification and re-enforcement of particular perceptions of black male students. He also reminds us of the development and performance of masculinity as intentional and strategic, particularly within specific contexts such as schools and peer groups where boys need to negotiate their marginalization.

Lance McCready in Chapter Six, "The troubles of Black boys in urban schools in the United States," further complicates the analysis of racialized masculinities by drawing on feminist and gay men's perspectives. He explores the troubles of black boys in urban schools in the Unities States from a standpoint that problematizes conventional understandings of black masculinity. He draws out the implications of such queer and feminist analytic frameworks for both research and policy, particularly as they relate to addressing the educational and social needs of black boys in urban schools. Within this context, he draws attention to the failure to simultaneously address the structural and cultural dimensions of the plight of black boys in urban schools. Moreover, by drawing on the voices of queer, gender nonconforming black boys in schools, he highlights the extent to which race, sexuality, and social class intersect with gender in significant ways to illuminate the dynamics and hierarchical dimensions of masculinity in these minority boys' lives (see Martino & Pallotta-Chiarolli, 2003). His chapter highlights the need—within the politically charged context of boys' education—to attend to the complex ways in which the dynamics of masculinity and sexuality for black boys are deeply embedded in class-based and racialized forms of inequality. This becomes even more pertinent, as McCready outlines, given the normalizing tendencies at the heart of reform initiatives which resort to promoting single-sex schooling and male teachers as central to addressing the troubles of urban black boys' engagement with schooling.

Chapter Seven reflects some similar themes and questions raised in previous chapters. In his chapter, "The beer and the boyz: Masculine transitions in a post-industrial economy," Anoop Nayak identifies a series of tensions emerging among British working-class men confronted by a changing economy, one that has shifted dramatically from post-industrial to a service-oriented labor force. Emerging from the apparent ashes of the post-industrial labor force is a working-class masculinity "recuperated" and "refashioned." The "local lads" share a subcultural status with a tradition in hard manual labor. Nayak describes the difficulties for white men from working-class backgrounds who are caught negotiating their own identities that are bound up in a "legacy of labor" and a "sticky cultural residue" that are hard to undo. The connections between particular kinds of labor, such as "scholarly prowess and desk work," reflect deep-rooted histories that continue to conflict with these working-class boys' lived "cultural habitus." Nayak examines the process by which a drinking culture is connected to, and more importantly, symbolic of, an industrial heritage. At the same time, there is a new sheen on the veneer of masculinity that once was. Managed, calculated, and publicly orchestrated, the young men are engaged in a "hedonistic play" that promotes the recuperation of white masculine culture. These young men reflect a set of newly emerging tensions in the routine negotiation of their understandings of being men. They are an embodiment of a particular form of working-class masculinity clinging to an industrial past but struggling to fit within the present and the future. This is not unlike the kind of resistance and struggle documented by James in relation to black male students' experiences of oppression.

Chapter Eight, Michael Kimmel's "Hostile high school hallways," is a careful examination of the violence and hostility manifest in school hallways in the United States. His analysis focuses on different types of peer harassment including bullying, hazing, and sexual harassment in schools. One after the other he provides scenarios to illustrate how gender policing operates in relation to gender nonconformity. In the chapter that follows, Kehler similarly raises questions about the school context and the process by which boys negotiate identities in the face of current understandings young men have of what it means to be a guy and what it means to be gay or assumed to be gay. Kimmel makes the point that the hostile hallways of many schools give rise to an increase in violence in schools. The use of aggression by young men and the ways hazing has become accepted practice by, for example, coaches has further solidified a process of ritualistic performativity in which men prove they are men. This same process has also seen a response by some targets of bullying and harassment in schools who "don't get mad, they get even." Kimmel describes the tales and responses he heard from young men as "stories of cultural marginalization" connected to and informed by a perceived failure to perform and enact the codes of masculinity typically expected by their peers.

In "Boys, friendships and knowing: 'It wouldn't be unreasonable to assume I am gay,'" Kehler examines the role of homophobia in the regulation of high school masculinities as it intersects with how and when young men develop male-male friendships. His chapter, similar to those of Nayak, James, and Kimmel, draws on data to illustrate the tensions and struggles young men experience if and when they reject what Connell (1995) refers to as the offer of a "project of masculinity." Building on previous research, his chapter challenges the assumptions about boys being boys and instead reminds us of a kind of gender work boys do to convince their peers that they are "real men." Traditional masculine codes are negotiated in exchange for the safety of heternormative masculinity. The fears for this group of high school young men are numerous as they attempt to develop closeness and intimacy while maintaining their positions as men among their peers. The messiness of being men and enacting particular codes of masculinity amid a culture of fear and homophobia are evident as these boys are variously named and located by their peers as "gay" or "freaks."

Emma Renold, in her chapter, "Tomboys and female masculinity: (Dis)Embodying hegemonic masculinity, queering gender identities and relations," provides a further critique of approaches that essentialize gender and sexual difference by focusing on what it means for girls to "do boy." She provides knowledge about how a small group of girls embody hegemonic masculinity as a response to negotiating and resisting heterosexualized femininities. In investigating how girls do masculinity, Renold highlights the need to conceptualize gender as "by no means fixed to a sexed body." Her contribution raises important questions about the need for educators to carefully consider the emotional and social consequences for both boys and girls who do gender and sexuality in normative and non-normative ways.

The final two chapters, by James King and Wayne Martino, include a focus on male teachers. King, in his chapter entitled "What can he want? Male teachers, young children and teaching desire," foregrounds the issue of desire for elementary male school teachers and the significance of this for teaching young children. He draws particular attention to the narratives and discourses circulating in the culture about the desiring male teacher. These representations of the male teacher, combined with a particular construction of the child, he claims, detract from the real business of teaching young children and a failure to interrogate "the sexist devaluing of childcare work." He raises important questions about how our sexual and gendered commodification of children influences teaching behavior.

Martino's chapter, "Beyond male role models: Interrogating the role of male teachers in boys' education," also focuses on male teachers. However, he draws attention to the limitations imposed by educational stakeholders and policy makers who invoke a particular conception of normative masculinity, as a basis for establishing certain truth claims about the role of male teachers in their capacity to turn boys around and to recuperate their failing masculinities. Martino highlights the gap between policy and research-based knowledge about male teachers, which draws attention to the restrictions that dominant constructions of masculinity impose on both male teachers and boys at school in terms of "the impulse to normalize." This knowledge about the dominant construction of masculinities and the gendered construction of teaching is presented as a necessary basis for pedagogical reform within the context of boys' education.

Viewed together, the contributors to this book offer invaluable insights that support the urgent need to move beyond a recuperative masculinity politics in boys' education and hence beyond the backlash against progressive and feminist gains in education. Rather than resorting to the impulse to normalize boys, what is needed is a more sophisticated research-based knowledge about the impact and constraints imposed by dominant understandings about it means to be "acceptably" male. As many of the contributors illustrate, this must necessarily involve employing analytical frameworks that enable educators to consider the politics of difference in boys' lives. It entails addressing emotional and social costs and benefits of hegemonic masculinities for both boys and girls and male and female teachers in schools. It also involves building teacher knowledge about both the structural and cultural factors impacting the lives of boys and girls in schools. As Fraser (1997) argues, this means "theorizing the ways in which economic disadvantage and cultural disrespect are currently entwined with and support one another" (p. 12). Connell (1995) has also stipulated that gender, as "a way of structuring social practice" is "unavoidably involved with other social structures" in that it "intersects" or rather "interacts" with race and class (p. 75). Thus, the problem with boys' education, in our view, has been the tendency for a reform agenda to collapse into a project of normalizing and homogenizing boys (and, relationally, girls). We believe that a cultural project of de-gendering and re-gendering masculinities needs to be undertaken in conjunction with a commitment to embracing both analytic frameworks and a research-based knowledge about pedagogical reform that is capable of interrupting these normalizing tendencies that reinstate a white, idealized, normalized, and heterosexualized masculinity for boys (see James, Chapter 5; Lopez, 2003; Pascoe, 2007). This critical framework for addressing the problem of cultural definitions and appropriations of hegemonic masculinity in boys' lives in school need not be at the expense of or detract in any way from a commitment to anti-racist education. This focus on the interplay of masculinities with sexuality, race, ethnicity, social class, disability and geographical location indeed provides a platform from which to implement a reform agenda in boys' education that is committed to gender justice as opposed to a recuperative masculinity politics.

Wayne Martino (The University of Western Ontario)
Michael Kehler (The University of Western Ontario)
Marcus B. Weaver-Hightower (The University of North Dakota)

References

Britzman, D. (1998). *Lost subjects, contested objects*. New York: State University of New York Press.

Connell, R. W. (1996). Teaching the boys: New research on masculinity, and gender strategies for schools. *Teachers College Record, 98*(2), 206–235.

Connell, R. W. (1995). *Masculinities*. Sydney: Allen & Unwin.

Darling-Hammond, L. (1997). *The right to learn: A blueprint for creating schools that work*. San Francisco: Jossey-Bass.

Davis, J. E. (2001). Transgressing the masculine: African American Boys and the Failure of Schools. In B. Meyenn and W. Martino (Eds.), *What about the boys? Issues of masculinity in school* (pp. 140–153). Buckingham: Open University Press,.

Fraser, N. (1997). *Justice interruptus: Critical reflections on the 'post-socialist' condition*. New York: Routledge.

Hayes, D., Mills, M., Christie, P. & Lingard, B. (2006). *Teachers and schooling making a difference: Productive pedagogies, assessment and performance*. Sydney: Allen & Unwin.

Haywood, C., & Mac an Ghaill, M. (1996). Schooling masculinities. In M. Mac an Ghaill (Ed.), *Understanding masculinities* (pp. 50–60). Buckingham, England: Open University Press.

Jackson, P. W. (1968). *Life in classrooms*. New York: Holt.

Kimmel, M. (2008). *Guyland: The perilous world where boys become men*. New York: HarperCollins.

Kumashiro, K. (2000). Toward a theory of anti-oppressive education, *Review of Educational Research, 70*(1), 25–53.

Lopez, N. (2003). *Hopeful girls, troubled boys: Race and gender disparity in urban education*. New York: Routledge.

Martino, W., & Kehler, M. (2007). Gender-based literacy reform: A question of challenging or recuperating gender binaries, *Canadian Journal of Education, 30*(2), 406–431.

Martino, W., & Pallotta-Chiarolli, M. (2003). *So what's a boy? Addressing issues of masculinity and schooling*. Maidenhead, UK: Open University Press.

McCreedy, L. (2004). Understanding the marginalization of gay and gender non-conforming black male students, *Theory into Practice, 43*, 136–143.

Mills, M., Martino, W., & Lingard, B. (2007). Getting boys' education 'right': the Australian government's Parliamentary Inquiry Report as an exemplary instance of recuperative masculinity politics, *British Journal of the Sociology of Education, 28*(1), 5–21.

Newmann, F., et al. (1996). *Authentic achievement: Restructuring schools for intellectual quality*. San Francisco: Jossey-Bass.

Noguera, P. (2008). *The trouble with black boys: And other reflections on race, equity and the future of public education*. San Francisco: Jossey-Bass.

Ontario Ministry of Education. (2004). *Me read? No way!* Toronto: Queens Printer for Ontario.

Pascoe, C. J. (2007). *Dude you're a fag: Masculinity and sexuality in high school*. Berkeley: University of California Press.

Price, J. (1999). Schooling and racialized masculinities: The diploma, teachers, and peers in the lives of young African American men, *Youth and Society*, *31*(2), 224–263.

Weaver-Hightower, M. B. (2008). *The politics of policy in boys' education: Getting boys "Right."* New York: Palgrave Macmillan.

Weaver-Hightower, M. B. (2003). The "boy turn" in research on gender and education, *Review of Educational Research*, *73*(4), 471–498.

1 Issues of Boys' Education in the United States

Diffuse Contexts and Futures

Marcus B. Weaver-Hightower

Introduction

When I go to cocktail parties in Australia and tell people I study the education of boys, normally I get stories about my new acquaintances' own children or mention of a newspaper account they read recently on the subject. At the very least, there will be a look of familiarity on their faces, or sometimes suspicion, until they figure out on which "side" of the issue I am. Conversely, when I go to cocktail parties in the United States and tell people I study the education of boys, there is normally a moment of silence, a cock of one eyebrow, and the inevitable question: "Boys?! What's the issue there?" This has slowly changed in recent years as boys' issues gain more public attention in the United States, but there is still a qualitative difference between the two countries. Why should this be?

In many countries around the world, especially wealthier, industrialized countries, much concern has been expressed over boys and their education. From Canada to Wales, England to Australia, and New Zealand to Japan, anxieties over boys' faltering literacy scores and grim social indicators have gripped the attention of the media, parents, administrators, teachers, and politicians. In many of these countries, widespread alarm and concerted local and national interventions have been apparent, even difficult to ignore. As I have described at length elsewhere (Weaver-Hightower, 2008b), Australia's world's-first federal-level attempt at policymaking on boys' education resulted in a lengthy report, *Boys: Getting It Right* (Australian House of Representatives Standing Committee on Education and Training, 2002), and several national initiatives to create a research base and corpus of teaching practices (for other critiques, see Gill, 2005; Mills, Martino, & Lingard, 2007). Australian federally funded research reports (Alloway, Freebody, Gilbert, & Muspratt, 2002; Collins, Kenway, & McLeod, 2000a; Lingard, Martino, Mills, & Bahr, 2002) and a nation-wide Boys' Education Lighthouse grant program (see Commonwealth Department of Education Science and Training, 2003), have helped create such knowledge bases. However, Australia is not alone or unique in this regard. In England, for example, articles on boys appear almost weekly in the *Times Educational Supplement*, and teacher-targeted books offering advice for raising boys' academic achievement have flooded the market (e.g., Bleach, 1998; Head, 1999; Noble & Bradford, 2000). Also, numerous English local educational authorities have commissioned reports to consider boys' issues (e.g., Arnot & Gubb, 2001). Similarly, in Canada, reports have been commissioned on boys (Bouchard, Boily, & Proulx, 2003; see also Frank, Kehler, Lovell, & Davison, 2003, p. 120) and, in New Zealand, the right-wing National Party has made repeated calls for a federal inquiry into boys' education (Fox, 2006; Ross, 2003). In Iceland, boys' education discourses similar to those in England are prevalent among teachers, and some universities are teaching classes especially for training male teachers (Jóhannesson, 2004). These movements are all part of what I have elsewhere (Weaver-Hightower, 2003b) noted is a more general "boy turn"—a refocusing from girls' issues to boys' issues—in research on gender and education internationally.

What about the state of boys' education issues in the United States, though? Despite the high visibility of debates internationally (which are admittedly more tense, complex, and sometimes contradictory than I have presented here), issues of boys and masculinity in education are still relatively nascent discussions in the United States. High-profile exceptions and certain movements around boys' education have been present for many years, but the United States has yet to see the concerted governmental and public panics and policy characterizing the topic in other countries. No U.S. governmental reports have appeared. No inquiries. The U.S. context for boys' education issues, stated simply, is diffuse, conservative, structurally and legally constrained, and localized. Finding causes requires exploration of the complex circumstances of U.S. education.

In this chapter, then, I seek to answer this overarching question: Why has the United States not seen boys' educational panics and policy movements to the same extent other countries have? Certainly many have expressed concerns about boys in the United States, but why have such movements been less "successful," less a part of public consciousness? What differences in context might explain the difference in concern over boys? In this chapter, I will not present critiques of whether boys *should* elicit concern or interventions at all (a legitimate question, but one which I have addressed elsewhere; see Weaver-Hightower, 2003a, b). Rather, in this chapter, I want to examine whether and how boys' issues have been or might be taken up in the very complicated, disparate, structurally determined U.S. context. I start by laying out the history of gender and education events within the United States, connecting it to the emerging concern over boys particularly seen in popular press books. From there, I explore the specific issues of concern regarding U.S. boys, including both academic and social indicators often used to argue boys' needs. Despite these emerging anxieties, I argue that numerous factors either prevent large-scale interventions and policy or quarantine interventions at the local level. The chapter explores the structural factors in the United States that prevent or contain large-scale or governmental concerns over boys' education, and it looks at some of the more successful and high-profile U.S. cases of educational work for boys, particularly focusing on African-American examples. Finally, I consider current momentums within education and government that could cause boy debates to gain wider attention within U.S. educational and public circles in the future, and I sound a few cautions about any growth of attention.

Gender and Education Matters: A U.S. History

The United States has a long history of debates over education and gender. The lion's share of controversy throughout this history has been over the mixing of the sexes in schools and, relatedly, girls' access to educational institutions and resources. In the last third of the nineteenth century, as girls began entering public schooling and consternation over the supposed ills of coeducation followed, educationalists began seriously considering gender issues. Much early work was critical of coeducation and its deleterious effects on boys and girls alike. Edward Clarke's *Sex in Education* (1873) is perhaps the most famous example. In the book, Clarke decries the threat to girls' "catamenial functions," or reproductive abilities, from excessive use of the intellect during coeducation. Not so for boys; in fact, exercising the intellect was thought to be a good way to redirect boys' biological urges.

Anxieties were not only expressed over the presence of female *students*. As Gail Bederman (1995) recounts, boys' contact with female *teachers* was also a worry, particularly clear in the turn-of-the-twentieth-century work of G. Stanley Hall. Hall recommended early primary teachers allow boys to act like "savages" to help counteract the physical weakening from female teachers' undue civilizing influence. Similar panics over the "feminizing" of boys by women teachers have never since gone away. From Patricia Sexton's (1969) influential polemics on the "decline of manliness" to recent diatribes against "progressive" education's attempts to make boys more like girls (Sommers, 2000b), the arguments blaming female teachers for boys' difficulties filter across the decades in differing forms.

At the beginning of the twentieth century, attention shifted to boys specifically. William Byron Forbush (1901/1907) led the way with his popular book, *The Boy Problem,* and others followed in quick succession (e.g., Gibson, 1916; see Kidd, 2004, for a fuller discussion). Such books decried apathetic boys with no direction and little contact with religion or traditional boy pursuits. Though some today suggest that this concern is new or a result of feminist interventions for girls, crisis discourses for boys are well established. Responses to the perceived crisis—efforts to remasculinize boys—have also taken differing forms then as today, including giving boys access to "traditional" knowledge and activities (e.g., Iggulden & Iggulden, 2007), the use of physical education (e.g., Sadker & Sadker, 1994, pp. 214–215), boys' organizations like the Boy Scouts (Kimmel, 1996), and even military training. Contemporary boys' programs cannot help but confront or be seen in light of the continuing legacy of both fears over the taint of female teachers and efforts to instill a manufactured, traditional masculinity in boys. Put simply, panic still characterizes gender in education issues.

Not completely outside of this crisis character, a decided turn to girls' educational issues began in the United States in the early 1970s. The successful addition of Title IX to U.S. civil rights legislation in 1972, prohibiting discrimination by sex in institutions receiving federal funds, both capitalized on and created renewed interest in girls' access to schools and educational resources, most visibly in athletics. At the same time, closer scrutiny fell on the representation of females in the curriculum (e.g., Women on Words and Images, 1972) and the treatment of girls in schools (e.g., Frazier & Sadker, 1973). The Women's Equity in Education Act (WEEA) soon followed, and a resource center providing guidance for improving girls' educational experiences and achievement was set up. Attention to girls' issues ebbed and flowed in subsequent years, but the early 1990s saw a firestorm erupt over girls' needs again.

The catalyst for this renewed crisis was the release of the report by the American Association of University Women (AAUW), *How Schools Shortchange Girls* (1992). In it, the AAUW charged that policymakers had left out girls' issues in the United States's educational reform flurry following the watershed *A Nation at Risk* report (National Commission on Excellence in Education, 1983). The neglected issues, they argued, include girls' declining self-esteem, gender-biased testing, achievement gaps in math and science, and the absence of women and women's issues in the curriculum. The U.S. media quickly took up the report, often characterizing it as a first glimpse at a major crisis. Other research, both from the AAUW (1993; 1995) and others (Orenstein, 1994; Pipher, 1994; Sadker & Sadker, 1994) built on themes from *How Schools Shortchange Girls,* emphasizing the dangers of girls' depression and low self-esteem and the role schools play in these. Legislation again resulted when the U.S. Congress in 1994 passed the Gender Equity in Education Act, largely in response to the renewed attention to girls' issues.

More recently, starting in the late 1990s, a distinct shift in attention toward boys' educational issues began in earnest, though unlike girls' issues no significant legislation has yet been proposed or passed. Largely, concentration on boys has come from a spate of popular trade books dealing with the raising of boys and polemical texts about alleged failures and deceptions of feminist educational reforms (see also Foster, Kimmel,

& Skelton, 2001, pp. 12–18). The former, parent-focused tomes on raising boys, have been most visible; several, in fact, have made the bestseller lists.

One of the first of the raising-boys ilk was William Pollack's *Real Boys* (1998). In it, Pollack presented a picture of boys' mental health just as bleak as Pipher's earlier bestseller appraisal of girls, *Reviving Ophelia* (1994), a book Pollack explicitly attempted to answer. Boys, he said, are also suffering from low self-esteem, shame, loneliness, and depression, but owing to strictures of the "boy code," a kind of "toxic" male sex role, boys are more at risk but less likely to reach out for help. Schools, too, play a part, for *"the very structure of most coeducational schools tends unwittingly to favor female students"* (p. 239; emphasis original), particularly in teachers' attitudes, negative stereotyping of boys, and failure to account for boys' learning styles. Other books of this genre, including Gurian's *A Fine Young Man* (1998), Kindlon and Thompson's *Raising Cain* (2000), Thompson's *Speaking of Boys* (2000), and a slew of others, have made many of the same arguments, presenting parents and teachers with advice and strategies to help boys deal with the complexities of emotional life in a supposedly toxic new age.

Yet another million-copy seller, *Bringing up Boys* (2001), was written by James Dobson, host of *Focus on the Family,* a conservative Christian radio show claiming (as of early 2004; see www.family.org) to be on more than 3,000 radio stations daily in 12 languages and in 95 countries. *Bringing up Boys* frames raising boys within the same conservative Christian ideologies of *Focus on the Family,* with emphasis on traditional Christian sex roles and God-ordained gender differences. In Dobson's view, harmful media, valueless schooling, and lax parenting unduly influenced by feminism and postmodern theory (which he incorrectly conflates with moral relativism) all have left boys with no moral compass. The solution, he claims, rests on returning to parenting styles of old ("Parents a century ago had a much better 'fix' on these long-term objectives and how to achieve them" [p. 7]), with the ultimate objective being to help children understand "who God is and what He expects them to do" (p. 248). Religiosity does not characterize all of the raising-boys books (c.f., Weaver-Hightower, 2008a), but many are based in conservative, right-wing ideologies. Many suture neoconservative pining for an idyllic past (Apple, 2006) with a spiritualist view of masculinity as inherent in a biology created by God (see Clatterbaugh, 1990).

A particularly important example of such conservative texts, one Dobson echoes with his criticisms of feminism, is Christina Hoff Sommers' *The War Against Boys* (2000b). Sommers, a long time critic of left-leaning feminism (see also Sommers, 1994), charged in *The War Against Boys* that "misguided feminism," often through calculated deception, has turned the educational system counter to the "natural" proclivities and needs of boys. She proposed fixing this by "returning" to moral education and "basic values, well-proven social practices, and plain common sense" (p. 209); this represents a wished-for return to traditional masculinity.

Michael Gurian holds similar critiques of progressive education in his book *Boys and Girls Learn Differently!* (2001). In his estimation, educators have forgotten or ignored the "natural," brain-based differences between boys and girls to the detriment of both. Though some of his recommendations for teachers and parents dealt with learning style differences that could indeed be considered brain-based (pacing of lessons or using manipulatives, for instance), many crossed the line into highly social interventions such as using school uniforms (not traditionally a part of U.S. public education, though increasing in use), character education programs, and "rites of passage" experiences.

More recently, Peg Tyre's (2008) *The Trouble with Boys* provided another best seller–list argument on boys in crisis. In it, Tyre argued numerous reasons for boys' being at the short end of a "new gender gap," from "thinking with a boy brain" to excessive video game playing, but most of her focus was on the misunderstandings and unrealistic expectations of boys' behavior by teachers and schools. Tyre combined a number of conservative discourses but focuses on parents—mothers specifically—as advocates for their children against such educational malfeasance.

Several key points should be kept in mind when considering these books—and others of their kind—as central players in the U.S. context for boys' education. First, they are often practice-oriented (Weaver-Hightower, 2003a, b), and relatively few theoretically oriented works on boys' schooling and masculinity have originated in the United States (notable exceptions include Brown, 2001; Ferguson, 2000; Kimmel, 1996; King, 1998; Lesko, 2000; Newkirk, 2000; 2002; M. W. Smith & Wilhelm, 2002; Thorne, 1993; Young, 2000). This is key, for boys' education debates in the United States have primarily taken place at the popular rather than academic level; U.S. academics have had little public answer to the most regressive elements of such books, though this is changing as the research community begins to turn more toward boys' education research (Weaver-Hightower, 2003b). Right or wrong, the small amount of non-advocacy research limits the nuance of these issues and constrains the impact of work on boys to individuals rather than institutions. Popular boy books encourage individual parents and educators toward activism, but they elide the possibility of structural and political change. Still, the texts' practical focus and ease of reading has very effectively distributed *one particular version* of boys' problems. These books, in the absence of response from education research, have been left to define boys' education for the entire country. Worse, in an era of site-based management absent state guidance on boys' education, such books have become *"de facto policy"* (Lingard, 2003) for schools. Put simply, the absence of formal policy about boys has left teachers and administrators to look to such texts (though not uncritically) for solutions to the very real problems they face with boys every day.

Second, the books' conservative nature deserves scrutiny. As mentioned earlier and as Martino and Berrill (2003) point out, much of the popular discourse around boys in the United States and internationally has a distinctively Rightist standpoint. Most rely on stereotyped or biological views of masculinity. Many are explicitly anti-feminist; Mills (2003), in fact, calls this genre the "backlash blockbusters," a reference to bestseller Susan Faludi's (1991) notion that media's slanted reporting often perpetuates backlash against the gains of feminism. Most boy books also appeal to "common sense" and a neoconservative desire for "simpler times" when people "knew their roles" in society. Of course, many groups, particularly but not only girls and women, were underserved or oppressed by education in the "golden age" such books venerate; serious problems still exist for girls; and argument about "nature," brains, and testosterone have been used as rationales for discrimination for thousands of years. That such rightist texts have enjoyed near-free reign to define the issues represents a potentially critical mistake by social justice movements. Those parents and educators who have valid concerns for boys and who otherwise might be allies of progressive reform have often been "pushed right" (Apple & Oliver, 1996) to conservative positions because the U.S. left—perhaps afraid of giving them legitimacy—has largely ignored boys' issues until recently.

Third and finally, these books have not appeared from or been contained within a vacuum. As I have argued in greater detail elsewhere (Weaver-Hightower, 2003b), a number of etiologies of the "turn" to boys must be taken into account if the regressive portions of the backlash blockbusters are to be effectively countered. Media panic, boy books, and news events are one cause (and, simultaneously, an effect) of the turn. Other phenomena have also caused the shifted attention. Early feminist formulations of gender discrimination in education (such as those mentioned earlier) revolved on test score gaps and other simple indicators and set a tone of panic and blame—compare schools "shortchanging" or "failing" girls with a "war against boys"—easily leading to boy panics when test scores in literacy were considered (see the following section). Certain conservative, neoliberal reforms in education have exacerbated these worries, particularly the ascendance of high-stakes testing in conjunction with severe penalties for poor performance (see Gillborn & Youdell, 2000). That is, boys' problems are more evident in a context where test scores matter so much. Economic changes and shifts in the workforce have also created a context of "masculine crisis" across the globe, and security threats real and perceived have increased popular attention on the need for new generations of masculine men to protect us (Weaver-Hightower, 2002). The political economy of publishing, too, feeds on and has fed the popularity of boy-rearing books. The controversy such texts garner benefits sales, and the notoriety often garnered benefits authors, their careers, and sometimes their bank accounts. Also, it is clear from other countries' examples (see especially Weaver-Hightower, 2008b, for the Australian context) that governmental initiatives and pressure as well as the development of micro-economies around boys' issues (such as through the sales of books, conferences, and professional development) similarly push boys' education issues to the fore. A small but growing economy has been created around boys' education in the United States, but the governmental pressure and initiatives are currently quite limited, though as I will explain later, there are signs that these, too, are growing.

Still, the issues boys face in the United States, just as elsewhere, are not simply manufactured crisis, backlash against feminism, or a bid to return to religious orthodoxy. Parents and educators are not dupes, after all. A number of indicators of boys' achievement, social status, and health have been cause for major concerns among well-meaning groups in the United States.

Where the Boys Are: Issues For and About Boys in the United States

In the spring of 2002, I was a panelist for a discussion of "The Boy Crisis" held at the University of Wisconsin-Madison. As a couple of 12-year-old boys who had been invited to share their experiences fidgeted beside me at the panelist table, the adults talked about school systems and teachers unresponsive to their sons' needs. These parents and educators talked about pedagogy that ignored the hands-on activities their sons thrive on and the topics boys are interested in, like guns and motorcycles. Instead, their boys were forced to talk about how they "feel" (said with a sneer) about characters in books. (The 12-year-olds were now simulating bodily noises and giggling). The parents talked about the many hours their sons spent in detention because the teacher really did not understand boys' needs, did not have the patience for their energy. One thing that became clear—other than that my protestations were being taken as just another feminist-deluded academic ignoring boys' needs—was that these parents had serious complaints. They were not (to my knowledge) religious zealots intent on rolling back girls' educational gains. They had very real, very specific concerns about their own children they felt were going unheeded. Are they correct, though? Do boys in the United States have demonstrable educational needs based on gender?

Most of the issues of concern regarding boys in other countries have also been of concern in the United States. Broadly, these fall into two often-overlapping categories: academic issues and social issues. Both categories contain valid points of concern, though causes of these difficulties and fixes for them are highly disputed. The following analysis is not meant to imply that boys' issues are more numerous or important than those of girls; there are no clear-cut "answers" here, and every point has its counter. As well, gender is ultimately relational, with complex interconnections between what happens to boys and what happens to girls, so it is difficult and deceptive to pull out one gender's indicators and make claims from them. These caveats in mind, however, it is important to give the reader a sense of the issues often cited in U.S. debates as cause for worry over boys.

Academic Issues

Literacy

Academic issues for boys in U.S. schools have focused mainly on literacy, though boys also lag behind girls in other subjects. In literacy, boys' scores trail girls' in the National Assessment of Educational Progress (NAEP), often called "the Nation's Report Card" as the only nationally comparable literacy test. Boys' reading scores trail girls' by 10 points (on a 500-point scale) for the 2007 test of eighth graders, seven points for fourth graders (National Center for Educational Statistics, 2007). In perspective, the much-discussed gender gap favoring boys in math has not been more than three points in fourth or eighth grade tests going back to 1992, the same year as the release of the AAUW's (1992) *How Schools Shortchange Girls*. The reading score gap, however, has been shown to be true longitudinally by the long-term trend version of the NAEP (National Center for Educational Statistics, 2005); boys have been behind girls since the test was first administered in 1971. These gaps are also present internationally (Ogle et al., 2003; Wagemaker, Taube, Munck, Kontogiannopoulou-Polydorides, & Martin, 1996). Thus, given the long-term, cross-cultural nature of these score gaps and concerns for boys' literacy—stretching back further than even the data presented here (Cohen, 1998)—educators, researchers, and policy makers should decisively discount claims of feminist conspiracies and progressive reforms away from past success.

In writing, the other tested component of literacy, boys' scores appear even worse. On a 300-point scale in this instance, the 2007 NAEP writing test gaps between males and females were 20 and 18 points in eighth and twelfth grades, respectively (National Center for Educational Statistics, 2008).

These gendered score gaps, in a politically telling way, have been a featured element of the reporting of NAEP results, until recently preceding even race- and class-based gaps, which are actually more pronounced. The 2007 reading gap between white and black students was 27 points for fourth and eighth grades, and for those receiving free lunch and those not—a rough indicator of socioeconomic status—it was 29 and 25 points

(National Center for Educational Statistics, 2007). Privileging gender over these issues is in line with a general absence of talk about the racial and classed dimensions of achievement among groups of boys. I return to this point shortly.

Also of particular note, boys' literacy has garnered much recent practitioner attention in the United States. Books such as *"Reading Don't Fix No Chevys": Literacy in the Lives of Young Men* (Smith & Wilhelm, 2002); *Teenage Boys and High School English* (Pirie, 2002);[1] *Misreading Masculinity: Boys, Literacy, and Popular Culture* (Newkirk, 2002); and *To Be a Boy, To Be a Reader: Engaging Teen and Preteen Boy in Active Literacy* (Brozo, 2002) have all capitalized on the recent concern for boys' reading and writing. Each argues in different ways—often with limited empirical evidence—that boys' literacy is distinct from girls' literacy, and each suggests strategies for more closely aligning the language arts curriculum to the specific needs of boys. Brozo (2002), for example, suggests having boys study "archetypes" of masculinity—in a Jungian sense—as a way to counteract harmful cultural stereotypes. Pirie (2002), on the other hand, suggests both boys and language arts must change in ways more aligned to modern roles for men, such as giving boys the "vocabulary" to talk about emotion.

Other Outcomes of Education

Most educators agree that test scores are not the only indicators of a complete education. Though often debates over boys in the United States rely on anecdotal evidence of boys' disengagement and social ills, several indicators of civic and lifelong learning attitudes also suggest boys are faring more poorly than girls in specific areas. According to the U.S. Department of Education's *Condition of Education* report (hereafter, *CoE*; http://nces.ed.gov/programs/coe/index.asp; accessed October 2008), men are less likely to have read a book in the last six months or to claim they "read regularly," even though they do read newspapers more often than women (indicator 15-2001). These, too, are long-term historical indicators (see Kaestle, 1991). Women are also more likely to self-report being registered to vote and actually voting (indicator 15-2003). Females in grades six through 12 were more likely to participate in community service (indicator 16-2001) and more likely to participate in non-athletic extracurricular activities than boys (Bae, Choy, Geddes, Sable, & Snyder, 2000). Bae and colleagues (2000) also report girls are more likely to take advanced placement exams, tests that confer college credit to high school students.

Dropouts, Retention, and Exclusion

In the United States, boys are more likely to drop out of school than girls (Bae et al., 2000, p. 34), and African-American and Hispanic students are far more likely to drop out than white students. Boys are also more likely to repeat a grade (p. 40), a predictor highly correlated to dropping out of school and other educational risks. Boys suffer disproportionately from disciplinary measures, suspension, and expulsion from school, particularly levied against and harmful to boys of color (Ferguson, 2000).

Access to and Retention in Noncompulsory Education

Access to education, once the major target of girls' advocates, has recently become an issue for boys. Again according to the *CoE* (indicator 9-2008), women outnumber men in undergraduate enrollment at both 2- and 4-year colleges, and the gap is expected to increase through at least 2017. Women also made up 60 percent of all graduate students in 2006, up 2 percent since 2000 (indicator 11-2008). Men's enrollment in first professional degree programs, such as dentistry, theology, chiropractic, medicine, podiatry and so on, while still about 51 percent of total enrollment—down 2 percent since 2000—has declined overall by 8.5 percent since 1976, with 16,000 fewer men now pursuing first professional degrees (indicator 11-2008). Still, women and men tend to enroll in differing fields, with the male-predominant fields tending to accrue more social and economic status. Access issues are not only germane to higher education. Women older than 16 are also more likely to participate in adult education programs (indicator 10-2007).

Some readers have likely been thinking all along, "Yes, but women do not do as well in the workforce, even with their degrees." They are, of course, right. Still, though women's economic success has not kept pace with their greater educational attainment— a point I return to shortly— credential inflation could eventually change men's advantage in this regard.

Social Issues

Socio-Educational and Well-Being Indicators

A number of social and non-academic educational issues facing boys have caused significant concern in the U.S. context. Boys, for example, make up two-thirds of U.S. special education students (Office of Special Education and Rehabilitation Services, 2005). Though one could partly explain this by the under-identification of girls in need of special services, many are worried that boys are targeted more for their behavior problems than for their needs. This is particularly relevant to arguments over attention deficit disorder—disproportionately diagnosed in boys—as well as the use of medication on children (see, e.g., Gurian, 2001). Boys are also more likely to commit suicide (http://www.cdc.gov/ncipc/dvp/Suicide/SuicideDataSheet.pdf; accessed January 15, 2008). They are more likely to be treated for substance abuse (http://www.drugabusestatistics.samhsa.gov/NSDUH/2k6NSDUH/tabs/Sect2peTabs1to42.htm#Tab2.42B; accessed January 15, 2008), they are far more likely to be caught up in criminal justice institutions (http://www.ojp.gov/bjs/glance/cpgendpt.htm; accessed January 15, 2008) and to be victims of violent crime (http://www.ojp.usdoj.gov/bjs/glance/vsx2.htm; accessed October 18, 2008). Boys are more prone to behavior, habits, and attitudes that conflict with school success. Teachers, for instance, report kindergarten girls were more likely to persist at tasks, be eager to learn, and pay attention than were their male peers (West, Denton, & Germino-Hausken, 2000). Boys themselves are less likely to report finding school work "meaningful" and more likely to say courses are "dull" (Freeman, 2004). Support for boys' learning is also an issue, for the 2003 *CoE* survey shows boys have a lower mean home literacy index, a score based on being read to or told stories as well as the presence of children's books and other media in the home (p. 163). The survey similarly showed that boys were less likely than girls, three or more times the week before the survey, to have been read to; told a story; taught letters, words, or numbers; or taught songs or music (p. 164). These findings are consistent with research showing that parents interact differently with boys and girls in ways influential to learning (e.g., Gleason, 1987; Heath, 1983). Though these indicators do not necessarily implicate a cultural devaluation of males (cf., Faludi, 1999; Farrell, 1993; Sommers, 2000b), these are serious markers deserving attention.

Violence and "Crisis Masculinity"

Advocates cite other social indicators, as well, to make claims for reform on behalf of boys. Chief among these is violence. Males in the United States are vastly more likely to be both the perpetrators and victims of violent crime. Violence as a men's issue has been particularly publicized, with school shootings, bullying, and harassment garnering significant attention in the late 1990s and early 2000s (Newman, 2004). The publicity around violence has racialized dimensions, as well, with media presentation of black violence over-reported and white violence, such as toward African-Americans and Arab-Americans in the form of racial profiling, often under-reported. Racializing violence in this way serves, partly, to elide the gendered nature of violence. Rather than challenging the masculine nature of violence (Mills, 2001), the mass of attention in education has been on bullying prevention, higher surveillance over what students write or wear (Newkirk, 2000), and criticism of media and cultural violence.

Highly publicized violence contributes to panics over a so-called crisis of masculinity in society. This is a worldwide phenomenon, typically caused or characterized by economic distress, nationalism, war, and feelings of social exclusion among men (Comaroff & Comaroff, 2000). Susan Faludi indexes this in her book *Stiffed: The Betrayal of the American Man* (1999), where she attributes the rise of public and private violence to the "broken promises" of good jobs and civic roles that were to accrue to men. Terrorism and responses to it have also been attributed to the perceptions of masculinity in crisis (Kimmel, 2002; McClintock, 2002; Weaver-Hightower, 2002). But are men and masculinity really in crisis in the United States? The question is perhaps unanswerable, but some indicators do suggest men as a whole are not, for example, as economically stable as they once were. According to the 2004 *CoE* (p. 133), in constant year 2000 U.S. dollars, the average man is making $5,389 *less* than he was in 1971 when the statistics were first taken. That is a 15 percent decrease in real dollars. Though the average woman still makes only $1 to the average man's $1.39, women are earning 40 percent more than they did in 1971. Let me stress that women's gains have *in no way caused* men's declining average. Perceptions of a shaky future, however, are a reasonable response to men's own declines.

Male Teachers

The state of male *teachers* in the United States has also attracted publicity, just as it has in other countries (Mills, Martino, & Lingard, 2004). Though some analysis has centered on the gendered experiences of male teachers (e.g., Johnson, 2000; King, 1998, 2000), most has focused on the numerical dearth of males at the primary level. The *Status of the American Public School Teacher 2000–2001* report by the National Education Association (NEA Research, 2003), the United States's biggest teacher union, shows males make up only 21 percent of all U.S. teachers. Most males gravitate toward secondary school, however, leaving only 9 percent of elementary school teachers being male. When the NEA released the report, the media particularly emphasized the gender result, not completely surprising given the problem's framing as a "40-year low" in the number of male teachers. The media, however, has given causes limited analysis, largely focusing on economic and social decision-making: Pundits blame the low pay and stereotypically female-appropriate nature of teaching. Discussions about male teachers often center, though, on the presumed effects on *students* more so than on teachers (e.g., Dee, 2006). Advocates typically assert potential role-modeling benefits for boys from having more male teachers, but little empirical evidence exists for these claims (see Zirkel, 2002, for an exception).

In spite of advocacy attention to social issues, the United States has seen less attention to crucial questions asked in other countries. Particularly absent from the majority of boy debates in the United States is asking "Which boys?" are disadvantaged (cf., Collins, Kenway, & McLeod, 2000b; Epstein, Elwood, Hey, & Maw, 1998; Jackson & Salisbury, 1996; Katz & Jhally, 1999; Kenway & Willis, 1998; Lingard et al., 2002; Martino & Pallotta-Chiarolli, 2003; Mills, 2001). In general, asking this question acknowledges that not *all* boys are disadvantaged in schools. Those boys who are non-Anglo, working-class, non-heterosexual, stereotypically "feminine," or disabled are far more likely to face disadvantage (Connell, 1995; Martino & Pallotta-Chiarolli, 2003). Little concerted attention to differences *between* boys has thus far been given in the United States, though. That is, when the specter of boy crises appear, little is typically said about, say, gay or bisexual boys or boys with physical disabilities, despite the research done on these issues in and of themselves. The "backlash blockbusters" are focused—*because they do not say otherwise* (Morrison, 1992, p. 72)—on white middle-class boys, and they are largely consumed by white, middle-class parents and teachers. The paucity of systematic research *inside* U.S. schools, looking at the ways boys experience education "on the ground" (like those done in the United Kingdom, such as Mac an Ghaill, 1994; Willis, 1977), accounts for perhaps the biggest reason for the lack of attention to diversity. Eliding such differences holds dangers of further targeting resources to groups who are already the biggest winners at school.

U.S. educators and scholars have not completely overlooked boys' diversities, though. In fact, several notable and influential works have shed light on the particular problems of African-American boys. Ferguson (2000), for example, shows the ways disciplinary regimes in schools construct black masculinity in harmful, entrenching ways. Importantly, Ferguson demonstrates that such constructions, including panics over black boys in even well-meaning circles, relegate African-American boys to the equally damaging roles of "endangered species" or "criminal." Dance (2002), similarly, illuminates the ways African-American students, particularly boys, confront and adapt to the stereotypes "mainstream" U.S. culture has of them. They instrumentally use street culture to survive the racial, gendered, classed, regional, and educational oppressions confronting them. Numbered among these are lower achievement and social indicators (as listed earlier) and a vast disproportion of students of color in the criminal justice system. Works from the United States such as Ferguson's and Dance's—along with many others (e.g., Fashola, 2005; Fordham & Ogbu, 2000; Ladson-Billings, 1994; Murtadha-Watts, 2000; Price, 2000; Tatum, 2005)—give the theoretical underpinnings of possible interventions into the education of boys of color, focusing attention on identity and social oppression rather than on blame and deficits.

The indicators I have used in this section are not the only ones possible, nor do all scholars accept their general use. Using testing data, for example, is questionable on a number of grounds (Weaver-Hightower, 2003b). Also, many scholars suggest a focus on outcomes of education like work and higher levels of educational attainment is a much more sound measure of "disadvantage" than test scores and suspension rates (Collins et al., 2000a; Epstein et al., 1998). Boys' poorer literacy scores, for instance, do not translate into poorer job market success (Collins et al., 2000a). Such indicators initially gained use to demonstrate the educational disadvantage of girls (e.g., AAUW, 1992). Asking parents and educators now to disregard statistics like test scores and drop out rates, particularly when such indicators have become "common sense" gauges of educational equity and success—not to mention deeply implicated in accountability and sanctions—is what I call the "counter-intuitive big ask." Though changing indicators from test scores to, say, economic success might reflect a growing understanding of the nuance of gender's impact on education, it can appear to the general public to be self-serving for girls' advocates. Nevertheless, researchers and the public must continue to ask, as these scholars request, what indicators are important and what these gauges really mean in the larger context of educational equity.

Constraints to the Growth of Boys' Education Issues

Given the varied concerns just cited—and returning to my foundational question—why have boys' educational issues not commanded more ubiquitous attention in U.S. media, educational research, and policy? Though such countries as Australia and England are embroiled in heated, very public debates about boys, the United States has only a relative few popular press books and a handful of scholars attending to the issues. In this section, I argue that a mélange of contextual factors in the United States and its educational system have served to contain—at least to some extent—the moral panics so many other countries have faced. Readers should not regard this as an exhaustive list.

Governmental and Educational Structures

The United States uses a version of federalism for its governance, meaning the federal and state governments have distinct areas of responsibility. The Tenth Amendment to the *Constitution of the United States of America* guarantees these separate responsibilities, preventing the federal government from exercising dominion over states except in those areas specifically mentioned in the Constitution. Thus, waging war against other nations is a federal role, but education, because the Constitution does not mention it, is a state responsibility. This has interesting consequences. For example, the U.S. government was able to mandate desegregation of schools in the 1950s as a *civil rights* issue (a federal role mandated by the

Fourteenth Amendment), but it could not force Arkansas or Virginia to school black and white students together; these states simply shut down schools rather than integrate them. They could legally do this because the provision of schools is solely at the discretion of individual states.

The United States's history of interventions in gender and education issues is inextricably bound up with such issues of federalism. Proponents advanced Title IX (see above) as a civil rights issue under the Fourteenth Amendment's mandate for "equal protection under the law." Though the scope of Title IX is limited to those institutions accepting federal money—private schools and businesses are exempt—its provisions are broad, ensuring not only almost universal access to education and resources (because the private school sector in the United States is small) but limiting the ways in which single-sex programs, for instance, can be provided. These regulations are under threat, as I will explain later, but presently Title IX restricts what gender-related programs schools can do and how they do them. Interventions targeted to boys, such as the Detroit all-male schools discussed in the next section, fall under Title IX rules, and this is part of what has prevented concerted boy-specific interventions.

Federalism, in the same vein, has also ensured the diffuse nature of boy concerns. Because no federal-level policy is permissible—barring additional civil rights legislation for males, which would be unlikely—states are left to create their own policies concerning boys. As movements for boys' education have been fractured and small, state-level policy has not been feasible, and again such policies would run up against Title IX regulations against sex discrimination. The only state, at the time of writing, to have attempted policy on boys' education has been Maine (Maine Task Force on Gender Equity in Education, 2006), and their process quickly turned from one on boys to one that considered gender broadly (boys *and* girls) owing, some contended, to the political climate (Wack, 2006).

A related constraint in the U.S. context not present in other nations is the frequent reliance of U.S. educational policy on judicial precedent.[2] In the United States's overtly litigious context, district courts (in cases such as the Detroit all-male academies discussed below) and the U.S. Supreme Court arbitrate most important education policy in regard to equity, civil rights, and religion's presence in schools. *Brown v. Board of Education* (1954), for example, mandated all U.S. schools desegregated by race, whereas *Engel v. Vitale* (1962) and others have prohibited school-sponsored prayer. The reliance on court precedence in the United States—whereas other nations largely develop and implement policy at the level of bureaucracy—limits the ability for so-called "equity" work for boys. Little or no precedent exists for considering males a disadvantaged group in U.S. law, and the effort, resources, and time involved in litigating for boys' educational issues has thus far been prohibitive.

Boys' education issues might be taken up within the homeschooling (see Young, 2000) or private school sectors, outside the bounds of federal regulation and legal precedence, but little public attention has come from any such programs. Again, the U.S. private school sector is small relative to the public sector; approximately 6.8 million students attend private schools (according to the 2007 *Digest of Education Statistics*; http://nces. ed.gov/programs/digest/d07/tables/dt07_001.asp; accessed October 18, 2008), whereas home-schooled students account for just over one million (http://nces.ed.gov/programs/digest/d07/tables/dt07_037.asp). The vast majority of students in the United States—90 percent, or more than 53 million—attend public schools. The private sector's relative size thus limits the exposure the U.S. populace has had to programs for boys and to single-sex schooling, and it thus limits the amount of attention boys' issues have gotten relative to other countries with large private sectors (Australia and England, especially).

Social and Cultural Constraints

Another potential constraint on the growth of boys' issues in the United States is simply the population size. Whereas New Zealand has 4.2 million inhabitants, Australia 20.6 million, Canada 33.2 million, and the United Kingdom 60.9 million, the U.S. population has reached nearly 303.8 million (all July 2008 estimates; https://www.cia.gov/library/publications/the-world-factbook). Capturing the attention of such a large population and getting them to act in a unified, direct way presents no small challenge.

Other social and cultural factors, though, are likely more influential in containing boys' education discourses. First, the U.S. populace tends to think of "gender" issues as exclusively *women's* issues. Despite cultural movements in the United States that have increased awareness about masculinity and men's roles, particularly the early 1990s mythopoetic men's movements (see, e.g., Bly, 1990; Keen, 1991; Moore & Gillette, 1990) and the Promise Keepers (e.g., Janssen & Weeden, 1994), "gender" is still largely equated with women. This potentially limits receptivity to any notion that boys might face problems *because they are male*. In the same vein, the lingering disadvantages of girls have far to go before they are solved, so focuses on boys can seem a distraction from or threat to more "traditional," accepted notions of gender equity.

Second, and akin to distraction, the focus among the U.S. public in the mid- and late-2000s is almost myopically on school reform writ large. Since 1983, when the watershed *A Nation at Risk* (National Commission on Excellence in Education) report appeared, the major reform movements in the United States have concerned the setting of "standards" and the establishment of "accountability" and "choice" programs (M. L. Smith, 2004), typically centered around standardized testing. After passage in

2002 of the No Child Left Behind (NCLB) Act, the federal law mandating testing and accountability measures to an unprecedented degree, U.S. educators have focused even more on such reforms. With these large, looming issues in view, gender has taken a back seat even for girls. This could, ironically, lead to increased attention to gender in the future, as I will explain later, but currently U.S. public attention is elsewhere.

Third, men's and boys' *gendered* concerns largely lack institutional infrastructures in the United States. There are some good reasons for this, not the least of which is that social justice is aligned *against* men's interests (see Connell, 1995, Chapter 10).[3] U.S. movements around men's issues have been fragmentary and local, often with little funding, few lobbyists, and thus scant impact on legislation. One possible exception is movements around divorce and custody support for men. Otherwise, no influential organizations on the scale of the National Organization for Women (NOW) or the AAUW exist to forward boys' educational issues, and this has necessarily limited the spread of such concerns and limited any influence on policy.

Fourth and finally, movements toward boys' education tread a tense, ambivalent cultural ground in the United States owing to their position within larger, sometimes contradictory ideologies of masculinity. Pollack's (1998) warnings, for example, about not shaming boys for attachments to their mothers fits well the "masculinity therapy" model (see Connell, 1995; Kenway & Willis, 1998; Lingard & Douglas, 1999). The notion of shame as a root cause of problem masculinity even harkens to mythopoetic constructions of masculinity (e.g., Bly, 1990). Conversely, Dobson (2001, p. 122, quoting J. Nicolosi), suggests fathers do what they can to force separation of a boy from his mother after the age of three; failure to do so risks turning boys homosexual, he claims. Here there are vestiges of Muscular Christianity (see Kimmel, 1996) as evident in organizations such as the Promise Keepers, a group endorsed by Dobson. Others reject altogether the kinds of therapeutic approaches to boys evident in Pollack's work because they pathologize the "natural" ways of being a boy. Sommers' *The War Against Boys* (2000b) does so, arguing instead that teachers and the deceptions of feminists—not anything to do with boys themselves— are responsible for the slipping achievement of boys. Hers is a strongly biological view, with definite tones of Christian conservatism. The point here is that arguments about boys must filter through such sometimes tense and contradictory cultural politics about the origins and place of masculinity in U.S. society. Though some might lament the "poor boys" who suffer toxic gender roles, others perceive such lamentation as just another way to "soften" boys and to turn them away from God's plan for virile masculinity. At one level, the diversity of views on masculinity could serve to increase the pool of those concerned about boys, for there is an explanation to suit many tastes. On another level, though, such ideological conflicts ensure the diffuse, fragmentary nature of the boy debates and limit the possibilities for unifying the public in a singular direction.

Boys' Education "on the Ground": Local Interventions

Earlier I argued that responsibility for education at the state and local level in the United States is a constraint on targeting boys' education issues in a concerted, coherent way. This is true at the federal and state levels in terms of *explicit* policy. The history of local control of schools in the United States, however, along with growing movements toward site-based management, where principals and staffs are responsible for almost all decision making and policy, have facilitated growth in boys' educational at the *local* level. Indeed, local interventions, *not policy*, are the chief sites for action around issues of boys' education in the United States.

The primary mechanism explaining this local growth of boys' education is what Bob Lingard (2003) terms "*de facto* policy," mentioned earlier. Again, when the state abandons (or never takes up) the role of central policy maker, schools must find alternative sources to create policies to solve the real needs and problems they face from day to day. The glut of available and accessible texts within the raising-boys genre, discussed earlier, has provided such alternative sources for educators and concerned parents. Individual classrooms and schools around the United States, though largely invisible to the public eye, have gleaned ideas from these conservative texts, along with popular-rhetorical books' teacher- and parent-friendly "workbook" versions. Pollack's *Real Boys* (1998), for example, has a companion *Real Boys Workbook* (Pollack & Cushman, 2001) including advice and worksheets to guide parents and teachers. Gurian's *The Boys and Girls Learn Differently Action Guide for Teachers* (Gurian & Ballew, 2003), similarly, extends his previous work on providing "ultimate" classrooms for boys and girls (Gurian, 2001) with teacher-friendly—that is, short and accessible to meet the intense demands on teachers' time—worksheets and checklists. Though we can be relatively sure of the *content* of these endeavors to spread boys' issues in education, it is impossible to estimate the numbers of educators who have taken up such ideas or the extent to which educators have recontextualized (Bernstein, 1977)—that is, altered through practice—such discourses to fit their needs and beliefs.

Not all efforts at pedagogical and curricular interventions for U.S. boys have been under the radar or based in conservative texts, though. In fact, a number of arguably more progressive initiatives have been created to deal with the unique and sometimes dire social and academic needs of African-American boys (e.g., R. A. Smith, 2002). Such programs are endemic to and representative of the U.S. context of localized programs for boys. Though other programs for boys are afoot, these African American–created and –centered programs stand out because they are in some cases heavily publicized and because they offer glimpses of programs that resist notions that all boys are equally disadvantaged in schools.

Perhaps the most visible example of Afro-centric programs for boys was the contentious creation of three all-boy, African-American schools in Detroit, Michigan in the early 1990s. A district court ruled, in *Garrett v. Board of Education,* that the schools were in violation of the rights of girls. Though advocates for the all-boys academies cited the unique educational needs of African-American boys, the plaintiffs argued that the academies' establishment, because they were public schools, violated the Fourteenth Amendment's equal protection guarantee, Title IX, and several other federal and state ordinances. Though the all-boy schools were prohibited, chilling the hopes of single-sex schooling advocates in the United States, the issues of boys—particularly African-Americans— were put in the spotlight through this case.

Other programs for African-American boys have received less attention but demonstrate the possibilities and realities of local, non-governmental programs in the United States. Such programs have spawned from concerns for the lagging educational achievement of African-American boys and the increasing social ills growing from this. Such programs often provide male mentors, often particularly targeting boys without fathers at home, along with academic enrichment opportunities and (sometimes religious) counseling that are culturally relevant to the participants (Ladson-Billings, 1994), integrated into local institutions, staffed by people who live and work in the communities and schools, and responsive to local needs. The Paul Robeson Institute as described by Dance (2002) is another such program in Cambridge, Massachusetts. Boys Booked on Barbershops (called B-BOB; see http://www.midsouth.rr.com/kjob/bbob/bbob.html; accessed March 2004), part of the nationwide African American Read-In Chain, provides another example of responses from within the African-American community to boys' needs, in this case particularly focused on literacy skills and attitudes. Started in Memphis, Tennessee, using barbershops—traditionally one of the most stable businesses in African-American communities—the program seeks to provide high-interest books and have men and boys read together. Such a program is an innovative use of community resources to tackle the community's educational needs.

Caution is in order about such programs, despite whatever benefit and innovation they represent. First, the success of such programs, diffuse as they are and dependent upon the efforts of committed but often overworked community members, is never assured. Also, as Murtadah-Watts (2000) shows in her analysis of one of the Detroit academies intended to be all-male, discussed earlier, even programs *within* African-American communities can unintentionally replicate racist regimes of control, particularly control over the bodies of black males.[4] Such findings suggest vigilance even when implementing purportedly "progressive" reform.

Contexts for Future Growth of Boys' Education Issues

Though much of the debates and interventions surrounding boys' education, as I have shown, have been constrained by governmental and social contexts and have been relegated to the local level, things are changing; *contexts are always already in a state of transformation.* Though results of changes are notoriously difficult to predict, there are noticeable trends within the United States potentially bearing on the future of boys' education issues.

First, I mentioned that testing and accountability movements at both the state and federal level were suppressing or containing the discourses of boys' education by monopolizing the public's and the medias' attentions. Contradictorily, though, the testing and accountability measures currently in ascendance could well serve as a mainspring for increased growth in boys' education movements and policy. As Gillborn and Youdell (2000) have shown in the English testing and accountability context, a process of "triage" results when schools are judged on exams. That is, those students who are "on the bubble" of passing the tests accrue the majority of funding and intervention; in short, they take extra resources. Those most likely to be "on the bubble" are boys. Given the NCLB mandates to disaggregate test scores by sex, race, and class, the lagging performance of boys will be more apparent.[5] Given also the NCLB penalties for poor performance or even lack of progress for already well-performing schools, educators concerned for their jobs and their schools' survivals will increasingly need to attend to poorly performing boys.

A second condition for future growth of boys' education discourses, one powerfully interconnected with testing, is the increasing control exerted over education at the federal level in the United States. Though, as mentioned earlier, the U.S. federal role in education is constitutionally limited, new policy levers within the NCLB are changing this (see M. L. Smith, 2004, pp. 239–241). Though federal funding accounts for only about 7 percent of total U.S. educational spending, the long-term under-funding of public schools makes even this amount indispensable, so the NCLB holds sway over all educational authorities accepting federal monies. Similarly, the shift in federal funding from lump-sum distributions for states to targeted, competitive grants creates a situation in which the federal government can control what gets funded and can control what research corpuses and methods can be used. In this way, the government not only can control ideologies and create affinity groups (Gee, 2000–2001) but it can reward those supportive of its ideological positions. Because the state is a *deeply gendered* institution primarily oriented to the benefit of already dominant males, such a situation definitively advantages movements for boys' education.

Australia's recent meteoric rise in boys' education anxieties provides a compelling example of what can happen in a similar context of increasing federal control (Weaver-Hightower, 2008b). Like the United States, Australia's educational system is primarily a state and territory responsibility, though increasingly the Commonwealth government is exerting influence over the specificities of education (Lingard & Porter, 1997). I argue this increasing federal role in education has in many ways amplified the influence of the Australian government report *Boys: Getting it Right* (Australian House of Representatives Standing Committee on Education and Training, 2002)—the world's first federal-level inquiry into boys' education issues—and its resulting programs. Through direct grants to schools, the Boys' Education Lighthouse Schools Programme acted to produce affinity groups (e.g., Gee, 2000–2001), granting money to those accepting *a priori* that boys are disadvantaged and in need of interventions, a notion endorsed by the House report. Through financial incentive, the federal position becomes *de facto* policy even though the federal role is limited. The corollary with the U.S. context is clear: As the U.S. federal government increases its role through financial and other means, advocates for boys' education have new access to broad avenues of influence, namely federal rather than locally contained funding and policy, whether *de facto* or *de jure*.

Third, the growth of boys' education discourses, third, are encouraged by the current state of cultural politics in the United States.[6] Within an era of conservative restoration (Apple, 2000) and conservative modernization with strong moves toward the Christian Right (Apple, 2006), educational discourses critical of feminism and other forms of equity—on sexuality, especially—are gaining broader use and acceptance. Such discourses, harkening in many instances to Muscular Christianity and other traditional gender order beliefs, espouse advocacy positions on boys' issues partly to "return" education to the traditional, conservative Christian values existing before the impacts of feminism.

A fourth context for growth of boys' education discourses in the United States is recent rollbacks of women's policy infrastructure, reasonably termed a backlash against women's gains. The Bush (the younger) administration, for example, within two months of assuming office in 2001, closed the White House Office of Women's Initiatives and Outreach, the office closest to the President's ear dedicated to women's and girls' concerns. Bush's budgets every year since 2004 have proposed the elimination of the Women's Educational Equity (WEE) Program; though it has survived elimination, WEE has been reduced from $3 million to $1.8 million annually. Bush has also annually advocated lowering the budget of the Violence Against Women Program through the Department of Justice. The Bush administration has also twice commissioned reviews of Title IX. The first review (The Secretary of Education's Commission on Opportunity in Athletics, 2003) sought to clarify rules for university athletic programs, a reaction in part to high-profile cases of disbanding male athletic teams allegedly owing to Title IX "restrictions." The second review targeted Title IX rules limiting single-sex education programs, a review that eventually made it legal to create single-sex public schools (Davis, 2006). Given multiple attempts to modify Title IX and defund WEE, women's groups are, with good reason, feeling besieged. Considering also the dwindling resources, infrastructure, and oversight for women's concerns, conditions are ripe for increasing governmental programs for boys.

Fifth, boys' education panics and policies are finding fertile ground in recently stepped-up large-circulation, mainstream media attention in the United States. *Newsweek*, a large-circulation weekly news magazine ran a cover story in January 2006 proclaiming "The Boy Crisis" (Tyre, 2006), accompanied by a photograph of a group of scowling young toughs. *Business Week*, a conservative-leaning magazine for business news also with a large national circulation earlier ran a cover proclaiming a "New Gender Gap" in which "boys are becoming the second sex" (Conlin, 2003), accompanied by an image of a huge girl, arms folded and with a cocky grin, looming over a reduced-size boy with a downcast expression. Earlier, the *Atlantic Monthly*—also a widely circulated magazine—ran an abridged preview (Sommers, 2000a) of Sommer's *The War Against Boys* (2000b). *Education Week*, the United States' largest newspaper devoted solely to educational issues, periodically runs opinions and analyses focused on boys' score gaps (e.g., Galley, 2002; Newkirk, 2003; Riordan, 1999). Of key concern, the continuing interest in boys' issues is still markedly conservative, this interest generally lacks focused empirical study, and there is a dearth of high-profile U.S. voices of opposition— with the exception of scholars such as Michael Kimmel (e.g., 2000) and David Sadker (e.g., 2002) and high-profile reports by the think-tank Education Sector (Mead, 2006) and by the AAUW (Corbett, Hill, & St. Rose, 2008). Combined with a perceptible decline in the publicity around girls' remaining educational inequalities, the high profile of boys' issues has the potential to shift what the public and educators consider "real" gender issues.

Sixth, there are important public movements toward boys' policy. Perhaps the most telling example was a high-profile civil rights complaint filed with the U.S. Department of Education in December 2005. Doug Anglin, a student at Milton High School in Massachusetts, and his lawyer father filed the claim, arguing that boys at his school are disadvantaged. As Anglin told the *Boston Globe,* "From the elementary level, they [schools] establish a philosophy that if you sit down, follow orders, and listen to what they say, you'll do well and get good grades. Men naturally rebel against this" (Jan, 2006). Anglin also suggests, for example, that boys should be allowed to go to the bathroom whenever they want and that making boys decorate their notebooks is discriminatory. The complaint garnered local, national, and even international media coverage, with Internet sites of every ideology commenting on the story. (In line with the cultural tensions discussed above, even conservative pundits, interestingly, were often dismissive of Anglin's claims of victimhood.) Most relevant to my argument, the complaint is clearly geared to trigger national policymaking As the *Boston Globe* article says, "Anglin ... said he brought the complaint in hope that the Education Department would issue national guidelines on how to boost boys' academic achievement." The Department of Education's Civil Rights Office dismissed Anglin's complaint in 2006, but clearly the pressure is on to bring federal policymaking to bear. It appears to be working.

Indeed, it appears that panic discourses have been used by high-profile politicians in the United States. For example, in the press release announcing the publication of the 2004 biannual, Congressionally mandated report on the education of girls and women (Freeman, 2004), then-U.S. Secretary of Education Rod Paige said of the current state of gender in education:

> It is clear that girls are taking education very seriously and that they have made tremendous strides ... The issue now is that boys seem to be falling behind. We need to spend some time researching the problem so that we can give boys the support to succeed academcally.
> (November 19, 2004, press release, retrieved from http://www.ed.gov/news/pressreleases/2004/11/11192004b.html)

Paige's successor in the Secretary post, Margaret Spellings, has also made public comment on boys' education concerns, being quoted in the *Newsweek* story above (Tyre, 2006) as saying that boys' achievement gap "has profound implications for the economy, society, families and democracy." Though these are high-level officials signaling possible policy moves on the horizon, concern over boys has merited mention at the highest level of the U.S. government. In the 2005 State of the Union speech, annually the most watched and dissected political speech both in the United States and sometimes overseas, George W. Bush also voiced his concerns over boys:

> Now we need to focus on giving young people, especially young men in our cities, better options than apathy, or gangs, or jail. Tonight I propose a three-year initiative to help organizations keep young people out of gangs, and show young men an ideal of manhood that respects women and rejects violence. Taking on gang life will be one part of a broader outreach to at-risk youth, which involves parents

and pastors, coaches and community leaders, in programs ranging from literacy to sports.

Though this speech does not directly address some of the core concerns of boys' education that circulate in popular-rhetorical and practice-oriented literatures on boys' education, it represents a clear concern for masculinity crisis at the very highest levels of the U.S. government. It signals a significant chance of further policy and funding targeted to boys, a context to watch in the coming years.

Still, despite heavy growth in conservative discourses around boys' education, it is important to also note that some resistance has also grown up around such limiting discourses. A widely publicized report from Education Sector, a nonpartisan education policy think tank, entitled *The Truth About Boys and Girls* (Mead, 2006), for example, refutes the notion that boys are in crisis in schools as is popularly represented in the media. The report also critiques the notion that there is a crisis in college enrollment for males. This report, the increase in publications from a (pro)feminist perspective in journals, and the holding off of the most reactionary tendencies in Maine's policy formulation indicates that the issue of boys' education is more complex and tense than any simple analysis of its conservative dimensions would suggest. Though largely conservative pundits and movements have advanced the boys' education issue, those movements have not been monolithic or totalizing.

Cautions for Moving Forward

Given conditions favorable to those who would target educational resources to boys specifically, I should note several cautions. First, the possibility that test scores could be the primary evidence for turning to boys' issues is problematic. Are tests valid? Do they measure what is truly of concern? Though parents and educators are understandably concerned about achievement data, such indicators can elide social ills (risk taking, for example) and skill and attitude deficiencies (such as citizenship attitudes) in boys that deserve serious consideration. These indicators can also paint a more sanguine picture of girls than is actually the case.

Girls' needs may not show up on a test, but they are still very real. I join a chorus of those cautioning against the misguided conclusion that girls' needs have been solved. Girls still struggle with access to technology and technological literacy, access to high-status fields, and equitable outcomes from schooling such as workforce and economic indicators. Serious problems also remain in interpersonal relations girls have with boys. Many boys would benefit from anti-sexism, anti-harassment, antiviolence, anti-homophobia, and antiracism programs just as much as they would literacy programs. Because boys' issues are relationally tied to girls' issues, these interventions serve the best interests of all students. Our ability to see indicators of need for such interventions, however, is weakened in a context of declining women's policy infrastructure, governmental devaluing of all but experimental research, and rhetorical competition for "victim status."

Recent changes to Title IX to allow single-sex education are also of particular concern. Though not advertised as such, changes to Title IX are necessary to clear hurdles for the public subsidizing of private single-sex schools through vouchers, a reform unambiguously supported by the Bush administration despite low public support. The changes to Title IX call for a two-part test when evaluating the need for single-sex schools: (A) that such schools would help provide school choice for parents, and (B) that such schools would serve the learning needs of the students. The order of those goals—and this is how they are ordered in the official changes—should make clear the intention to further a rightist educational reform agenda. Indeed, like NCLB section 5131.a.23's establishmet of "innovative programs" for school choice including single-gender schools as well as sanctions elsewhere in the Act for anything less than achievement of standards by 100 percent of children (which no psychometrician will say is possible), most of NCLB's provisions work toward a system friendly to vouchers and privatization (see M. L. Smith, 2004, p. 234–235). Despite language within the revisions to Title IX calling for "substantially equal" opportunities and the application of "even handedness" in program offerings, many of the current protections for both girls and boys are undercut, and the ethic of "separate but equal," so hotly denounced in fights for civil rights by African-Americans, is reinscribed on the basis of gender. Well-meaning people from across the political continuum have differing ideas about single-sex education. Indeed, progressives in the African-American community have advocated single-sex schools for boys, such as the case of Detroit schools mentioned earlier. Some feminist groups advocate single-sex schools as well. Yet, research has shown that the benefits of single-sex education are not assured (AAUW, 1998; Mael, 1998; Riordan, 2002; U.S. Department of Education, 2005). In fact, such schools and classes can have disastrous consequences for teachers and students alike, for such programs may exacerbate hypermasculine cultures that are harmful to non-dominant boys and female teachers (Askew & Ross, 1988), may entrench stereotypes of gender (e.g., Kaminer, 1998), and may create dumping grounds for misbehaving boys (Kenway & Willis, 1998). These are not, of course, certain outcomes, but they can occur without vigilance and care in the programs' creations.

Possible racial implications, too, could follow from increasing attention to boys' issues. As Gillborn & Kirton (2000) have shown in England, racism among white working-class boys has increased in conjunction with discourses of "white victimhood" following from the "underachieving boys" debate. White victimhood discourses circulate in the United States as well, so boy panics could potentially exacerbate racial tensions. Any focus on, or alternately exclusion of, African-American boys could increase tensions, too, especially in view of the competitive nature characterizing boy debates thus far. Whether they are or are not, the resources of education are at least *perceived* to be part of a zero-sum game, where one group wins to the degree others lose. Such a perception accompanies gender as well as race.

Again, each of these cautions is only that: a caution. Boys' education issues are neither inherently conservative nor inherently dangerous. Indeed, working with boys has tremendous potential for progressive, socially just education. Thus far, however, rightist movements and conservative authors have indeed co-opted these issues. Their conservative adherents do not, though, permanently taint such issues. With care and alertness, interventions can serve the interests of both boys and the society they help make up.

Conclusion

As I have argued in this chapter, boys' education issues in the United States, just as elsewhere, are complex matters. Significant contextual differences exist between the U.S. reception of such matters and those of other countries around the world. For the most part, movements concerned with boys' issues have had less "success" in the United States. Concern for boys has been diffuse, conservative in nature, locally contained, and structurally constrained. Yet, as this context evolves, boys' issues have high potential for growth. Comprehending this context requires an understanding of the history, governmental structure, and social and cultural peculiarities of education in the United States. Understanding these contextual traits also suggests certain strategies dependent on that context. For the U.S. context, such strategies might include, among many others, targeting the local and diffuse sites of boys' education reform, usually individual schools and classrooms; working through the judicial system—rather than, say, the bureaucracy, as one might in Australia—to protect gender equity gains; and working toward putting out (pro)feminist messages in lay language and in sources that are popular and easily accessible. In the end, with due caution sensitive to the policy ecology, any programs or interventions need not be conservative or destructive to already vulnerable groups. Rather, such programs *could* enrich us all.

Author's Note

Significant portions of research for this essay were funded by a Fulbright fellowship from the United States Department of State in conjunction with the Australian-American Fulbright Commission. Special thanks are due to Rebecca Weaver-Hightower, Michael Apple, Fazal Rizvi, and members and visitors of the Friday Seminar at the University of Wisconsin-Madison for their comments on the draft. Remaining flaws are solely the author's responsibility.

Notes

1. Pirie is a Canadian, but this book, unlike many other Canadian works, has been widely available to U.S. practitioners.
2. I am indebted to Fazal Rizvi for this insight.
3. Compelling arguments can be made that the vast majority of institutions—any, in fact, not explicitly for women—serve the interests of men. I would agree with such a contention. My reference here is to infrastructure with explicit charter to serve men's interests *as gendered actors*.
4. As Murtadha-Watts (2000, note 3, p. 69) explains, after the ruling against the Board of Education of Detroit, girls were allowed into the school, but their enrollment makes up only 5 percent.
5. NCLB legislation does not provide for sex/gender as a category for reporting as part of its Annual Yearly Progress measure, the most direct link to accountability punishments. It does however, in Title I, part A, subpart 1, section 1111, (b)(3)(C)(xiii) require that states disaggregate scores on tests by gender and, in (h)(1)(C)(i), that states report these disaggregated numbers to the U.S. Secretary of Education and the public. Thus, though NCLB does not provide direct sanctions for gender gaps, the relative scores of boys and girls—and the resulting effect on overall scores—will stand out.
6. I thank Michael Apple for this point.

References

Alloway, N., Freebody, P., Gilbert, P., & Muspratt, S. (2002). *Boys, literacy and schooling: Expanding the repertoires of practice.* Canberra, Australia: Commonwealth Department of Education, Science and Training.

American Association of University Women. (1992). *How schools shortchange girls.* New York: Marlowe & Company.

American Association of University Women. (1993). *Hostile hallways: The AAUW survey on sexual harassment in America's schools.* (AAUW Report No. 923012). Washington, DC: AAUW.

American Association of University Women. (1995). *Growing smart: What's working for girls in school.* Washington, DC: AAUW.

American Association of University Women. (1998). *Separated by sex: A critical look at single-sex education for girls.* Washington, DC: AAUW.

Apple, M. W. (2000). *Official knowledge: Democratic education in a conservative age* (2nd ed.). New York: Routledge.

Apple, M. W. (2006). *Educating the "Right" way: Markets, standards, God, and inequality* (2nd ed.). New York: Routledge.

Apple, M. W., & Oliver, A. (1996). Becoming Right: Education and the formation of conservative movements. *Teachers College Record, 97,* 419–445.

Arnot, M., & Gubb, J. (2001). *Adding value to boys' and girls' education: A gender and achievement project in West Sussex*. Chichester, UK: West Sussex County Council.

Askew, S., & Ross, C. (1988). *Boys don't cry: Boys and sexism in education*. Milton Keynes, UK: Open University Press.

Australian House of Representatives Standing Committee on Education and Training. (2002). *Boys: Getting it right. Report on the inquiry into the education of boys*. Canberra, Australia: The Parliament of the Commonwealth of Australia.

Bae, Y., Choy, S., Geddes, C., Sable, J., & Snyder, T. (2000). *Trends in educational equity of girls and women* (NCES 2000-030). Washington, DC: U.S. Department of Education, National Center for Education Statistics.

Bederman, G. (1995). *Manliness and civilization: A cultural history of gender and race in the United States, 1880–1917*. Chicago: University of Chicago Press.

Bernstein, B. (1977). *Class, codes and control (Volume 3: Towards a theory of educational transmissions)* (Revised ed.). London: Routledge & Kegan Paul.

Bleach, K. (Ed.). (1998). *Raising boys' achievement in schools*. Stoke-on-Trent, UK: Trentham Books.

Bly, R. (1990). *Iron John: A book about men*. Reading, MA: Addison-Wesley.

Bouchard, P., Boily, I., & Proulx, M. C. (2003). *School success by gender: A catalyst for masculinist discourse* (No. SW21-103/2003). Ottawa, Canada: Status of Women Canada.

Brown, J. A. (2001). *Black superheroes, Milestone Comics, and their fans*. Jackson: University Press of Mississippi.

Brozo, W. G. (2002). *To be a boy, to be a reader: Engaging teen and preteen boys in active literacy*. Newark, DE: International Reading Association.

Clarke, E. H. (1873). *Sex in education, or, A fair chance for girls* (5th ed.). Boston: Houghton Mifflin.

Clatterbaugh, K. (1990). *Contemporary perspectives on masculinity: Men, women, and politics in modern society*. Boulder, CO: Westview Press.

Cohen, M. (1998). "A habit of healthy idleness": Boys' underachievement in historical perspective. In D. Epstein, J. Elwood, V. Hey & J. Maw (Eds.), *Failing boys?: Issues in gender and achievement* (pp. 19–34). Buckingham, UK: Open University Press.

Collins, C., Kenway, J., & McLeod, J. (2000a). *Factors influencing the educational performance of males and females in school and their initial destinations after leaving school*. Canberra, Australia: Commonwealth Department of Education, Training, and Youth Affairs.

Collins, C., Kenway, J., & McLeod, J. (2000b). Gender debates we still have to have. *Australian Educational Researcher, 27*(3), 37–48.

Comaroff, J., & Comaroff, J. L. (2000). Millennial capitalism: First thoughts on a second coming. *Public Culture, 12*(2), 291–343.

Commonwealth Department of Education Science and Training. (2003). *Meeting the challenge: Guiding principles for success from the Boys' Education Lighthouse Schools Programme Stage One 2003*. Canberra, Australia: Australian Government Department of Education, Science and Training.

Conlin, M. (2003, May 26). The new gender gap. *Business Week*, pp. 74–80.

Connell, R. W. (1995). *Masculinities*. Berkeley: University of California Press.

Corbett, C., Hill, C., & St. Rose, A. (2008). *Where the girls are: The facts about gender equity in education.* Washington, DC: American Association of University Women.

Dance, L. J. (2002). *Tough fronts: The impact of street culture on schooling.* New York: RoutledgeFalmer.

Davis, M. R. (2006, October 24). Single-sex classes, programs authorized under final education department regulation. *Education Week.*

Dee, T. S. (2006, Fall). The why chromosome: How a teacher's gender affects boys and girls. *Education Next,* p.68–75.

Dobson, J. (2001). *Bringing up boys.* Wheaton, IL: Tyndale House Publishers.

Epstein, D., Elwood, J., Hey, V., & Maw, J. (1998). Schoolboy frictions: Feminism and "failing" boys. In D. Epstein, J. Elwood, V. Hey, & J. Maw (Eds.), *Failing boys?: Issues in gender and achievement* (pp. 3–18). Buckingham, UK: Open University Press.

Faludi, S. (1991). *Backlash: The undeclared war against American women.* New York: Anchor Books.

Faludi, S. (1999). *Stiffed: The betrayal of the American man.* New York: William Morrow & Co.

Farrell, W. (1993). *The myth of male power: Why men are the disposable sex.* New York: Simon & Schuster.

Fashola, O. S. (Ed.). (2005). *Educating African American males: Voices from the field.* Thousand Oaks, CA: Corwin Press.

Ferguson, A. A. (2000). *Bad boys: Public schools in the making of Black masculinity.* Ann Arbor: University of Michigan Press.

Forbush, W. B. (1907). *The boy problem* (6th rewritten ed.). Boston: The Pilgrim Press. (Original work published 1901.)

Fordham, S., & Ogbu, J. U. (2000). Black students' school success: Coping with the "burden of 'acting white.'" In R. Arum & I. R. Beattie (Eds.), *The structure of schooling: Readings in the sociology of education* (pp. 303–310). Mountain View, CA: Mayfield Publishing.

Foster, V., Kimmel, M. S., & Skelton, C. (2001). "What about the boys?": An overview of the debates. In W. Martino & B. Meyenn (Eds.), *What about the boys?: Issues of masculinity in schools* (pp. 1–23). Buckingham, UK: Open University Press.

Fox, R. (2006, May 20). Boys—the classroom timebomb. *The New Zealand Herald.*

Frank, B., Kehler, M., Lovell, T., & Davison, K. (2003). A tangle of trouble: Boys, masculinity and schooling—future directions. *Educational Review, 55*(2), 119–133.

Frazier, N., & Sadker, M. (1973). *Sexism in school and society.* New York: Harper & Row.

Freeman, C. E. (2004). *Trends in educational equity for girls and women: 2004* (NCES 2005-016). Washington, DC: U.S. Department of Education.

Galley, M. (2002, January 23). Research: Boys to men. *Education Week, 23,* 26–27.

Gee, J. P. (2000–2001). Identity as an analytic lens for research in education. *Review of Research in Education, 25,* 99–125.

Gibson, H. W. (1916). *Boyology, or boy analysis.* New York: Association Press.

Gill, Z. (2005). *Boys: Getting it right:* The 'new' disadvantaged or 'disadvantage' redefined? *Australian Educational Researcher, 32*(2), 105–124.

Gillborn, D., & Kirton, A. (2000). White heat: Racism, under-achievement and white working-class boys. *International Journal of Inclusive Education, 4*(4), 271–288.

Gillborn, D., & Youdell, D. (2000). *Rationing education: Policy, practice, reform, equity.* Buckingham, UK: Open University Press.

Gleason, J. B. (1987). Sex differences in parent-child interaction. In S. U. Philips, S. Steele, & C. Tanz (Eds.), *Language, gender, and sex in comparative perspective* (pp. 189–199). Cambridge: Cambridge University Press.

Gurian, M. (1998). *A fine young man: What parents, mentors, and educators can do to shape adolescent boys into exceptional men.* New York: Jeremy P. Tarcher/ Putnam.

Gurian, M. (2001). *Boys and girls learn differently! A guide for teachers and parents.* San Francisco: Jossey-Bass.

Gurian, M., & Ballew, A. C. (2003). *The boys and girls learn differently action guide for teachers.* San Francisco: Jossey-Bass.

Head, J. (1999). *Understanding the boys: Issues of behaviour and achievement.* London: Falmer Press.

Heath, S. B. (1983). *Ways with words: Language, life, and work in communities and classrooms.* Cambridge: Cambridge University Press.

Iggulden, C., & Iggulden, H. (2007). *The dangerous book for boys* (1st U.S. ed.). New York: Collins.

Jackson, D., & Salisbury, J. (1996). Why should secondary schools take working with boys seriously? *Gender and Education, 8*(1), 103–115.

Jan, T. (2006, January 26). Schoolboy's bias suit: Argues system is favoring girls, *The Boston Globe.*

Janssen, A., & Weeden, L. K. (Eds.). (1994). *Seven promises of a promise keeper.* Colorado Springs, CO: Focus on the Family Publishing.

Jóhannesson, I. Á. (2004). To teach boys and girls: A pro-feminist perspective on the boys' debate in Iceland. *Educational Review, 56*(1), 33–42.

Johnson, R. T. (2000). *Hands off!: The disappearance of touch in the care of children.* New York: Peter Lang.

Kaestle, C. F. (Ed.). (1991). *Literacy in the United States: Readers and reading since 1880.* New Haven, CT: Yale University Press.

Kaminer, W. (1998, April). The trouble with single-sex schools. *Atlantic Monthly,* 23–26, 34.

Katz, J., & Jhally, S. (Director). (1999). *Tough guise: Violence, media, and the crisis in masculinity* [motion picture]. Northampton, MA: Media Education Foundation.

Keen, S. (1991). *Fire in the belly: On being a man.* New York: Bantam Books.

Kenway, J., & Willis, S. (1998). *Answering back: Girls, boys and feminism in schools.* London: Routledge.

Kidd, K. B. (2004). *Making American boys: Boyology and the feral tale.* Minneapolis: University of Minnesota Press.

Kimmel, M. S. (1996). *Manhood in America: A cultural history.* New York: Free Press.

Kimmel, M. S. (2000, November 7–8). What about the boys? *WEEA Digest,* 1–2.

Kimmel, M. S. (2002, February 8). Gender, class and terrorism. *Chronicle of Higher Education*, 48, B11–B12.

Kindlon, D., & Thompson, M. (2000). *Raising Cain: Protecting the emotional life of boys*. New York: Ballantine Books.

King, J. R. (1998). *Uncommon caring: Learning from men who teach young children*. New York: Teachers College Press.

King, J. R. (2000). The problem(s) of men in early education. In N. Lesko (Ed.), *Masculinities at school* (pp. 3–26). Thousand Oaks, CA: Sage.

Ladson-Billings, G. (1994). *The dreamkeepers: Successful teachers of African American children*. San Francisco: Jossey-Bass.

Lesko, N. (Ed.). (2000). *Masculinities at school*. Thousand Oaks, CA: Sage.

Lingard, B. (2003). Where to in gender policy in education after recuperative masculinity politics? *International Journal of Inclusive Education*, 7(1), 33–56.

Lingard, B., & Douglas, P. (1999). *Men engaging feminisms: Pro-feminism, backlashes, and schooling*. Buckingham, UK: Open University Press.

Lingard, B., & Porter, P. (Eds.). (1997). *A national approach to schooling in Australia?: Essays on the development of national policies in schools education*. Canberra, Australia: Australian College of Education.

Lingard, B., Martino, W., Mills, M., & Bahr, M. (2002). *Addressing the educational needs of boys*. Canberra, Australia: Commonwealth Department of Education, Science and Training.

Mac an Ghaill, M. (1994). *The making of men: Masculinities, sexualities, and schooling*. Buckingham, UK: Open University Press.

Mael, F. A. (1998). Single-sex and coeducational schooling: Relationships to socioemotional and academic development. *Review of Educational Research*, 68(2), 101–129.

Maine Task Force on Gender Equity in Education. (2006). *Draft report*. Augusta, ME: Maine Department of Education.

Martino, W., & Berrill, D. (2003). Boys, schooling, and masculinities: Interrogating the "Right" way to educate boys. *Educational Review*, 55(2), 99–117.

Martino, W., & Pallotta-Chiarolli, M. (2003). *So what's a boy? Addressing issues of masculinity and schooling*. Maidenhead, UK: Open University Press.

McClintock, A. (2002). Masculinity and other war zones. Paper presented at the Visiting Distinguished Faculty Award Lecture, University of Kentucky, Lexington, KY, January.

Mead, S. (2006). *The truth about boys and girls*. Washington, DC: Education Sector.

Mills, M. (2001). *Challenging violence in schools: An issue of masculinities*. Buckingham, UK: Open University Press.

Mills, M. (2003). Shaping the boys' agenda: The backlash blockbusters. *International Journal of Inclusive Education*, 7(1), 57–73.

Mills, M., Martino, W., & Lingard, R. (2004). Attracting, recruiting and retaining male teachers: Policy issues in the male teacher debate. *British Journal of Sociology of Education*, 25(3), 355–369.

Mills, M., Martino, W., & Lingard, B. (2007). Getting boys' education 'right': The Australian Government's Parliamentary Inquiry Report as an exemplary instance of recuperative masculinity politics. *British Journal of Sociology of Education*, 28(1), 5–21.

Moore, R. L., & Gillette, D. (1990). *King, warrior, magician, lover: Rediscovering the archetypes of the mature masculine*. San Francisco: HarperSanFrancisco.

Morrison, T. (1992). *Playing in the dark: Whiteness and the literary imagination*. New York: Vintage.

Murtadha-Watts, K. (2000). Theorizing urban black masculinity construction in an African-centered school. In N. Lesko (Ed.), *Masculinities at school* (pp. 49–71). Thousand Oaks, CA: Sage.

National Center for Educational Statistics. (2005). *NAEP 2004 trends in academic progress: Three decades of student performance in reading and mathematics*. Washington, DC: U.S. Department of Education.

National Center for Educational Statistics. (2007). *The nation's report card: Reading 2007*. Washington, DC: U.S. Department of Education.

National Center for Educational Statistics. (2008). *The nation's report card: Writing 2007*. Washington, DC: U.S. Department of Education.

National Commission on Excellence in Education. (1983). *A nation at risk: The imperative for educational reform*. Washington, DC: National Commission on Excellence in Education.

NEA Research. (2003). *Status of the American public school teacher 2000–2001*. Washington, DC: National Education Association.

Newkirk, T. (2000). Misreading masculinity: Speculations on the great gender gap in writing. *Language Arts*, 77, 294–300.

Newkirk, T. (2002). *Misreading masculinity: Boys, literacy, and popular culture*. Portsmouth, NH: Heinemann.

Newkirk, T. (2003). The quiet crisis in boys' literacy. *Education Week*, September 10, 34.

Newman, K. S. (2004). *Rampage: The social roots of school shootings*. New York: Basic Books.

Noble, C., & Bradford, W. (2000). *Getting it right for boys and girls*. London: Routledge.

Office of Special Education and Rehabilitation Services. (2005). *25th annual (2003) report to Congress on the implementation of the Individuals with Disabilities Education Act, vol. 1*. Washington, DC: U.S. Department of Education.

Ogle, L. T., Sen, A., Pahlke, E., Jocelyn, L., Kastberg, D., & Roey, S., (2003). *International comparisons in fourth-grade reading literacy: Findings from the Progress in International Reading Literacy Study (PIRLS) of 2001* (NCES 2003-073). Washington, DC: National Center for Educational Statistics.

Orenstein, P. (1994). *School girls: Young women, self-esteem, and the confidence gap*. New York: Anchor Books.

Pipher, M. (1994). *Reviving Ophelia: Saving the selves of adolescent girls*. New York: Grosset/Putnam.

Pirie, B. (2002). *Teenage boys and high school English*. Portsmouth, NH: Heinemann.

Pollack, W. (1998). *Real boys: Rescuing our sons from the myths of boyhood*. New York: Random House.

Pollack, W., & Cushman, K. (2001). *Real boys workbook*. New York: Villard.

Price, J. N. (2000). Peer (dis)connections, school, and African American masculinities. In N. Lesko (Ed.), *Masculinities at school* (pp. 127–159). Thousand Oaks, CA: Sage.

34   *Marcus B. Weaver-Hightower*

Riordan, C. (1999, November 17). The silent gender gap: Reading, writing, and other problems for boys. *Education Week*, pp. 46–49.

Riordan, C. (2002). What do we know about the effects of single-sex schools in the private sector?: Implications for public schools. In A. Datnow & L. Hubbard (Eds.), *Gender in policy and practice: perspectives on single-sex and coeducational schooling* (pp. 10–30). New York: RoutledgeFalmer.

Ross, T. (2003). Nats call for inquiry into boys' education. Retrieved October 27, 2003, from http://www.stuff.co.nz/stuff/0,2106,2668521a7694,00.html

Sadker, D. (2002, November). An educator's primer on the gender war. *Phi Delta Kappan, 84*, 235–244.

Sadker, M., & Sadker, D. (1994). *Failing at fairness: How our schools cheat girls*. New York: Touchstone.

Secretary of Education's Commission on Opportunity in Athletics. (2003). *Open to all: Title IX at 30*. Washington, DC: U.S. Department of Education.

Sexton, P. (1969). *The feminized male: Classrooms, white collars and the decline of manliness*. New York: Random House.

Smith, M. L. (2004). *Political spectacle and the fate of American schools*. New York: RoutledgeFalmer.

Smith, R. A. (2002, October 30). Black boys. *Education Week*, pp. 40, 43.

Smith, M. W., & Wilhelm, J. D. (2002). *"Reading don't fix no chevys": Literacy in the lives of young men*. Portsmouth, NH: Heinemann.

Sommers, C. H. (1994). *Who stole feminism?: How women have betrayed women*. New York: Simon & Schuster.

Sommers, C. H. (2000a, May). The war against boys. *The Atlantic Monthly, 285*, 59–74.

Sommers, C. H. (2000b). *The war against boys: How misguided feminism is harming our young men*. New York: Simon & Schuster.

Tatum, A. (2005). *Teaching reading to Black adolescent males: Closing the achievement gap*. Portland, ME: Stenhouse Publishers.

Thompson, M. (2000). *Speaking of boys: Answers to the most-asked questions about raising sons*. New York: Ballantine Books.

Thorne, B. (1993). *Gender play: Girls and boys in school*. New Brunswick, NJ: Rutgers UP.

Tyre, P. (2006, January 30). The trouble with boys. *Newsweek, 147*, 44–52.

Tyre, P. (2008). *The trouble with boys: A surprising report card on our sons, their problems at school, and what parents and educators must do*. New York: Crown Publishers.

U.S. Department of Education. (2005). *Single-sex versus coeducational schooling: A systematic review*. Washington, DC: U.S. Department of Education.

Wack, K. (2006, March 29). Thorny politics drive panel studying gender. *Portland Press Herald*.

Wagemaker, H., Taube, K., Munck, I., Kontogiannopoulou-Polydorides, G., & Martin, M. (1996). *Are girls better readers? Gender differences in reading literacy in 32 countries*. Amsterdam: The International Association for the Evaluation of Educational Achievement.

Weaver-Hightower, M. B. (2002). The gender of terror and heroes? What educators might teach about men and masculinity after September 11, 2001. *Teachers*

College Record. Retrieved September 9, 2002, from http://www.tcrecord.org/Content.asp?ContentID=11012

Weaver-Hightower, M. B. (2003a). Crossing the divide: Bridging the disjunctures between theoretically oriented and practice-oriented literature about masculinity and boys at school. *Gender and Education*, *15*(4), 407–423.

Weaver-Hightower, M. B. (2003b). The "boy turn" in research on gender and education. *Review of Educational Research*, *73*(4), 471–498.

Weaver-Hightower, M. B. (2008a). Inventing the 'all-American' boy: A case study in the capture of boys' education issues by conservative groups. *Men and Masculinities*, *10*(3), 267–295.

Weaver-Hightower, M. B. (2008b). *The politics of policy in boys' education: Getting boys "Right"*. New York: PalgraveMacmillan.

West, J., Denton, K., & Germino-Hausken, E. (2000). *America's kindergartners* (NCES 2000-070). Washington, DC: National Center for Educational Statistics.

Willis, P. (1977). *Learning to labor*. New York: Columbia University Press.

Women on Words and Images. (1972). *Dick and Jane as victims: Sex stereotyping in children's readers*. Princeton, NJ: Women on Words and Images.

Young, J. P. (2000). Boy talk: Critical literacy and masculinities. *Reading Research Quarterly*, *35*(3), 312–337.

Zirkel, S. (2002). Is there a place for me? Role models and academic identity among white students and students of color. *Teachers College Record*, *104*(2), 357–376.

2 Gender Policies in Australia and the United Kingdom

The Construction of "New"
Boys and Girls

*Martin Mills, Becky Francis, and
Christine Skelton*

Introduction

Since the early 1990s, concerns about boys' underachievement have dominated gendered policy concerns in the United Kingdom and Australia. However, the take-up of the boys' issue in each country, though often grounded in similar backlash politics, have of late taken different turns in relation to their constructions of "boys." In the U.K. context, boys have been simultaneously positioned as "at risk" (because of their masculinity) and (if this is not attended to) as "problem boys" (Francis, 2006; Francis & Skelton, 2005). However, in the Australian context, while there are some aspects of this "therapeutic turn" apparent in references to boys' abilities to cope with change, and a demonization of particular groups of boys (for example, Muslim boys), there is still very much a construction of boys as an oppressed group dominating the policy agenda (Mills, Martino, & Lingard, 2007). In this chapter, we examine these two national take-ups of the boys' debate and situate them within the histories of their relevant local contexts and within global anti-feminist discourses. We argue that though these two different national trends in the educational "boy-turn" (Weaver-Hightower, 2003) indicate the differing concerns of each national context, underpinning each trend is an anti-feminist politics that works toward undermining girls' educational experiences by constructing them as undeserving of their achievements.

Within both national contexts, achievement is a key concern. In the United Kingdom, an (albeit somewhat notional) quasi-market in education has foregrounded credentialized educational achievement to the exclusion of virtually any other concept of "quality." Moreover, neoliberal preoccupations with human capital and with individual responsibility and meritocracy saturate policy and produce "underachieving pupils" as a grave potential impediment to a competitive economy. In Australia, data demonstrating boys' supposed underperformance on a range of national tests, especially those relating to literacy, are regularly rolled out to justify boys' educational initiatives at the national and local level. This concern is indicative of neoliberal discourses of human capital growth and associated regimes of efficiency and economy that are shaping educational policy in many Western countries. As in the United Kingdom, where national economic well-being is discursively associated with academic achievement and where schools are judged on their ability to contribute to this economic well-being, students who regularly fail to achieve at school can be constructed as a liability. However, in Australia the quasi-market and credentialization of education seen in the United Kingdom are less well-established (possibly owing to aspects emanating from the federal governance in Australia; for example the influence of the more progressive politics of many state governments). Moreover, conservative anti-feminist discourses have worked alongside these neoliberal discourses to position boys' underachievement as the product of the attention that has been paid to girls' education over the last two to three decades.

The Australian Context: The Location of Boys within a Gender Equity Agenda

In Australia, there have been two distinct strands of the anti-feminist move toward a focus on boys' education. On the one hand, there has been what Connell (1995) and others (see for example, Kimmel, 1995) have referred to as a mythopoetic politics working its way through boys' educational discourses. These politics take a therapeutic approach to boys' education and suggest that boys' natural ways of being a boy, their "deep masculinity," have been affected by the rise of feminism that has troubled boys' sense of self. Hence, as Titus (2004) indicates in relation to the ways in which the debate has been taken up in the United States, there has been a push to "rescue," "protect," "heal," and "save" boys (see for example, Gurian 1999; Kindlon and Thompson, 1999; Pollack, 1999; and see Mills, 2003 for a critique of these texts). Within many of the "foundation" texts of this movement (for example, Bly, 1991 in the United States and Biddulph, 1995 in Australia), there is a plea for men to take responsibility for leading boys into a "healthy" and "appropriate" manhood: that is, the raising of boys is constructed as a form of "men's business." It is only recently that constructions of boys as requiring "help" to develop into "healthy males" has made an appearance in the U.K. policy literature (Department of Health, 2003). However, there are differences in the Australian and U.K. contexts. In the United Kingdom the relative lack of feminist influence on policy (see Arnot, 1989) means that no "backlash" against feminist informed policy has been required: The production of boys as "at risk" is more to do with a general "therapeutic turn" in approaches to pedagogy (Ecclestone, 2004). The same discourses used in these texts (by Pollack, Gurian etc) can be seen in many of the various Australian and U.K. educational policy concerns that connect a lack of male teachers with current concerns about boys' education (see Francis & Skelton, 2001; Martino & Frank, 2006; Mills et al., 2004, 2007; Skelton, 2001, for critiques of this position). Many working within this mythopoetic tradition, though often claiming that they support feminist concerns for improvements in girls' education, also blame feminists for the current status of boys' education. As Titus (2004) has suggested: "Conferring victim status on males also makes it obligatory to designate perpetrator(s) of harm." It is feminists who are being constructed as the perpetrators of this supposed victimization in many of the Australian policy frameworks.

The other strand of anti-feminist men's politics to be found in many of the discourses shaping the current gender and education policy moment are often referred to as "men's rights" (Connell, 1995) and are reflected in the claims that a supposed discrimination against boys has been the order of the day since feminists have supposedly captured the state, and education departments in particular (see Farrell, 1993, and Hoff Sommers, 2000, for examples of these politics). Men's-rights politics tend to be more vitriolic than mythopoetic politics. These politics are not based upon presumptions that boys need to be healed or even "protected" from one another. Indeed, as Francis and Skelton (2005, p. 46) note, Hoff Sommers is particularly scornful of therapeutic approaches to boys' education; instead, she has sought to attack the structures that have supposedly been set in place to prevent boys from being boys. Hence, men's-rights politics usually contain an angry attack on feminists and the supposed "feminisation of schooling" (see Skelton, 2002 for critique of this notion) and claim that boys should now be a social justice concern as they have been systematically oppressed by the historical concern with girls' education. These men's-rights discourses are evident in the United Kingdom within many of the strategies recommended by educational consultants and the like for use by teachers (e.g., producing "boy friendly" reading materials and seating boys next to girls so that girls' language skills might "rub off" on boys (Bleach, 1998; Noble and Bradford, 2000). Yet interestingly, in Britain, such "men's rights" (and, indeed, mythopoetic) discourses have largely *not* been incorporated in official education policy documents. Conversely, these themes were prominent in many of the submissions to the Australian Parliamentary Inquiry into boys' education, *Boys Getting it Right*, and though there is often an explicit rejection of the extremes of this movement by policy makers, men's-rights politics clearly impact upon the way in which some documents are shaped and in the direction that boys' policies are taken up in schools. For instance, in one Australian high school, it was reported to one of us how at the end of the 2005 school year there was much lamenting on the part of the school administration about girls outperforming boys in the matriculation results, whereas at the end of the 2006 school year, senior administrators in the school were cheering because their efforts to improve boys' academic results had led to the boys outperforming the girls!

Australia has a long history of engagement with gender issues in education. In the 1970s, this engagement began as a feminist one concerned about the ways in which girls were disadvantaged and discriminated against by the education system and in which their experiences of school were often negative ones as a result of the behaviors of boys and sometimes male teachers (Commonwealth of Schools Commission, 1975). However, coinciding with the advent of a conservative men's backlash against feminism in many Western countries there has been, since the 1990s, a growing interest in the education of boys, where boys have been constructed as the new victims of schooling.

The morphing of the gender agenda in Australia from one that is concerned with the education of girls into one focused on boys is apparent in the changing titles of major policy documents and programs from the 1970s through to the present moment. Girls' figured prominently in the titles of policy documents from 1975 to 1993: *Girls, School and Society* (Commonwealth of Schools Commission, 1975); *National Policy for the Education of Girls in Australian Schools* (Commonwealth of Schools Commission, 1987); *Listening to Girls, Review of the National Policy* (Milligan et al., 1992); and the *National Action Plan for the Education of Girls 1993–97* (Australian Education Council, 1993). However, in 1997, a key national policy document that had the support of all Australian states washed *girls* from the title and replaced it with the term *gender*: This was the *Gender Equity: A Framework for Australian Schools* (Gender Equity Taskforce, 1997).

The *Gender Equity Framework* was a pivotal moment in Australian policy development in that boys as boys were now also made a focal point of educational policy. In a number of ways this policy, despite being criticized by many within the growing boys' lobby, was seen by feminists who had been working in girls' education for many years as representing a partial surrendering of ground by the State governments, and their departments of education, to the boys' lobby groups (see, for example, Daws, 1997). Interestingly, the take-up of boys in this policy drew on similar discourses shaping the earlier concerns of feminists working within the educational bureaucracy (often referred to in positive terms as "femocrats"; see Eisenstein, 1997). For as Daws (1997) has stated:

> So far, satisfactorily incorporating boys' issues under the banner of gender equity, without diminishing the emphasis on the continuing challenges facing girls, has eluded the Gender Equity Taskforce. The current statement of strategic directions runs the risk of being interpreted as a restatement of early liberal positions on equality of

opportunity, rather than a progressive statement which moves beyond divisive debates about who is more disadvantaged and most in need of educational interventions and resourcing (p. 105).

However, though this policy document drew on what Foster, Kimmel, and Skelton (2001) have referred to as a "presumptive equality,"(i.e., that boys and girls were treated as equally disadvantaged), the dominance of "boys" in Australian gender policy was not made complete until 2002 with the release of *Boys: Getting it Right* (House of Representatives Standing Committee on Education and Training, 2002). This report was highly critical of *Gender Equity: A Framework for Australian Schools* as a document that had been overly concerned with girls' issues at the expense of boys. Its recommendation that there be a review of the Framework to make it more "boy-friendly" was taken up by the former federal government. However, it has been a review that has been in progress since 2003 and had still not been completed by mid-2006 owing to its unpalatability to the States. The *Boys: Getting it Right* report was the stimulus for the then federal government's 2003–2005 *Boys' Lighthouse Schools Project* and the 2005 *Success for Boys Project*. These two latter programs were funded to the tune of $7 million and $19.4 million, respectively, a far cry from previous funding amounts allocated to girls' schooling! The Australian focus in this chapter will be on the politics contained in these two programs (see Mills et al., 2007 for an analysis of *Boys: Getting it Right*). The chapter argues that though human capital theory influences much of this Australian agenda, anti-feminist mythopoetic and men's rights discourses, unlike the United Kingdom, are still the driving force behind policy concerns for boys.

The U.K. Context: Boys and Education as an Issue of Standards

As we have already intimated, in the United Kingdom, the emphasis is on reaching (or exceeding) the prescribed standards in public examinations and, as boys are seen to be failing in reaching those standards, then strategies and recommendations are aimed at this group. Thus, the *policy* concern about boys is foremost about standards rather than social justice objectives. A number of booklets have been produced for schools to enable them to directly target the attitudes, behaviors, and learning styles of boys (e.g. *Yes He Can—Schools where boys write well* [Ofsted, 2003a]; *Boys' Achievement in Secondary Schools* [Ofsted, 2003b]; *National Healthy School Standard to Raise Boys Achievement'* [DfES, 2003]).

This targeting of boys began in the mid-1990s with the introduction and publication of league tables whereby the performance of a school's pupils in standard assessment tasks (SATs) were measured and compared between schools, ostensibly to inform and facilitate 'consumer' (parent) choice. These league tables were published for the first time in 1994 for secondary schools and 1996 for primary schools—which provides an explanation as to why "boys' underachievement" began to hit the media headlines in 1995. This was the culmination of a sustained effort towards the marketization of education.

A Conservative government, under the leadership of Margaret Thatcher, introduced the major shift in education that was later to be developed under New Labour. After the Second World War, education was seen to have a social and economic function that involved the development of economic growth, equality of opportunity, and social justice. However, a series of acts culminating in the Education Reform Act 1988 replaced this with a notion of education as a means of enabling individual aspirations through the rough justice of market forces (Haywood & Mac an Ghaill, 1996). Thus, the notion of education as a means of securing social democracy—in which the eradication of inequalities was perceived as necessary for the collective good—was replaced with one of meritocratic social diversity, promoting ideas of individual entitlement and freedom of choice. When New Labour came to power in 1997 and Prime Minister Tony Blair pledged "education, education, education" as central to his Third Way policies, schooling became of even greater significance. The neoliberal tenets that underpin Third Way politics locate responsibility with individuals rather than social structures (Rose, 1999), and hence position it as the 'duty' of each individual to achieve.

Though both Australia and the United Kingdom place "boys and schooling" as an "educational priority," there are significant differences between the two countries. It has already been commented that social justice objectives were evident at least in the early days of the debates in Australia, but that in the United Kingdom in recent years, the official priority has been economic determinants (followed by social objectives such as addressing the tendency of boys toward destructive behaviors). As Pat Mahony (2003, p. 75) from the UK points out, "One obvious difference between Australia and the UK is that we have had no tradition of a "femocracy" working within the central State." The accuracy of this statement can be clearly seen when contrasting government policy intervention over boys' underachievement and the lack of willingness on the part of government to become involved in strategies to tackle girls' underachievement in an earlier period (Arnot & Weiner, 1987). Furthermore, Mahony comments on how a change in U.K. government (i.e., the winning of power by New Labour in 1997 marking the end of 18 years of Conservative rule) has not altered the general drift in policy, and indeed, "inequality" has increasingly been redefined in New Labour policy as "social exclusion" (Mahony, p. 76). The situation then in the United Kingdom is that the "achievement" agenda has dominated, and continues to dominate, educational policy.

Current Directions in Australia and the United Kingdom

Boys as Victims

The first major funding to schools specifically for boys' education in Australia came under the federal government's *Boys' Lighthouse Project* in 2003. The purpose of this project was to foreground those approaches to boys' education occurring in schools that had been effective in addressing boys' supposed educational needs. Approximately 350 schools were involved (some of these obtained funding as part of a cluster group). Schools were selected on the basis of their ability to provide evidence on how their strategies and programs improved boys' education. The selected schools included those that had introduced mentoring programs based upon men (or sometimes older boys) working with boys; that had developed a range of strategies for motivating boys; and that had made boys' literacy a school priority. The justification for the $7 million funding for this project was provided by the Commonwealth Government (2003) in *Educating boys: Issues and information*. Reasons included the following:

- Boys underperform on key literacy measures (p. 2).
- Though girls' performance in literacy results has remained relatively stable over the past 25 years, overall boys' results have fallen to a significant degree (p. 2).
- Girls are achieving higher average marks in the majority of subjects at year 12, and the "gap" between boys' and girls' total marks has widened (p. 3).
- Boys are less engaged with their school and enjoy school less than do girls (p. 3).
- For the past 25 years, more girls than boys have completed schooling (p. 4).
- More girls than boys go on to study at higher education institutions (p. 4).
- Males make up an overwhelming proportion of students experiencing disciplinary problems and school exclusion (p. 4).

These grounds indicate that the concerns are with achievement (especially literacy), enjoyment, retention, post-school options, and behavior. However, these indicators of boys' problems do not take into account issues of curriculum selection, later distribution of wealth and power, sexual harassment of girls, and so on (see Yates, 2000).

The constant reference to the "last 25 years" is indicative of the anti-feminism that underpins much of the recent policy development in boys' education. The suggestion is that in that 25-year period, "something" has happened to bring about change for boys and girls; implicit within that suggestion is that that something is "feminism." The constant comparison of boys' social and academic outcomes with those of girls is also indicative of the treatment of this gender debate as a zero sum game. For instance, that boys may be enjoying school less than girls (as debatable as this might be) does not mean that girls enjoy school (see Hallam and Rogers, 2006); further, that the gap between girls and boys is supposedly widening does not mean that boys are achieving less: It could mean that girls are improving. And finally, boys' behaviors are constructed as a concern for boys, with little concern expressed about the ways in which these behaviors may have negative experiences on the educational experiences of girls. Further, the suggestion that boys are "experiencing" discipline problems and school exclusions removes their agency from their behaviors—it is something that is done to them. (One is left to wonder, by whom?) The notion that boys are experiencing behavior problems represents a key distinction in the turn that the boys' debate is taking in the United Kingdom from that currently shaping the boys' agenda in Australia. In the United Kingdom, as Francis (2006), and others (for example, Elwood, 2005) have noted, new constructions of boys tend to focus on the "problem boy." However, in the Australian context, this notion of experiencing leaves the "poor boy" discourse intact by suggesting that even their poor behaviors are not their fault.

This poor boys discourse in Australian policy documents often works to construct boys as being uncertain about what it means to be a boy in contemporary times. The reported experiences of the various lighthouse school projects were used to produce *Meeting the Challenge Report: Guiding Principles for Success from the Boys' Education Lighthouse Schools Programme Stage One 2003*, a document that provides to schools a number of principles for implementing effective strategies for improving boys' education. The opening words in the foreword to this document by the former federal Minister for Education, Science and Training, Dr. Brendan Nelson, were: "Where masculinity was once seen as a virtue, it is now seen as an obstacle to be overcome" (Department of Education, Science and Training, 2003, p. iii). Here are echoes of the mythopoetic movement that constructs not "masculinity" as a problem but its devaluing. Questions obviously arise as to what form of masculinity Nelson is referring to. However, it is probably fair to say that he was concerned about the undermining of traditional forms of masculinity that have been brought into question by changing times, including by challenges from various sections of the feminist movement. The response to this devaluing of traditional forms of masculinity has been in line with those of the mythopoetic movement, with its focus on male mentors, by stressing the importance of male teachers in the education of boys. One of the guiding principles for success with boys is thus to "Provide opportunities for boys to benefit from positive male role models from within and beyond the school." This is supported in Nelson's foreword, which stated:

Only one in four students studying to be a teacher is a man. When you walk into a school to find the only man on site is the gardener, how does that affect the development of both boys and girls?

(Department of Education, Science and Training, 2003, p. iii)

The slippage between mythopoetic and men's-rights politics is apparent in the comments of Nelson in his support for this document. Both forms of politics are anti-feminist (see Mills, 2003) and this is evident in Nelson's claims. There are clear links made between the rise of the feminism and boys' supposedly declining levels of achievement and problematic social behaviors. For instance, Nelson states that "Between 1975 and 1995, the literacy achievement of fourteen year-old boys declined" (iii). The 1970s are, of course, when the second-wave feminist movement was first beginning to impact upon Australian society, as in many other Western countries. He then goes on to say that "The problem is not that girls are doing better than boys—it is instead that boys are not doing as well as they once did." Here the argument is constructed not as one that has seen boys and girls improving at different rates but a construction of boys as having been set back by gender policies designed to improve girls' education. This is also evident in his comments about the *Gender Equity Framework:*

Methods adopted to achieve long overdue progress in relation to the educational needs of girls under the national policy document *Gender Equity: A Framework for Australian Schools*, written in 1996, may have come at the expense of boys.

(Department of Education, Science and Training, 2003, p. iii)

This suggestion, that advances in girls' education have possibly come at the expense of boys, ties into the men's-rights politics that claim that structural arrangements have been put in place that work against the interests of boys: that is, that they been structural arrangements that have supported the "war on boys." The former federal government's *Success for Boys* project sought to address this structural imbalance.

Success for Boys grew out of the *Boys' Lighthouse* project and draws upon the principles outlined in *Meeting the Challenge.* The *Success for Boys* document notes that "Over the period 2005-2008 the government is to provide grants averaging $10,000 to 1,600 schools in the compulsory years of schooling (kindergarten to grade 10)" (Department of Education, Science and Training, 2003, p. i). The project is supported by a set of professional development activities constructed by James Cook University in Queensland and the Curriculum Corporation. The grants to schools are designed to assist schools to take up the professional learnings contained within the set of modules provided in the professional development packages with the intention of embedding them in practice. A series of supporting conferences have also been set up across the country.

It is interesting to note some changes between the former Minister's foreword for *Meeting the Challenge* and the one he constructed for the *Success for Boys* document outlining the project for those intending to complete the tender for funds. In *Meeting the Challenge* he suggests that "From teachers and parents in remote Aboriginal communities to prestigious independent schools, there is a concern with what is happening to boys" (Department of Education, Science and Training, 2003, p. iii). However, this is qualified somewhat in the *Success for Boys* document:

> While we want all our boys to succeed, we know that some boys experience more challenges than others. Some boys are at a particular risk of disengaging from school. This may include boys from backgrounds such as Indigenous backgrounds, who are geographically isolated, who are from disadvantaged socio-economic backgrounds and boys with a disability (p. i).

In the *Success for Boys* brochure encouraging schools to apply for the $10,000 grants, it indicates the areas of concern regarding boys' education: "Some areas of concern for boys compared to girls are their lower literacy achievement, lower school retention and lower participation in higher education." It indicates that the money will be for professional learning that "will have a focus on three key intervention areas that research indicates are of particular benefit to boys":

- Giving boys opportunities to benefit from positive male role models and mentors from both within and beyond the school.
- Effective literacy teaching and assessment.
- The use of information and communications technology (ICT) as a means of improving boys' engagement with active learning.

These key intervention areas are all reflected in the modules constructed for the *Success for Boys* program to accompany a core module that provides a theoretical framework for the remaining modules: Boys and literacy; Mentoring for success; Boys and ICTs; and Indigenous boys' transitions.

It is significant that Indigenous boys are raised as a key issue. However, there is a failure to recognize the severe disadvantages faced by Indigenous girls in Australia. The "which boys" approach that appears to have had some impact upon the shaping of this document, and the construction of some of the associated modules also does not appear to be reflected in the distribution of funds from this project, which have gone to, among other schools, some quite exclusive private schools. The anti-feminism of the *Success for Boys* project has been somewhat mediated by the influence of academics from James Cook University, including Nola Alloway (see Alloway, 1995; Alloway, Freebody, Gilbert, & Muspratt, 2002) and Rob Gilbert (see Gilbert & Gilbert, 1998), who have worked on the construction of modules for this project. However, the modules also begin with data similar to those presented to justify the *Boys' Lighthouse* project. For instance, drawing on the *Boys: Getting It Right* parliamentary inquiry, *Success for Boys* indicates that there are concerns about boys' early literacy achievement, school retention, results in subjects at years 10 and 12, boys' entry into tertiary education, and suspensions and exclusions. However, the core module makes the point that:

> The above data reveal only the *average* performance of boys compared with the *average* performance of girls. Thus, while the data may suggest that many, or even most, boys in Australian schools perform less well than girls on a range of measures, it would be incorrect to assume that *all* boys do so.... We need to ask *which* boys are, or are at risk of, underachieving in school; and *which* boys are, or are at risk of, disengaging from school. We need, for example, to consider potentially influential factors such as socioeconomic status, cultural background and whether the boys are Indigenous.
>
> (Alloway, Dalley-Trim, Gilbert, & Trist, 2006, p. 28)

It is unfortunate that this boys discourse is not supported by the current context that is positioning boys as disadvantaged. Many of the schools that have been awarded funding for this project have been done so on the grounds that they are seeking to improve boys' outcomes. The focus here is clearly on improving boys' literacy, and other, outcomes. The ICT module is designed to develop ICT strategies that promote boys' success in terms of engagement with schooling and academic outcomes. So, too, the mentoring module; this is about encouraging men to work with boys to improve their academic success. There is a failure in these modules to address issues of boys' misogynist and homophobic behaviors that have an impact on the quality of educational experiences that all students, girls and boys, experience.

The particular school contexts in which these modules will be implemented will have a significant effect upon the way in which they engage with particular forms of gender politics. It is possible that the modules can be implemented in critical ways through a (pro)feminist framework. However, given the current climate, it is far more likely that these modules will be implemented in schools where the focus is very much on boys and their achievement. Furthermore, the material support that has been provided to this program ensures that *something* will be done as schools will be held accountable for raising boys' achievement. This is very different from many previous girls' policies, and indeed the

Gender Equity Framework, so derided by many sections of the boys' lobby, which was largely symbolic. The impact of the *Success for Boys* on girls has also been ignored. Though the core module states that "Many of the strategies will also be of benefit to girls," there is a failure to recognize the ways in which girls will feel their educational needs are being neglected as schools begin to advertise their success in obtaining one of these grants to improve boys' education (Alloway et al., 2006, p. 1).

Boys as a Problem

In the United Kingdom, however, the mythopoetic eulogizing of boys has largely been left to educational consultants and journalists. The discursive construction of the "fragile inner-boy," at risk of underachievement, *does* emerge within policy texts (Francis & Skelton, 2005), but policy on boys' underachievement is simultaneously underpinned by "moral-contractual discourse" (Fairclough, 2000) based on concepts of a "something for something" pact. This neoliberal perspective, referred to in Australia as "Mutual Obligations" (between individual and state), permeates policy in the United Kingdom. Fairclough provides an illustrative quote from former Prime Minister Tony Blair:

> Our welfare system must provide help for those who need it but the deal that we are trying to create in Britain today is something for something. If we provide jobs we expect people to take them.
>   (Blair, 1999, quoted in Fairclough, 2000, p.39)

As we saw earlier, this neoliberal perspective positions individuals as responsible for taking up the opportunities apparently made available to them to thrive in the neoliberal economy. If they fail to thrive, this failure is seen to lie with them as individuals, rather than with socio-economic structures and circumstances. As Bauman (2005) observes, a benefit for the neoliberal state in the transference of responsibility for "failure" from the state to individuals is that these discursive practices justify a "washing clean of hands" in relation to those underperforming. These practices are also applied in relation to education. Francis and Skelton (2005) have argued that though a "poor boys" discourse continues to be applied to boys generally, these neoliberal policy drives are beginning to position some boys differently, with an increasingly sour note developing in the policy documents on "failing boys."

It is notable, for example, that the "boys will be boys" discourse identified by Epstein et al. (1998) as justifying and celebrating boys' rebellious, anti-school behaviors has recently been in decline (Francis & Skelton, 2005). The wane of the boys will be boys discourse that valorized and celebrated boys' roguishness and antipathy for diligence has been precipitated by the rise of new discourses that are beginning to position boys' roguishness and antipathy for diligence as points of grave concern. Neoliberalism is dependent on individuals' buying into notions of meritocracy (via educational credentialism), flexibility, individual responsibility, economic competitiveness, and so on—all of which evoke the "good" hard-working pupil rather than the errant school-boy "rogue" or "lad."

So, increasingly, boys are being positioned as problems or as in danger of becoming problems. The "boys at risk" narrative presents boys as vulnerable and confused and their apparent bad behavior and/ or underperformance as expressing or masking their insecurity and alienation. Boys are presented in this literature as lacking self-esteem and even as socially excluded as a group (Francis & Skelton, 2005). They are in need of attention and remedy to save them from becoming *problem boys*. Problem boys are constructed throughout the U.K. social policy arena in relation to delinquency, crime, unemployment, and other "social ills." However, focusing specifically on education, we are witnessing a shift in the positioning of particular groups of disruptive and low-achieving boys. Where the behaviors of such boys might have previously been wryly accepted as boys being boys, increasingly such boys are now being positioned in the U.K. policy literature as irresponsible and inadequate (Francis & Skelton, 2005). From a neoliberal human capital perspective, these "underachieving" boys appear to be unable or unwilling to thrive in the meritocratic educational system that perpetuates achievement— achievement vital for both individual and national economic success. Within the "something for something" social ethos discussed earlier, underachieving boys do not appear to be upholding their side of the bargain. In fact, further to their own lack of application, they are increasingly identified as distracting their classmates and teachers, hence impeding those better-intentioned pupils doing their best to progress:

> Boys who are failing to reach their full potential often cause problems in the classroom through disruptive and anti-social behavior ... Every day people working in and with schools are spending valuable time and money picking up the pieces after routine acts of disruption and vandalism which are mostly carried out by boys.
>
> (*Boys Will Be Boys?* 1996 p. 2)

> Secondary schools often contain groups of boys who create a culture that is anti-work, anti-establishment and disruptive to both boys' and girls' education—the antithesis of the positive achievement culture and ethos that a school is hoping to create.
>
> (*Using the National Healthy School Standard to Raise Boys' Achievement*, 2003, p.14)

Hence "problem boys" are beginning to be positioned as "beyond the pale" in the policy discourse. And as Francis (2006) has observed, these boys produced as a "problem" in the policy literature are indicatively working-class, white, African-Caribbean, and Pakistani boys (these groups hold the largest proportions of low-achieving boys; Gillborn & Mirza, 2000).

That the largest groups of "failing boys" are working class substantiates Francis's (2006) claim that the delineation between boys at risk and problem boys in education policy is comparable to Bauman's (2005) and Mendes's (2003) analyses of the processes of dissection of the "deserving" from the "undeserving" poor. A raft of recommended measures has been produced in policy documents for teachers to introduce pedagogies that will apparently raise boys' achievement (e.g. Qualifications and Curriculum Authority [QCA], 1998; Ofsted, 2003a, b; DfES, 2003). Government money has been invested in research, resources, training, and interventions to address the government's educational priority of narrowing the gender gap (see Francis & Skelton, 2005 for elaboration). Yet, as research has documented, the outcomes of many of these strategies for "raising boys' achievement" are inconclusive—indeed some have been identified as thoroughly counterproductive (Francis & Skelton, 2005; Younger, Warrington, & McLellan, 2005). Given that efforts to raise boys' achievement are not bearing fruit, there is a clear incentive for policy makers to view boys who persist in their underachievement in spite of resourcing as hopelessly and deliberately wanton. Rather than question the logic of the strategies adopted, blame for failure is beginning to be apportioned to certain groups of boys. The suggestion being that the measures to facilitate attainment are in place—if they are not working, this must be owing to boys' willful refusal to cooperate. The evidence that the maintenance of dominant constructions of masculinity encourages boys to avoid working hard for fear of being seen as "boffins" (and hence effete; see Epstein, 1998; Martino, 1999; Francis, 2000; Mills, 2001; Skelton, 2001; Martino & Pallotta-Chiarolli, 2003), is largely ignored as too complex and difficult to confront.

The view that these (indicatively working-class white, African-Caribbean, and Pakistani) boys are those en route to becoming the "yobbish" social problems of the future is sometimes overt in the English policy documents. For example, the report *Boys Will Be Boys?* (1996) refers to the "increasing numbers of young people—mainly boys—who have effectively ceased to be part of mainstream society" (p. 2). These problem boys are positioned as the architects of their own failure and consequently as undeserving of sympathy. Indeed, in line with the punitive approaches to social problems encouraged in neoliberal policy (see Bauman, 2005), recommended stern measures for such schoolboys and their behaviors are beginning to appear. As the Department for Education and Skills document *Using the National Healthy School Standard to Raise Boys' Achievement* (2003) declares:

> The existence of an anti-swot culture is regarded as a major threat and is [to be] addressed not only through the development of an achievement culture, but also on a day-to-day basis through school policy and appropriate sanctions which are widely documented and distributed (p. 14).

Implications for Girls

So far we have focused on the way in which the boys' debate in each of the two locations works with slightly different takes on the "new boy." However, there are many similarities in the construction of the "new girl" contained within the broader policy agenda on boys. This new girl, as Elwood (2005) indicates, is the "overachieving girl." In Australia, the construction of this new girl within the policy environment means that girls can be ignored in relation to their educational needs, even Indigenous girls who as a group are perhaps the most oppressed group of students in Australia. There is also a way in which this construction of girls serves to "put girls in their place." The continued focus on boys can work to suggest that schools are not really interested in girls any more and that girls have only achieved better than boys because of an unfair system. That the current situation could be the product of girls now getting what they deserve (Boaler, 1998) does not rate a mention. Indeed, there is very little within this new policy environment that has anything to commend it to girls. The failure to address boys' oppressive behaviors toward girls, the lack of concern with the ways in which misogynist and homophobic discourses have trivialized curriculum areas associated with femininity, and the essentializing of traditional forms of masculinity and femininity being cases in point (see Charlton, Mills, Martino, & Beckett, 2007 for an example of the boys' debate impacting negatively upon the education of girls).

The subtle differences between the construction of boys and girls in the two locations stems from the ways in which human capital theory is shaping gender debates in these places. Within the broader policy agenda in Australia, the achievement debate often foregrounds lost human capital as a result of low levels of achievement and student retention. In Queensland, for instance, the new "learning or earning" agenda that keeps 17-year-olds at school unless they have secured full-time employment is founded upon the notion that education is about ensuring the future economic success of that State. However, this concern with future economic prosperity rarely spills over into the boys' debate in Australia. The marketization of schools has also tended to be unaffected by this gender debate, apart from a few instances wherein schools have marketed themselves on what they are doing for boys, although there is at least one instance where an elite girls' school marketed itself drawing on the problem boy discourse (see Mills, 2004). In the main, anti-feminist discourses hold sway in both the policy production and the school-based implementation of policies such as *Success for Boys*. Whether this will be the case should the significant financial investment in boys' education not "pay off" remains to be seen.

The situation is somewhat different in the United Kingdom. There, the increasing use of league tables to market schools has worked to construct some boys as a liability and girls as an asset in this competitive environment. For instance, Elwood says in relation to the United Kingdom:

> In these days of the education market place, league tables and targets, the overachieving girl is a valuable commodity and she finds herself wooed by single-sex and mixed-sex schools alike (Ball & Gewirtz, 1997). Schools are keen to recruit girls and competition for this precious resource is tough, so much so that schools (especially mixed schools) will "use" the presence of girls in their schools to market their establishments to prospective parents; girls are schools' unique selling positions.
>
> (Elwood, 2005 p. 378)

However, as Elwood indicates, the valuing of girls does not continue once girls have arrived at the school. Once there, it is business as usual.

Conclusion

Clearly there are some key similarities in the ways in which "the boys' achievement debate" has been constructed in Australia and the United Kingdom and in the politics behind the policy concerns (neoliberal and anti-feminist). The dominance of poor boys discourse within debates in both countries is clear. Yet, here already, a subtle difference arises: We have argued that whereas in the Australian case the poor boys discourse permeates through to policy, with mythopoetic and men's-right's perspectives being articulated in key documents, in the United Kingdom, such articulations have been largely left to journalists and education consultants. We hope to have teased out some of the explanations for these and other differences in the policy manifestations between the two locations. We have argued that the advancement of the quasi-market in education via neoliberal policy drives in the United Kingdom, in which standards and achievement become important commodifications, and underachievement is produced as individual irresponsibility, is beginning to problematize groups of underachieving boys. Conversely, the political history of Australia (where feminists have had a greater impact on educational policy than in the United

Kingdom) may to some extent account for (if not explain) the "backlash" tenor of recent policy making around gender and achievement and the mythopoetic and men's rights themes therein.

References

Alloway, N. (1995). *Foundation stones: The construction of gender in early childhood.* Carlton, Victoria:Curriculum Corporation.

Alloway, N., Freebody, P., Gilbert, P., & Muspratt, S. (2002). *Boys, literacy and schooling: Expanding the repertoires of practice.* Canberra: Commonwealth Department of Education, Science and Training.

Alloway, N., Dalley-Trim, L., Gilbert, R., & Trist, S. (2006). *Planning guide and core module: Success for boys.* Melbourne: Curriculum Corporation.

Arnot, M. (1989). Political lip-service or radical reform? Central government responses to sex equality as a policy issue. In M. Arnot & G. Weiner (Eds.), *Gender and the politics of schooling* (pp. 309–331). London: Unwin Hyman.

Arnot, M., & Weiner, G. (Eds.). (1987). *Gender and the politics of schooling.* London: Hutchinson.

Australian Education Council. (1993). *National action plan for the education of girls 1993-1997.* Carlton, Victoria:Curriculum Corporation.

Bauman, Z. (2005) *Work, consumerism and the new poor,* second edition Buckingham: Open University Press.

Biddulph, S. (1995). *Manhood: An action plan for changing men's lives* (2nd ed.). Sydney: Finch.

Bleach, K. (Ed.). (1998). *Raising boys' achievement in schools.* Stoke-on-Trent: Trentham Books.

Bly, R. (1991) *Iron John: A book about men,* Shaftesbour: Element.

Boaler, J. (1998). Mathematical equity: Underachieving boys or sacrificial girls? *International Journal of Inclusive Education, 2*(2), 119–134.

Charlton, E., Mills, M., Martino, W., & Beckett, L. (2007). Sacrificial girls: A case study of the impact of streaming and setting on gender reform. *British Education Research Journal, 33*(4), 459–478.

Commonwealth Government of Australia. (2003). *Educating boys: Issues and information.* Canberra: Commonwealth Government of Australia.

Commonwealth of Schools Commission. (1975). *Girls, schools and society, Report of the study group to the Schools Commission.* Canberra: Commonwealth of Schools Commission.

Commonwealth of Schools Commission (1987). *A national policy for the education of girls in Australian schools.* Canberra: Commonwealth of Schools Commission.

Connell, R. (1995). *Masculinities.* Sydney: Allen & Unwin.

Connolly, P. (2004). *Boys and schooling in the early years.* London: RoutledgeFalmer.

Daws, L. (1997). The quiet achiever: The national policy for the education of girls. In B. Lingard & P. Porter, (Eds.), *A national approach to schooling in Australia: Essays on the development of national policies in schools education* (pp. 95–110). Canberra: Australian College of Education.

Department of Education, Science and Training. (2003). *Meeting the challenge: Guiding principles for success from the Boys' Education Lighthouse Programme Stage One 2003*. Canberra: Department of Education, Science and Training.

Department of Education, Science and Training. (2005) *Success for boys: Helping boys achieve*. Canberra: Department of Education, Science and Training.

Department of Health. (2003). *Using the national healthy school standard to raise boys' achievement*. Wetherby, UK: Health Development Agency.

DfES (2003) *National healthy school standard to raise boys achievement*. London: Health Development Agency.

Ecclestone, K. (2004) Learning or Therapy? The Demoralisation of Education, *British Journal of Educational Studies*, 52(2): 112–137.

Eisenstein, H. (1997). *Inside agitators: Australian femocrats and the state*. Sydney: Allen & Unwin.

Elwood, J. (2005). Gender and achievement: What have exams got to do with it? *Oxford Review of Education*, 31(3), 373–393.

Epstein, D. Elwood, J. Hey, V. & Maw, J. (Eds.) (1998). *Failing Boys? Issues in Gender and Achievement*. Buckingham: Open University Press.

Fairclough, N. (2000) *New Labour, new language?* London: Routledge

Farrell, W. (1993). *The myth of male power: Why men are the disposable sex*. New York: Simon & Schuster.

Foster, V., Kimmel, M., & Skelton, C. (2001). What about the boys? An overview of the debates. In W. Martino & B. Meyenn (Eds.), *What about the boys?: Issues of masculinity and schooling* (pp. 1–23). Buckingham: Open University Press.

Francis, B. (2000). *Boys, girls and achievement: Addressing the classroom issues*. London: Routledge.

Francis, B. (2006). Heroes or zeroes? The discursive positioning of 'underachieving boys' in English neo-liberal education policy. *Journal of Educational Policy*, 21(2), 187–200.

Francis, B., & Skelton, C. (2001). Men teachers and the construction of heterosexual masculinity in the classroom. *Sex Education*, 1(1), 9–21.

Francis, B., & Skelton, C. (2005). *Reassessing gender and achievement: Questioning contemporary key debates*. London: Routledge.

Gender Equity Taskforce for Ministerial Council for Employment, Education, Training and Youth Affairs. (1997). *Gender equity: A framework for Australian schools*. Canberra: Publications and Public Communication, Department of Urban Services, ACT Government.

Gilbert, R., & Gilbert, P. (1998). *Masculinity goes to school*. Sydney: Allen & Unwin.

Gillborn, D., & Mirza, H. (2000). *Educational inequality: Mapping race, class and gender*. London: HMI.

Gurian, M. (1999). *A fine young man: What parents, mentors, and educators can do to shape adolescent boys into exceptional men*. New York: Jeremy P. Tarcher/ Putnam.

Hallam, S., & Rogers, L. (2006) Gender differences in approaches to studying for GCSE among high achieving pupils, *Educational Studies*, 32(1), 59–72.

Haywood, C. & Mac an Ghaill, M. (1996). Schooling masculinities. In M. Mac an Ghaill (ed) *Understanding masculinities: Social relations and cultural arenas*. Buckingham: Open University Press.

Hoff Sommers, C. (2000). *The war against boys: How misguided feminism is harming our young men*. New York: Touchstone.

House of Representatives Standing Committee on Education and Training. (2002). *Boys' education: Getting it right*. Canberra: Commonwealth Government.

Kimmel, M. (Ed.) (1995). *The politics of manhood: Profeminist men respond to the mythopoetic men's movement (and the mythopoetic leaders answer)*. Philadelphia: Temple University Press.

Kindlon, D., & Thompson, M. (1999). *Raising Cain: Protecting the emotional life of boys*. London: Michael Joseph.

Mahony, P. (2003). Recapturing imaginations and the gender agenda: Reflections on a progressive challenge from an English perspective. *International Journal of Inclusive Education*, 7(1), 7–81.

Martino, W. (1999) 'Cool boys', 'party animals', 'squids' and 'poofters': interrogating the dynamics and politics of adolescent masculinities in school, *British Journal of the Sociology of Education* 20(2): 239–263.

Martino, W., & Frank, B. (2006). The tyranny of surveillance: Male teachers and the policing of masculinities in a single sex school. *Gender and Education*, 18(1), 1–33.

Martino, W. & Pallotta-Chiarolli, M. (2003) *So what's a boy? addressing issues of masculinity and schooling*. Maidenhead: Open University Press.

Mendes, P. (2003) *Australia's welfare wars: the players, the politics and the ideologies*. Sydney: University of New South Wales.

Milligan, S., Thomson, K., & Ashenden and Associates. (1992). *Listening to girls: A report of the consultancy undertaken for the review of the National Policy for the Education of Girls conducted by the Australian Education Council*. Carlton, Victoria: Curriculum Corporation.

Mills, M. (2001) *Challenging violence in schools: An issue of masculinities*. Buckingham: Open University Press.

Mills, M. (2003). Shaping the boys' agenda: The backlash blockbuster. *International Journal of Inclusive Education*, 7(1), 5–73.

Mills, M. (2004). The media, single sex schooling, the boys' debate and class politic. *Journal of Educational Policy*, 19(3), 33–352.

Mills, M., Martino, W., & Lingard, B. (2004). Issues in the male teacher debate: Masculinities, misogyny and homophobi. *British Journal of Sociology of Education*, 25(3), 35–369.

Mills, M., Martino, W., Lingard, B. (2007). Getting boys' education 'right': The Australian Government's Parliamentary Inquiry Report as an exemplary instance of recuperative masculinity politic. *British Journal of Sociology of Education*, 28(1), 21.

Noble, C., & Bradford, W. (2000). *Getting it right for boys … and girls*. London: Routledge.

Ofsted (2003a). *Yes he can: Schools where boys write well*. London: Ofsted Publications.

Ofsted (2003b). *Boys' achievement in secondary schools*. London: Ofsted Publications.

Pollack, W. (1999). *Real boys: Rescuing our sons from the myths of boyhood*. New York: Henry Holt.

Qualifications and Curriculum Authority. (1998). *Can do better: Raising boys' achievement in English*. London: Qualifications and Curriculum Authority.

Rose, N. (1999) *Powers of freedom: Reframing political thought*. Cambridge: Cambridge University Press.

Skelton, C. (2001). *Schooling the boys: Masculinities and primary education*. Buckingham: Open University Press.

Skelton, C. (2002). The 'feminisation of schooling' or 'remasculinising" primary education, *International Studies in Sociology of Education, 12*, 7–96.

Titus, J. (2004). Boy trouble: Rhetorical framing of boys' underachievement. *Discourse: Studies in the Cultural Politics of Education, 25*(2), 14–169.

Weaver-Hightower, M. (2003). The 'boy turn' in research on gender and education. *Review of Educational Research, 73*(4), 47–498.

Yates, L. (2000). The 'facts of the case': Gender equity for boys as a public policy issue. In N. Lesko (Ed.), *Masculinities at school* (pp. 30–322).Thousand Oaks, CA: Sage.

Younger, M., Warrington, M., & McLellan, R. (2005). *Raising boys' achievement in secondary schools*. Maidenhead: Open University Press.

3 What Can We Expect?

A Strategy to Help Schools Hoping for Virtue

*Michael C. Reichert, Peter Kuriloff,
and Brett Stoudt*

Introduction

In 2001, five U.S. independent schools came together to create a new consortium, the Center for the Study of Boys' Lives (CSBL), in collaboration with the University of Pennsylvania's Graduate School of Education. A sixth school was added in 2005. Two of the member schools were day schools for boys, one a boys' day school in a coordinate relationship with a contiguous girls' school, one a coed day school that converted from a girls' school in the 1970s, and two that are top-tier boarding schools that became coeducational in the 1970s and 1980s after long careers as boys' schools. Each of the schools, in short, had a considerable track record dedicated to boys' education and reasonable claim, on that basis, to success and expertise in that work. Yet, their support for the new center reflected their desire to put a finer point on that expertise. The mission of the center was "... to conduct research, encourage public discussion, and advocate on behalf of boys. Using research tools that give voice to boys' lived experiences, the center will strive to promote the widest sense of possibility and greatest hope for integrity in boys' lives ..." (www.csbl. org).[1]

This group of schools was motivated by the recognition that despite their success with boys, not all was well with their charges. The coeducational schools had strong impressions that their girls were increasingly outperforming their boys in most academic subjects. Awards of all kinds seemed to be strongly tilted toward girls as well. The all-boys' schools were concerned that, despite continuous efforts to eradicate hazing and bullying, those behaviors seemed enduring features of the schools' landscapes. Further, all the schools were concerned that boys seemed to engage in high-risk behaviors, both in and out of school, that sometimes put them in real danger.

Founding members of the CSBL recognized that despite their privileged position and the privileged positions of many (though not all, as each school has made a significant investment in diversity) of their boys, their historic curricula for educating boys might unwittingly feed both their students' risk taking and whatever educational struggles they experience. More dimly, perhaps, but more courageously, at some level they wished to be sure that their own gender curricula were not implicated in the problems boys were experiencing. By helping these schools to excavate their "hidden" masculinity curricula through a process of school-based action research, the CSBL hoped to help them address their concerns about their young men and to expand the recognitional offers made to them.

In this chapter, we develop the perspective that problems boys present in schools reflect schools' more or less implicit gender regime. We describe what we perceive to be a tension between schools' man-making commitments and their desire to cultivate boys' character strengths. We then elucidate an alternative approach to school curricula for boys: an evidence-based approach, built upon school research employing multiple methods, including quantitative and qualitative analysis, the training and support of teacher-based inquiry teams, the inclusion of boys as researchers, and cross-school conversation and critique. To illustrate this approach in action, we briefly describe several examples of projects under way at member schools. As we hope to show, the effort to fill in gaps in our understanding of boys' lives is at the heart of our work and the basis for our hope that schools can become more adept at schooling boys in general and supporting the development of their virtue.

Troubles with Boys' Experience

Boys' problems in school can be summarized briefly. Poor academic achievement, disciplinary problems, over-diagnosis and referral to special educational services, athletic over-injury, bullying, peer harassment, and school violence: These are some of the issues that raise concerns about the effectiveness of schooling for boys. These outcomes stand in stark contrast to girls' successes in schools. This contrast has become news of late, to the point that a recent front-page *New York Times* article (Lewin, 2006) detailed how, across every major ethnic group in the United States and throughout most of the industrialized countries, girls now earn a growing percentage of college degrees. The author is careful to say the "achievement gap" has not developed because boys' performance has changed in any dramatic way. In fact, a report from a U.S.-based educational think tank argued persuasively that "The real story is not bad news about boys doing worse; it's good news about girls doing better" (Mead, 2006, p. 3).

However, the same report sadly acknowledged that college rates are relatively lower for males in large measure because of boys' greater likelihood to drop out before graduation and the fact that fewer male students enroll in college to begin with. College, in essence, represents the final chapter in a boys' educational story going all the way back to primary grades. In a cover story for *Newsweek* magazine, Tyre (2006) wrote that from elementary years all the way through graduate and professional training programs, patterns in boys' achievement reveal that more boys than ever appear to be turning off to education. The article cites one study indicating that the number of boys who said they "didn't like school" has risen 71 percent over the last two decades (2006, p. 46).

Many boys, in short, do not embrace educational aspiration. And, though they suffer through required schooling, they do not seem to be otherwise quiet and well-behaved. Research on boys' behavior in school reveals even more dramatic and perhaps more alarming gender contrasts. Some years ago, in one of the schools where the authors have worked, a gender audit showed remarkable though not uncommon disparities in discipline: demerits—the primary response of school staff to students' rule infractions—were skewed toward males at a rate of nearly 20,000 to 100! The 200 or so male students averaged 100 demerits each. Even granting that such disciplinary practices as the use of demerits are gendered to begin with (i.e., that the system cues on behaviors more likely for males), many of the infractions were truly over any reasonable line for civil behavior. In one instance, for example, a popular, well-respected, and usually well-mannered boy one evening sent an e-mail to all of his classmates graphically inventing a sexually explicit story about one of his female classmates, who had the misfortune to be the sister of a buddy with whom he was arguing.

Such conduct by boys in schools, in fact, reflects a greater problem of male incivility. Both in their impact on their own lives and on the lives of others around them, male behaviors are often troubling and hurtful. Over the past several decades, as the influence of other socializing agencies has diminished, schools have become more a default choice to manage this problem. One popular response has been to add programming aimed at values. Since 1996, character education programs have become ubiquitous (Howard, Berkowitz, & Schaeffer, 2004). However, importantly for those looking to affect boys' school troubles, when Berkowitz (1997, 2002) reviewed such programs for "what works in schools," he concluded that the "primary influence on a child's character development is *how people treat the child*" (italics in original, 2002, p. 58).

This finding, that students develop civic virtues and character strengths from their experiences, requires that schools ascertain, as a baseline, how students perceive their experiences. As they investigate boys' experiences, schools' gender regimes—the "pattern of practices that constructs various kinds of masculinity and femininity among staff and students" (Kessler, Ashendon, Connell, & Dowsett, 1985, p. 42)—will be observed to play a critical role in shaping the pressures, relationships, and experiences of boys in schools. At the broadest level, the concept of a gender regime teaches that schools are both active agents in promoting particular ideas of masculinity ("masculinizing practices," according to Connell, 1996) and sites within which boys act out certain gender scripts in relation to each other. The various identities available to boys within a particular school culture are almost always organized hierarchically (Reichert, 2000, 2001). The dominant identity is not necessarily the most common type of masculinity but will be the most influential and is usually organized around qualities such as physical size and skill, affluence, emotional control, social confidence, and latent, sometimes overt, violence (Stoudt, 2006; Kuriloff & Reichert, 2003). Spending so much time in their particular school, boys' experiences of the school's regime, while generally unconscious, are highly consequential: "It confronts them as a social fact, which they have to come to terms with somehow" (Kessler et al., 1985, p. 42).

Boys' experience of schools' gender curricula bears directly on their relationship to educational aspiration in the sense that, as they "do gender," students adapt themselves to the opportunities afforded them by the pressures, inducements, and punishments of the school community's norms and gender possibilities (Swain, 2005). Some boys find room to care about academic achievement and establish positive relationships with the reward and authority structures of schools. Others have more difficulty. Chu (2000), in a careful microstudy, closely accompanied a small group of boys through school and described the "overcompromise" some of them made with this masculinity structure of their school and the attendant "psychological costs and social consequences" of this adaptation (Froschl and Sprung, 2005, p. 5).

For the past several decades, concerns for equity and justice have properly focused on ensuring that schools' gender curricula eliminate bias and barriers to equal rights, equal access, and fairness for girls. This work has "come a long way" but must now extend even further, researchers from the Wellesley Center for Women proposed, to "a conceptualization of gender as a set of social constructions and societal assumptions about the possibilities and limits of male and female experience and behavior" (Spencer, Porche, & Tolman, 2003, p. 2). In particular, among the societal assumptions still limiting girls' educational experience is a "public-private dialectic in social life and schooling itself, and men's and women's assymetrical relations with that dialectic" (Foster, 1998, p. 1). Addressing such myths and social constructions is necessary if societies are to continue to make schooling and its rewards fully accessible to girls, these writers argue. Even more crucially, in terms of the moral lessons students absorb from school communities, Fine (1992) has argued for an expanded understanding of equality of opportunity: "With access to this moral community established as legitimate and universal, the issue of social justice has shifted to the process of exclusion, that is, students' differential experiences and outcomes once inside these communities" (p. 102).

As Sizer and Sizer (1999) and others such as Fine and Berkowitz have suggested, students absorb their moral instruction from what happens, or does not happen, for them in schools. In the case of boys, basically schools get the men they grow. The close relationship among boys' experience of their schools' gender regimes, their moral relationships, and civic behavior suggests the critical importance of ensuring that boys find schools welcoming, safe, supportive, and hopeful spaces in which they can see possibilities for, in terms of Young's "enabling" theory of justice, "the development or exercise of capacities" (1990, p. 39). Access to educational opportunity, in other words, must take account of social and school conditions that can either enable the exercise of boys' capacities or create insurmountable barriers to their educational investment. For the many boys who struggle to fit themselves to the structures, pedagogy, and relationships of schools, are there biases and barriers impeding the exercise of their abilities, woven into the practices, beliefs and very ways we "recognize" boys in our schools (Mann, 1994)? More practically, how well are we enabling boys to learn?

To our minds, despite all the current buzz associated with the subject of boys' education, it seems that much of what happens for boys in schools still largely escapes notice, much less good explanation. Over the past several decades, social science has helped developmentalists and educators realize the key role of methods of inquiry for generating solutions to problems of inclusion and equity. Gilligan (1982), for example, discovered her insights into girls' lives by cultivating a new sensitivity to their voices. Dynamics of power, she concluded, were woven into all social interactions, including research efforts to capture girls' experience, requiring methods that account for the impact of the research context itself on subjects' ability to name and describe their experience. Fine (1992) said it well: "[T]he only way to do activist research is to be positioned explicitly with questions, but not answers; as mobile and multiple, not static and singular; within spaces of rich surprise" (p. 230). Or, as another feminist researcher put it, "If we want someone to tell it like it is, you have to hear it like it is" (Reinharz, 1988, p. 16). To ensure schools that can offer grounded solutions to problems of boys' education, we must position ourselves more willingly with our questions about their lives.

Methods to Surprise Ourselves

The CSBL hoped in its work to challenge common, taken-for-granted assumptions about boys to help schools reevaluate their gender regimes and establish more evidence-based programming. Thus, the Center encourages research strategies that can unearth the phenomenological experiences of boys and their school contexts, to "give voice" to their perspectives. Through collaborative, action-oriented research, using multiple methodological strategies, the CSBL helps schools discover a more grounded understanding to guide their work with boys.

Although the CSBL was founded within single-sex and co-ed schools, the work avoids simplistic boy-girl dichotomies common in deterministic depictions of gender. In our view, collapsing within-group variation to calculate an "average" for boys and girls forces generic interpretations of gender (James, 1997) and attempts to universalize experience by building on the assumption that gender differences are "a set of fixed, stable, and enduring traits or qualities" (Shields, 2002, p.22). Such dichotomizing approaches fail to explain why the differences occurred, in particular overlooking the importance of driving forces such as context, history, power, and identities. The CSBL has avoided this binary trap by devoting its efforts to understanding boys in particular, attempting to illuminate the questions "for whom, when and under what circumstances?" and examining the variability within and between subsets of boys.

Pledged also to avoid merely reproducing traditional representations of gender, the CSBL is committed to research methods adequate for the task. Thus, we have placed an emphasis on triangulation, coming at our study of boys in schools from a number of angles. In this approach, we have found Alford (1998) helpful: "Developing coherent arguments that recognize historical processes, symbolic meanings, and multivariate relations is the best way to construct an adequate explanation of a complex social phenomenon" (p. 19). To capture the effect of "historical processes" on boys' experience within schools, we gather data from such sources as archives, texts, and narrative accounts. To appreciate boys' "symbolic meanings," we employ qualitative methods (e.g., interviews, ethnographies, thematic coding), aiming to answer the generic question, "How are meanings constructed in interaction and in social worlds? (Alford, 1998, p. 51). And using more quantitative tools (e.g., surveys, statistics), we can answer the generic question "What factors explain an outcome?" and take into account the multiple ways a phenomenon (such as achievement) may vary in relation to other important factors in boys' lives.

The research model that the CSBL recommends to schools emphasizes participatory action research (PAR), as we feel that PAR can best mobilize a school's commitment to evaluating its current curriculum and to developing best practices. This model can help improve the validity and reliability of the conclusions as it enables school-based teams to examine change over time from multiple levels and helps these researchers to become better acquainted with the students, the faculty, and the school. When it comes to the payoff—the action phase—recommendations are informed by a set of findings discovered in close interaction with boys.

As a collaborative effort, our model strives to be democratic. The CSBL does not impose a patented research protocol on schools, nor does it steer findings toward a particular direction. Rather, we work within each school to develop a research team made up of teachers, administrators and, sometimes, students. This team generates an area of inquiry, establishes research questions, selects unit of analyses and appropriate research methods, and finds outlets for distribution of results. The unfolding of the research protocol is school-driven. Qualitative analyses are conducted in a partnership between the CSBL and the teacher research group. Quantitative analyses are analyzed by the CSBL and then discussed with the research group. Spending time on the ground in the school over an extended time provides all with an understanding of the educational environment: its rhythms, politics and history. Using teachers' institutional memory and historical knowledge further embeds the current work in a larger context.

Schools' action research projects create opportunities for within-school and between-school conversations. Interviews, focus groups, and surveys are designed to privilege the voices of boys under the assumption that an authentic understanding of boys' experiences begins with their knowledge and interpretation. We think of this stage as the first conversation in the overall action research process. Analyses of the collected data create the context for the second conversation. Engaging with evidence affords an opportunity for the research team to contrast their personal experiences with a collective experience. These conversations create a space for the research team to critique and learn, to be surprised or vindicated. Most important, they create opportunities for dialogue about the selected topic, which was deemed important and immediately relevant to the larger school community. The third space for conversation comes with the distribution of findings to the school. These presentations come in various forms: presentations at staff meetings or with school trustees, student assemblies, and written summaries, as examples. This step in the research process takes the data beyond the research group into the school community to expand the dialogue and increase awareness. A fourth occasion for conversation comes with the annual CSBL Roundtable, which provides a space for research teams from schools across the country to become aware of and to discuss each school's projects. Cross-school conversations, among schools historically quite unique, creates a learning community and a research support network, built upon the common commitment to evidence-based, teacher-driven "best practices" for boys.

In guiding schools through the "what, so what, now what" of their research, the CSBL considers the last—"now what"—intervention phase the most important. The entire research process was designed to facilitate this last phase. The research questions were based on concerns close to the hearts of teachers and important to their school. The research team's collection and analysis of the data created an ownership and curiosity about the outcomes. The numerous spaces for dialogue created a critical meta-awareness and expertise. In these and other ways, the research enterprise within each school represented a two-tiered intervention. At the first level, the act of research itself creates spaces within and between schools to discuss important issues that are otherwise not likely to be discussed. Further, at the second level, outcomes of the research process produce evidence of best practices for boys that lead to changes within schools.

Three Exemplary Projects

The Problem of Peer Harassment

At one of the schools that had earlier conducted several assessments of student peer culture, a team of faculty and students set out to explore in more detail the complexities of peer mistreatment and harassment (defined in the study as insulting, ridiculing, bullying, hazing, fighting behaviors). Through conversations about their perceptions of school life, the student research team developed a 15-minute interview protocol, composed of both qualitative and quantitative elements, that was undertaken throughout the school (e.g., halls, cafeteria, classrooms). This protocol enabled the student researchers to collect a large and representative sample (N = 100) of their fellow students in the ninth through twelfth grades. The interview data were analyzed through multiple discussions, in which students and faculty used their own expertise as citizens of the school juxtaposed with patterns that emerged from their data. The teachers and students summarized their analyses with formal letters addressed to one another ("Dear Teachers ..." and "Dear Students ..."), discussing what they found and its potential implications for future intervention.

Most notably, the teams discovered that peer harassment (particularly insults and ridicule) was pervasive and often subtle and helped to define, teach, (re)produce, and discipline rigid boundaries of masculinity and other forms of privilege. From their survey, the team discovered that 84 percent of its sample reported having experienced ridiculing-teasing, 33 percent experienced bullying-intimidation, 9.6 percent reported hazing-initiations, and 10 percent experienced fighting-physical violence. Harassment and peer violence were embedded in the social fabric of the school and implicated in power relations among peers, teachers, and the institution.

Data from both students and teachers complicated crude dichotomies such as aggressor-victim, described emotionally ambiguous experiences that were at the same time hurtful and bonding, and revealed peer harassment as contextually dependent upon when, where, and from whom it was received-given-observed. The results illuminated intersections of violence, privilege, and boys' socio-emotional relationships with peers, coaches, and teachers. They validated the use of participatory research as a method to create dialogue, awareness, and action about-for-with boys. Not surprisingly, the results of this process described clearly how the culture involved pervasive peer policing to ensure boys stayed within acceptable norms, which represented clear and prescriptive ideas about masculinity. Exclusion and censorship were the most potent instruments of peer policing evident in these findings. The exclusion and censorship of "unacceptable" masculine displays were conveyed through the school's tacit curriculum, in which boys learn to "suck it up, bear the pain, evince no sweat while working."

Beyond these tacit messages, the qualitative elements in the student peer interviews uncovered how a preferred form of masculinity was promulgated and policed through forms of teasing and ridiculing. Much of the teasing-ridiculing established either in-or-out, us-and-them distinctions that had the effect of elevating the preferred standard. One boy described a typical experience this way:

> Take chemistry, there is such a low level of white noise of bullying when he is a little too late for class. They say, "Is your train late?", pointing out that he has to take the train, while they get driven from [affluent neighborhood] but he came from another neighborhood … . There are all these ways that you never quite cut it, the way you dress, where you live, the way you live … all these ways you're not quite good enough.

As another student explained, homophobic remarks were common to the point that they were taken for granted:

> Students subconsciously put pressures on other students: pressures that include making sure your tie is not considered a gay tie because of its coloring, or that the car you are getting out of is up to the standards of [our rich] community. On a dress down day there is the added pressure of wearing a certain pair of jeans because they won't be considered tough enough, or the saying on your sweatshirt is as gay as the pink tie you wore two days ago.

Many of the students both acknowledged the stressful environment this creates and, yet, still appreciated the masculine curriculum it reflects:

> This school is riddled with insults and fierce competition, yet, in my mind, I think that most of it is good. The reasons for this are that male interaction is founded upon a system of hierarchy … a hierarchical system of respect and popularity built from these interactions.

Another student agreed, writing:

> Beneficial teasing has aided in development of friendships. It may
> sound funny, but I am honored when others pick on me.

There appeared to be "hot-spots" for harassment in the school,
generally away from the carefully monitored academic spaces of the
school. In locker rooms and areas in the gym, in fact, coaches gave boys
the impression, perhaps simply by their absence, that forms of hierarchy
and harassment were permissible. One boy, a student-athlete, admitted
that he and his teammates were generally reluctant to interfere with
locker room fights, for a host reasons: the appropriateness of disciplining
others who "deserve it," the masculine understanding that each boy is
independent and responsible for himself, the wish not to get anyone in
trouble (i.e., to "narc"), the desire to fit in, and the very real fear of having
the bullying turned on you.

But it was not just coaches and students who used verbal put-downs,
insults, ridicule, and even bullying to control boys. The research team was
surprised and quite affected by evidence that suggested faculty collusion,
encouragement, and even participation in forms of harassment. In the
team's interviews with other faculty members, some teachers confessed to
the belief that "boys respect the teachers who are quick ... and it is hard to
turn it off on the weekend with our own families ... people who haven't
developed that end up leaving." Another female teacher added,

> I'm a very small and petite women—if you are a big athletic looking
> man you can, in this school, walk into a classroom and have a presence
> ... the only way that those kids weren't going to run me over was if
> I found a way to be quick and clever ... . I have to say things to
> these boys that I would have never considered saying to girls ... they
> would have been in tears ... parents would be in school saying this is
> a horrible teacher.

Even a senior administrator acknowledged the school's tacit sanctioning
of harassment within the school's regime:

> There's a real premium on appropriately sarcastic teasing, finding a
> weakness and playing on it without exploiting it. That's a skill I think
> the kids relish. The kids who really struggle here are those who are
> not verbal. Since there is such a clear line of nothing physical allowed
> at school, since they cannot push each other around physically, they
> do push each other around verbally.

The research team concluded the first phase of its intervention by
presenting their research at the CSBL Roundtable, at a school trustees
meeting, and at a faculty meeting. It became very clear to both groups

on the research team—students and teachers—that phase two of their intervention must begin with the faculty. The team concluded that if their work helps teachers and coaches become aware of their collusive reinforcement of the culture, they can undermine unconscious support for these practices within the school culture. It might also increase the school's sense of responsibility for the hot-spots for peer policing within the school. Consequently, the team has begun a project in which they will ask their fellow faculty members to interrogate their own practices and to work toward alternative ways of managing their students. After that, the team envisions peer-run projects with students to reduce reliance on these forms of self-policing.

Boys at the Bottom

Another of our schools, a boarding school that went co-educational in the 1970s, now serves 500 students of great socioeconomic and racial range. The school research team became concerned with how new students were adapting academically to what many consider a highly demanding, hot-house academic and social environment. An initial review revealed that 70 percent of those students receiving Ds and Fs during their first year were boys. To figure out what was going on, the team conducted a "gender audit" of 34 years' data contrasting boys and girls across a large number of variables from overall grade point average and subject grade averages to awards to scores on entrance exams and both PSATs and SATs.

The gender audit found consistent gendered patterns over the entire 34 years. When overall grade point average (GPA) was broken into quartiles, boys outnumbered girls in the lowest quartile whereas girls outnumbered boys in the highest quartile. Further, the number of girls grew as the quartiles rose whereas the number of boys decreased. This V-shaped pattern is expressed in Figure 3.1 and repeated itself for every subject except math and science but, even in those subjects, there were significantly more boys than girls in the bottom quartile.

Given these findings, the school's research team wanted to know what the boys experienced of their life at the school: How did they feel about the workload, their efforts to "make it" and their efforts to establish themselves among their fellow students and faculty? Using a blocked random selection process, the team interviewed boys from high- and low-achieving groups. Though these interviews with boys told a very nuanced story about their struggles to satisfy the academic requirements of their schooling, making a place for themselves socially at the same time, two themes in particular emerged that shed light on this lower performing group.

One insight that emerged was that, though many came to school wanting to get "straight As," those who did poorly initially attributed it to a rocky start, as this boy described:

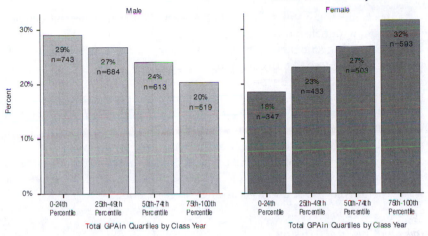

Figure 3.1 Overall GPA by Class Year

> I haven't quite made it. I got off on a rocky start. I was having trouble jumping in … . This was a new experience, managing my own schedule and all the stuff you have to do. But I think I am better off this term than I was last term.

Despite this generally optimistic spin, in fact, once they landed in the bottom quartile, boys were six times more likely to graduate in the lowest quartile than others in their cohort. One result for the school was that there was a group of boys in the lowest quartile who could not maintain their initial optimism and hopefulness and who came to express a general sense of disappointment in themselves. Jason captured the defeated quality of these boys when he said, "I don't really see myself excelling right now in anything." Not experiencing rewards of recognition or mastery, the boys in this bottom group ultimately come to accept their relatively poor achievement, giving up on their initial aspirations.

Yet it wasn't just the boys at the bottom who felt disappointed. A second major theme to emerge from the data was that for many boys, regardless of quartile, the struggle to keep their heads above water and to succeed was never over. Not one boy, at any age or achievement level, expressed a sense of mastery over the work. Indeed, even academically accomplished boys felt that they regularly sacrificed learning to keep up: "… it's like when you have so much work, it doesn't matter—getting it done instead of learning it or something." Undercutting the inspiration of outstanding teachers and a highly motivated peer group, an overwork drill that seemed to rob students of their ability to enjoy the intellectual experience. The drill was so demanding, it seemed, that where some boys may achieve mastery at the expense of their engagement in their schooling, boys at the bottom seemed unable or unwilling to make those particular sacrifices.

These interview and audit findings were sobering for the school, adding a new dimension of compassion and appreciation for the group of underperforming students. Perhaps, faculty wondered, some of the boys at the bottom, who told stories of coming to feel dispirited and even personally disparaged, were simply unwilling to traffic with the unreasonable nature of these pressures. As a next step, the team planned to present the data to the entire faculty and begin to focus on how to address profound issues given voice by the boys in the study. How can the school help boys adjust more successfully so they do not experience such rocky starts? How can they help all boys develop more of a feeling of mastery and satisfaction? And finally, and most important for such a successful school, does it make sense that boys feel like they must give up learning to "get it done?"

A School's Moral Mission

Though all of the CSBL member schools are values-based, one puts special emphasis on its mission of preparing boys for life. Character education has long been an integral part of the school's curriculum, beginning in the youngest grades with a program enumerating a particular set of values that are affixed to students' uniforms. Yet, a series of teacher-led investigations revealed that, by the high school years, students seemed unaffected by this values transmission approach. When asked by the teacher researchers how they would improve the school, faculty overwhelmingly expressed frustration that they could not influence what they viewed as their students' moral behavior: cheating, weekend partying and sexual escapades, other forms of risk-taking, petty misconduct such as leaving trash or placing graffiti on school furniture. They were also concerned about boys' treatment of one another.

The team responded by exploring these questions with students, conducting several focus groups with a carefully selected sample. In these focus groups, the team tried to map the school's moral territory by asking about bullying or scapegoating they had observed, about cheating, petty misconduct, and about risk taking. Findings from these exploratory conversations indicated the important role peer groups played in boys' out-of-school lives, especially prominent for the group of weekend partiers. In school, the boys indicated that they saw a significant amount of cheating on tests, and they acknowledged that there was an ongoing but small amount of petty misconduct and vandalism in the school.

To deepen these insights into boys' moral behavior, the team next conducted in-depth individual interviews with a random sample of senior boys. Overall—and not surprisingly—these interviews revealed that families played a big part in the boys' experiences in school and in their social lives. Their relationships with their families flavored, and sometimes determined, how boys viewed, and "did," school, how they made decisions about what was important, what they could and should do, who they should hang out with, and what they valued. They affected under what circumstances boys cheated, how they would and would not take responsibility and, in general, what principles they lived by.

However, the interviews also revealed that by the time boys reached the high school division, their peers had begun to play a bigger part in their on-going construction of their selves than their families. The interviews helped the school appreciate the developmental impact of boys' experience of its gender regime, manifested both in school policies and within peer group play. The following insights added critical dimension, grounded in boys' actual experience, to the school's understanding of its moral curriculum.

The Nature of Cheating

Boys in the focus groups and interviews talked about cheating in ways that went beyond concerns that had been expressed by teachers on the research team. Though some merely said, "It happens sometimes," others said, "It happens a lot." Caleb summarized the types of cheating that occur:

> Oh, cheat sheets, people sitting next to each other, people talking to each other. Um, that's pretty much it, like, people will write the answers down on a piece of paper, hide the paper.

Other boys described people writing notes on the inside of their ties, sleeves, and casts, holding cheat sheets between their knees, looking over their classmates shoulders and looking things up when teachers left the room. By and large, while boys agreed that cheating takes place, some expressed how they hate it when it happens and others said it doesn't bother them as it only puts the cheater at risk. Hamilton expressed the common sentiment:

> The problem is if you are ... in class with them, you're surrounded by kids that don't think it is that big a deal.

The Nature of Petty Misconduct

Boys described the same kinds of misconduct as their teachers. They talked about observing other boys writing graffiti on public surfaces in the school, littering, and engaging in small acts of defiance. However, they attributed these behaviors to a variety of causes, more innocent than immoral: playfulness with each other, boredom or passing time, defiance stemming from a macho resistance and the desire to be cool, and finally to a kind of consumerism. Oren, for example, characterized it this way:

Some kids are just like sometimes it's a joke. They write something about somebody else on a bathroom stall or on a table, or something like this. I don't know, some kids are just disrespectful and vandalize things...

Other boys were quite clear that much of the petty misconduct at the school arose from being bored, not having much to do and passing time. Alan said, "I think it is just boredom. Like, if you have free time or something and you're bored." But aspects of this kind of behavior were also understood by boys to reflect resistance to authority. Oren captured this view:

I guess you could say it is defiant because it is sort of like, not hate, but along those lines between the students and the teachers. Like some students just don't like teachers ... . You're rebelling against the people you don't really like ... . If you don't like a teacher, you are going to write on the desk or something like that. And you piss them off and I guess that is sort of like your sense of accomplishment that you made their life a little worse for that period of time.

The Significance of Boys' Peer Groups

Boys lived within a variety of somewhat fluid, often overlapping, peer groups, which were key to their identities. For example, members of the football team defined themselves as football players and hung out together whereas subgroups defined themselves as African-American football players, "smart" football players, recruits, weekend warriors, or jocks. Boys derived support, comfort, and solace from each other as they chilled, hung out, partied, and otherwise found ways to have good times with each other. Most of the most popular boys were on major sports teams and being a member of these meant that the party culture was easily passed on to first-year students by older team members.

Besides being jocks, the most popular boys were the "the guys who get called to hang out every Friday and Saturday." They were the "weekend warriors" whose partying was notorious. These parties took place at the homes of parents who were out of town or in the nearby woods, and involved heavy drinking. The weekend warriors were perceived as affecting a cool, unruffled manner, as having serious family money, as not working hard, and as expressing much bravado. They had a rebellious streak and showed they were not "pansies" by playing games of hurting each other, mildly resisting authority, and bending school rules.

The peer group performances of the most popular group of boys involved both heavy drinking and in "getting girls." Getting the girls meant having sex with them in "hook-ups" at parties, where boys would "get lucky" and "go off to a bedroom with a girl." Seldom would these hook-ups reflect anything more than one night stands. Their girls came from a core group of about 10 to 12 from a nearby school who partied with the boys. Our informants said they were the "cutest" and "most popular" girls who "respected the macho boys." Over the course of their tenure at the school, the weekend warriors would have sex with many of them. Within the peer status system, girls became trophies. Indeed, some of our informants saw a "video incident" (what came to be a very public incident in which a female student was conned into having sex with a male student, filmed by a hidden crew) as an extreme expression of macho scoring. They made it clear that they believed some boys on the football team had planned the event, announcing it at lunch the day before. The idea was to video the boy and girl having sex and then show it to the team. The boys described this as done with much hilarity, joking, and cheering. The event was planned for a wider audience apparently to demonstrate the ring leader's prowess to the rest of the school while enshrining the team's masculine hegemony.

The School's Conscious Effect on Boys' Behavior

By the time boys reached middle school, their ethics were determined more by family values and the pressures and circumstances of their peer group situations. Gamel expressed the limited impact of the school's moral instruction: "I don't think people go around the school saying I shouldn't do this because the school code says not to. I don't think it affects the decisions that the kids make that much."

Boys tended cynically to believe that the school's values were much less for the boys and much more for the outside world. Bob explained, "The (lower school program) are really, I think, something that the school likes to bring up in functions where they're speaking to parents and stuff, to try to make the school seem like totally abiding by these rules and stuff."

Though they did not see school's values program as central to their moral choices, strong connections with teachers, together with teachers' supportiveness and availability to help, their creation of safe places to talk, and their capacity to talk about moral questions honestly made a real difference to boys. Boys described the value of the small school in knowing their teachers, being known by them, and being able to find them when they wanted to talk. They appreciated how teachers were available to speak with whenever they needed them. And, they emphasized that they could find ones to talk with them about very difficult subjects. Hamilton captured these thoughts well: "Kids have such close interaction with the teachers here. That is one of the strengths. I mean you can go to teachers after classes and kids are talking to teachers in the hallways."

The School's Less Conscious Influence on Boys' Behavior

Students also recognized that the school sometimes both created problems that compounded students' dilemmas and missed opportunities to use events to help boys with these choices. In particular, they pointed to inconsistency in the application of rules, favoritism toward elite athletes, and policies and structures that encouraged misconduct. Boys complained when the school was inconsistent. For example, as did many others, Sam noted that during the 'video incident', the school had not followed its own due process:

> The school kind of violated its own policy to me. And I was like: How can you say you uphold all these morals and you want to protect the girl and you want to throw him out automatically?" But yet we are supposed to have students on the disciplinary committee.

Boys also complained about hypocrisy. Caleb pointed out, "There's alcohol at every party ... that's just a given." He went on to say that if the school didn't realize that, there was something wrong: "I mean the teachers aren't dumb, they're not blind. The teachers know who the kids are that do what."

Perhaps the informants' most vociferous complaints involved their perceptions of unfairness. They said that teacher-coaches and some disciplinarians held ordinary boys to different standards than boys who played elite sports. Matt made this observation about the privilege of certain athletes:

> I honestly didn't see one ... football player ever...in a detention. Like dress code violations ... . I specifically remember one time, my best friend, he's a pretty good baseball player (he's playing baseball in college), and he was walking in the hallway and he had a hooded sweatshirt on and there was probably three or four football players next to him had the same exact hooded sweatshirt things on, and [a teacher-coach] just walked up to my friend and told him to take it off.

In a variety of ways, boys told us that the elite sports, especially football, occupy a special place in the life of the school. They noted that the best athletes became team leaders, often school leaders, and certainly leaders of the hegemonic party crowd. The informants perceived that such teachers can be more lenient when enforcing the disciplinary and dress codes, when holding students to deadlines, and when looking the other way if students leave campus without proper authority. Boys also noticed that some teachers form special relationships with these students, joke around with them more, and give them more academic help.

In addition to the negative lessons boys seem to draw from the privilege accorded to athletes, the school's academic tracking system, creating a pervasive "smart-boy, dumb-boy" discourse, also appeared to fuel student misbehavior. All of the informants attributed other boys' places in the academic order of things to a combination of hard work, brains, parental expectations, and personal choices about how to spend one's time or to their status as (athletic) recruits. However, in a fascinating way, they differentiated according to how they explained their own success. Boys who were very successful attributed their achievement not only to brains but to having Ivy League parents and implied—though they didn't use this term—that they were the recipients of considerable cultural capital. Some of the less successful boys, however, seemed acutely aware that early tracking had cost them opportunities. They complained about the fact that because they had not taken school seriously as middle-schoolers, their capacity to take advanced courses as high-schoolers was severely limited. These boys regretted the school's failure to take into account their development and their potential.

Overall, what these qualitative research processes uncovered was a much more complex moral calculus influencing students' behavior. Quite clearly, the team felt, there were implications for the school's moral programming. These themes were presented, in a more detailed and elaborate way, to the school's administrative team at the end of the year and to a full faculty meeting the following fall. In the faculty discussions that followed, the school concluded that it was too often unaware of and disconnected from the realities of these moral development processes. One result was the commitment to put together a two-year grant proposal to develop a comprehensive, community-based character education program for the high school division, which began at the start of the next school year. The project has included students, parents, teachers, and alumni working together on research teams to conduct a more thorough baseline understanding of the school culture and to develop a multidimensional curriculum for a pilot program, which will also be carefully evaluated.

Schools' Will to Virtue

One of the member schools received a good bit of public attention for their work with the CSBL. In response to press about their new approach to boys, a widely read local columnist made sport of their willingness to rethink things. He mocked the fact that the school "... is out to liberate boys from the awful bonds of gender. Boys shouldn't have to be brave. They shouldn't have to be competitive. They shouldn't have to 'strive to produce'. Boys should be allowed to be more like ... well, girls, I guess" (Spencer, 1997). A mother of three boys at the school took issue with the column, writing in a letter to the editor of the paper:

Was what I saw in print for real? In a country where violence among young men is at a record high? Where young men kill each other as weekend entertainment? Were you actually writing an article criticizing a school for teaching young men that fighting is not a natural instinct? Were you really stating ... (the school's) program was something to be ashamed of?

Smelling blood, the columnist printed her letter in a follow-up column and added, "Gee, Ann, OUCH! You might really have hurt me if I were a girl," going on to further mock the school's approach and offering, finally, to make lunch for the program's leaders: "How's a spinach quiche and a tofu salad sound?"

More poignantly, at the same school, respondents to an alumni survey sent back questionnaire forms with very substantial and often passionate comments scribbled in the margins, clearly indicating that the school had struck a nerve. One man wrote:

My own experience at (school) started out very badly ... . I'd been pulled from the comfortable womb of a coed public school where I seemed to do well enough, socially and academically, without much effort, and was thrown into the totally uncaring, all-male, stiff-upper-lip, cold-showers-in-the-morning, violent, almost brutal world of the British upper-class public school. As a 12 year old, I was dismal at sports and (school) required us to do sports. I am proud of this project that my dear old school has taken on. If it results in insights that will relieve just a little of the suffering of some future bewildered 12 year old wondering why they are making him play football, it will have been worth many times its cost.

However, not all welcomed the school's new exploration and many, with the columnist, reacted with attack and upset. They were especially upset that the school should inquire about aspects of their lives—ideas about themselves as men, relations with women—which they viewed as distinctly separate from the school's realm, off limits, private.

Concluding Remarks

These pointed lessons about the politics of inquiry into boys' lives are an important part of the story of schools' investing in efforts to improve boys' experience and the moral lessons they draw from that experience. In fact, in many ways, the upset the project has created at more than one school is more immediately instructive than its successes. What we have come to appreciate is the considerable investment individuals and institutions make in their ideas about boyhood. The landscape of ideas about masculinity and manhood boys encounter in schools is not neutral, not open to imagination or tampering. Challenging these dominant codes, which have been systematically and historically woven into school curricula—into subject area, personnel practices, school rules, rituals and reward systems—even if just to examine their actual impact on boys, is not perceived as an innocent activity. However persuasive the link between virtue and experience may be, we have found that there are many barriers to schools discovering a grounded theory for boys' education. As Dale (1982) cautioned, "Hegemony is not so much about winning approval for the status quo, winning consent for it or even acceptance of it. Rather, what seems to be involved is the prevention of rejection, opposition or alternatives to the status quo through denying the use of the school for such purposes (pp. 156–157)." From being "too busy" to reflect on their curricula for boys to becoming entangled in internal politics, schools can generate lots of avoidance and take many missteps. Additionally, though usually there is no single individual opposing progress for boys, the overall effect of all of these systemic reactions can be to tie up or diminish the threat of change. Creating a school community that offers boys more experience of encouragement and fairness has required courage, persistence, and confidence on the part of schools. Here is a beginning list of reactions schools have evinced, as they set out to do this work, offered to normalize and to prepare others for what may follow.

Disparaging the Messenger

As the reaction of the newspaper columnist illustrated, a first reaction to the disturbance created by the challenge of new ideas has been to discredit or attack whoever may be importing the ideas. There are many ways that this has happened, all having the effect of isolating and extruding the disturbance, to keep the infection of new perspectives from being implanted into the mainstream of the school community. At one school, widely regarded for its expertise with boys, the recent launch of a survey of faculty attitudes toward boys occasioned numerous comments by colleagues about the point person himself: his masculinity, trustworthiness, his "switching to the other side." Though this person was a trusted member of the faculty, has coached boys, is raising a son himself, his new leadership of a project aimed at illuminating dark recesses of thought and practice at this venerable school left him vulnerable to "Othering," as if he were suddenly, somehow, different. This phenomenon of attack reminds us how carefully protected knowledge about boyhood can be, boundaried by clear lines of taboo and threat.

"Ideologies," Fine (1991) wrote upon completing her study of New York City high schools, "pull our attention to particular representations of social conditions, even as they deflect from others ... . Ideology pervades what happens and what doesn't, what is said and not, what is noticed and obscured" (p. 180). By leading a team to examine the school's tacit curriculum for boys, individuals such as this research team leader become, as Giroux (1997) puts it, "boundary crossers" or "border pedagogues," who come

> to recognize that schooling is really an introduction to how culture is organized, a demonstration of who is authorized to speak about particular forms of culture, what culture is considered worthy of valorization, and what forms of culture are considered invalid and unworthy of public esteem" (p. 239).

In an instinctual, often visceral way, violations of long-established taboos and carefully observed boundaries have frequently generated reaction, usually aimed at the individual perceived to be leading the effort.

Reverting to the Familiar

Given the considerable institutional investment schools make in their gender curricula, they may be leery of proposals for self-examination and change. One result of such leeriness in our experience has been a search for non-controversial explanations of boys' school behavior, the "mirror construction": ways of thinking that merely reflect popular assumptions. One such popular assumption currently enjoying wide play is that of biological sex differences. Where sociologists of gender see masculinities as "the ways bodies are drawn into a historical process" (Connell, 2000, p. 206), essentialists interpret brain difference findings to conclude that "Girls and boys behave differently because their brains are wired differently" (Sax, 2005, p. 28). Schools may feel more comfortable with such interpretations because they validate commonly held, comfortable practices, as if they are based in "boys' *natural* learning style" (Gurian and Stevens, 2005, p, 38, italics in original).

The CSBL is often asked, simply, to prescribe "boy-friendly" programming, an impulse at once promising and short-sighted. Our work has taught us that the only way for schools to arrive at a clear picture of what their boys need is to allow themselves to listen and to see, to be "surprised." By contrast with the over-generalized prescriptions offered on the basis of an essentialist read of boys' (or girls') biology, a pedagogy based upon careful examination of boys' actual experience of, say, literacy education may present, in the words of Smith and Wilhelm (2002), "a profound challenge to American schooling and the traditional teaching of English" (p. xxii). Where prescriptions based upon biological characteristics have the satisfying certainty of pseudo-scientific fact, our epistemological approach asks schools to venture into uncharted territories. A commitment to evidence-based programming for boys requires that schools agree, in advance, to surrender a measure of control over their historic curricula to a research process that is unpredictable, democratic and, therefore, threatening. As our schools created inquiry teams and invited these teams to explore pedagogical questions of their own, with an expectation of recommendations for change, they opened their gendering practice to conscious inspection and likely reform.

This is the conundrum that faces schools embarking on evidence-based programming for boys: Data about boys' actual experiences must be discovered and evaluated as a basis for educational practice, yet these very data may reveal aspects of a curriculum that is "hidden" from conscious view and not necessarily flattering. Schools' phenomenological commitment to the CSBL begins with discovering their actual impact of schools' curricula upon their male students. It is the power of these curricula to dominate the minds and hearts of boys seeking to set trajectories for their lives that compels schools to achieve more conscious control over these curricula. There are lots of good questions for schools to pursue about their boys. One school recently conducted a faculty inventory of questions about the boys in their care—what did they want to understand better about their boys?—and came up with a list several pages long! From how they read and manage time, to their relationships on every level, to their grasp of the lives of females, to their participation in the cyber world, and so on, schools could inform their pedagogy with knowledge discovered systematically, in actual contact with boys. However, to do so require openness and an investment of resources and necessitates an institutional willingness to be moved by the stories of young men.

Chasing Comfort

Writing in a chapter on "The Politics of Change in Masculinity," Connell (2000) warned against a desire for gender change to be pleasant or comfortable:

> I do not think men seeking progressive reforms of masculinity can expect to be comfortable, while we live in a world marked by gender violence and inequality. Masculinity therapy, of the kind promoted by pop psychologists who are currently the best-selling authors about men and masculinity, offers personal comfort as a substitute for social change (p. 204).

Some changes schools must make on behalf of boys will not be without some degree of pain. Sports programs are an example. By contrast with the hazing, bullying, and various other forms of abuse common among sports programs (Messner, 2005; Messner & Sabo, 1994; Sabo, 1986),

Marx (2003) describes the altogether different approach taken by the football program at a school in Maryland—the Building Men for Life program at the Gilman School, which emphasizes service, compassion, and love as key traits. In many schools, this approach would be a radical departure. Sports and the curricular space dedicated to its pursuit was usually a "hot-spot" for peer problems and boys' experience of mixed, often confusing, moral messages.

In his classic on school change, Sarason (1971) cautioned about the prospects for the widespread embrace of such school reforms: "Near impossible" for most school people, he wrote, "because it confronts them with the necessity of changing their thinking, then changing their actions, and finally, changing the overall structure of the setting" (p. 13). At one of the coed schools, initial research on an attrition problem with younger boys led to the disturbing awareness that older boys each year inherited rituals and the historic rationale for the systematic and at times brutal harassment of younger students. Despite the fact that many alumni, board members, and current parents supported these "traditions," a faculty survey led to the realization that there was widespread support across all groups of faculty that the practice was malignant and counter to the values of the school. Over the next several years, a concerted effort was made to end the practice, by separating and protecting younger students in horizontally organized dormitories, with hand-picked staff and student leaders and a host of new supports. Eventually, new boys reported only the infrequent instance of hazing. This school's example reveals the uncontrollable nature of an inquiry process that asks boys about their lives and commits itself to discovering theory from a phenomenological process. Not all that will be unearthed will be pretty or flattering. Boys' lives, in fact, can be quite gritty, and schools can expect to turn out stories and practices that reflect a seamier side to their man-making curriculum. However, we argue, if it is a goal to invite boys to justice and the cultivation of other social virtues, exposing the spaces and practices within our schools in which boys are learning to fear and to abuse is a necessary first step.

Beyond these examples of some more common temptations, however, our work encourages us that despite significant barriers, the claims of virtue can motivate schools to invest in discovering the realities of boys' lives. We—and they—have been encouraged by the goodness, the remarkable compassion, and the care exhibited among boys whose experience encourages healthy ways for being male. There are actually countless examples, in all of our schools. Enough examples, we feel, that we can promise schools that if they can address themselves to aspects of their curricula that produce injustice, violence, selfishness, and self-destructiveness, they will be rewarded with boys who can evidence, from their own lives, a reliable concern for caring and fairness. Connell, speculating on the future of change in masculinity, argues for "prefigurative politics": "at least samples of paradise, at least little bits of justice, here and now" (2000, p. 211). The glimpses of boys' lives we have seen in these schools, as fleeting and unsteady as they may be, prefigure the more just society we long for.

Notes

1. In 2007, to serve coed member schools more fully and their female students more fairly, the Center adopted a new mission, becoming the Center for the Study of Boys' and Girls' Lives, and added three more schools, including two single-sex girls' schools (www.csbgl.org).

References

Alford, R. R. (1998). *The craft of inquiry: Theories, methods, evidence.* New York: Oxford University Press.

Berkowitz, M. W. (1997). The complete moral person: Anatomy and formation. In J. M. DuBois (Ed.), *Moral issues in psychology: Personalist contributions to selected problems* (pp. 11–42). Lanham, MD: University Press of America.

Berkowitz, M. W. (2002). The science of character education. In W. Damon (Ed.), *Bringing in a new era in character education* (pp. 43–63). Pala Alto, CA: Hoover Institution Press.

Chu, J. Y. (2000). Learning what boys know: An observational and interview study with six four year old boys. Unpublished doctoral dissertation, Boston: Harvard University.

Connell, R. W. (1996). Teaching the boys: New research on masculinity and gender strategies for schools. *Teachers' College Record, 98*(2), 206–235.

Connell, R. W. (2000). *The men and the boys.* Berkeley, CA: University of California Press.

Dale, R. (1982). Education and the capitalist state: Contributions and contradictions. In M. Apple (Ed.), *Cultural and economic reproduction in education* (pp. 127–161). Boston: Routledge and Kegan Paul.

Fine, M. (1991). *Framing dropouts.* Albany: State University of New York Press.

Fine, M. (1992). *Disruptive voices: The possibilities of feminist research.* Ann Arbor: University of Michigan Press.

Foster, V. (1998). *Gender, schooling and post-school pathways: Beyond statistics and populist discourse.* Paper presented at the Australian Association for Research in Education. Adelaide, Australia.

Froschl, M., & Sprung, B. (2005). *Raising and educating healthy boys. A report on the growing crisis in boys' education.* New York: Academy for Educational Development.

Gilligan, C. (1982). *In a different voice.* Cambridge, MA: Harvard University Press.

Giroux, H. (1997). *Pedagogy and the politics of hope.* Boulder, CO: Westview Press.

Gurian, M., & Stevens, K. (2005). *The minds of boys.* New York: Jossey-Bass.

Howard, R. W., Berkowitz, M. W., & Schaeffer, E. F. (2004). Politics of character education. *Educational Policy, 18*(1), 188–215.

James, J. (1997). What are the social issues involved in focusing on difference in the study of gender? *Journal of Social Issues, 53*(2), 213–232.

Kessler, S., Ashendon, D. J., Connell, R. W., & Dowsett, G. W. (1985). Gender relations in secondary schooling. *Sociology of Education, 58*, 34–48.

Kuriloff, P. & Reichert, M.C. (2003). Boys of color, boys of class: Negotiating the academic and social geography of an elite independent school. *Journal of Social Issues, 59*(4), November.

Lewin, T. (2006, July 9). At colleges, women are leaving men in the dust. *New York Times*, p. A1.

Mann, P. S. (1994). *Micropolitics.* Minneapolis: University of Minnesota Press.

Marx, J. (2003). *Season of life.* New York: Simon and Schuster.

Mead, S. (2006). *The evidence suggests otherwise: The truth about boys and girls.* Washington, DC: Education Sector.

Messner, M. (2005). Still a man's world? In M. S. Kimmel, J. Hearn, and R. W. Connell (Eds.), *Handbook of studies on men and masculinities* (pp. 313–325). Thousand Oaks, CA: Sage.

Messner, M. A., & Sabo, D. F. (Eds.). (1994). *Sex, violence and power in sports.* Freedom, CA: The Crossing Press.

Reichert, M. C. (2000). Disturbances of difference: Lessons from a boys' school. In M. Fine & L. Weis, (Eds.), *Construction sites: Excavating class, race and gender among urban youth* (pp. 259–274). New York: Teachers College Press.

Reichert, M. C. (2001). Rethinking masculinities: New ideas for schooling boys. In W. Martino & B. Meyenn (Eds.), *What about the boys?: Issues of masculinity in schooling.* (pp. 38–52). Philadelphia: Open University Press.

Reichert, M. C., & Kuriloff, P. (2003). Boys' selves: Forging identities in the looking glass of school life. *Teachers' College Record, 106*(3), 547–576.

Reinharz, S. (1988). The concept of voice. Paper presented at meeting of Human Diversity, Perspectives on People context, University of Maryland, College Park.

Sabo, D. (1986, Summer). Pigskin, patriarchy and pain. *Changing Men: Issues in Gender, Sex and Politics, 16*, 24–25.

Sarason, S. B. (1971). *The culture of the school and the problem of change.* Boston: Alllyn and Bacon.

Sax, L. (2005). *Why gender matters.* New York: Doubleday.

Shields, S. A. (2002). *Speaking from the heart: Gender and the social meaning of emotion.* Cambridge, UK, Cambridge University Press.

Sizer, T. R., & Sizer, N. F. (1999). *The students are watching: Schools and the moral contract.* Boston: Beacon.

Smith, M. W., & Wilhelm, J. D. (2002). *Reading don't fix no chevys.* Portsmouth, NH: Heinemann.

Spencer, G. (1997, March 5). Snobbery will get you nowhere. *Delaware County Times*, p. 2.

Spencer, R., Porche, M. V., & Tolman, D. L. (2003). We've come a long way-maybe: New challenges for gender equity in education. *Teachers College Record, 105*(9), 1774–1807.

Stoudt, B. G. (2006). "You're either in or you're out": School violence, peer discipline and the (re)production of hegemonic masculinity. *Men and Masculinity, 8*(3), 273–287.

Swain, J. (2005). Masculinities and education. In M. S. Kimmel, J. Hearn, & R. W. Connell (Eds.), *Handbook of studies on men and masculinities* (pp. 213–229). Thousand Oaks, CA: Sage.

Tyre, P. (2006, January 30). The trouble with boys. *Newsweek*, pp. 44–52.

Young, I. M. (1990). *Justice and the politics of difference.* Princeton, NJ: Princeton University Press.

4 Why Does She Need Me?

Young Men, Gender, and Personal Practice

Rebecca Priegert Coulter

Introduction

As young men engage in school-based gender equity work, do they also begin to remake their own lives, particularly with respect to gender relations? As they intellectualize the personal as political, do they also enact the political as personal? Put another way, to what extent do they make their learnings about gender real through their practices in living out relationships? By exploring these questions with young men who took up anti-sexist work as secondary school students, I came to see how they struggled to make sense of who they were, what they believed, and how they should act. Their talk provides insights into the ways in which a political consciousness about gender can develop among young men and how they theorize the gendered nature of their own lives. Their observations also reveal the power of deeply rooted, hegemonic beliefs about masculinity and gender relations and clearly suggest the pedagogical work that confronts educators committed to making a more equitable world.

Elsewhere I have discussed how 10 young men, ages 15 to 20, attending publicly funded secondary schools in London, Ontario, Canada, voluntarily came to take up gender equity work in their classrooms and through extra-curricular activities such as equity clubs or the White Ribbon Campaign, a pro-feminist male initiative to oppose violence against women (Coulter, 2003). The young men described how learning experiences in schools were central to developing their interest in gender equity, understood in the Canadian context as an array of policies and practices designed to promote and protect women's equality (Coulter, 1999). Here, however, I want to move beyond looking at why the young men got involved in gender equity work to probe what impact their own changing understandings of gender had on the way they explained and made sense of personal relationships with young women. Ultimately, this chapter is about the messy business of change and the struggles of young men to reconstruct themselves (Kenway, 1995) while situated "within the self-evidence of relations of domination" (Bourdieu, 2001, p. 11).

The young men who participated in the research were interesting and thoughtful individuals who spoke openly about their ideas, their relationships and their lives. Selected from three different schools—an academic collegiate catering to the university-bound offspring of the business and professional-managerial classes and two comprehensive secondary schools, one located in a mixed-income area and the other in a working-class neighborhood—these young men had become successful students who generally anticipated enrolment in post-secondary institutions. With one exception, a young Métis (of mixed Aboriginal and European heritage), the participants were white and all self-identified as heterosexual. Six came from middle-class backgrounds, and four came from working-class families. One of the young men in the latter group had, at an earlier point in his life, lived on the streets for a period of time.

Each of the young men in this study participated in an interview lasting about 90 minutes, and half of them (i.e., five) agreed to take part in a focus group discussion, which, like the interviews, was recorded and transcribed. All of the young men had reflected on their own personal gender relations, and all of them had both male and female friends with whom they had talked about relationships in the concrete and the abstract. Indeed, the open sharing of some of the most intimate details of one's relationships seemed to be a hallmark of these mixed-sex friendship groups, and this tendency spilled over into the interviews and the focus group discussion. The frank and free way in which the young men, whose identities are protected through the use of pseudonyms, exchanged views with me and with one another resulted in a large pool of data. The material from the group discussion was especially rich. In the group, the young men spoke freely, working out ideas together but also occasionally challenging one another's claims or interpretations. Thus, though I use some evidence from the individual transcripts for context and background, I draw primarily on the exchanges in the focus group to reveal, through their own words, how the young men attempted to understand gender and gender relations. I begin by exploring their discussions about what it means to be a man and then turn to an examination of their struggles to make sense of relations between men and women, both in general and in the more personal and immediate way.

Being a Man

The young men easily listed stereotypical male characteristics, chiming out in the focus group discussion, for example, such descriptors as "the macho," "the protector," "the unemotional, uncaring guy," "the tall-standing, supportive" one. They attacked media images of men, particularly those in television advertisements, and labeled them as often "evil and sexist." They were especially irate about portrayals of men as being incompetent in the household. However, in commenting positively about a commercial showing a man "who's bright enough to, you know, use the product that allows him to do the least amount of work," they also recognized a certain ironic turn in this message about men and housecleaning. And, on the whole, they acknowledged but rejected constructions of masculinity that denied males the full range of emotions and the right to cry. Using an expression now common in North American popular culture, the young men talked about the difficulties in being able to show their "feminine side" and noted they were best able to do that in conversations with female friends or with girlfriends. Of course, the very use of the descriptor "feminine side" situates emotion, feelings, caring as belonging to women and uncritically reinforces dualistic constructions of women and men. It is a rhetorical strategy that conveys a desire to be allowed the "softer" expressions of emotion while protecting the male speaker from being taken too seriously by drawing on a somewhat jocular and ultimately dismissive categorization of male feelings. Put another way, for men to talk about their feminine side is a way for them to express an honest need "to feel." However, it comes labeled in a way that can be read as essentialist, sexist, and even misogynist, though I do not claim here that the young men consciously saw this dilemma. In describing their wish to draw on their feminine side, they were simply using the language made available to them by their cultural location.

In the end, all the young men had difficulty deciding what it really meant to be a man. Eighteen-year-old Casey poignantly described his own struggles to establish the meaning of masculinity as "travellin' around in a grey area."

> Like you have people who are saying, "Well, a man's supposed to be this way," and then you have people saying, "Well, you know, you could also do this," or "You should show more of this. You should do more of that." Where's like … where's the actual definition of what it's supposed to be? So, I mean, if you don't know then you're sort of just like travellin' around in a grey area tryin' to just be yourself.

This understanding from lived experience of the fluidity of gender identities was confirmed by Dave, who observed, "I think the rules that exist are sort of, I don't know, sort of liquid," a conclusion, of course, that is well-supported in the scholarly literature (see, for example, Brickell, 2005; Connell, 1995, 2000; Frank, Kehler, Lovell, & Davison, 2003; Martino, 1999; Swain, 2006), a body of work that was, however, unknown to the young men as they engaged in their own theory building.

These young men tended to believe there are rules about manhood but that the rules are difficult to pin down, and it is hard to figure out where and how you learn them. In other words, they had a glimpse of the way in which learning and practicing gender is very often liminal (Martin, 2006). Robert observed there are pressures for "meeting up to society's expectation of that classification of a man," but Derek followed this comment by observing that "over the course of the past twenty, thirty years the roles of men and women have been changing so much it's really hard to get any sort of identity." The young men gnawed away at what they recognized as a contradiction in their own beliefs that there were rules but, then again, there were no rules. Their talk revealed an open recognition that as they went about their lives, they were "doing masculinity." As with the Australian young men in Martino's (1999, 2000) and Martino and Pallotta-Chiarolli's (2001) studies, masculinity is very much about performance. In the words of one participant, "Like when I'm with one group I'm one person, and when I'm with the other, I have to act a different way, be a different person."

In the course of the group discussion, Casey discussed his lived experience of multiple masculinities (Connell, 2000; Lingard & Douglas, 1999). He talked about the different ways of being male on the football field, in the school band, and in the classroom.

> Like it sort of changes from being physical to academic, more skill-based in like math and English and that, than the actual body aspect of it ... . You have to look at it, it's like yes, there is a lot of power base under the male image, you know. You have to be this kind of strong person that can go out and do the things that a lot of people think men should be able to do, where it's like in the other aspect, it's like, well, you just, you know, be yourself. You try and get the good grades and the, you know, that other academic aspect of being male, I guess.

Derek responded by saying,

> I think ... . I think [Casey] just answered the question from earlier on when we had two conflicting opinions between men having to live up to the expectations of society and me saying there is no defined expectation. I think what the problem is is that there are too many different groups within society that have different sets of expectations, and we have to try to mesh amongst them all, and it's really hard with contrasting things, like being physical out on the field, and no matter how fast a runner you are on the field, that doesn't help you play a clarinet, you know. It's a totally ... [interruption].

Aaron took up this question of trying to mesh conflicting expectations by struggling to understand why, as someone who saw himself as a kind, nonviolent person, he took pleasure in playing North American football. He compared playing the game with going to war:

...you're in reality, and then you're put onto the field and you're not in reality any more. It's like a war. You have, you know, your two coaches or like generals or whatever, and you've got your armies, and, you know, you've got your strategic plays, you know, and then you try to win, you know, as much land as you can.

In a stunning example of how a patriarchal culture teaches young men to separate their lives into self-contained pieces and suppress certain emotions in order to act (Kaufman, 1999), Aaron talked about having a "split personality" and "going crazy" playing the game because "it's kind of like it's not real life." Openly speaking of the pleasures he found in sport, Aaron commented, "the harder I'd hit someone, the better I felt, you know, and I used to love hitting people as hard as I could." It was, he said, "just that whole domination, male domination thing that maybe football has in it, you know." But this was explained in his life as "not reality" until the day he actually knocked an opposing player unconscious and experienced conflicting emotions. That day, Aaron said, he felt "good for myself" but "bad for him." However, in feeling sorry for the other young man and empathizing with him, Aaron could no longer compartmentalize the pleasures he took in physical power and domination as "not real" and began to think more deeply about the meaning of physicality and force in men's lives. Aaron's obvious ambivalence in speaking about this experience led the young men in the group to take up an analysis of male power, competition and violence and, in doing so, they linked this discussion to their own responses to young women.

Competition, Power, and Fear

Referring back to earlier observations that he and Robert had made about the ways in which male students use their physical presence and psychological strategies to dominate or "overpower" young women in classrooms, Casey connected sports to competing for marks in school and edged up to acknowledging, even for himself as a gender-conscious young man, the presence of potential or actual male violence in gender relations. Coincidentally, Casey also challenged the notion that young men do not care about succeeding in school:

You can be the best on the field, but if you get into a situation where you're competing for math marks or something with a girl that's like better than you, and she's like constantly beating you, but you bring the mentality from the field of like, you know, the competition kind of thing and you want to beat them, but you're clear, but they clearly outmatch you in the skill, then you're sort of like, well, then you kind of revert back, maybe, to the more physical ... . It's sort of like, "Well, if that's the only thing I can do [inaudible interruptions], if that's my only strength here," then you build on that, and that's where the overpowering comes in. Like if you can't compete with them on your level, on their level, then, then you sort of lean towards what you're best at.

The young men suggested they could accept being beaten by other males but had high levels of discomfort when they were bested by young women in any way. As they probed their feelings, which they recognized as problematic, Aaron suggested, "Maybe it's subconscious, that we're afraid of powerful women." After providing an example where someone surpassed him in acting talent and achievements, Derek admitted that he was particularly annoyed that it was a young woman and agreed "there might be something there about power." He went on to recount another story of seeing a large, muscular woman coming out of a gym and feeling afraid of her. Because he was taller and stronger than most women, he had never thought about a physical confrontation with a woman but

then all of a sudden there was one woman ... that I knew could physically, you know, throw me around, and there was nothing I could do about it, and it just kind of, you know, gave me an eerie feeling in the gut of my stomach, you know.

As these young men, who believed they had "good, positive ideas and ideals about women," contemplated what they had just admitted about their own potential for violence and about their fears around women challenging male superiority, Dave turned quickly to sociobiology for explanations about the "naturalness" of masculine competitions for women, the desire to protect women, and the "genetic predisposition" to hunt and kill, now converted to activities on the playing fields.

Robert made an unsuccessful attempt to interrupt this self-justifying and rationalizing discourse, suggesting that physical violence is a male response that often occurs but is not inevitable.

Men revert back to physical violence, that was said, when all else fails. If you're not intellectually or socially or politically, I don't know, whatever you want to say, if you're not superior to a woman in any of those categories, you have to revert back to your physical self, and that's what I think the main trouble with males is today. They can't learn to adapt ... .

Opposing voices were immediately raised, with Dave, in particular, putting the case for men being genetically programmed for competition to ensure that "the strongest DNA is passed on, and to be, you know, to have this need to pound things into a pulp is a sort of survival trait." He argued that if women became stronger than men, it would be a dangerous thing from an "evolutionary standpoint." Men would lose their role in the human chain if they could not be "protectors, hunters and, you know, attackers," Dave argued, suggesting that men had "a deep-laden fear in the back of our minds that we're going to lose [interjection: 'our identity'] who we are, because that's what we were designed by nature to be." Several of the young men went on to make comments such as "It's still like you want to be able to protect that person." If women do not need protection, "we're expendable," said one to nervous laughter. Things may be changing, the young men agreed, but it is "kind of scary." As Derek frankly observed, "If this person's better than me at like everything I can offer [slight laugh], then why does she need me? So it's kind of that scare factor of like, wow … ."

bell hooks (2004) has argued that men are both willing to change and afraid of change. This is clearly the case for these young men. They are happy to participate in large, floating mixed-sex groups of peers, to enjoy the close friendships with young women that allow young men to speak openly about their emotions, to support activities for fairness and equality, to work for a safer world for women. However, despite their concern for gender equity, the young men find it difficult, not so much to compete with women but to be "defeated" by women. They admit to personal fears about powerful, high-achieving, independent women even as they recognize how this stands in tension with their intellectual beliefs about equality. Out of this tangled web, wafting the odor of the "crisis in masculinity" (Arnot, 2002; Lingard & Douglas, 1999) and reeking of the influence of the mytho-poetical movement (Connell, 2000; Kaufman, 1999; Lingard & Douglas), creeps a set of patriarchal attitudes and ideas about men and women. The dualism of the "battle of the sexes" lives among these young men despite their political commitment to and honestly professed desire for a more equitable world. Nowhere is this more clear for the young men than in the realm of personal, intimate relationships with young women.

Girlfriends, Cunning Women, and Sexual Predators

Connell (2000) has pointed out that because "change in gender requires reconstructing personal relations as well as public life, there are many opportunities for personal hurt, mistaken judgments, and anger" (p. 204). As we already have seen, young men easily revert back to the very stereotypes they earlier condemned, most particularly in their wish to retain the role as "protectors" or "guardians" of women. However, more troubling is the hostility and suspicion many of the young men directed toward young women during discussions about relationships. A number of accusations about the cunning woman who cannot be trusted or the woman intent on springing the matrimonial trap came quickly to the fore.

In discussing efforts in Canada to develop legislation to combat sexual exploitation by controlling and limiting the range of age differences allowed in dating relationships for teenagers, the young men initially admitted some senior male students took advantage of younger female students. However, they also pointed out that young people could be active agents in their own lives. Derek, in noting that he had recently broken up with his girlfriend who was four years younger than he was, commented that "because of her beliefs we had a non-pre-marital sexual relationship [but] if that two-year rule applied, it wouldn't matter whether or not I'm having sex with her. People would still look at me." In commenting on the proposed legislation, Robert argued that, "It's a dangerous thing to try and categorize people like that." He described a situation involving a 19-year-old young man he knew who was dating a young women five years younger than himself.

> One of the things that was very noticeable about their relationship was they basically decided that there's not gonna' be any sex in the relationship until she reaches sixteen, just as a way of sort of defining their relationship from the beginning. And the thing is that she's a very strong-minded person, she knows exactly what she wants and she's probably about the only person who can keep this guy in check because he's sort of a jerk. She's the only person who can really turn him into a normal person. And, you know, if they were having sex it wouldn't be because he had impressed it on her. It would be because she had basically decided, "O.K., I'd like to do this now." And if somebody came along and said, "You're under arrest," [slight laugh] because she had decided that she was ready, then that … . It's like some sort of weird fascism, you know … . If you differentiate from the norm in any way, you will be put in jail.

However, this conversation quickly changed directions when Aaron commented, "I don't know about anybody else, but I have a lot of trouble finding out or figuring out, you know, whether a girl is sixteen or twenty-one" [expressions of agreement and nervous laughter from others in focus group]. Aaron went on to talk about how girls he had met at parties turned out to be much younger than he had assumed, but they would phone him anyway and try to get him interested in dating. He concluded:

> I think there's gonna' be a lot of problems with that [the proposed legislation] because girls are very manipulative and they know how to lie and they know how to set, you know, how to set guys up and, and,

and … well, no, maybe not, maybe that's not what they're trying to do but … there's gonna' be a lot of problems with that.

The shift in Aaron's discourse here shows how, because of his experiences as a very good-looking, athletic, and popular young man who had just broken up with a girlfriend who responded by making false claims about pregnancy, he is struggling with and against specific constructions that situate women as always scheming to get their man. When asked what he thought women were manipulating to get, he replied, "I don't know [interruptions]. I just know woman are manipulative." Dave, the resident sociobiologist, jumped in by citing the work of Desmond Morris to explain how these situations were "all about genetics" and young women "wanting social status" that they achieved through attachment to a high-status male, which in high school meant an older, more senior student. Women were "genetically predisposed to getting themselves status through their mates," said Dave, a position that was immediately challenged by Robert, who argued social determination was more important than biology.

At this point, I reminded Robert that he had said in his individual interview that having "a nice-looking girlfriend that's the right height and the right size" is a status symbol for young men. In fact, he had gone further to argue, "It's all public image with your girlfriend, and if you have a good-looking girlfriend, then somehow you're better than the other boys." In the focus group, however, one of the young men suggested that having an attractive girlfriend can sometimes "backfire on you." One went so far as to claim, and others laughed and agreed, "If you have a bad-looking girlfriend, you don't really want to bring her out." At the same time, "When you do bring out the girls who are good-looking, you kind of get very protective of them." When asked if they meant "jealous" rather than "protective," Robert tried to explain, but his struggle with language reveals he was beginning to recognize the conversation had moved into troubling territory and was revealing problematic attitudes towards women that countered their intellectual commitment to equity.

Maybe jealous. Maybe. You know, you want to, you want to kind of let everyone know that, they're with you and, you know, that girl, well, you know, you shouldn't be, well, you should be looking but not a long time, I guess. [Laughter from most of the other young men] You know what I mean? Like…

Here a series of rapid interjections ensued from the others in the focus group: "Yeah. We permit quick glances, you know. Yeah, Yeah. Ogling. Yeah", and so on. This admission then lead to the following over-lapping exchange among the young men:

You kind of want everyone to know that, you know, this is … . It's
kind of like, kind of, I hate saying this, but not like possession but …
Hey, world, I'm a happy guy.
You were strong and skilled enough to …
But yet this is …
This woman is mine. Get your own. You know?
[Slight laugh] Get your own.

Robert concluded, "Yeah. It's kind of weird to say it, like it's kind of
hard to say that, but it's kind of like the way you do kind of think about
that, you know." Thus, the young men came to admit, however abashedly,
that they did tend to think of girlfriends as possessions and as status
objects. However, they also very quickly painted young women with the
same brush, arguing that women were even more possessive and more
inclined to jealousy than males. As one said,

The women are far more vicious than guys, I think, in that aspect. I
mean, they're very vengeful and devious. [interjection: "conniving"]
You just pound the shit out of some guy, but the girl has to sort of
[slight laugh; interjection: "do it mentally"]. Mentally. Yeah. Exactly.
She has to figure out a whole plot too and stuff. [laugh] Yeah. There's
a plan.

For the young men, "pounding the shit out of some guy" seemed like
a reasonable response when one felt threatened, but young women acting
out their feelings of jealousy in a verbal manner were described harshly
as "vengeful and devious" or "conniving." This discrepancy in how the
young men felt males and females acted in relationships reproduced the
most traditional of stereotypes. Indeed, the young men, at least initially,
reinforced the very image of men as rather clueless, put-upon, and unable
to understand women.

For example, despite having acknowledged their own feelings of
possessiveness toward girlfriends, the young men claimed to be puzzled
when those same girlfriends demanded public displays confirming their
relationship. Dave commented:

I don't sort of strut at all, especially when it comes to my girlfriend,
and this seems to disappoint her because she wants me to strut and
show off the fact that I do have her because she wants to know that,
you know, other people are jealous of me. I think this is sort of weird
because I don't understand the motivation for it, because I don't like
to show off anything of mine.

Aaron added his experience:

> I used to notice something with my ex-[girlfriend]. Like she used to,
> whenever there was a group of girls, like especially good-looking girls,
> and we were together at the movies or something like that, you know,
> or anywhere we were, and they were lookin' at me or checkin' me out
> or something like that, she'd be hangin' all over me and wanting me to
> show affection to her, you know, and she would get upset if I didn't,
> if I didn't, you know, you know, let these other girls know that I was
> with her. And she used to think that, you know, I used to do it on
> purpose or whatever, that, you know, I wasn't showin' any affection,
> but you know, it was just, I just didn't really notice … .

We have seen that the young men agreed that having and displaying a
good-looking girlfriend was an important status marker for them. Why,
then, did they have trouble understanding that the reverse might be true
for heterosexual young women?

Initially, the young men also claimed not to understand why their
girlfriends were insecure about their looks or why they would try to create
themselves as the objects of their boyfriends' expressed desires. Dave
observed that his girlfriend was

> a little bit obsessive about her looks. Like she's worried that I'm
> attracted to somebody else more so she's very … like I don't know
> why she is, she just seems to have this idea that if she doesn't look
> perfect, then I'm going to find someone else who is … .

In talking about and then analyzing what was going on, Aaron began
to grasp how patriarchal power works in intimate relationships. Although
he claimed "not to mean anything by it," he told his girlfriend, who had
brown hair, that he liked redheads. She began to dye her hair red even
though he "wasn't trying to say to her, you know, … . I'm gonna' go
for a redhead and if you don't change your hair, you know … ." Aaron
continued to reveal how this dynamic worked itself out after he also
commented to his short girlfriend that he liked "tall girls."

> I never was trying to insinuate that I was gonna' go for someone else,
> but she, in the back of her mind, thought that she was never good
> enough, you know, and she always thought like, well, "I have to start
> changing myself for him or else he's gonna' go and find it somewhere
> else," you know. And I always just thought, you know, "Well, wow,
> I have a lot of power that I don't even realize," you know. Or if I …
> even girls I'm not going out with, I'll just say something like, "That
> dress, you know, that you're wearing today is nice" 'cause at [name
> of his secondary school] they don't wear a lot of dresses, it's kind of
> like a hippie school anyway. The girls there, you know, whenever I see

a girl who looks half decent or, you know, wears, you know, a nice dress or looks very feminine or something like that or looks good, I'll comment on it and say, you know, "You look good today," or "You look nice today," or something like that, and then the next week or the next whatever, they're like, they're always wearing dresses and stuff like that, and I just kind of noticed that, and I just kind of said, "Whoa. I have power over girls I'm not even goin' out with," you know. You know what I mean? It's kind of, it's kind of a power trip but [inaudible] I don't know.

This is a very clear example of how young men learn about their power to influence and control women who have already been primed by culture to please men (Firminger, 2006). Through the very ordinariness and everydayness of interactions such as the ones described by Aaron, gender is created and performed and, in that process, male dominance is reiterated and reinforced. It is, as Aaron said, "a power trip" and one that the young men find both puzzling and satisfying.

At the same time, as they reflected on how their power played out in heterosexual relationships, they acknowledged their own feelings of insecurity about measuring up as the kind of men women would want. Aaron, despite realizing that he could and did exercise power over the young women in his life, observed that he often felt "like I have to better myself" to respond to women's demands. Verbalizing anxieties about what would happen if he did not have the things women wanted (a car, the right clothes), he worried that he might be seen as less desirable or inferior to other men. Others in the group picked up on this theme, acknowledging, for example, that

you do become very self-conscious about how you look and who you are and like, especially for a guy, how big you are, how fast you are, how … ., you know, can you fit the role that some people think you should be in? And that's where … and the thing that comes back to you is like, you know, like we were saying, it's the power.

For the most part, the young men were concerned about power as it related to their positioning within the male peer group but, more significantly, with their power to attract the kind of women they wanted, which, of course, also contributed to where they would be placed among other males in the school social circle. Casey was blunt about this: "It's kind of a status thing, you know. If you're on the sports team and you've got the body and you've got these things [i.e., a car, the right clothes], it's sort of like you're almost a step above a lot of people." In this context, several of the young man wanted to be able to tell younger brothers to "just be yourself" but admitted that, in reality, this did not work and you had to compete with a lot of other people to be somebody. Casey talked about "being the best at both worlds," the world of who you really were and the world of publicly performed masculinity. In other words, there was some sense in which young men felt they lived a bifurcated existence, although they acknowledged that in doing so, they questioned who they really were and felt that they no longer knew what it meant "to be yourself." In struggling for survival and status in their youthful worlds, they had lost the certainty of knowing who they were. They illustrate clearly "the deep *splitting of selves* that boys and men sometimes elect, sometimes are forced to undertake, as they negotiate the treacherous terrain of becoming a man" (Fine & Kuriloff, 2006, p. 259).

Because their consciousness of gender had been raised as part of their schooling and they had some tools with which to explore, analyze, and understand events in their lives (Coulter, 2003), these young men strained to work against the grain of the dominant form of masculinity in their secondary schools while, at the same time, making their own compromises with it. There was a real tension at work in their lives, revealed, for example, when they talked about their younger sisters. Dave, for example, said,

> … being a big brother, I'm protective of her. I don't like the thought of anybody bothering her—teachers, other students. She does get her fair share of taunting and stuff because she's so shy, and it just, it riles me. I just want to step in and say, you know, "All you people who annoy my sister, you're gonna' have to mess with me before you mess with her." But I trust her because I know that she's intelligent and she has good judgement about things even if she is a bit, you know, off in her own little world sometimes. But I know she is going to be great one day.

Casey commented that if he had a younger sister, he would be very protective and would issue warnings to potential boyfriends to be nice to his sister. After acknowledging that as a male he could never really know what growing up female was like, he concluded that

> … it's sort of like the only thing you can do is be the role model of the protector, you know. Make sure that if they [i.e., sisters] get hurt that you can go out and beat up whoever hurt them, 'cause like that's all [slight laugh] almost, you know, one of the things that you'd be looked at for.

Resorting to a traditional mode of masculine expression, both Dave and Casey returned to the theme of men protecting women, in this case sisters, and identified physical violence as the means to effect that protection. Dave, however, recognized that his female sibling might not desire this intervention and had resources of her own with which to protect herself, thus revealing his ability, in this instance, to distance himself from hegemonic or sociobiological constructions of masculinity. Later in the discussion about what the young men would tell sisters about men, he went even further:

> I don't want to breed in my sister some paranoia about men, because I know that there's a lot of bad men out there, but I don't want her to go into the world like some people seem to, thinking that men are sort of the enemy and not to be trusted because there's only one thing they want and they'll go to any ends to get it, because I don't even know many men like that. But I want her to understand that men are just, you know, other people, that she needs to, you know, not trust implicitly but not have this paranoia that they're going to harm her in some way, because it'll just make her unhappy forever.

Robert, on the other hand, offered a different view of men and, inadvertently created a bit of a shock wave in the group by raising the specter of incest.

> I do have a younger sister. Scares the hell out of me. She's started talking to me about boys and I thought, "god!" [slight laugh]. It's tough, because you have a younger sister and every other woman you talk with in your entire life you've just wanted to have sex with, but you can't have sex with your younger sister [nervous laughter from some young men]. Not that I'd want to, but … . So, when she asked me about boys, she just started to and she's in a bad relationship right now … . Jeez, it's like a magician giving away his magic tricks almost, eh? The information I have to give her about what guys do and the manipulations they go through and everything like that. I try to tell her honestly what we as males do, stereotypically, and hope that she can have foresight and see into the relationship. That's about it.

In contrast to Dave, Robert did fall back on a portrayal of men as hyper-sexual beings who have tricks they use to get women to agree to have sex with them. However, he met with considerable resistance from the rest of the group, with members revealing a sense of injustice that young males were always labeled as having voracious sexual appetites whereas young women were not. Many of the young men commented on female desire and made admissions in the group that would likely have set off a furor in locker rooms. One said, "My girlfriend thinks about sex much more than I do. Sex is not a big part of my life, but she's very, you know, interested in … ." Others in the group contributed similar observations, with one noting that his girlfriend "sometimes finds it a bit insulting that I'm not constantly, you know, wanting to have sex with her, because this seems to be something that's expected of me." Another commented,

> Yeah. Yeah. I've found that. I mean, there was this one time this one girl I was seeing, whatever, and I refused like to have sex or whatever, I refused to make out or to have sex or whatever, and she hated me. She hated me for that. And I said, "Well, you know, it's not you. It's just because, you know, I just don't feel like it or I just don't want to." Or if, or when I was goin' out with my girlfriend for two and a half years or whatever, if I refused it there would, you know, she really felt like she'd, like she [interruption "the knife"] ... . It was like I was takin' a knife and stabbin' her with it, you know. It was like [interruption: Yeah. It's like you're making them feel ...] Like it was like [she felt] completely undesirable, and it was totally expected of me whenever she wanted to, I had to produce.

Another young man put it this way: "We're supposed to be virile sex monsters who are always ready for it, you know."

Young men's resistance to constructions of themselves as hyper-sexual beings has been noted by other researchers (see, for example, Allen, 2003; Clements-Schreiber, Rempel & Desmarais, 1998) who, from varying theoretical positions, confirm Robert's claim that there are "contradictions here about how in society, society thinks that men are the pro-sexual and always thinking about sex, but it turns out that women think about it a lot ... . It's just [pause] fun." Thus, after complaining about the insatiability of female desire, the young men went on to talk about the pleasures and joys of sex for them. Comments such as "it's basically an emotion sort of pumping up," "it gets you energized," "it's a high you sort of get on to" were prevalent. One young man commented, "It's kind of like a drug. Once you've done it, you can't stop." Here Derek intervened with the observation,

> That was the rough part about stepping into a non-premarital sexual relationship, having been sexually active through my teenaged years and all of a sudden it's like [interruption: yeah, yeah], all of a sudden [it can] turn into a pressure cooker, you know, it's hard.

A little later, however, in the midst of a discussion about birth control and the use of condoms, Derek also commented, "Personally, I think that sex is overrated" and another young man agreed, "Yeah. So do I." Derek went on to explain:

> The act of sex. Thinking about it is great [laugh]. It's one of those things that, to quote Oscar Wilde, "The only thing worse than not

getting everything you want is getting everything you want" and sex is the same way. I mean, you're watching TV and you get these subtle clues, you know like [sigh] or if a woman walks down the street, no problem, OK, but when it comes to the actual thing it's not as fantastic as you built it up in your mind to be.

After a number of interjections of agreement, Robert said, "That's a pretty bold thing to say." Derek responded:

I'd say that that's a pretty damned accurate thing to say, is that you know, we're taught that sex is like an UNBELIEVABLE, EARTH SHATTERING EXPERIENCE [his emphasis], but it's not.

This observation hung in the air, one jocular comment was made ("well, there have been occasions …"), and the young men moved on to another topic, clearly unwilling to address further whether sex was or was not all it was cracked up to be.

In fact, the young men were clearly ambivalent about sex and their relationship to it. On the one hand, they complained about young women constructing them as "sex machines," although here the unspoken subtext may have been more about who gets to control sexual encounters in the relationship and make decisions about when, where and how. On the other hand, they acknowledged the pleasures and joys of sexual intimacy, but at least some of the young men were prepared to conclude that sex was not the all-encompassing, amazing experience popular culture led them to believe it was. When it came to sex, there was general agreement with Derek's statement, "Everything is on an individual basis when it comes to sex. There's nothing that you can say in general that applies to more than like a small fraction of the population."

Conclusion

Allen (2003) and Frosh, Phoenix & Pattman (2002) have argued that focus groups with young men are particularly helpful both for understanding how masculinities are made and for helping boys learn about themselves and others. In fact, research with young men allows them to speak to one another in a setting different from their usual places of encounter and provides a unique learning environment. The young men themselves recognized how participating in the research process had changed them. For example, Casey observed,

Well, it's kind of funny, like before this all came about [i.e., the research project] it was sort of like, yeah, I knew about the issues and sort of was like, yeah, this is something that goes on. But it's like when you really got down and thought about it, like having to get into a situation like this, and actually talked about it, a lot more stuff comes to light, that maybe some stuff that you do, that you don't really think about, and I think that's what ... like, yeah, it's good to go out and tell people, "Hey! This is what's wrong." But until they see it as wrong, nothing's gonna' change. ... . The importance of all of this is, like you can do all the studies in the world and write all the stuff that you want, but until somebody picks up the book and says, "Hey! This does pertain to me," nothing will change. And that's what's kind of funny, is like, you know, I can start to see things in my friends that I never saw before, 'cause I never thought of it as being wrong, that this is something they do that might not be correct, and that's just something that you have to learn.

The pedagogical implications of Casey's observations are clear. Approaches to gender equity or, for that matter, other school-based social justice or antiviolence campaigns are doomed to failure if young people themselves are not engaged in the process in ways that allow them to work freely through their own ideas with their peers. Young people grounded in their own social context need to struggle with the realities of their own lives, they need to see that "this does pertain to me." That is not to say that teachers and other adults should abrogate their responsibilities to provide settings, materials and ideas to facilitate consciousness-raising among the young. However, it is to suggest that pedantic, adult-designed and -driven equity programming often fails to connect with young people in any way that is transformative.

In fact, there are indications in the young men's talk about protecting young women that imply a need to reexamine the messages adults currently may be conveying through anti-bullying, antiviolence, and anti-harassment programs. Traditional notions of chivalry and gentlemanly conduct convey the idea that males should protect females, but this position fails to problematize the source of the violence women need to be protected from and does not critically examine the dependency relationship created when "strong" men are needed to protect "weak" women. Are these traditional gender binaries being reinforced, whether consciously or inadvertently, by teachers and social workers offering antiviolence programs? What shift has occurred when anti-sexist programs of the 1990s designed to help young men "recognize their ability to work toward becoming anti-sexist men involved not just in supporting women's struggles for equality, but in challenging the very construction of a sexist society" (Novogrodsky, Kaufman, Holland, & Wells, 1998, pp. 196–197) become the zero tolerance, antiviolence campaigns of the neoliberal present with their emphasis on individual behaviors and draconian measures of correction? The emphasis on the individual, on the "good" and "bad" choices the lone subject makes, surely can be seen to encourage the attitude that "good" boys protect girls. Thus are traditional gender roles reinforced and more complex understandings of social contexts and possibilities for political action and systemic change suppressed.

The trope of "protection" can also reinforce traditional notions of gender in another way. Riley (2003), in a study of professional, white, heterosexual men, examines how an "attachment to the role of breadwinner in the production of a masculine identity" (p. 100) persists despite women's presence in the paid workforce. She argues that, for men, the provider role has become infused with power and status, continues to bestow legitimacy on the male identity, and narrows possibilities for alternative constructions of masculinity. Furthermore, she demonstrates how men, when defending the concept of provision, use discursive "warranting" strategies to position themselves "as egalitarian while not necessarily promoting an egalitarian argument" (p. 110). The "protector" role acts in rather the same way for the young men who see themselves as protectors and reveal a real fear about losing that role. "Why would she need me" if she can protect herself? Thus, though the young men challenge many traditional understandings of masculinities and femininities, they also are able to retain elements of male identity that continue to reinforce existing power structures. And, because gender is a set of social relations, the young women who are taught to respond to men in particular and usually pleasing ways, to make themselves desirable to men, also contribute to reinforcing those same power structures. Unfortunately, neither young men nor young women have easy access to examples or language that would help them imagine and create a more equal world. This is a failure of schooling, although schooling alone cannot be held responsible.

Burdened with some deeply embedded gender constructs (for how could they not be?), the young men in this study are working both to understand who they are as men and what this means for their relationships with one another and with women. At one and the same time, they both reinforce the male-female binary by defining themselves against women and challenge that same binary by claiming shared space with women as fellow human beings with similar desires and goals. They both see and do not see how existing social structures produce young women who behave in ways the young men find maddening and reproduce male power in ways that shape social and intimate relationships. In their struggles to make sense of a complex world, the young men are sometimes angry, sometimes sanguine, sometimes confused but always present. "We're not," one said, "stereotypical males. Like we're the *actual* 'stereotypical' [laughter] males."

References

Allen, L. (2003). Girls want sex, boys want love: Resisting dominant discourses of (hetero)sexuality. *Sexualities, 6*(2), 215–236.

Allen, L. (2005). Managing masculinity: Young men's identity work in focus groups. *Qualitative Research, 5*(1), 35–57.

Arnot, M. (2002). *Reproducing gender: Essays on educational theory and feminist politics.* London & New York: RoutledgeFalmer.

Bourdieu, P. (2001). *Masculine domination* (R. Nice, Trans.). Stanford, CA: Stanford University Press.

Brickell, C. (2005). Masculinities, performativity, and subversion. *Men and Masculinities, 8*(1), 24–43.

Clements-Schreiber, M. E., Rempel, J. K., & Desmarais, S. (1998). Women's sexual pressure tactics and adherence to related attitudes: A step toward prediction. *Journal of Sex Research, 35*(2), 197–205.

Connell, R. W. (1995). *Masculinities.* Berkeley & Los Angeles: University of California Press.

Connell, R. W. (2000). *The men and the boys.* Berkeley & Los Angeles: University of California Press.

Coulter, R. P. (1999). "Doing gender" in Canadian schools: An overview of the policy and practice mélange. In S. Erskine & M. Wilson (Eds.), *Gender issues in international education* (pp. 113–129). New York & London: Falmer.

Coulter, R. P. (2003). Boys doing good: Young men and gender equity., *Educational Review, 55*(2), 135–145.

Fine, M., & Kuriloff, P. (2006). Forging and performing masculine identities within social spaces. *Men and Masculinities, 8*(3), 257–261.

Firminger, K. B. (2006). Is he boyfriend material? Representations of males in teenage girls' magazines. *Men and Masculinities, 8*(3), 298–308.

Frank, B., Kehler, M., Lovell, T., & Davison, K. (2003). A tangle of trouble: Boys, masculinity and schooling–future directions. *Educational Review, 55*(2), 119–133.

Frosh, S., Phoenix, A., & Pattman, R. (2002). *Young masculinities: Understanding boys in contemporary society.* New York: Palgrave.

hooks, b. (2004). *The will to change: Men, masculinity, and love.* New York: Atria.

Kaufman, M. (1999). Men, feminism and men's contradictory experiences of power. In J. A. Kuypers (Ed.), *Men and power* (pp. 59–83). Halifax, NS: Fernwood.

Kenway, J. (1995). Masculinities in school: Under siege, on the defensive and under reconstruction. *Discourse, 16*(1), 59–79.

Lingard, B., & Douglas, P. (1999). *Men engaging feminisms: Pro-feminism, backlashes and schooling.* Philadelphia: Open University Press.

Martin, P. Y. (2006). Practising gender at work: Further thoughts on reflexivity. *Gender, Work and Organization, 13*(3), 254–276.

Martino, W. (1999). 'Cool boys', 'party animals', 'squids' and 'poofters': Interrogating the dynamics and politics of adolescent masculinities in school. *British Journal of Sociology of Education, 20*(2), 239–263.

Martino, W. (2000). Policing masculinities: Investigating the role of homophobia and heteronormativity in the lives of adolescent boys. *Journal of Men's Studies*, 8(2), 213–236.

Martino, W., & Pallotta-Chiarolli, M. (2001). Gender performativity and normalizing practices. In F. Haynes & T. McKenna (Eds.), *Unseen genders: Beyond the binaries* (pp. 87–119). New York: Peter Lang.

Novogrodsky, M., Kaufman, M., Holland, D., & Wells, M. (1998). Retreat for the future: An anti-sexist workshop for high schoolers. In S. Repo (Ed.), *Making school matter: Good teachers at work* (pp. 193–213). Toronto: James Lorimer.

Riley, S. C. E. (2003). The management of the traditional male role: A discourse analysis of the constructions and functions of provision. *Journal of Gender Studies*, 12(2), 99–113.

Swain, J. (2006). Reflections on patterns of masculinity in school settings. *Men and Masculinities*, 8(3), 331–349.

5   Masculinity, Racialization, and Schooling

The Making of Marginalized Men

Carl E. James

Introduction

The August 8, 2005 issue of *Time* magazine (Canadian Edition) featured a special report on what it means to be 13 years old. Joseph Charles, an African-American male living in Los Angeles, United States, and one of the many youth profiled in the magazine (p. 41), commented that "Life as a 13-year old is hard. There is a lot of responsibility. Everyone wants you to be perfect ... . Thirteen is the beginning of a different stage of life." It is, according to Charles, when "interest in girls changes [and] you start wanting them to do stuff for you." However, it is not any girl that Charles thinks would qualify to be his girlfriend; she has to be someone who is "pretty." This expectation corresponds with what Cameron (1997) found in her study of the construction of heterosexual masculinity among young American men. As she notes, "Proper masculinity requires that the object of public interest be not just female, but minimally attractive" (p. 53). Seemingly with the notion of responsibility in mind, and likely reflective of his classed environment (one which is conflict-ridden and rough), Charles continued to say that his girlfriend must know "how to fight" because he would not "want her to be getting punked and then I have to jump in." Also at 13 years, said Charles, "most teens like sports"—his preference is basketball. However, sounding a note of logic and sobriety, he added, "They want to be the best on the team, but there is always somebody better than you ... . The only way you can get to play sports is if you get a good education." About school, Charles said,

> Being 13 is very hard at school. I have to be bad in order to be considered cool. I sometimes do things that aren't good. I have talked back to my teachers and been disrespectful to them. I do want to be good, but it's just too hard. Since I've been in junior high, I have been to four different schools. Some schools really tried to help me, but I have been suspended so many times, they just had to kick me out (p. 41).

Charles's story, which tells of his responsibilities, demands, and hardship as a student; interest in girls; and expectations as an athlete, is quite similar to that of many African (or black) Canadian youth. In Canada, as in the United States, the idea of being "cool," as Charles points out, is not only related to how some black youth negotiate and navigate school in Canada, and Toronto in particular, but also how many of them understand and perform their constructed gender identities, or masculinity, which is intimately connected to their socialization in a society that operates to marginalize them (see Dance, 2002; Ferguson, 2000; James 2005; Majors & Billson, 1992; Noguera, 2003a, b; Odih, 2002). Using the term *cool pose* to capture this understanding and performance of masculinity by African-American youth, Majors (1990) explains that

> black men often cope with their frustration, embitterment, alienation, and social impotence by channeling their creative energies into the construction of unique, expressive, and conspicuous styles of demeanor, speech, gesture, clothing, hairstyle, walk, stance, and handshake. For the black male, these expressive behaviors, which are a particular manifestation [of cool pose] ... offset an externally imposed invisibility, and provide a means to show the dominant culture (and the black male's peers) that the black male is strong and proud and can survive, regardless of what may have been done to harm or limit him ... It is adaptation rather than submission. In that sense, then, cool pose is an attempt to carve out an alternative path to achieve the goals of dominant masculinity" (p. 111).

Majors and Billson (1992) further point out that

> cool pose is constructed from attitudes and actions that become firmly entrenched in the black male's psyche as he adopts a façade to ward off second class status. It provides a mask that suggests competence, high self-esteem, control and inner strength. It also hides self-doubt, insecurity and inner turmoil" (p. 5).

Ferguson (2000) also writes of how black boys get labeled by their schools as "troublemakers" and how, in their embrace of this oppositional social identity and "bad boy" behavior, they challenge this assigned image and in the process earn respect and status among their peers (see also Dance 2002; Noguera, 2003a). However, as a number of scholars remind us, to understand the experiences and performances of males generally, and black males in particular, the emphasis should be on masculinities, more precisely heterosexual masculinities, bearing in mind that masculinities are not culturally universal but vary according to context, time, and within cultural groups depending upon a variety of factors (see Cameron,

1997; Epstein, 1998; Kimmel, 1999; Martino & Pallotta-Chiarolli, 2003; Price, 2000; Sewell, 1998). The resulting performance, then, of the "multilayered dimensions" and array of constructed Black masculinities (Price, p. 128) will be "fluid, multifarious, shifting and hybrid" (Sewell, p. 111; see also Cameron, 1997; Conchas & Noguera, 2004).

In this chapter, I discuss how the heterosexual masculinities of black males get constructed in relation to a process of racialization to which they are subjected in Canadian schools and which in turn serve to socialize them into the marginalized men that they become. I argue that working with the construction of black male students as underachievers, athletes, "at risk," and immigrants (i.e. foreigners), schools (teachers, principals, counselors, and coaches) operate with a form of "racial profiling"[1] or stereotyping that helps to reinforce and maintain these social and cultural constructs, which ultimately affect the educational participation, aspirations, possibilities, and outcomes of students. Additionally, though students pragmatically and in other ways (including what is often identified as resistance) use these constructs in their negotiation and navigation of schooling structures, they are often unable to escape the ineradicable impact of their schooling experiences. In the section that follows, I discuss the role that racialization plays in the construction and performance of black masculinities.

Racialization and the Performance of "Black Masculinities"

For many black males, the performance of masculinity—"the cultural interpretation of maleness, learnt through participation in society and its institutions" (Leach, 1994, p.36)—is based on a racialized script that, as Stevenson (2004) writes, is a script "designed within white society's projected fears of Black manhood, not the self-determined efforts, experiences, and potential of Black manhood" (p. 13). This racialized notion of masculinity is part of a process of manufacturing and utilizing the category of race to structure and explain the cultural attitudes and behaviors of black males. It is a form of racialization in which, as Martinot (2003) states, "race is produced and bestowed on people by institutional social actions, and not simply as a condition found in people as their racial category ... ." (p. 13). This emphasis of race is imbued with lasting social, political, cultural, economic, and even psychological meanings and significance that are produced and reproduced through ideological and institutional practices that impose a particular reading or construction of difference on ethno-racial group members (Dominguez, 1994; James, 2003; Kimmel, 2003). Essentially, all individuals are part of a racialization process; hence, we experience our societies, communities, or world in "color-coded ways" (Dalal, 2000, p. 27), the constructions of which operate either to support the privileges of those in the dominant group or to marginalize those who do not fit into that group in the society.

Marginalization refers to the situation in which individuals or groups of individuals are prevented from effective participation in the social, educational, cultural, and political life of the community and/or society and consequently are limited in (or deprived of) their bid to realize their potential (Young, 1990). The process of marginalization is influenced by individuals' location in the social hierarchy of the society. So, in cases whereby white heterosexual males of European or British origin continue to be seen as the embodiment of the values, norms, traits, and standards of masculinity, black males will remain marginalized with the possible consequence of being placed in a "double bind"—existing in a situation wherein they are expected to provide "evidence of their manhood while being denied access to the means of achieving the status that would provide such evidence" (Hatchett, Black, & Holmes, 1999, p. 72). The evidence expected is that of heterosexual masculinity that, according to Theodore and Basow (2000),

> is the cultural pressure exerted on males to be masculine in traits and heterosexual in orientation or else be viewed as feminine and socially unacceptable .... It is the cultural ideology which extends the belief that masculinity and femininity consist of two bipolar sets of behaviors, traits, and social roles.
>
> (p. 32; see also Kimmel, 2003, p. 76)

The idea then is that heterosexuality—the emphasis here is on gendered as opposed to sexualized notions of heterosexualities—is an essential trait of masculinity. Hence, to avoid marginalization, and for black youth, further marginalization, young men will seek to internalize and make visible (in words, dress, and action) their gendered attributes of heterosexuality with the hope of fitting cultural expectations and measuring up to the standards of masculinity[2] (see Cameron, 1997; Davis, 2001; Davison, 2000; Noguera, 2003a; Theodore & Basow, 2000). Related to this process of fitting in and measuring up is the tendency of young men to participate in sport that is often presented to them as a means of becoming men. As such, sport continues to be the bastion of males' masculine socialization and site of performance (Abdel-Shehid, 2005; Davison, 2000; Lenskyi, 2003; Messner & Sabo, 1990; Pronger, 1992).

Abby Ferber (2007), in his article, "The construction of Black masculinity," questions, "How can a White supremacist nation, which subjects Black men to ongoing racism and demonization, at the same time admire and worship Black men as athletes?" He argues that though black male bodies are admired for their entertainment value gained through music—such as rap and hip hop—and in certain sports, at the same time these commodified bodies continue to invoke contempt and fear. Nevertheless,

> within the contemporary context of color-blind ideology, the embrace of Black athletes helps White fans to assure themselves that America is not racist after all ... . Although seemingly harmless entertainment, mainstream sports culture reiterates the common themes evident in White supremacist constructions of Black masculinity.
>
> (Ferber, 2007, p. 12)

This reading of black male athletes is also evident in the Canadian context and in schools in particular where educators operate with a color-blind ideology (James, 2005).

Furthermore, in Canada, constructions and variations (including hybrids) of masculinities related to black males (as in the case of other minorities) are informed by the discourse of official multiculturalism.[3] This discourse at times operates to essentialize or homogenize minority group or "Other" Canadians holding that their values, beliefs, and behaviors are rooted in their *cultures* from elsewhere (the places from which they or their ancestors immigrated), which purportedly sets them apart from "Canadians"—typically considered to be people of British and French backgrounds (James, 2003). It is evident in schools' multicultural educational programs, materials, curricula, and pedagogical approaches, which sustain the Anglo-male cultural hegemony and justify black males' differences in school participation and educational attainments (Dei, Karumanchery, & Karumanchery-Luik, 2004; James & Haig-Brown, 2001; Henry & Tator, 2006). So, in this schooling situation, it is understood that black males' disengagement from the schooling processes, poor academic but successful athletic performance, high rates of suspensions from school, and inappropriate educational choices lead to unsuccessful educational and career outcomes (Bhattacharjee, 2003; Codjoe, 2001; Dei, 1997; James, 2005; Odih, 2002). Moreover, these choices are considered to be a consequence of these boys' "foreign" or "immigrant"cultures— cultures related to their Caribbean and (continental) African origins and/or upbringing.[4] This construction of blacks as immigrants or foreigners is part of the racialization process that operates to maintain a perception of black males as lacking the values, norms, and attitudes of "mainstream"masculinity—something into which they will always have to be socialized but might never acquire.

Though indeed black youth masculinities will be informed by the cultural origins of their parents and their parents' immigrant experiences and expectations, so too are their masculinities a product of, or constructed in response to, their experiences with inequity, racism, and discrimination and their desire to conform, live up to, or challenge (as opposed to admitting failure or inability to meet) the expectations of white hegemonic masculinity. Further, media images of African-American masculinities, represented in such things as sports, comedies, movies, and music (e.g., rap, hip hop, and reggae), become references or models for black Canadians who construct their masculinities in a similar context of hegemonic heterosexual masculinity. This is why it is fair to say that in some ways, 13-year-old Charles's perceptions and experiences are similar to many black Canadian youth who are growing up in a society in which racialization and marginalization are part of their experiences. Additionally, however rigid the social norms and expectations by which masculinities are policed, it is to be expected that individuals will exercise agency in their gender roles, resulting in variability, diversity, and hybridity in masculinities and the behaviors through which various masculine identities are performed.

In what follows, I try to show (1) the role that schools and educators play in contributing to the construction of masculinities through a process of racialization and the resulting marginalization of black youth, and (2) how in their responses to these processes, the youth, invariably help to affirm the perceptions of their masculinities that operate to construct them as underachievers, athletes, "at risk," and immigrants (foreigners) in the first place. In a way, these constructions are part of a complex circular system that operates to inform educators' perceptions and interactions with black youth and the youth responses and interactions with educators.

The Role of Schools and Educators in the Making of Marginalized Men

In her study of black males in an elementary school in the United States, Ferguson (2000) illustrates how the school's daily routines and practices are premised on principles of racism (sustained by media images) that present black males as erratic, intimidating, violent, dangerous and, hence, in need of control. Such an image helps to construct black boys as "troublemakers" and "bad boys" who must be disciplined, punished, and controlled if they are to be in school. Ferguson contends that this constructed oppositional identity "adultifies" and pathologizes the childhood expressions and attitudes that otherwise would be considered common for the age of these students. The resulting fears and suspicions of black males that are to be found among educators and students operate to impede and frustrate their participation in school and access to educational opportunities and possibilities (Ferguson). Similarly, based on her study of urban youth, Dance (2002) indicates that students adopt tough self-images as a way to avoid being bullied in schools or picked on in the neighborhood. And lacking realistic and empathetic understandings of their students' lives, schools contribute to the "high suspension, expulsion, and dropout rates for inner-city youth, especially Black and Brown males" (p.10).

In a similar way, Dei (1997) writes of the high school "push out" as opposed to "dropout" rates of black students in the Toronto school system resulting from the "complex dynamics of cultures, environments and organizational lives of mainstream schools" (p. 246). Dei found that students become disengaged from school and drop out because of "differential treatment based on race, having to deal with an exclusive curriculum, and poor communicative and pedagogical practices that failed to adequately explore the complexities of their experiences that have shaped their lives" (p. 246). Caribbean-born Richard who dropped out of school at grade 10 said that part of his difficulty with school was related to restrictions on self-expression:

> ...because you have to assimilate and you have to be like everyone else ... . If you didn't, then you're a troublemaker, again, or you're the strange kid that's got this, you know, psychological problem ... . Because you want to learn your identity and when something other than [in a] class[room], where you feel ... wrong ...; and you bring it up and "Oh well this didn't really happen." You're a troublemaker now because you're going against the school ... .
>
> (Dei 1997, p. 247)

Hence, like the African-American boys in Ferguson's study, Richard was not only labeled a troublemaker but was considered to be a "strange kid with psychological problems." This attempt to explain the constructed oppositional identities and behaviors of black male students, who simply wished to have their experiences and social differences recognized and addressed in schools, becomes part of what might be termed the construction-response cycle. That is, constructed as immigrants or foreigners (even though they might not be), African-Canadian students experience a schooling situation—as represented in the school program, curriculum, and pedagogical approach—that is structured to socialize them into the dominant norms, values, and practices of Canadian society. In responding to this schooling situation by insisting, in whatever way they do, on having space and recognition of their social difference, African-Canadian males contribute to their construction as troublemakers, strange kids, and students with "psychological problems." Convinced of the legitimacy and logic of their respective understandings and expectations of the teaching-learning situation and corresponding actions, schools—teachers, counselors, coaches, and principals—and students continue on a never-ending cycle in which both groups see the schooling problems as resulting from the values and behaviors of the other. However, it is the schools' interpretation of these students' attitudes and behaviors in relation to the normalized white heterosexual masculinity that remains paramount.

Related to the construction of black students as troublemakers is the perception of them as underachievers—students, especially males, for whom academics is not a priority, who have little interest in school, and, hence, tend not to do well academically. It is this lack of interest in academics that was, and still is, seen as responsible for their disruptive or oppositional behaviors in school. And as researchers have shown, cultural difference is often used to explain the resulting streaming or program-grade placements and educational outcomes of these students. On that basis, black males were being streamed into lower-level, vocational, or behavioral classes in schools: practices that parents, students, and educators claimed to be not so much a consequence of the students' inability, interest, ambition, or knowledge but of systemic racism and discrimination that operated in the stereotyping (or racial profiling) of these students, particularly males, as academically incompetent and unsuited for academic work (Brathwaite & James, 1996; Codjoe, 2001; Dei, 1997; Solomon, 1992). Consequently, being constructed as academic underachievers, black males do not have the benefit of building on their academic abilities and potentials. As such, in a society in which level of educational attainment largely determines occupational and economic outcomes, with their limited education, black males are likely to remain in a marginalized position.

However, there are educators who, on the basis of what might be perceived as "good intentions," do support black males in their schooling, particularly in the area of sports. In doing so, educators claim to be building on the youth's interests, motivations, and abilities in sports and facilitating their stay and participation in school (James, 2005). For example, a *Toronto Star* newspaper article (June 9, 2000) reported the story of Jamaican-born, 15-year-old, "6-foot-1, 200 pound" Dwayne James who was returning to school having dropped out earlier because of, as reporter, David Grossman wrote, "disciplinary problems." Dwayne was a successful shot put athlete, having tossed a personal best of 15.61 meters, capturing the Ontario provincial title and a third gold medal that year. This success in the shot put so impressed Dwayne's school principal, his teacher, and his coach and the reporter that they were optimistic his hard work in athletics would translate into educational success.

Not surprisingly, the route by which it was thought that Dwayne would attain success is typical. As a way of addressing Dwayne's problems with school, the school coach encouraged him to take up sports[5] and, in doing so, engaged in a dialogue with which many black students, especially basketball players, are familiar (see James, 2005). The coach was reported to have said, "I remember meeting him for the first time and after seeing his size, encouraged him to take part in sports." The coach described Dwayne as "very athletic, can dunk a ball, has a great vertical leap and seems to be comfortable playing the game." The coach also said that he believed that sports has given Dwayne "a lot of confidence because Dwayne's a quiet and very shy kind of person." However, according to the coach, what impressed him the most was Dwayne's "work ethic in sports"—explaining that Dwayne "never missed a practice and his attendance is excellent." Noting Dwayne's confidence, motivation, and dedication to sports, his school principal said that he is "convinced that, with proper mentoring, the sky is the limit for what he [Dwayne] is capable of doing." The idea here, as the reporter mentioned, Dwayne was on the "right track" toward achieving an athletic scholarship to a university in the United States— again a typical expectation that educators, especially coaches, and student athletes tend to hold (see also James, 2005).

However, attending school and playing sports with the sole purpose of eventually winning a scholarship to an American university or college are ideas and practices that are fraught with numerous problems—problems that are likely to result from the fact that the vast majority of student athletes with such ambitions will not win scholarships. Further, having failed to invest equal time and effort in their academic work, they will be left without adequate preparation for an alternative educational and career path. There is also the reality that having concentrated on a single athletic activity is likely to limit opportunities and possibilities for student athletes, especially when we consider the precariousness of sporting careers and the sporting market (James, 2005). In many of these cases therefore, schools, through the blind encouragement and support that coaches, teachers, and principals give to students for their athletic as opposed to their academic performance, help contribute to students' not acquiring the appropriate and necessary education for life, a situation that could result in their marginalization.

Apart from the support that educators give to black students as they pursue their sporting interests, there is also educators' and students' involvement in Career Days/Fairs, "Multicultural Days," and the annual Black History Month celebrations through which many educators believe they provide students opportunities to learn about themselves and their history. Often during these events, "black role models" are invited to schools to talk to students about their careers and jobs, their national origin or "homeland," their experiences as black persons in Canada, the "history of African/Black peoples," or activities of black organizations. It is on such occasions that black males are invited to "model" for the black students, especially males, how they were able to rise above racism to become the athletes, doctors, lawyers, or professors that they are. I recall being invited by a high school teacher to talk to his media class, one-third of whom were black, mostly males, because he wanted them to meet "someone who holds a position in a university" and who represented "a successful Black male who has also experienced systemic racism" (James, 2000, p.

89). So it fell to me, as to many of the other role models whom teachers, including black teachers, invite into their classes to be an example and give advice to the students about how they too can "overcome" the effects of racism by focusing on their academic work. I did go to talk to the group of students recognizing the problematics of the role and contradictions that I represented. I think here of how often we are used as exhibits, and in some cases as tokens, to affirm that achievement within the existing structure of school is possible and that racism can be "overcome": All that students have to do is to work hard and meet the expectations set out for them. Typically, this approach denies the layered complexity of and variation in experiences among students that are often beyond the scope of any role model program. Indeed, as Marquese (1995) points out, role models are expected to demonstrate that they have "achieved personal success on the basis of the existing laws and customs of the society. Yet all but a tiny minority can ever hope to achieve such success within those laws and customs" (p. 9-10). Furthermore,

> ...the conceptualization and practices of role modeling are part of a hegemonic system in which educators inadvertently participate. [It is one] that encourages young people to conform to prevailing values, role expectations and beliefs about the education system. Role models are expected to collude with the education system to produce uncritical students who will have no sense of the complexity and contradiction of the racial construction of identities, their relationship to the histories of colonialism and social structures, and as Britzman (1999, p. 39) writes, "their own proximity to the histories and experiences of racism and sexism."
>
> (James, 2000, p. 92)

In this regard, *Boys to Men*, a program initiative (Spence, 2002) that is structured around role modeling and mentorship for "at-risk" black middle and high school male students in the Toronto area, will do little to reverse the negative effects that black males' schooling experiences have on them (p. 5). Merely exposing boys, as Spence (2002, p. 71) writes, especially those from "fatherless homes," to "positive images of ... male teachers, mentors, advocates and other role models" in a bid to build their self-esteem that has been "battered by the pervasive negative images of people like themselves ..." will not necessarily prevent these boys from developing "negative attitudes toward life and academic achievement;" for the hegemonic structure of the normalized white male masculinity into which these black males are being socialized and expected or forced to fit is not critically engaged. Neither are these young males provided with the critical skills and tools to understand and assess how their black heterosexual masculinities are constructed and performed in relation to that hegemonic structure. In the absence of such education, the *Boys to Men* program merely helps to build and maintain, possibly unwittingly, these "at-risk" youth's sense of confusion about the ways in which the cultural forces in schools interact with and shape their race and gender identities, school performance, and marginalization. The point is, role models and mentors must provide the males with whom they work a critical understanding of their relationship to the power structures of society and the ways in which those structures function to inform their responses and constructed identities.

The situation in which the identified at-risk students find themselves mirrors a larger trend in education for black Canadian students, and males in particular. Rather than serving as a source of hope and opportunity, some schools are sites wherein black males are racially profiled and marginalized (Dei, 1997; Noguera, 2003a; Odih, 2002). In fact, in his research on the impact of the *Safe School Act* on Ontario students for the Ontario Human Rights Commission, Bhattacharjee (2003) found that disciplinary policies in schools "have always had a disproportionate impact on Black students, but the Act and 'zero tolerance' policies have made the problem much worse, with significantly higher numbers of Black students being suspended and expelled" (p. vi). These high rates of suspensions and expulsions are, in part, related to the fact that, as one educator in the Toronto area told me:

> Some students become pawns in the designation of a "high needs" school. High needs school equals more money. More money means more resources, more teacher assistants, more teachers, and in some cases an additional vice principal. More money also means that you may be able to obtain special education support and resources for your school … . Teachers are required to document the students who are recommended for specialized support. Therefore, students who may receive detentions or conferences with teachers for misbehavior, will now receive frequent formal suspensions. Students who may require remedial support in schools would now receive failing grades on their report cards. Students who have English as a Second Language needs and placed in mainstream classrooms are given failing grades for not "understanding" the material. These actions take place in schools to provide a paper trail behind all students who are deemed to have high needs academically or socially. This paper trail justifies the need for more money for special programs … in areas such as school safety, literacy, English as Second Language, and/or behavioral needs … . And the more defined the high needs image or profile of the school, the more readily additional funding will be given. The more readily the funding is given, the more defined the "high needs" profile becomes. The result for many schools is lower expectations

of students in certain schools, more suspensions and more stringent enforcement of consequences.

(M. M. August, 2005, personal communication)

Therefore, the ways in which schools are funded contribute to the identity construction, schooling situation, educational outcome, and subsequent marginalization of students. Additionally, as this teacher observes, in many cases, black students are the ones who are labeled as at-risk students with behavioral problems and academic and social needs.[6] Therefore, in such a context, the perceptions of black male students as underachievers, troublemakers, immigrants, and less academically inclined is solidified or reinforced by the schooling structures.

Becoming Men: How Black Youth Negotiate their Schooling

The structure of schools, as shown through their programs and policies, and the cultural values, beliefs, and norms into which students have been socialized both inside and outside of school, combine in complex ways to influence black males' constructed identities in relation to, among other characteristics, race and gender. As such, it is important to give attention to how black males are seen and treated in school and, as we take up in this section, how in turn they see, position themselves, and act—in short, exercise agency—in their respective school settings. Relevant to this discussion is how what Steele (1999) refers to as "stereotype threat," that is, the threat of being viewed through the lens of a negative stereotype, or the fear of doing something that would, inadvertently, confirm the stereotype that is held of black people (pp. 44–54). Stereotype threat also functions to shape the identities, behaviors and academic performance of black male students, who in contrast to whites are acutely mindful of their race and related stereotypes.

Charles, as mentioned earlier, said that at school he had to be "bad in order to be considered cool." For this reason, he engaged in a number of disrespectful and disruptive behaviors that got him suspended from school many times. Charles's "cool pose" (Majors, 1990) or "tough front" (Dance, 2002) provided him the mask necessary to negotiate the marginalizing schooling structures, hide his insecurities and inner turmoil, and avoid being bullied or picked on. This might not have won Charles the understanding and support he needed from teachers, but he was more likely to gain the support of his friends, for being "one of the guys," to quote Noguera (2003b, p. 20), is important to how young black males cope with their "social marginalization within and beyond the walls of school" (Dance, 2002, p. 52). To this end, they would work hard to prove to their friends that they are cool or tough—doing things that are expected of them like playing sports, hanging out with friends, being defiant to teachers, congregating in particular areas of school, and fighting when necessary (Cunningham & Meunier, 2004; Dance, 2002; James, 2002a; Noguera 2003b). However, as Price (2002) indicates, the idea that the peer group functioned as a refuge is open to question, for not all black youth view and/or use the peer group in the same way. The trusting and caring relationships that black youth develop with their peers, albeit tenuous at times, function in crucial and different ways to influence the identities they construct in relation to white hegemonic masculinity. That is, their behaviors tend to reflect varying degrees of black or white cultural practices (Price, 2002).

The fact is that the development and performance of masculinity among black youth are neither homogeneous nor universal. Indeed, as Sewell (1998) asserts with reference to inner-city African-Caribbean boys in a London (England) high school, they are not "one big lump of rebellious, phallocentric underachievers" (p. 111; see also Ohih, 2002). On the contrary, depending on context, they engaged with school using one or more of four strategies. Sewell found very few (less than 15 percent) respondents who outright rejected school, disassociating themselves from any intellectual pursuits. He refers to this group as the "rebels"—the ones in whom the hyper-masculine and machismo characteristics were most evident. There was an even smaller group (less than 10 percent) who were categorized as "retreatists." They were the ones who rejected schoolwork but tended not to engage in other types of oppositional actions. It might seem that it is with one of these two groups that Charles and the other troublemakers, truants, and dropouts might be identified. However, as we see with Charles, he did not give up on school, he kept returning to different schools, evidently because he understood the value of education. It is likely that it is for this reason that he wanted "to be good, but," as he said, "it's just too hard." It might have been hard because of both peer pressure and the alienating school curricula, discriminatory treatment, and oppressive disciplinary measures.

So Charles and others cannot be solely categorized as troublemakers, rebels, or "retreatists" who simply reject school; instead, in complex and paradoxical ways, their actions are an indication of their refusal to engage school exclusively on the school's terms. For instance, as I found in a study of university students from an urban working-class area of Toronto (James & Haig-Brown, 2001), even as the identified "troublemakers" (most of them males) refused to attend class and do their schoolwork, they would encourage and insist that their university-bound friend, Rebecca, not socialize with them but concentrate on her work, for in her, as she stated, they placed their "hopes and dreams" for success. It is possible that these supportive males perceived that Rebecca was much more able to live with the rules and meet the expectations of the school, and in so doing, Rebecca represented for them as she termed it "a breakthrough"—an opportunity to demonstrate to teachers that black students were able to succeed in school and go to university. Represented here is not only these males' sense of community but their way of contributing to the development of a community reputation—black students are not merely troublemakers, they are also good at academics—which they seemed to be taking on as a responsibility. In a way, the actions of these male students helped to complicate and challenge the stereotype or essentialized notions that were held of black students in that school. Rebecca's male friends could be termed "accomplices," students who appreciated the importance of education but were unwilling to compromise their values, and in so doing, lived vicariously through their peers whose aspirations they supported.

The second largest group of students (little more than one-third of the respondents) in Sewell's (1998) typology were the "innovators"—boys who were pro-education but were opposed to the rules and practices of school. According to Sewell, these males walked a tightrope between pursuing academically oriented activities and being perceived as being too academically oriented. Based on studies of students in the Toronto area, Canada, (James, 2005; Solomon, 1992), it would appear that many of those who might be considered "innovators" are athletes. Solomon refers to the African-Caribbean males in his study as "jocks" for whom school was the means by which they would get the chance to play sport so that they might attain their postsecondary aspirations. "For the Jocks," writes Solomon, "sports serve three main functions: it helps in the formation of Black culture and identity; it observes machismo; and it is pursued as a viable channel for socioeconomic advancement." (p. 76). To an extent, these functions might explain why a significant number of black males are to be found on the sports teams—especially basketball—in schools.

Saying that many of his male peers cannot relate to school, one research participant, Kirk, commented:

> ...You go to school to learn yes, but sports is the extra thing and that is the ticket out ... . With basketball, a lot of Black youth are given scholarships to universities. So that you can say is our ticket out of school because a lot of us do not have the money to pay tuition fees.
>
> (in James, 1990, p. 45)

For many male student-athletes, then, sport is not only a means of coping with school but their ticket out of a poverty situation. However, their athletic interests and aspirations could be a double-edged sword, in that while their participation in sports and the support they receive from their coaches, teachers and principals, as in the case of Dwayne above, can help to build confidence and cultivate hope for a prosperous economic and social future, their investment in sports often comes at the expense of their academic activities. So, in the case of injuries and/or failure to attain the athletic opportunities and scholarships that black males seek, the situation could result wherein they remain marginalized by not having the necessary education to attain a job and consequently the money to live the lives to which they aspire.

Sewell also notes that "innovators" often have to negotiate the resentment of many of their black peers who might see their participation in school activities and their academic successes as not conforming to the prevailing notions of black masculinity. This means that innovators, like many other black male students, constantly have to negotiate their marginalization—from both their school and their peer group. Caught in this double-bind situation, some black males will opt to protect, and hence maintain, their relationships with their peers. Take the case of Jamal, for example.[7] He recalled an incident in his high school wherein a friend of his was in a fight with a Persian student. He stood back and was watching the fight when some friends of the Persian students jumped in. Feeling that this was not fair, Jamal jumped in, and as he said, started to "take people off." In dealing with the situation, the vice principal "spoke to the Persian students ... [and] suspended the three Black students"—the one who was fighting and two others. Jamal continued to explain:

> Myself, I didn't get in trouble, I'm not even sure why. I asked her [the vice principal] ..., 'why aren't you giving me the same.' But at that time, I was a better student, like you know what I mean – my grades were all in order, teachers knew me as a good student. But the other two [males] weren't doing as well in school, and some teachers didn't really like them, I guess you could say. So just that, that persona of those two students gave them less of a chance ... . So although I wasn't white, I had good academics so that was a plus; so that subtracted me from that situation, and I thought that was so unfair. And for the longest time I fought it, and I was starting to lose the respect that I had for some of the teachers because they didn't understand why I'm trying to defend the two other students that aren't doing as well in school, or whatever the case. But I was just doing it because we're all Black, we all need to advocate for each other, you know what I mean, especially when we're being treated unfairly, and for the longest time it went on.

Interestingly, Jamal was not prepared to simply take pride in the fact that as a "good" student he was saved from a suspension. He was concerned about the preferential treatment that he received, for it was not on the basis of fair or equal treatment but because he was known to teachers as a good student. Hence, from his perspective, on the basis of race—after all, the Persian students were not suspended—he should also have been suspended. This sentiment is reflected in Jamal's statement: "We're all Black", and for that reason alone, he felt that as someone to whom teachers would listen, he had a responsibility to advocate for his peers, even though the teachers did not understand why—something that was causing him to loose respect for his teachers. Clearly, Jamal understood that because of systemic racism, he was not inoculated from racist treatment, hence his actions, likely a response to his perceived stereotype threat, were not only a result of his efforts to demonstrate his commitment to his peers that he was not a conformist (will be discussed later), but a matter of self-protection and self-preservation.

To an extent, Jamal's ideas and actions are reflective of those of a "rudebwoy," a term originating in Jamaica referring to black Caribbean diasporic males' counter-hegemonic stance against their marginalization. Campbell (2005) writes that "rude" here should not be confused with being a "thug," which refers to those whose stance against oppression tends to take on criminal characteristics. Rather rudebwoy, writes Campbell, "is a way of thinking and acting that satisfies the individual's desire to exist outside of the subjectivities exerted by individuals and society's dominant institutions." He observes that through dress, language and the performance of cool, Canadian black males challenge the ways in which they are disciplined by the hegemonic structures in their effort to attain personal freedom (p. 12). Similarly, a group of teacher-candidates with whom I worked observed that among their black male (and other working-class) students in the downtown Toronto schools in which they were placed, there was a high rate of absenteeism from classes, lack of punctuality, talking, sleeping and eating in classes, and walking out of classes whenever they chose. Those students who conformed by wearing uniforms (if uniforms were required) would roll up their pant legs and shirt sleeves, wear earrings, necklaces, baseball caps, and bandanas and decorated their school uniforms with accessories, logos, and other symbols in defiance of the rules of the school. In school, they congregated in specific spaces where they played rap, hip hop, and reggae music as well as dominos. They spoke in a contrived African-American language or what Ibrahim (2000) refers to as "Black-stylized English.",[8] One black male student was quoted as saying, "I don't care if I fail. I don't care 'cause school is bullshit anyways. All the teachers really care about are those perfect A+ students, and I'll tell you one thing, they ain't Black" (James, 2002a, pp. 13–14). The cultural expressions of these students and many black males draw on their Caribbean (specifically Jamaican) and/or African origin and on American media images and messages of African-Americans with whom they tend to identify. In this regard, aspects of the "cool pose" construct will be evident in the ways in which black Canadian males relate to schooling and to the world around them. However, taking their Canadian existence and their Caribbean-immigrant origin into consideration, we get a hybrid rudebwoy construction. The fact is, unlike the United States, the majority of black Canadian youth are of

Caribbean-origin living in a country where American media beam information that contributes to their construction of blackness.

Canadian studies indicate that the children and grandchildren of immigrant Caribbean and African parents tend to have a high commitment to education and correspondingly high educational aspirations (Brathwaite & James, 1996; Codjoe, 2001; James, 2005; Solomon, 1992). So, though the rudebwoys, rebels, retreatists, troublemakers, and innovators will engage in activities that make their interest in, and commitment to, education seem questionable, the fact is many of them are influenced by the sacrifices of their parents in immigrating to Canada so that their children can have better lives than they had. Moreover, on the basis of their understanding of their parents' early lives, their respect and love for their parents, and their desires to take advantage of the opportunities and possibilities that they know their parents envisioned for them, many black Canadian males will conform to the principles and expectation of schools (James, 2002b). Indeed, in his categorization of his African-Caribbean respondents living in Britain, Sewell (1998) indicates that the largest group was the "conformists" (about 40 percent of the research participants). This means that most African-Caribbean students were not rebelling against the school but, to varying degrees, accepted its values and expectations.

Noguera (2003a) makes a similar point with reference to African-Americans. Such acceptance sometimes takes the form of pragmatism: an understanding that they have to conform to realize their educational academic aspirations, but at the same they challenge the fact that they are not represented in the curricula and educational materials and question the inequity and lack of democracy in the ways in which schools function. I refer to this group of students, or when students respond in such ways to their schooling situation (for, of course, their responses are not fixed), as "critical participants" or "pragmatists," for they knowingly and pragmatically engage with the system understanding that despite their successes in school, they are not immune from racial stereotypes as black males. Jamal (discussed earlier) is an example of this.

The point to be made is that the categorization of black Canadian males cannot be taken as fixed, as their identities, cultural expressions, and engagement with the school system vary according to time, space, cultural context, and their reading of what circumstances demand. The paradox is that as they seek to avoid their marginalization and assert their voices and legitimacy as full participants in their educational process and, in the society generally, their actions will cause them to be labeled as troublemakers and rebels, and in this regard they remain locked into these stereotypes or identity constructs and are treated accordingly.

Conclusion

The racialization process to which black males are subjected in their schooling process plays a significant role in the masculinities that emerge. These masculinities are a product of the "patriarchal white supremacist" (hooks, 2004) structure of the society that constructs them as underachieving, athletic, "at risk," and immigrant students and their attempts not only to challenge such racial profiling but simultaneously demonstrate their capacity to function within the very white male heterosexual paradigm that operates to marginalize them in the first place.[9] As hooks (2004) points out, any intervention in helping black males to live healthy, productive, and satisfying lives should not be to give them access to "patriarchal white supremacist" vales but rather to help and encourage them to adopt new notions of masculinity that do not embrace capitalism, competition, winning, and aggression—all of which exemplify normalized white heterosexual masculinity. With this perspective, teachers, coaches, and principals and role models and mentors (these two latter roles should be with the cooperation of the youth with whom they work) can help black male youth to become "critical participants" in their educational and schooling processes whereby they develop an understanding of the mechanisms that contribute to their identification as underachievers, athletes, troublemakers, "at risk," and foreigners. To this end, educators must work to alter the negative images of black youth and the view that they are "damaged" individuals who need to be "undamaged" or "cured" with the help of role models and mentors (Marquese, 1995). The reality is, black youth are caught in a disaffirming, inequitable, and marginalizing schooling structure that understandably they are resisting or will resist in their struggle for an education that is just, affirming, and empowering. Therefore, educators have a responsibility to work to change the structure and culture of schools such that black males are regarded with respect and provided with support and resources so that they develop a sense of hope, possibilities, and empowerment.

Notes

1. Racial profiling is stereotyping that is typically used to refer to police targeting of minorities, and blacks in particular, as trouble-makers and criminals. The Ontario Human Rights Commission (2003) defines racial profiling as "any action undertaken for reasons of safety, security or public protection that relies on stereotypes about race, colour, ethnicity, ancestry, religion, or place of origin rather than on reasonable suspicion, to single out an individual for greater scrutiny or different treatment" (p. 6). I use the term here to refer to similar approaches that teachers and administrations use in the constructions and interaction with black male students.
2. This process often leads males to reject those characteristic considered gay—a deviance (see Cameron, 1997).

3. The official multicultural policy of Canada is, in part, premised on notions of "colour-blindness" (race does not matter in Canada) and cultural democracy— the myth that "Other" Canadians are free to maintain and practice their cultures (from elsewhere).

4. The irony here is that blacks (like other minority and immigrant groups) are perceived to have "maintained" their cultural values, attitudes, and practices from elsewhere even though they were born here (most black adolescents are second-generation Canadians) or have ancestors that go back generations. So, unlike white immigrants who are seen as being able to adopt, change, or take on the culture of the new society, blacks are seen as unable to do the same.

5. Ogden and Hilt (2003) write that today athletes and celebrities are cast by mass media as the major, if not only, success stories among African males. As such, they are often perceived as role models for black youth to emulate.

6. The Toronto District School Board defines "at risk" students as those performing "below grade expectations" and are "disengaged from school with very poor attendance" (p. 4).

7. Jamal is a 24-year-old Canadian-born black male of Caribbean origin living in Toronto, where he was interviewed. He was one of 120 participants in the qualitative study for a five-year CIHR funded research project in which I am co-investigator, with Wanda Thomas Bernard as principal investigator and David Este, Akua Benjamin, Carol Amaratunga, and Bethan Lloyd also co-investigators. The study examines the experiences of a cross-section of the Halifax, Toronto, and Calgary black communities, particularly those of young males, in terms of racism and violence, noting the impact of both on individual, family, and community health and well-being; Web site (www.dal.ca/rvh).

8. Ibrahim (2000) was referring to his study of 'continental' African-Canadian youth in a French school. He argues that the language used, or the "lexical expressions" of the youth are "performances of hip hop identity which students take up" (p. 66).

9. In his discussion of power and masculinity, Kuypers (1999) writes: "As a plague, however, the quest for power becomes an incessant drive and an unattainable goal. For those of us who cannot satisfy the expectation (and that logically must include all of us who come in second), the struggles with failure are deep" (p. 7).

References

Abdel-Shehid, G. (2005). *Who da man? Masculinities and sporting cultures.* Toronto: Canadian Scholars' Press.

Bhattacharjee, K. (2003). *The Ontario Safe Schools Act: School discipline and discrimination.* Toronto: Ontario Human Rights Commission.

Brathwaite, K. S., & James, C. E. (Eds.) (1996). *Educating African Canadians.* Toronto: Our Schools/Our Selves & James Lorimer Ltd.

Cameron, D. (1997). Performing gender identity: Young men's talk and the construction of heterosexual masculinity. In S. Johnson & U. H. Menhof (Eds.), *Language and masculinity* (pp. 47–64). Cambridge, MA: Blackwell.

Campbell, M.V. (2005) Rudebwoy Alien. Paper presented at the conference "Caribbean Migrations: Negotiating Borders," Ryerson University, Toronto, Canada.

Codjoe, H. M. (2001). Fighting a "public enemy" of Black academic achievement: The persistence of racism and the schooling experiences of Black students in Canada. *Race, Ethnicity and Education, 4*(4), 343–375.

Conchas, G. Q., & Noguera, P. A. (2004). Understanding the exceptions: How small schools support the achievement of academically successful Black boys. In N. Way & J. Y. Chu (Eds.), *Adolescent boys: Exploring diverse cultures of boyhood* (pp. 317–337). New York: New York University Press.

Cunningham, M., & Meunier, L. N. (2004). The influence of peer experiences on bravado attitudes among African American males. In N. Way & J. Y. Chu (Eds.), *Adolescent boys: Exploring diverse cultures of boyhood* (pp. 197–218). New York: New York University Press.

Dalal, F. (2002). *Race, colour and the process of racialization: New perspectives from group analysis, psycholanalysis and sociology.* New York: Routledge.

Dance, L. J. (2002). *Tough fronts: The impact of street culture on schooling.* New York: Routledge.

Davis, J. E. (2001). Transgressing the masculine: African American boys and the failure of schools. In W. Martino & B. Meyenn (Eds.), *What about the boys?: Issues of masculinity in schools* (pp. 140–153). Buckingham, UK: Open University Press.

Davison, K. (2000). Masculinities, sexualities and the student body. In C. E. James (Ed.), *Experiencing difference.* Halifax, NS: Fernwood Publishing.

Dei, G. J. S. (1997). Race and the production of identity in the schooling experiences of African-Canadian youth. *Discourse: Studies in the Cultural Politics of Education, 18*(2), 241–257.

Dei, G. J. S., Karumanchery, L., & Karumanchery-Luik (2004). *Playing the race card: Exposing white power and privilege.* New York: Peter Lang.

Dominguez, V. R. (1994). A taste for the other. *Current Anthropology, 35*(4), 333–338.

Epstein, D. (1998). Real boys don't work: 'underachievement,' masculinity, and the harassment of 'sissies.' In D. Epstein, J. Elwood, V. Hey, & J. Maw (Eds.), *Failing boys?: Issues in gender and achievement* (pp .96–108). Buckingham, UK: Open University Press.

Ferber, A. L. (2007). The constriction of Black masculinity: White supremacy now and then. *Journal of Sport and Social Issues, 31*(1), 11–24.

Ferguson, A. (2000). *Bad boys: Public schools in the making of Black masculinity.* Ann Arbor: University of Michigan Press.

Hatchett, B. F., Black, L., & Holmes, K. (1999). Effects of citizenship inequalities on the black male. *Challenge: A Journal of Research on African American Men, 10*(2), 65–77.

Henry, F., & Tator, C. (2006). *The colour of democracy: Racism in Canadian society.* Toronto: Harcourt Brace & Company.

hooks, b. (2004). *We real cool: black men and masculinity.* London: Routledge.

Ibrahim, A. (2000). Whassup homeboy? Black popular culture and the politics of curriculum. In G. J. S. Dei & A. Calliste (Eds.), *Power, knowledge and anti-racism education: A critical reader* (pp. 57–72). Halifax, NS: Fernwood Publishing.

James, C. E. (1990). *Making it: Black youth, racism and career aspiration in a big city.* Oakville, ON: Mosaic Press.

James, C.E. (2000). "You're doing it for the students": On the question of role models. In C.E. James (ed), *Experiencing difference*, pp. 89–98. Halifax, NS: Fernwood Publishing.

James, C. E. (2002a). You can't understand me: Negotiating teacher-student relationships in urban schools. *Contact, 28*(2), 8–20.

James, C. E. (2002b). Achieving desire: Narrative of a Black male teacher. *International Journal of Qualitative Studies in Education, 15*(2), 171–186.

James, C. E. (2003). *Seeing ourselves: Exploring race, ethnicity and culture*. Toronto: Thompson Educational Publishing, Inc.

James, C. E. (2005). *Race in play: Understanding the socio-cultural worlds of student athletes*. Toronto: Canadian Scholars' Press.

James, C. E., & Haig-Brown, C. (2001). Returning the dues: Community and the personal in a university/school partnership. *Urban Education, 36*(3), 226–255.

Kimmel, M. S. (1999). Masculinity as homophobia: Fear, shame and silence in the construction of gender identity. In J. A. Kuypers (Ed.), *Men and power* (pp. 105–128). Amherst, NY: Prometheus Books.

Kimmel, M. S. (2003). I am not insane; I am angry: Adolescent masculinity, homophobia, and violence. In M. Sadowski (Ed.), *Adolescents at school: Perspectives on youth, identity, and education* (pp. 69–78). Cambridge, MA: Harvard Education Press.

Kuypers, J.A. (1999). *Men and power*. New York: Prometheus Books.

Leach, M. (1994). The politics of masculinity: An overview of contemporary theory. *Social Alternatives, 12*(4), 36–37.

Lenskyi, H. J. (2003). *Out on the field: Gender, sport and sexualities*. Toronto: Women's Press.

Majors, R. (1990). Cool pose: Black masculinity and sports. In M. A. Messner & D. F. Sabo (Eds.), *Sport, men, and the gender order: Critical feminist perspectives* (pp. 109–114). Champaign, IL: Human Kinetics Books.

Majors, R., & Billson, J. M. (1992). *Cool pose: The dilemmas of black manhood on America*. New York: Lexington Books.

Martino, W., & Pallotta-Chiarolli, M. (2003). *So what's a boy?: Addressing issues of masculinity and schooling*. Maidenhead, UK: Open University Press.

Martinot, S. (2003). *The rule of racialization: Class, identity and governance*. Philadelphia: Temple University Press.

Marquese, M. (1995). Sport and stereotype: From role model to Muhammad Ali. *Race & Class, 36*(4), 1–29.

Messner, M. A. & Sabo, D. F (Eds.). (1990). *Sport, men and the gender order*. Champaign, IL: Human Kinetics Books.

Noguera, P. A. (2003a). The trouble with black boys: The role and influence of environmental and cultural factors on the academic performance of African American males. *Urban Education, 38*(4), 431–459.

Noguera, P. A. (2003b). Joaquin's dilemma: Understanding the link between racial identity and school-related behaviors. In M. Sadowski (Ed.), *Adolescents at school: Perspectives on youth, identity, and education* (pp. 19–308). Cambridge, MA: Harvard Education Press.

Odih, P. (2002). Masculinities and role models: Masculinity and the educational "underachievement" of young Afro-Caribbean males. *Race, Ethnicity and Education, 5*(1), 91–105.

Ogden, D. & Hilt, M. (2003). Collective identity and basketball: An explanation for the decreasing number of African American on America's baseball diamonds, *Journal of Leisure Research* 35, 213–228.

Ontario Human Rights Commission. (2003). *Paying the price: The human cost of racial profiling.* Toronto: Ontario Human Rights Commission.

Price, J. N. (2000). Peer (dis)connections, school, and African American masculinities. In N. Lesko (Ed.), *Masculinities at school* (pp. 127–159). Thousand Oaks, CA: Sage Publications.

Pronger, B. (1992). *The arena of masculinity: Sports, homosexuality, and the meaning of sex.* Toronto: University of Toronto Press.

Sewell. T. (1998). Loose canons: Exploding the myth of the "black macho." In D. Epstein, J. Elwood, V. Hey, & J. Maw (Eds.), *Failing boys?: Issues in gender and achievement* (pp. 111–127). Buckingham, UK: Open University Press.

Solomon, R. P. (1992). *Black resistance in high school: Forging a separatist culture.* Albany, NY: State University of New York Press.

Spence, C. M. (2002). *On time! On task! On a mission!: A year in the life of a middle school principal.* Halifax, NS: Fernwood Publishing.

Steele, C. M. (1999). Thin ice: "Stereotype stress" and Black college students. *Atlantic Monthly, 284*(2), 44–54.

Stevenson, H. C. (2004). Boys in men's clothing: Racial socialization and neighbourhood safety as buffers to hypervulnerability in African American adolescent males. In N. Way & J. Y. Chu (Eds.), *Adolescent boys: exploring diverse cultures of boyhood* (pp. 59–77). New York: New York University Press.

Theodore, P. S., & Basow, S. A. (2000). Heterosexual masculinity and homophobia: A reaction to the self? *Journal of Homosexuality, 40*(2), 31–48.

Time (2005, August 8) pp. 7–11. Canadian Edition.

Young, I. M. (1990). *Justice and the politics of difference.* Princeton, NJ: Princeton University Press.

6 Troubles of Black Boys in Urban Schools in the United States

Black Feminist and Gay Men's Perspectives

Lance T. McCready

Introduction

In this chapter, I explore the troubles of black boys in urban schools in the United States from a perspective informed by writings of black feminists and gay men.[1] My purpose for doing so is to begin theorizing a more progressive research and policy agenda for these troubles. My analysis is guided by the question "How do black feminists and gay men's critical perspectives on black masculinity inform what are considered to be the 'troubles' of black boys in urban schools?" I focus on the work of Patricia Hill Collins and Joseph Beam. These writers, mostly uncited in the literature on urban education, problematize conventional understandings of black masculinity and therefore have influenced my thinking about a range of black sexual politics in urban education.

I began to be exposed to the writings of black feminists and gay men as an undergraduate and through my work with Gay Men of African Descent (GMAD), a grassroots social/support, HIV/AIDS organization for black men in New York City. During the summer of my junior year in college, I started attending Friday night meetings of GMAD. After "coming out" (openly identifying as a gay man), I was hungry for affirming images and rhetoric that made the connections between my burgeoning race, class, gender, and sexuality consciousnesses. After my graduation from college, I became heavily involved in GMAD as a youth board member where I gained invaluable experience organizing Friday night "rap sessions," poetry readings, fashion shows, and HIV/AIDS outreach. Through these events, I met several black gay artists such as Djola Branner and Brian Freeman of the performance troupe PomoAfroHomo; poets Craig Harris, Donald Woods, and Assotto Saint; short story writer Melvin Dixon; and filmmaker Marlon Riggs. These men, who drew on the work of black feminist writers such as Audre Lorde, bell hooks, and Pat Parker, showed me how my social group identities were both personal and political.

When I entered graduate school in the fall of 1992, full of hope and enthusiasm gained from my GMAD friends, comrades, and lovers, I quickly learned that my academic colleagues had a difficult time understanding the significance my activist experiences in the black and lesbian, gay, bisexual, and transgender (LGBT) communities. Black male graduate students who I knew were gay from clubbing and house parties chose not to "come out." Senior colleagues were baffled by the connections I was making between the arts, activism, and urban school reform. When I suggested taking a year off to teach in elementary school to gain classroom experience, a senior professor in my department suggested this wouldn't be a good idea for two reasons: "your hair (I had dreadlocks at the time), and your sexual orientation. Students need Black men who are going to be disciplinarians in the classroom," she said, assuming that because I was openly gay, I couldn't also be a disciplinarian. This was the first time in the context of urban education that I realized my sexuality gave meaning to other social identities, here my race and masculinity, and it angered me. I felt judged and stereotyped, and most of all held back. In this faculty member's eyes, I couldn't possibly be a good role model for young black children because I had dreadlocks and was gay.

Discrimination against single mothers, gay men, lesbians, and transgender folk owing to sexism, classism, and homophobia (such as in the incident described here) continues to exist in black communities, so it comes as no surprise that black feminists' and gay men's perspectives are underutilized in urban education. Moreover, very little of the literature on the troubles of black boys in urban schools is written from a feminist or "queer" (an umbrella term that includes gay men, lesbians, bisexuals, and transgendered people) perspective, despite the fact that there are feminists and gay male scholars present in urban education. Why aren't the insights of queer educators drawn on more in urban education? Perhaps black women and men marginalized by their race, gender, and sexual identities feel speaking from this place on the "borderlands" (Anzaldâua, 2007) of urban education would jeopardize their reputation and therefore their ability to effectively work toward social change.

So, through writing this chapter as an openly gay man of African descent who works to improve the lives of residents in urban school communities, I hope to "make space" for black feminists and gay men who offer critical perspectives on black masculinities that hold tremendous promise for addressing the troubles of black boys in urban schools. Toward making this argument, the chapter is structured as follows. The first part provides a conventional review of the troubles of black boys, followed by a discussion of Pedro Noguera's notion of the structural and cultural dimensions of risk that lead to these troubles. Noguera's framework is a good starting point because he is considered to be one of the leading authorities on the relationship between the identities of black male students and academic performance. He has appeared on several nationally syndicated radio and television talk shows to discuss this topic and therefore has gained a national reputation. He and I currently work on a research project that looks at the effectiveness of single-sex schools for black and Latino male students. I will provide more details of the project in the final section of this chapter. These friendships and affiliations, personal and professional, do not stop me, however, from making the criticism that Noguera's rubric fails to adequately theorize the ways masculinity and heteronormativity are aspects of structural and cultural risk. I describe the experiences of two gay and gender nonconforming black male students who make this clear.

The second part of the chapter focuses on the work of black feminist scholar Patricia Hill Collins and black gay male writer Joseph Beam, who write critically about black masculinity and, in doing so, theorize the ways gender and sexuality oppression are part of the structure and culture of urban communities. I draw on these critiques to reinterpret the troubles of black boys and think about a more progressive research and policymaking agenda that might address black boys' troubles in urban schools. I do this mostly by raising questions about the research I am currently conducting on single-sex schools, a reform that has been touted as promising by educators and policymakers. Overall, this chapter is meant to provide a rationale for why black feminists' and gay men's perspectives are crucial for developing a more progressive research and policy agenda to address the "troubles" of black boys in urban schools.

The Troubles of Black Boys In and Out of School[2]

All of the most important quality-of-life indicators suggest that black and Latino males are confronted by a wide variety of hardships. They lead the nation in homicides, both as victims and perpetrators (Blumstein, Rivera, & Rosenfeld, 2000; Roberts, 2004; Skolnick and Currie, 1994), and in what observers regard as an alarming trend Black males now have the fastest growing rate of suicide (Poussaint and Alexander, 2000). For the last several years, black males have been contracting HIV and AIDS at a faster rate than any other segment of the population (Centers for Disease Control, 2007), and their incarceration, conviction, and arrest rates have been higher than all other groups in most states for over a decade (Department of Justice, 2006; Roper, 1991; Skolnick and Currie, 1994). Even as babies, black males have the highest probability of dying in the first year of life (Auerbach, Krimgold, & Lefkowitz, 2000; National Research Council, 1989) and as they grow older, they face the unfortunate reality of being the only group in the United States experiencing a decline in life expectancy (Spivak, Prothrow-Stith, & Hausman,1988). In the labor market, they are the least likely to be hired and, in many cities, the most likely to be unemployed and discriminated against for job opportunities

(Hacker, 1992; Holzner, 2007; Massey and Denton, 1993; Moss and Tilly, 1993; Kirschenmann and Neckerman, 1991; Wilson, 1987).

Beset with such an ominous array of social and economic hardships, it is hardly surprising that the experience of young black males in education evidences similar signs of crisis. This is true with respect to educational attainment and most indicators of academic performance. Nationally, black males are more likely than any other group to be suspended and expelled from school, and they are more likely to be arrested in a school setting (Meier, Stewart, and England, 1989; Skiba, 2002). Though from 1973 to 1977 there was a steady increase in black male enrollment in college, since 1977 there has been a sharp and continuous decline (National Research Council, 1989; Carnoy, 1994). Today, far too many black males between the ages of 18 and 24 are in prison rather than in college (Boothe, 2007; Cook & Cordova, 2007).

Black males are more likely to be classified as mentally retarded or suffering from a learning disability and placed in special education (Frankenberg, Lee, & Orfield, 2003). They are also less likely to be in gifted and talented programs and advanced placement and honors courses (College Board, 2008; Pollard, 1993). In contrast to most other groups wherein males commonly perform at higher levels in math and science-related courses, the reverse is true for black males (Pollard, 1993). Though males generally are enrolling in colleges and universities at lower rates than females, for black and Latino males, the disparities are widest and growing (Coley, 2001). Even class privilege and the material benefits that generally accompany it fail to buffer black males from low academic performance. When compared to their white peers, middle-class black males lag significantly behind in both grade point average and standardized tests (Jencks and Phillips, 1998).

Structural and Cultural Explanations

In *The Trouble with Black Boys: The Role and Influence of Environmental and Cultural Factors on the Academic Performance of African American Males*, Pedro Noguera (2005) argues that explanations for the risk factors or "troubles" of black male students in urban communities and schools tend to be polarized between structural and cultural explanations of behavior. Noguera describes "structuralists" as researchers and policymakers who lean toward explanations of political economy such as the availability of jobs, economic opportunities, class structure, and social geography. From the structuralist perspective, holding black male students responsible for their poor performance in school makes little sense as forces beyond the control of any particular individual shape their behavior. An example of a scholar who relies on primarily structural explanations of the troubles of black boys would be William Julius Wilson (1987) who argues that the problems of joblessness and neighborhood organization, including crime and drug trafficking, are reflected in black male students' lack of effort in school.

In contrast, "culturalists" downplay the importance of political economy and treat human behavior as a product of beliefs, values, norms, and socialization. From the culturalist perspective, expanding employment opportunities or providing more money to less affluent, predominantly black school districts would do little to improve the academic performance of black male students as their attitudes toward school are shaped by the culture brought from home and the neighborhood (Murray, 1994). Harvard sociologist Orlando Patterson wrote a searing opinion editorial for the *New York Times* in which he takes the position that the structuralist perspective is

> a deep-seated dogma that has prevailed in social science and policy circles since the mid-1960s: the rejection of any explanation that invokes a group's cultural attributes—its distinctive attitudes, values and predispositions, and the resulting behavior of its members—and the relentless preference for relying on structural factors like low incomes, joblessness, poor schools and bad housing.

Patterson claims academics are "allergic" to cultural explanations because they "blame the victim," are wholly deterministic, and suggest that cultural patterns cannot change. He dismisses all of these critiques in favor of his own analysis that black males fall into a "Dionysian trap" in which they worship hip-hop, professional basketball, and homeboy fashions, mainstays of U.S. mainstream culture that feed their pride and self-esteem, but cannot see beyond these icons when "it is time to turn off Fifty Cent and get out the SAT prep book."

Noguera points out that rather than taking an either-or position, a growing number of researchers, himself included, are trying to find ways to work between the two sides of the debate. Dissatisfied with the determinism of structuralists who render individuals as passive objects of larger forces and with the "blame the victim" perspective of the culturalists who view individuals as hopelessly trapped within a particular sociocultural milieu, some educators and researchers aim to synthesize important elements from both perspectives while simultaneously paying greater attention to the importance of individual choice and agency. For example, John Ogbu (2003) and Signithia Fordham (1996) employ a "cultural-ecological" analysis to explain the underachievement of black males. Cultural-ecology incorporates a global and socio-historical perspective and acknowledges the influence of race as a structuring phenomenon both educationally and more broadly in society. From this perspective, the notion of "blocked opportunities" helps explain divergent educational outcomes of blacks,

Latinos, and Asians vis-à-vis whites, addressing relative academic success and failure (Ogbu, 1983). Ogbu maintains that African-American male students, as members of a "caste-like minority" that historically entered the United States involuntarily through slavery, cope with and respond to their race-based domination or oppression in particular ways. New forms of identity, behaviors, and meanings emerge in black male peer groups that are often oppositional to the majority culture and become markers of group identity. In other words, given such structural constraints as severe job ceilings and job market discrimination and the denial of other societal benefits commensurate with their level of education, black students and other involuntary minority groups perceive schooling as offering unequal returns.

Signthia Fordham (1996), Ogbu's colleague, found the anthropological concept "fictive kinship" useful when trying to understand the oppositional identities of black students. She observed that black students may or may not have been related by blood, but they maintained essential social relationships that served a political function as well. When black students used kinship terms such as "brother" or "sister" to refer to one another, it conveyed a sense of peoplehood or collective social identity. The fictive kinship systems of black students at Capital High School, the site for Fordham's research, included strategies for protecting their identity and maintaining boundaries between themselves and white students. Black students perceived certain behaviors and certain activities or events as inappropriate because whites had established the performance criteria in those areas. Academic tasks and school-related activities represented one such area. As black students were involved in the evaluation of group members' eligibility for membership in the fictive kinship system, they control the criteria used to judge one's worthiness for membership. Fictive kinship is also the medium through which black students distinguish who is really black and who is "acting white" (Fordham & Ogbu, 1986).

Possibly because both Ogbu and Fordham tend to view black students' identities through a patriarchal, heteronormative lens, they inadequately theorize how the dynamics of gender and sexuality affect oppositional identities and membership in the fictive kinship system. From a feminist perspective, one supposes that there are ideals of gender and sexuality that work simultaneously with racial norms to determine forms and types of resistance and group membership. What are these gender and sexuality norms, and what happens when black students transgress these ideals? Patricia Hill Collins's concept of intersectionality, meaning the way various forms of oppression are interlocking and social identities are co-constructed, could be helpful here (Collins, 2000). Collins has used intersectionality to understand and explain black women's resistance to oppression through blues music and everyday living. Intersectionality could push us to think about the ways black student resistances could be a response to not one but many forms of oppression including racism, heterosexism, and classism. However, interestingly, neither Ogbu nor Fordham draw on black feminist theory to theorize the oppositional behavior of black students at Capital High School.

Noguera does critique both Ogbu and Fordham for relying too heavily on the notion of "oppositional behavior" that is ultimately a cultural explanation of black students' troubles. He explains that

> They argue that Black students hold themselves back out of fear that they will be ostracized by their peers. Yet, what these researchers do not acknowledge is the dynamic that occurs between Black students, males in particular, and the culture that is operative within schools. Black males may engage in behaviors that contribute to their underachievement and marginality, but they are also more likely to be channeled into marginal roles and to be discouraged from challenging themselves by adults who are supposed to help them.[3]

In other words, from Noguera's perspective, Ogbu and Fordham overlook the ways the institutional structure and culture of schools marginalize black male students on the basis of race. However, what about the ways the institutional structure and culture of schools could marginalize black male students on the basis of gender and/or sexuality? The experiences of black male students who are gay and/or gender nonconforming are instructive here.

David and Antoine: Stories of Harassment and Abuse

During the fall semester 1997, I interviewed David, a black gay male senior at a high school in Northern California I call California High School or CHS. David was a 17-year-old when I interviewed him. He was a lanky 6' 4" with skin the color of honey. He had large, earthy brown eyes and meticulously arched eyebrows and usually dressed in jeans, sneakers, a T-shirt, and a hooded sweatshirt. Occasionally, I saw him wear something flashier such as a Hawaiian print shirt, but most times he wore standard Gap-inspired clothes with either a baseball or wool-knit cap, depending on how cold it was outside. The combination of David's light brown skin color, height, and what some students viewed as feminine-appearing eyes marked him as gender nonconforming and thus made him a target of abuse from his peers.

I was rapt with attention as David recounted multiple incidents of harassment he received in elementary and middle school. "I had long curly hair," he said, "so people used to think I was a girl and I used to get teased a lot because of that." When David got to CHS, the harassment became more physical. "People eventually started throwing things at me and shit." David approached Mr. Jones, a black man in his mid-forties and the director of CHS security, about the harassment he was receiving, particularly from his black male peers. Mr. Jones asked, "Well, what did you do to deserve it [the harassment]?" David replied, "I was walking out of the library and these [Black] boys threw a magazine at me and called me names." Mr. Jones replied, "Oh, well, usually someone does something to someone first before they're going to throw some books at you."

As a result of this harassment during the fall semester of his junior year, David no longer felt safe at CHS and decided, after much pleading with his mother, to finish high school in Independent Studies, a self-directed high school diploma program administered by the continuation high school in the school district. It is important understand that David's decision to leave was not based on his gender nonconformity alone. Rather, his gender nonconformity exacerbated marginalization emanating from multiple dimensions of his identity. For example, in my interview with David, I learned he had been identified as a "gifted" student in elementary school. For most of his time in school, David was in a separate academic track than the majority of black students. According to David, participating in gifted and talented programs was hard because he was one of the few students of color in his classes, and his black peers felt his participation in these programs symbolized he was trying to "act white" (Fordham and Ogbu, 1986). In addition, David was biracial: His mother was white, his father black. At times, David believed his skin color combined with his gender nonconformity seemed to position him outside the "boundaries of Blackness" in the eyes of his black peers.

Though David experienced enormous personal growth during his year in Independent Studies (he developed close friendships with other gay, lesbian, and gender nonconforming students of color), his academic progress was less than stellar. After giving it much, thought he decided to confront his fear of failure and give CHS a second chance. When he returned to CHS, however, David found it difficult to find a peer group that met his social and emotional needs. Even though he openly identified as gay, he felt alienated from the group of white female students who participated in Project 10, a group support for LGBT students. According to David, "It's [Project 10] about 4 or 5 girls who all know each other. They're all out, you know, within that group. And they go there I guess for social support." David felt that it was more difficult for guys, guys of color in particular, to "come out" and feel comfortable attending a queer support group. He attributed the difficulty of students of color openly identifying as gay or lesbian to cultural differences in the ways homophobia and heterosexism are expressed in black communities.

In addition to possible cultural differences in identifying as gay, David's experiences seem to reflect the tendency of white female students, like their black peers, to socialize with one another around a distinct set of racially defined concerns rather than build coalitions with students from different racial backgrounds who may have an entirely different set of interests. In the racially segregated environment of CHS, Project 10's lack of a social-support agenda regarding race seemed to inadvertently privilege those students who de-emphasized their racial identity. Fran Thompson, faculty advisor for Project 10, believed the strong participation of white female students was related to the fact that they were the most concerned about encountering discrimination for being openly queer. In contrast, queer students of color seemed to relate more to groups outside of CHS such as Lavender, a support group run by a local lesbian and gay community center. Admitting that "diversifying the ethnic composition of the group is very complicated," Fran questioned her own ability to fully understand the multitude of pressures queer students of color face. Her limited understanding of multiple dimensions of social support needed by queer youth of color may have unintentionally alienated David, encouraging him and others to seek resources outside the school. In this way, Project 10 and other queer youth programs in segregated school environments may privilege white students and marginalize queer youth of color. Thus, David's experiences at CHS and Project 10 suggest that whereas gender nonconformity caused much of his marginalization, multiple perceived differences such as his academic status and race triggered other forms of marginalization at CHS. To understand David's marginalization as due to gender nonconformity alone would be far too simplistic.

I reached a similar conclusion two years later after an interview and participant observation with another openly gay, gender nonconforming black male student, Antoine. At 18 years old, 5' 7" and 150 pounds, he was smaller than most of his black male peers. His medium brown skin, prominent nose, light brown eyes (from contact lenses), textured dark brown hair (with a bronze tuft in the front), and slightly nasal, lispy, baritone voice gave him a slightly feminine air. Despite these qualities, he dressed in the "uniform" worn by most of his black male peers: baggy jeans, T-shirt under an oxford-type shirt, plain baseball cap, pierced left ear, boots, and a backpack with a single arm sling. His clothing reflected his desire to fit in rather than to call attention to the ways his voice, stature, hairstyle, openly gay sexual identity, and participation in dance set him apart as gender nonconforming.

When Antoine came to CHS in the ninth grade, he lacked confidence. "I wasn't really good at like holding your head up and smiling and stuff like that," he said. When he met with a counselor about his class schedule, the counselor brought up the physical education (PE). Antoine asserted that "I'm not interested in any kind of sports or nothing like that, so don't put me in that." The counselor suggested classes in the African Dance Program (ADP), which at CHS fulfills the PE requirement. Antoine agreed to "give it a shot." During his first semester of ADP, he was nervous and danced in the back. Second semester he began to warm up, and by sophomore year, he remembered, "I was fine … and I gradually started coming to the front [of the class]."

Although participating in ADP gave Antoine a newfound celebrity, he continued to be socially reserved owing in part to openly identifying as gay and, as I later learned, being a special education student. His academic difficulties made him extremely self-conscious of his status relative to other black peers, many of whom were *not* special education students. According to one of Antoine's teachers, he had difficulty accepting his academic shortcomings. For example, Antoine routinely skipped his special education classes and instead served as an informal teaching assistant in beginning ADP classes. Even though Mama Mwingu, the director of ADP, knew he was skipping academic classes, she empathized with his desire to fit in with black students who were not in special education classes.

Like David, Antoine experienced harassment for being gender nonconforming. Some of the heterosexual-identified black male dancers liked to tease him by punching him on the arm or slapping him upside the head. When I asked Antoine about it, he said that he did not mind their behavior and instead viewed hitting as his peers' way of flirting with him. From my perspective, Antoine's nonconfrontational approach was a way of keeping the peace with heterosexual black male students who routinely asserted their power over gender nonconforming students through harassment and abuse. For instance, I often observed Chris, another black male dancer in ADP, jokingly hit Antoine upside the head during rehearsal. On another occasion, I observed Darrell, a CHS graduate who had been hired as one of the official drummers for ADP, hit Antoine repeatedly as Antoine yelled, "Stop!" at the top of his lungs. Antoine chuckled after both incidents.

On the one hand, my observations and interviews suggest that Antoine liked the attention his heterosexual peers showed him, regardless of whether or not it was abusive, because it made him feel like one of the guys. Even though the teasing and subsequent hitting was somewhat violent, it allowed him to interact with his peers and counteracted possible marginalization brought on by openly identifying as gay. On the other hand, it is possible the hitting reflected repressed same-sex desire, especially as Antoine viewed it as flirting. Antoine believed that any attention, even negative attention, symbolized desire:

> I think everybody has thought about it in a negative or positive way, being with the same sex. And when I say a negative way, if I was straight and I was like, "Ooh, I can't see myself doing it to another dude" or "I can't see myself being with a dude." That's still thinking about it..They be like, "Naw, no, we ain't never, we ain't never, I ain't never thought about being with another dude or whatever." And I'm

like, if you sit there and be like, "Eew, I can't see myself being with another dude, that's nasty," that's thinking about it. So c'mon, you have thought about it in a negative or in a positive, so you thought being with the same sex at least one time or more in your life.

Overall, Antoine's experiences in ADP suggest that gender nonconformity caused much of his marginalization and abuse, although other perceived differences such as being a special education student and having same-sex desire triggered other forms of oppression. The ongoing harassment of queer students of color like David and Antoine in urban schools suggests gender and sexuality are indeed components of the structure and culture of urban schools; however, in the literature on the troubles of black boys masculinities, heterosexuality, homosexuality, and gender nonconformity remain under-explored dimensions of the human experience.

In the recently published edited volume *Educating African American Males: Voices From the Field* (Fashola, 2005), a collection of presentations from the Conference on African American Male Achievement, only two chapters written by James Earl Davis and by Dena Phillips Swanson, Michael Cunningham, and Margaret Spencer even mention masculinity. Davis is the only one to argue that

> What has emerged from this focus on the educational problems of Black males is an archetype of masculine behavior that is either deficient or distorted under the weight of racism, economic marginality, and cultural pathology (Hunter & Davis, 1992). Although masculinity is generally seen as being important (Akbar, 1991; Connell, 1995), it is regarded, however, as unidimensional and implicitly universal. Thus, this framework obscures the diversity and complexity of the constructions of so-called masculinities and how they are played out for African American males in schools (p.132).

Davis's work should be applauded because he is virtually the only researcher of black boys' troubles who consistently addresses issues of masculinity and homophobia (e.g. 2001; Hunter & Davis, 1992; Polite & Davis, 1999). Much more work is needed on the range of black boys' masculinities and their relationship to academic outcomes such as achievement, engagement, and participation in school. To do this, we need to incorporate the insights from academic fields of study beyond education such as women's/feminist studies, masculinity studies, and LGBT studies. Black feminist scholarship on masculinities is helpful here because it uses the concepts of matrix of domination, intersectionality, and self-recovery, combined with insights from masculinity studies and queer theory, to make the case that black men must have a more progressive conceptualization of their gender identities to thrive in society. A black feminist scholar who is a strong advocate for more progressive notions of black masculinity is sociologist Patricia Hill Collins. Collins is best known for the award-winning book *Black Feminist Thought: Knowledge, Consciousness, and the Politics of Empowerment* (2000), in which she outlines American black feminism expressed in music, fiction, poetry, and oral history. Collins saw three themes: oppressions are interconnected; black women create alternative worldviews for self-definition and self-determination; and black women have often internalized imposed restricting definitions of who they are—especially racialized concepts of beauty, skin color, and physique. In *Black Sexual Politics: African Americans, Gender, and the New Racism*, Collins (2004) points to areas that have been overlooked: racialized gender roles within family and work, politics, violence—in the home, on the job, and in the street—and homophobia. She makes a radical argument that for black men and boys to develop more progressive notions of black masculinity, they have to learn to tell the difference between masculinity as dominance versus masculinity as strength. Making a distinction between the two is crucial so that African-American men and boys can stop doing damage to themselves, women, and children under the banner of protecting their manhood. Next, I summarize her argument toward posing a different set of questions to form the basis of research and policymaking designed to address the troubles of black boys in urban schools.

Telling the Difference Between Dominance and Strength

In the book chapter "A Telling Difference: Dominance, Strength, and Black Masculinities," Patricia Hill Collins presents a compelling case for black men's being able to tell the difference between dominance and strength. She begins by asserting that definitions of black masculinity in the United States "reflect a narrow cluster of controlling images situated within a broader framework that grants varying value to racially distinctive forms of masculinity" (p. 75). All of the representations, she argues, hinge on questions of weakness,

> whether it is a weakness associated with an inability to control violent impulses, sexual urges, or their black female, heterosexual partners or a weakness attributed to men whose lack of education, employment patterns, and criminal records relegate them to inferior social spaces (p. 75).

The possibility of masculinities being a form of weakness is based on hegemonic white masculinity that is fundamentally a relational construct wherein gender boundaries are defined through a series of oppositional relationships whereby normal masculinity becomes defined in opposition to women, gay men, poor and working-class men, boys, and black men. Each of these groups serves as an important social group for constructing the ideas of hegemonic white masculinity and actual social practices of dominance that maintain power relations that privilege elite white men. As social groups, women, gay men, poor, and working-class men, boys, and black men are socially stigmatized with a particular form of weakness that is juxtaposed to the seeming strengths of hegemonic white masculinity. Hegemonic masculinity reflects a cognitive framework of binary thinking that defines masculinity in terms of its difference from and dominance over multiple others (real men are not like women, real men are not gay, real men are not poor, real men are not boys, real men are not black). The dominance is the strength of hegemonic white masculinity.

Because many African-Americans implicitly accept the belief in complementary gender roles, they fail to challenge the strong women–weak men thesis associated with American racial ideology, not the strong men–weak men thesis associated with American masculinity. Instead, many African-Americans argue that black poverty, political powerlessness, and educational disparities could be addressed by approximating more closely the gender roles of dominant society. Collins laments that within this logic, gender normality becomes a sign of racial progress, and racial progress becomes measured in racially specific forms. If all masculinities, including those defined by African-American men, are evaluated by how closely they approximate dominant social norms, then not surprisingly, hierarchies of successful and failed manhood match up with the white normality–black deviancy framework that accompanies racism, to the heterosexual-homosexual binary that supports heterosexism, to structures of age that grant seniority to older males over younger ones, and to a class system that grants propertied individuals more power and status than those who lack it.

Collins believes strongly that black men are harmed and constrained by popular images that hinge on questions of weakness, and to the extent that they internalize this thesis, "their own strategies to combat their oppression will be misguided" (p. 75). From Collins' perspective, commonsense beliefs such as the strong black women–weak black man thesis played out in situation comedies such as *The Parkers* and the strong white men–weak black men thesis portrayed in buddy movies such as the *Lethal Weapon* and *Rush Hour* franchises are based on a system of power derived from hegemonic white masculinity that lead black men to embrace unrealistic strategies for dealing with relations of dominance. Collins asserts that progressive black masculinities require rejecting the images currently associated with black masculinity and the structural power relations that cause them. This includes rejecting images of physical dominance and aggressiveness celebrated by hip-hop artists and professional athletes.

These entertainers' reputations are built on physically dominating others through living the "thug life" and playing sports. Developing progressive black masculinities also requires rejecting sexual dominance and the popular images associated with it such as "the playa" who has multiple sexual partners and the "baby daddy" who fathers children by more than one mother.

In addition to rejecting physical and sexual dominance, the development of progressive black masculinities requires the rejection of political and economic dominance as well. The fact that many African-American men work in the informal labor market, including the global drug industry, and have prison records that preclude them from invoking their voting rights as citizens to change labor laws, creates a situation wherein African-American men are less able to contribute financial support to their families and communities. In the context of globalization wherein job flight, mechanization and downsizing, and punitive domestic social welfare policies leave black boys in poor schools with bad housing and poor opportunities, economic dominance modeled by elite white men seems a distant dream. Collins's explanation of why it is important to consider alternative masculinities that reject the model of economic and political dominance is an excellent example of Noguera's (2005) recommendation to work between structuralist-culturalist perspectives. She considers both the structural conditions of black men and culturally based beliefs about gender relations used in black American communities.

Collins acknowledges that the process of moving beyond the notion of masculinity as dominance is challenging work because it requires black men to exhibit strength in two areas: relinquishing privilege and personal accountability. Progressive black masculinities recognize and subsequently relinquish real and imagined privileges gained through domination, "in particular the benefits and costs attached to sexism and heterosexism. Relinquishing benefits of dominance is difficult because it inevitably fosters marginalization and alienation from those very groups that long served as places of belonging" (p. 92).

The experiences of Kevin, another student I interviewed in ADP, serves as an example of this kind of alienation. Kevin lamented that even though he was popular among black female students in ADP, he felt alienated from the dance teacher, Nana, because she withheld support when he transgressed masculine codes of behavior. Kevin admitted that he liked to "shake things up" in class by pointing his toes when he was supposed to flex or wearing braided hair extensions that bounced when he danced. Kevin consciously transgressed hegemonic codes of black masculinity but knew doing so had a price. With sadness in his voice, Kevin explained, "I would say like, all the people who should know me the best, it should be Nana. But then I don't think she knows me very well. I don't think anybody really knows me, any of the teachers know me very well." Black male students such as Kevin who make conscious efforts to express progressive masculinities receive very little support for their actions. Teachers, peers, and family members who are more comfortable with the status quo may alienate gender nonconforming students, fearing what they don't understand. Ironically, at the same time they are being alienated, students such as Kevin are "making space" for other gender nonconforming youth to express themselves. Kevin's history teacher in eleventh grade, Bob Anderson, praised Kevin's bravery in the face of intense peer pressure to conform. "Kevin made it easier for others to be different," said Mr. Anderson, "Everyone benefited from the risks he took."

The second area black men must learn to exhibit strength in is "incorporating an ethic of personal accountability in relation to women, children, parents, siblings, and one another" (Collins, 2006, p. 92). Collins points out that "historical patterns of black sexual politics provide the overarching context for black men's behavior" but asserts that "each individual African American man is responsible for his actions and the choices he makes in everyday life" (p. 93). Personal accountability to self and others means rejecting the negative outcomes of the weakness thesis and redefining black male strength in terms of relationships with others. From this perspective, black men must work to become allies with those for whom middle-class, white, heterosexual male logic considers weak: men who identify as gay, men who are incarcerated, or men who put schoolwork ahead of sports and entertainment.

Black male students who are hegemonically heterosexual becoming allies with black male students who are gender nonconforming is a huge challenge. None of the students I interviewed reported having boys or men in their lives who valued their gender nonconformity as a form of progressive masculinity. All of the students I interviewed reported being rejected as soon as they started to exhibit any type of effeminate behavior. For example, Jamal, a student I interviewed about his non-participation in the school's social-support group for LGBT students, said his relationship with a neighborhood friend, Durrell, changed after he exhibited different interests than most boys his age. Jamal recalls,

> This guy [Durrell], like we were friends from 4th grade until age 13. But I mean like, like there was a difference. I was doing things differently. Like he was popping wheelies on his bicycle and I wasn't interested in popping wheelies. Or he would learn to play, he would learn to, um ride his skate board and I stuck with the skates and skates were considered, they weren't considered as like macho. He was like idolizing LL Cool J and I was like idolizing Diana (Ross) and Janet (Jackson) you know?"

These differences in masculinity become the grounds for hegemonically masculine black male students to eschew accountability to black males who are gender nonconforming. Overall, these kinds of divergences in identification make it difficult to imagine black male students, as a group, rallying around the notion of progressive black masculinities. This is made even more difficult when black male students are not exposed to the work of black gay men who have written extensively about value of transgressing dominant modes of masculinity.

Black Gay Men's Writing

In the late 1980s and early 1990s, black gay men, organizing on both the East and West coasts of the United States, were heavily influenced by the writings of black feminist scholars and activists who theorized that major systems of oppressions are interlocking and therefore fighting homophobia was not separate from fighting racism or sexism. In the introduction to *In the life: A black gay anthology*, Joseph Beam (1986) remembers,

> I was fed by Audre Lorde's *Zami*, Barbara Smith's *Home girls*, Cherrie Moraga's *Loving in the war years*, Babara Demings *We cannot live without our lives*, June Jordan's *Civil wars*, and Michelle Cliff's *Claiming an identity I was taught to despise*. Their courage told me that I, too, could be courageous. I, too, could not only live with what I feel, but could draw succor from it, nurture it, and make it visible (p. xix).

In my early twenties, before attaining my doctorate, I too was influenced by black feminist praxis. As one of the first youth board members of GMAD, I helped organize consciousness-raising workshops modeled after the black women's self-help movement, whereby we sought to educate ourselves about the ways black men discriminate against other non-black men of color. Guided by the poetry of Pat Parker, we held the belief that if bigots "come" for one of us based on our race, class, or sexual orientation, they have the potential to come for all of us based on any stigmatizing identity we claimed.

My work with black gay men enables me to destigmatize alternative sexualities, confront my own internalized homophobia, and challenge the normative assumptions of heterosexuality, including core ideas of black gender ideology. Through reading the work of black gay writers, I and other black gay men involved in HIV/AIDS education and political organizing began to think about the ways black men are bought into dominance through their uncritical acceptance of "Black macho," the term Michelle Wallace (1990) uses for hegemonic black masculinity. Joseph Beam's (1986) essay, "Brother to brother: Words from the heart" (pp. 180–191), was especially influential in this regard because it provides a language and framework for thinking about and discussing more progressive forms of black masculinity, in particular the notion of "Black men loving Black men" as the revolutionary act" (p. 190). For Beam, the notion of "Black men loving Black men" is simultaneously an "autonomous agenda call to action" and "acknowledgement of responsibility" (191) that progressive black men must take up. This powerful critique of hegemonic masculinity has the potential to inform the troubles of black boys in urban schools: however, urban educators rarely draw on black gay men's writing, one guesses, for a variety of reasons, ranging from homophobia in urban education to the relative obscurity of cultural studies texts in the professions. Through discussing Beam's essay in greater detail, I hope to introduce a new body of work to the field of urban education, one that will push educators and policymakers to think more critically about black masculinities and the troubles of black boys. Toward this end, in conclusion to this chapter, I use both Collins' and Beam's essays to reconsider the "troubles" of black boys and pose critical questions about single-sex schooling, one of the reforms currently being touted as a promising remedy for black boys' underachievement in urban schools.

Black Men Loving Black Men

Beam (1986) begins "Brother to Brother" by describing the pain and anger he feels because "I cannot go home as who I am" (p. 180). Home for Beam is more than blood-related family and relatives he grew up with, "but the entire Black community: the Black press, the Black church, Black academicians, the Black literati, and the Black left" (p. 180). Why can't Beam and black gay men like him go home? Because their sexual identity, which transgresses traditional codes of masculinity, is a source of alienation: "I am most often rendered invisible, perceived as a threat to the family, or am tolerated if I am silent and inconspicuous" (p. 181).

Rather than use the anger he feels destructively, Beam desires to use it to rebuild home as a place to which he can return: "Use it [anger] to create a Black gay community in which I can build my home surrounded by institutions that reflect and sustain me. Concurrent with that vision is the necessity to repave the road home, widening it so I can return with all I have created to the home which is my birthright" (p. 183). However, because many black men do not speak of the oppression they experience, and more importantly the love they have for one another, black men and boys struggle to survive anew, missing the opportunity to draw strength from one another. Beam asserts that the love black men feel for one another must be heard. Part of what makes this difficult is that black men, unlike black women, have few traditions that encourage the production of intimate spaces to explore feelings of love and friendship. Beam laments,

We gather in public places: barber shops, bars, lodges, fraternities, and street corners, places where bravado rather than intimacy are the rule. We assemble to do something rather than be with each other. We can talk about the Man, but not about how we must constantly vie with one another for the scant crumbs thrown our way. We can talk about dick and ass and pussy, but not of the fierce competition for too few jobs and scholarships (p. 186).

In the face of silence, Beam suggests giving voice to dreams, which is the first step toward their realization. Beam allows himself to dream that among black men "our blood is thicker than difference" (p. 187). As an example of being able to transcend gender differences among black men, Beam describes his correspondence with an incarcerated man, Ombaka, who is straight, from the South, and Muslim, compared to Beam himself, who is gay, from the North, and agnostic. Beam connected with Ombaka through their being able to discuss their dreams for the future, for instance their shared desire to be writers. This relationship gives him hope that gay and straight black men forge relationships that move from "survival to potential, from merely getting by to a positive getting over" (p. 188). Beam dares black men to dream that "we are worth wanting each other" (p. 189).

In the essay's conclusion, Beam points out that that black men loving black men is a revolutionary act not only because it challenges the homophobia that has historically existed in black communities but because "as Black men we were never meant to be together—not as father and son, brother and brother—and certainly not as lovers." Black men loving black men is an autonomous agenda because it "is not rooted in any particular sexual, political, or class affiliation, but in our mutual survival" (p. 191). Beam acknowledges that the ways black men manifest their love for one another will be "myriad as the issues we must address" (191); however, in doing so, they must acknowledge the responsibility to "take care of our own kind when the night grows cold and silent." Here, even though the essays were written in different eras (Beam in the late 1980s, Collins in 2005), Beam echoes Patricia Hill Collins's call for black men to develop an ethic of personal responsibility.

The erasure of homophobia from urban school reform agendas for black boys, and hence the need for an "ethic of responsibility" toward creating safe and comfortable places for gender nonconforming boys, is an important issue that I take up in the following section focused on single-sex schools. The accelerated development and implementation of public, single-sex middle and high schools for black and Latino boys is motivated by a deep concern to address structural and cultural dimensions of the inequities facing these students. Interest in single-sex schools, however, may not stem from more progressive approaches to issues of masculinity as outlined by both feminist and gay activists such as Collins and Beam. There remains a strong impulse to "normalize" black boys in these schools by promoting and legitimating particular versions of black masculinity without addressing the range of masculine identities that result from the ways gender intersects with race, class, culture, sexuality and other factors such as geographical location.

Single-sex Schools and the Troubles of Black Boys

Black feminist theory and black gay men's writings have had a significant impact on my research, in particular my work on the Black and Latino Male School Intervention Study (BLMSIS), on which Pedro Noguera is principal investigator and I am a lead researcher. BLMSIS which is based at New York University's Metro Center (http://steinhardt.nyu.edu/metrocenter), aims to assess the curriculum and overall effectiveness of single-sex schools targeting black and Latino male middle and high school students in New York City, Chicago, Dallas, and Atlanta. Single-sex schools aimed at black and Latino males are currently being touted as a promising reform to prepare more black male students for college.

There have been several reform efforts to improve the academic achievement of low-income and minority students, including Head Start preschools, comprehensive school restructuring plans such as Success for All and Accelerated Schools, tutoring, mentoring, and after-school programs (Fashola, 2005). However, more recently, as part of a plan to provide additional opportunities for students to choose a "better" school, the Bush administration lessened Title IX restrictions on single-sex schools (Salomone, 2006). This change renewed interest in establishing single-sex schools within the public school system as a way to address the needs of students who have not been successful in traditional coeducational schools (Hubbard & Datnow, 2005). In part, the interest in single-sex public schools as a solution for low-income students of color is supported by research indicating students' educational experiences vary by gender within and across ethnic groups. For example, Hudley (1995) notes that the safe and orderly nature of sex-segregated programs benefit some African-American boys. Overall, however, research findings are inconclusive, and both educators and policymakers agree that further research is needed (Salomone, 2006).

Despite the inconclusiveness of research findings, single-sex school for black boys has become increasingly popular as a solution to the national problem of black boys' low college enrollment rates and overall academic underachievement (Gewertz, 2007). From the perspective of black feminists and black gay men such Patricia Hill Collins and Joseph Beam, who advocate for more progressive forms of black masculinity, is there reason to believe that single-sex schools are a promising reform? I wonder whether in their efforts to address the troubles of black boys in urban schools, educators in single-sex schools promote the development of progressive black masculinities. More specifically, based on the work of Collins and Beam, I am concerned about whether single-sex schools for black and Latino male students promote dominance or strength and whether they are or are not a "home" for all faculty and students.

These questions highlight the need for critical reflection on the "knowledges" informing the implementation of programs designed to address the educational and social needs of black male students. (Martino, Mills, & Lingard, 2005, p. 250). In "Issues in boys' education: A question of teacher threshold knowledges?" Martino and colleagues use case study data of a junior secondary Australian school to examine what assumptions and knowledge about boys as gendered subjects informed teachers', administrators', and counselors' approaches to teaching, learning, and counseling in the school. Their research revealed that teacher belief systems about boys have a significant impact on the development of a specific program to address their educational needs. The principal appeared to play a crucial role in this process, using a "boy friendly philosophy" (p. 441) to push for an activities-based curriculum that emphasized the pastoral relationship between teacher and student. The authors point out that

> What remains unproblematized in the kinds of discourses informing such a view is an absence of the crucial effects and socializing influences of a particular model of masculinity, which actually encourages many boys to reject the feminine and expressive modes of relating and learning (p. 447).

Like Martino and colleagues, I am concerned with whether teachers and administrators in single-sex schools for black male students are aware of and interrogate the kinds of discourses that inform their views on black masculinities and the ways they might affect the curriculum. For example, a powerful discourse that is routinely mentioned by administrators in the BLMSIS schools is popular entertainment, specifically hip-hop. One administrator I interviewed laments,

> Have nice beats, have nice rhymes, get famous, boom, I can be Jay Z. Or just play ball all the time, be in as many tournaments as possible. You know, try to get my name in the paper, blah, blah, blah, I'll be in the NBA. You know, they think that's what it takes only.

On the one hand, the tone this administrator used to make this quote suggests he is critical of hip-hop discourses because they do not emphasize the importance of education. On the other hand, I question whether this administrator was truly critical of the violent, hyper-masculine models of manhood often employed in hip-hop performances, because later I saw one of the school's black male teacher's aides grab a student by the neck and pull him into the student support room, and his administrator did not interrupt, comment, or critique the incident.

The teacher aide's behavior is an example of the kind of physical dominance Patricia Hill Collins believes we need to abandon in favor of more progressive masculinities. Collins' framework for progressive black masculinities raises several important questions for schools in the BLMSIS, such as "Are school programs a vehicle for reproducing masculinities predicated on dominance, strength, or some combination of the two and with what effects?" For example, several of the schools in the BLMSIS have mentor programs that rely on "professional" black men who are doctors, lawyers, and businessmen as role models. What kind of masculine identities are these men modeling? Are professional masculinities modeled on elite white men to which black boys should aspire? How can urban educators encourage black boys to reject dominance and instead make space for them to craft progressive gender identities not predicated on being successful in a profession that encourages the exploitation of others?

I am also concerned that teachers and administrators may not interrupt the "pecking order" of masculinities expressed by boys, thereby reinforcing stereotypes of black macho as the most viable form of masculinity and making it difficult for boys such as Antoine, David, and Kevin (discussed earlier) who are gender nonconforming. Joseph Beam (1986) said , "I cannot go home as who I am" because he transgressed the hegemonic codes of black masculinity (p. 180). Do all students in the BLMSIS schools feel at home? Urban communities, despite being home to most social-support-education-legal resources for people who identify as lesbian, gay, bisexual, transgender, questioning, or intersex, are also spaces of homophobia. Recently, for example, the superintendent of Newark Public Schools, Marion Bolden, made the executive decision to black out a photo of Andre Jackson, a senior, kissing his boyfriend in the school yearbook. Ms. Bolden said she thought the photo was "suggestive" whereas Jackson said, "I didn't intend to say 'Oh hey look at me, I'm gay.' It was just a picture showing my emotion, saying that I'm happy you know. It was to look back on as a memory." (Fernandez, 2007). In Memphis, Tennessee, principal Daphne Beasley went as far as to make a list of student couples to see who was engaging in "public displays of affection" and, when she came across the names of two gay male students, she "outed them" or disclosed their sexual identity to their parents. One of the outed students, Nicholas, said it was "frightening to see a list with my name on it where not just other teachers could see, but students as well..I really feel that my personal privacy was invaded. I mean, Principal Beasley called my mother and outed me to my mother!"

Given the rampant homophobia in many single-sex schools, behavior that is predicated on certain masculine identities' being valued more than others, it is unlikely that queer youth would consider such single-sex schools home. However, is this even an issue for teachers and administrators in single-sex schools? Not one school of the seven schools in BLMSIS boasts a gay-straight alliance. Not one intentionally addresses issues of sexual identity, gender nonconformity, homophobia, or heterosexism. If single-sex schools are to "reflect and sustain" black boys who embody a range of masculine identities, some more effeminate than others, some homosexual and bisexual and heterosexual, then they must "repave the road home, widening it" so all boys can participate.

Conclusion

The masculinity issues and questions posed by black feminist scholars and black gay male writers should form the basis of a more progressive research agenda for the troubles of black boys and reforms to address those troubles. I have given examples of what a more progressive stance towards black masculinities might look like in my own research on single-sex schools for black and Latino male students when black feminist and black gay male perspectives are taken into account. These perspectives are absent in the literature on black boys' experiences in urban schools, even though they speak to both structural and cultural constraints that produce risk for black male students in urban schools. Incorporating the perspectives of black feminists and black gay men enables urban educators to think of school reforms through an intersectional lens that takes into account the interlocking nature of race, class, gender, and sexuality in the lives of black boys. In doing so, we are one step closer to developing an ethic of responsibility in our research, teaching, and policymaking that is predicated on the belief that there is room for all of us to thrive in urban schools, without any of us being marginalized.

Notes

1. I use the term "black" and "African-American" synonymously as Americans of African descent are nearly equally divided in their preference for either term (Sigelman and Tuch, 2005).
2. This section draws on the Executive Summary of the Black and Latino Male School Intervention Study (BLMSIS) research project based at NYU and funded by the Bill and Melinda Gates Foundation.
3. Both John Ogbu and Signithia Fordham approach issues of academic performance from an anthropological perspective that privileges a cultural frame of reference.

References

Akbar, N. (1991). *Visions for black men*. Nashville, TN: Winston-Derek Publishers

Anzaldua, G. (2007). *Borderlands: The new mestiza = la frontera* (3rd ed.). San Francisco: Aunt Lute Books.

Auerbach, J., Krimgold, B., & Lefkowitz, B. (2000). *Improving health: It doesn't take a revolution*. Washington, DC: National Policy Association.

Beam, J. (1986). *In the life: A black gay anthology*. Boston: Alyson Publications.

Blumstein, A., Rivara, F. P., & Rosenfeld, R. (2000). The rise and decline of homicide—and why. *Annual Review of Public Health, 21,* 505–541.

Boothe, D. (2007). *Why are there so many black men in prison?* Memphis, TN: Full Surface Publishing.

Carnoy, M. (1994). *Faded dreams: The politics and economics of race in America*. New York: Cambridge University Press.

Centers for Disease Control. (2007). Racial/ethnic disparities in diagnoses of HIV/AIDS-33 states, 2001–2005. *Morbidity and Mortality Weekly Report, 56*(09), 189–193.

Coley, R. (2001). *Differences in the gender gap: Comparisons across racial/ethnic groups in education and work*. Princeton, NJ: Educational Testing Service, Policy Information Center.

College Board. (2008). *4th Annual AP report to the nation*. New York: College Board.

Collins, P. H. (2000). *Black feminist thought: Knowledge, consciousness, and the politics of empowerment* (Rev. 10th anniversary ed.). New York: Routledge.

Collins, P. H. (2004). *Black sexual politics: African Americans, gender, and the new racism*. New York & London: Routledge.

Collins, P. H. (2006). A telling difference: Dominance, strength and black masculinities. In A. D. Matua (Ed.), *Progressive black masculinities* (pp. 73–97). New York: Routledge.

Connell, R. (1995). *Masculinities*. Berkeley, CA: University of California Press

Cook, B. J., & Cordova, D. I. (2007). *Minorities in higher education: 22nd annual status report*. Washington DC: American Council on Education.

Davis, J. E. (2001). Transgressing the masculine: African American boys and the failure of shools. In B. Mayeen and W. Martino (Eds.) *What About the Boys? :Issues of Masculinity in School* (pp. 140–153). Buckingham: Open University Press.

Department of Justice. (November, 2006). Prisoners in 2005. *Bureau of Justice Statistics Bulletin, 215092,* 1–12.

Fashola, O. S. (2005). *Educating African American males: Voices from the field*. Thousand Oaks, CA: Corwin Press.

Fernandez, M. (2007, June 24). School officials blackout photo of a gay student's kiss. *New York Times*. Available at http://www.nytimes.com/2007/06/24/education/24yearbook.html

Fordham, S. (1996). *Blacked out: Dilemmas of race, identity, and success at capital high*. Chicago: University of Chicago Press.

Fordham, S., & Ogbu, J. U. (1986). Black students' school success: Coping with the "burden of 'acting white.'" *Urban Review, 18*(3), 176–206.

Frankenberg, E., Lee, C., & Orfield, G. (2003). *A multiracial society with segregated schools: Are we losing the dream?* Cambridge, MA: The Civil Rights Project at Harvard University.

Gewertz, C. (2007). Black boys' educational plight spurs single-gender schools: New federal rules seen as chance for innovation. *Education Week, 26*(42), 1.

Hacker, A. (1992). *Two nations: Black and white, separate, hostile unequal.* New York: Charles Scribner and Sons.

Holzner, H. (2007). *The labor market and young Black men: Updating Moynihan's perspective.* Washington DC: The Urban Institute

Hubbard, L., & Datnow, A. (2005). Do single-sex schools improve the education of low-income and minority students? An investigation of California's public single-gender academies. *Anthropology & Education Quarterly, 36*(2), 115–131.

Hudley, C. A. (1995). Assessing the impact of separate schooling for African American male adolescents. *The Journal of Early Adolescence, 15*(1), 38–57.

Hunter, A. G., & Davis, J. E. (1992). Constructing gender: An exploration of Afro-American men's conceptualization of manhood. *Gender & Society, 6*(3), 464–477.

Jencks, C., & Phillips, M. (1998). *The black-white test scores gap.* Washington, DC: Brookings Institute.

Kirschenman, J., & Neckerman, K. M. (1991). "We'd love to hire them, but …": The meaning of race for employers. In C. Jencks & P. E. Peterson (Eds.), *The urban underclass* (pp. 203–232). Washington, DC: The Brookings Institute.

Martino, W., Mills, M., & Lingard, B. (2005). Interrogating single-sex classes as a strategy for addressing boys' educational and social needs. *Oxford Review of Education, 31*(2), 237–254.

Massey, D., & Denton, N. (1993). *American apartheid.* Cambridge, MA: Harvard University Press.

Meier, K., Stewart, J., & England, R. (1989). *Race, class and education: The politics of second generation discrimination.* Madison: University of Wisconsin Press.

Moss, P., & Tilly, C. (1993). *Raised hurdles for black men: Evidence from interviews with employers.* Working Paper, Department of Policy and Planning. Lowell: University of Massachusetts.

Murray, C. A. (1994). *Losing ground: American social policy, 1950–1980* (10th anniversary ed.). New York: BasicBooks.

National Research Council. (1989). *A common destiny: Blacks and American society.* Washington, DC: National Academy Press.

Noguera, P. A. (2005). *The trouble with black boys: The role and influence of environmental and cultural factors on the academic performance of African American males.* Thousand Oaks, CA: Corwin Press.

Ogbu, J. U. (1983). Minority status and schooling in plural societies. *Comparative Education Review, 27*(2), 168–190.

Ogbu, J. U. (2003). *Black American students in an affluent suburb: A study of academic disengagement.* Mahwah, NJ: Lawrence Erlbaum Associates.

Polite, V. C., & Davis, J. E. (1999). *African American males in school and society: Practices and policies for effective education.* New York: Teachers College Press.

Pollard. D. S. (1993). Gender, achievement and African American students' perceptions of their school experience. *Education Psychologist, 28*(4), 341–356.

Poussaint, A., & Alexander, A. (2000). *Lay my burden down: Unraveling suicide and the mental health crisis among African Americans*. Boston: Beacon Press.

Roberts, D. E. (2004). The social and moral cost of mass incarceration in African American communities. *Stanford Law Review, 54*, 1271–1306.

Roper, W. (1991, May-June). The prevention of minority youth violence must begin despite risks and imperfect understanding. *Public Health Reports, 106*(3), 229–231.

Salomone, R. C. (2006). Single-sex programs: Resolving the research conundrum. *Teachers College Record, 108*(4), 778–802.

Sigelman, L., & Tuch, S. A. (2005). What is a name? Preference for "Black" versus "African American" among Americans of African descent. *Public Opinion Quarterly, 69*(3), 429–438.

Skiba, R. J.(2002). Zero tolerance, zero evidence: An analysis of school disciplinary practice. In R. J. Skiba & G. G. Noam (Eds.), *New directions for youth development* (no. 92: Zero tolerance: Can suspension and expulsion keep schools safe?). San Francisco: Jossey-Bass.

Skolnick, J., & Currie, E. (1994). *Crisis in American institutions*. New York: Harper Collins.

Spivak, H., Prothrow-Stith, D., & Hausman, A. (1988). Dying is no accident. *Pediatric Clinics of North America, 35*(6), 1339–1347.

Wallace, M. (1990). *Black macho and the myth of superwoman*. London & New York: Verso.

Wilson, W. J. (1987). *The truly disadvantaged: The inner city, the underclass, and public policy*. Chicago: University of Chicago Press.

7 The Beer and the Boyz

Masculine Traditions in a Post-Industrial Economy

Anoop Nayak

Introduction

> I see all this potential—and I see it squandered. God damn it—an entire generation pumping gas, waiting tables: slaves with white collars. Advertising has its taste in cars and clothes, working jobs we hate so we can buy shit we don't need. We're the middle children of history, man. No purpose or place. We have no Great War, no Great Depression. Our Great War's a spiritual war. Our Great Depression is our lives. We've all been raised on television to believe that one day we'll be millionaires and movie gods and rock stars, but we won't. We're slowly learning that fact and we're very, very pissed off.
>
> (*Fight Club*, directed by David Fincher, 20th Century Fox, 1999)

The foregoing oratory, uttered by Hollywood actor Brad Pitt cast as the dark overlord of an underground fight club, epitomizes a number of recent concerns regarding the place of young men in Western society. In mainstream media and popular culture, it is tempting to believe that masculinities are in "crisis." Stripped of an industrial heritage and shorn of the heroic accolades attributed to men of war, contemporary masculinities appear as displaced subjectivities, alienated and ridden with insecurity about their purpose and role.

Although cognizant of the impacts that recent transformations have had upon the identities of young men, the populist idea of masculinities in crisis needs further interrogation. In particular, the fantasy that white collar workers—and other, alienated young men—should "discover" their masculinities through embodied acts of acute violence is problematic. On the one hand, it implies that masculinity is a tangible essence that, once released from the starchy rigmarole of polite society, is hell-bent on exerting violent fury. On the other, it suggests that such acts not only afford pleasurable release but are entirely natural. These ideas are little more than the myths of masculinity. It is now widely recognized in academic literature that masculinities are socially constituted phenomenon, they vary over time and place, being nuanced by ethnicity, generation, sexuality, and social class (Connell, 1995; Frosh, Phonix, & Pattman, 2002). Nevertheless, Fincher's engrossing film is symptomatic about the "new times" in which many young white men are growing up. For it asks, how do "boyz" become "men" in a post-industrial world filled with table-waiting jobs, public administration, bar work, call centers, and humdrum service sector employment?

In response, this chapter seeks to understand the historical, structural, and cultural changes that have impinged upon young men's labor market aspirations. In particular it explores interconnections between what Ball (1987) has called the "micro-politics" of schooling and the macro-processes of recent social and economic transformations. The study begins with a brief review discussing the changing nature of youth transitions in late-modernity. It highlights the increasingly fragile, complex, and contradictory choices open to young men as they seek to make the transition from formal education to the world of work. Preceding the ethnography, I then describe the changing economic geography of the study area, Northeast England, which has witnessed profound de-industrialization. More recently, the locale has seen an investment in cultural industries and the development of a burgeoning service sector economy. The re-branding of the region is palpable where a locality once famed for coal mining it now renowned for "clubbing." It would appear that hedonism has replaced heavy industry.

The ethnography focuses upon a group of young white men from skilled working-class backgrounds. It argues that the legacy of labor, distilled over successive generations, forms a "sticky" cultural residue that cannot be erased overnight from their identities. Instead, such "social sediments" are the dense accumulation of local cultures, familial values, working-class traditions, community histories, and school counter-cultures. The study explores the complex dissonance that exists between this popular "circuit of cultural production," the formal education system and the changing economic job market. To gain deeper insight into the "structural" and "cultural" processes of transition, the research investigates the role of drinking cultures and their relationship to what are evidently gendered, social class histories. Developing the work of Connell (1995), I go on to consider drinking as a "body-reflexive practice" through which the industrial past and the post-industrial future are materially and symbolically negotiated. For it is within the closed arena of "circuit-drinking" that the embodied spectacle of masculine excess is produced, performed, and exhibited. The cultural studies approach to drinking is then supplemented with an analysis exploring how "felt" attachments to industry are sustained in the post-industrial period.

New Youth Transitions[1]

For young white working-class men residing in the Western hemisphere, the transition to manhood was once inextricably linked to the movement from school to work. In the British postwar period, manufacturing employment was seen to offer viable, if restricted, opportunities for working-class males. However monotonous this work was, it was seen to provide the material benefits of regular pay, stability, security, and a "job for life." Within the complex registers of masculinity, industrial employment also accrued its own type of cultural capital, forged through notions of the patriarchal "breadwinner," physical "hardness," and a strict sexual division of labor that split the public "masculine" world of work from the private domestic realm of women's unpaid labor. For many young men, the financial independence ascribed to earning a wage enabled them to vacate household duties and instill a pride in either "craft" or "graft."

However, as de-industrialization began to set in, young men were increasingly less likely to be "learning to labor," as the title of Paul Willis's (1977) enduring ethnography previously suggested. Instead, working-class boys were caught in the uncertain transition that accompanied ill-paid, poorly structured government training schemes or, quite simply, were left "schooling for the dole" (Bates, 1984). For many working-class youth, this left a stark choice between what Coffield, Borril, & Marshall, (1986) matter-of-factly identify as "Shit jobs and Govvy schemes" (p. 86).

Recently the dearth of manufacturing jobs in Western nation states has in part been supplemented by an expanding service sector economy and the urban regeneration of old industrial quarters. Though this has seen an increase in youth participation in the labor market, this new shift is characterized by more casual forms of labor, marked especially by part-time working hours, fixed-term contracts, more "flexible" patterns of employment and, at least for EU countries, pay scales that barely hover above the minimum wage. At structural and cultural levels, then, the "pathways" open to young men as they attempt to make the transition to adulthood and the world of work are rapidly changing yet increasingly individualized. Chatterton and Hollands reflect upon the range of new, sometimes unaccomplished, transitions:

> The post-Fordist labour market has not only worked to delay and interrupt traditional youth transitions, but it has also worked to complexify them. Young people today make a bewildering array of labor market transitions, including moving through various training and educational routes through to temporary, contract and part-time work, and in some cases to secure employment (2003, p. 81).

Thus, though young working-class men are more likely to be "learning to serve" (McDowell, 2000) rather than "learning to labor," this has given way to new masculine subject positions that are highly contradictory. In the post-industrial period, contemporary masculine transitions continue to be marked by opportunity, "risk," uncertainty, and labor market insecurity (Vail, Wheelock, & Hill, 1999). However, rather than leading to the collapse of social class distinctions, theorists such as Ulrich Beck (1998, p. 35) argue that such "risks seem to *strengthen*, not to abolish the class society" in late-modernity. It is within these new times that young men are pursuing multiple, fragmented, or unaccomplished transitions. This includes complex, fractured, and "insecure transitions" (MacDonald, 1999. p. 171) mediating across school-work, local-global, boyhood-manhood, and so forth.

To elucidate the impact that recent transformations are having upon masculine identities, I draw upon material generated from ethnographic research conducted in school, neighborhood, and city-center sites. The ethnography combines three different methods: principally, *participant observation* of young men's daily lives in multiple settings. The aim is to investigate not only what respondents say they do (words) but to examine further what they actually do (deeds). It is suggested that by moving between talk/action, representation/presentation, and the discursive/embodied, we can enable a more comprehensive account of masculinities to emerge. Second, I utilize data derived from *semi-structured interviews* with young men that occurred in focus group settings and face-to-face interaction. Third, I draw upon *"thick" description* of people, places, and life events. In particular, this includes the use of local history and personal biographies. Finally, the ethnographic approach is complemented with historical, theoretical, and cultural analyses of education institutions, the labor market, and the leisure sphere.

From Coal Mines to "Clubbing": The Economic History of North East England

The Northeast of England is a region historically rich in economic resources and has long been associated with ship-building, coal mining, and heavy engineering. Even by 1961, the region employed double the number of workers in these industries than any other place in the country. Unlike many U.K. regions containing prominent port cities, the North East was less reliant upon established colonial trading links. Indeed, it has been suggested that there was even the potential for a hegemonic "genuine local ruling class" (Massey, 1995a, p. 194) to emerge. The mineral-based economy of coal mining, or what Hudson eloquently terms "carboniferous capital" (2000, p. 31), enabled the region to prosper throughout the nineteenth century, during the war periods, and well into the postwar era. Indeed, at one point, one-fourth of the nation's coal came from the Gibside district alone. By the end of the First World War, some 78,000 people worked for the ammunitions company Armstrong Whitworth, one of the largest employers in the area, making iron and high-quality steel for guns, armaments, battleships, hydraulics, and fuse-making facilities. Around this core industry grew lighter industries, workshops, and smaller stores distributing nuts, screws, bolts, springs, barrels, and a plethora of engineering machinery. Even by the 1970s, 40% of employment was still based in the manufacturing and primary industries of the area.

However, this picture was to change with a succession of pit closures in the 1980s to the extent that there is just one last remaining colliery. The once internationally renowned shipbuilding industry is today severely streamlined. This process of economic restructuring had been instigated by the demands of a competitive global economy, poor management, disinvestment, and overcapacity in the market. It was also tied to a ruthless New Right agenda to shut down pits, quash the old Labourite National Union of Miners, and invest in business rather than manufacturing. As the North-South regional divide intensified, the loss of local manufacturing, mining, and shipbuilding industries not only affected those made redundant at the time. Future generations of young men whose cultural worlds would once have been educationally shaped through a prism of schooling, training schemes, modern apprenticeships, and hard labor were now finding themselves viewed as unskilled, unemployable, redundant youth.

Despite the scale of these economic changes, the North East has more recently been re-branded. Traditionally associated with unions, cloth caps, leek growing, working-men's clubs, dog racing, and fog on the Tyne, the image of the region has since been radically transformed. From its representation as a bleak post-industrial area, the North East, and, in particular, its principal city Newcastle upon Tyne is now portrayed as a site for excessive drinking, partying, and wild stag and hen nights. An oft-sited report by Weismann Travel, a Texas-based travel consultant, remarkably declared the city to have the eighth best nightlife on the planet. The "Party City," as Newcastle is popularly termed, became a celebrated image used to promote the joint Newcastle and Gateshead European City of Culture bid of 2003, primarily through the slogan "feel the buzz." At the same time, there has been heavy investment in tourism, waterfront developments, the arts, and new cultural industries. In particular, this includes the building of the Millennium Bridge, the Regional Music Centre, as well as Baltic, an expansive arts centre designed in the former Gateshead flour mill. As the traditional "masculine" infrastructure has depleted, it has been replaced, then, by new developments, especially clubs, restaurants, and café bars in what amounts to the creation of a vibrant night-time economy (Chatterton & Hollands, 2001; Hollands, 1997).

However, this shift from coal mining to "clubbing" has had a profound affect upon the material landscape and the formation of local identities. In particular, processes of gender cannot be set apart from economic restructuring but instead are embedded within the restructuring process itself (Halford & Savage, 1997). Thus, the growth in a "soft economy" centered upon services, catering, and call-center work has transformed the region's economic base and at the same time led to significant gender transformations in the labor market. The so-called "feminization" of labor means that women now make up around 50 percent of the work force in a region where male employment has fallen. Although more than a third of these women work part-time, female employment has rarely been so high. Their willingness to service customers and work flexible hours, combined with the absence of a recalcitrant trade union history, has enabled young women to gain a smoother passage into this labor sector.

In contrast, as a number of education studies have shown, the bodies of working-class young men may be seen as "troublesome," nonconformist, and marked by resistance (Cohen, 1997; Corrigan, 1979; Hargreaves, Hestor, & Mellor, 1975; Willis, 1977). As a carrier of signals and a dense economy of signs, it has been stated that "the body is the most ubiquitous signifier of class" (Skeggs, 1997, p. 82). Moreover, young men may also be unwilling to surrender any real or imagined bodily capital they may accrue through physical toughness. As such, it is quite possible that they are guilty of treating part-time work, customer relations, and servicing in a disparaging manner. Regardless, figures for 1996 reveal that 40 percent of young men aged 16 to 24 years were likely to be seeking work, nearly double the rate of their female counterparts (Chatterton & Hollands, 2001, p. 7). In a culture where the supposedly "feminized" attributes of "deference and docility" (McDowell, 2002, p. 40) are in demand, it would appear that certain white working-class males may be out of step with an economy that values flexibility, keyboard proficiency, telephone communication skills, and personal presentation.[2] Post-industrial masculinities must now adapt, risk unemployment, or indulge in underground activity and criminal hyper-masculine displays (Campbell 1993; Nayak 2003a).

Local Lads and the Legacy of Labor

In his epic study of the history of English occupational relations, E.P. Thompson encourages us to move beyond monolithic conceptualizations. The phrase "Working classes," declares Thompson, "is a descriptive term which evades as much as it defines" (1982, p. 8). Thus, the historian goes on to emphasize the plurality of laboring styles harbored beneath this opaque label "working class." Writing about the industrial period, he notes how the concept "ties loosely together a bundle of discrete phenomena" (ibid) which in actuality comprise a variety of distinct laboring cultures, traditions, histories, and status markers. Here, I focus upon what is sometimes broadly portrayed as the "respectable" working class whose values are depicted as clean, thrifty, skilled, and upwardly mobile. Research with this cohort was undertaken as they displayed a staunch local pride and a white working-class masculinity that were generally resistance to change. Once regarded as prodigious workers, arguably it is this social stratum that is today most acutely experiencing post-industrial transformations.

The young men in this study are white working-class youth aged 16 years, all born and raised in the Northeast of England. The core members comprise Jason, Shaun, Steve, Filo, Carl, Fat Mal, Dave, Cambo, Duane, and Spencer, although others, including Jono and Bill, occasionally joined the group.[3] In a statement of regional pride, the respondents describe themselves as *Real Geordies*, that is, local lads who "tek nae shit" (Filo), "give as good as we get" (Duane), and, "kna who we are at the end of the day" (Cambo). Although the term *Geordie* has contested origins, it is associated with the parts of the locality and, among other definitions, is said to be the name given to coalminers, or possibly a nickname for George Stephenson's pit safety lamp (Colls & Lancaster, 1992, p. x). The question remains, then: If the Real Geordies could no longer be "Real" in the true occupational sense of the word, how exactly is this identity being performed and for what purpose is it being resuscitated? As we shall find, it is through working-class traditions such as "circuit-drinking" that a local, white masculine identity is being preserved, recuperated, and ultimately refashioned.

A prominent masculine legacy of manual labor ran through the familial biographies of these young men. With few exceptions, all spoke of fathers, uncles, and grandfathers who had developed specialist skills refined as sheet-metal workers, construction workers, offshore operators, glaziers, fitters, and mechanics. However, some members came from backgrounds where the tradition of manual labor had been sustained through the heavy industries of engineering, coal mining, and dock work. A smaller fraction also came from families connected to small businesses, including Jason's dad, who ran a fish stall in North Shields; Jono's dad, who was a cab driver for a local taxi firm; and Shaun's father, who was a publican. Even so, these individuals shared the same subcultural status as their peers and also had male relatives with an established tradition of hard manual labor in the North East. For these "local lads," the relationship between political economy and masculine subcultural status is implicitly one in which, "occupation serves as a mutual identification pattern" (Beck, 1998, p. 140). Aside from Carl, each of the *Real Geordies* came from families who were now classified as owner-occupiers, having purchased properties in the North East housing chain. As such, they can be distinguished from the unemployed "underclass" discussed by Campbell (1993) in that they were enmeshed in what has been described as a "culture of respectable familialism" (Skeggs, 1997, p. 63).

Indeed, the *Real Geordies* would at one time have formed the "aristocracy of labor" (Gray, 1981). This masculine heritage involved an element of craftwork in which laboring skills and techniques were acquired through apprenticeships and tutoring schemes. Skilled and semi-skilled occupations related to the construction industry and the higher echelons of the manufacturing economy liberally peppered their familial biographies. Cambo, Dave, Carl, and Spencer had fathers and elder brothers who were employed in recognized trades, including that of plumbers, plasterers, tilers, joiners, "brickies," and glaziers. Duane hoped to become a car mechanic like his father; Filo's dad had worked as a docker before gaining an engineering qualification that enabled him to fit and repair central heating boilers; Steve said his dad was a "sparky" (a skilled electrician); Fat Mal's was a foreman in a factory; and Bill's father was reputed to have a lucrative job in a sheet-metal plant. All of the young men lived at home at the time of the research, though a number had jobs to supplement what appeared an active social life. This work included part-time jobs such as working in petrol stations, supermarkets, fast-food chains, daily paper rounds, paid domestic labor, and casual work for friends and relatives when such opportunities arose. Although many had acquired work, there is a qualitative distinction between the types of work and education available to *Real Geordies* and those of their forefathers.

The Curriculum of the Body: Education, Labor and Society

> What actually does take place when in the course of historical development the identity of social classes rooted in the lifeworld melts away? When, on the one hand, the conditions and risks of wage labor become *generalized* and, on the other, *class loses its subcultural basis and is no longer experienced*?
>
> (Beck, 1998, p. 98)

Though the concept of "Geordie" has changed over time, the identity prevails despite the closure of collieries in the North East. We would be mistaken in believing that, because the *Real Geordies* could never be "Real" in the true occupational sense, a number of symbolic associations did not take place. As Cohen remarks, "Growing up working-class has for many meant an apprenticeship to such an inheritance—a patrimony of skill entailed in the body and its techniques, forging a quasi-congenital link between origins and destinies" (1997, p. 205). In this respect, scholarly prowess, desk work, and mental labor were viewed by the *Real Geordies* as "soft" and, in some cases, in conflict with their lived cultural habitus. Thus, young men labeled "stiffs," "boffs," and "anoraks" were widely disparaged by the *Real Geordies* as subordinate masculinities (Nayak, 2003b). They were described to me as "arse-lickers" (Duane) and "brown-nosers" (Jono) who "creep to the teachers and like reely suck up to them" (Carl). Even so, consistent underachievers at the lower end of educational performance were identified as "thickos" or "charvers" and regarded as equally detestable (Nayak, 2003a).

When it came to the world of labor, the *Real Geordies* were neither "work shy" nor "lazy," as some members of staff had claimed, nor were they devoid of employment strategies. Instead, they were negotiating various life-paths that would *preserve* rather than eradicate their subcultural allegiance to football, drinking, and going out. There is, then, a cultural dissonance between schooling and the laboring histories from which these young men descended. Inevitably, extending their education by entering into further/higher education (FE/HE) is not without consequences. According to Beck, "As schooling increases in duration, traditional orientations, ways of thinking, and lifestyles are recast and displaced" (1998, 93), so altering the landscape of working-class masculinities. It was still the case that such school activities tended to be treated with a degree of skepticism, unless directly related to a trade. The recent introduction of university student fees may further delay or curtail decisions to continue education. Indeed, some deemed it made little sense to apply oneself academically when reputations could be more quickly established within the accepted registers of working-class masculinity that valued strength, loyalty, humor, and physical stature. To this extent, in the North East region, "The legacy of a culture of waged labor has thus proved highly resistant to change" (Hudson, 2000, p. 82). Instead, for many working-class males, the post-industrial period has witnessed the surrender of lifelong labor with a company, firm, or factory, meaning that the socially cultivated attributes of the *Real Geordies*—loyalty, hard graft, and routine—would now go unappreciated.

In the main, the *Real Geordies* had already rejected the upwardly mobile passage into FE/HE, careers, and deskwork. However, this did not mean they had rejected the work ethic itself. Steve may have been exceptional in that he viewed A-levels as a means to improve his chances of working in a bank. Moreover, he spoke discretely to me about considering options for HE. Also, Duane wanted to do a higher national diploma in mechanical engineering at a local college, whereas a number of others showed preferences for vocational training courses including those related to the new microelectronic industries. Others such as Filo had learned much about fitting boilers from his father but at present lacked approved qualifications. Similarly, Cambo frequently speculated that there was "stacks" to be made in building conservatories but was unsure quite how to put this plan into action. Carl and Jason, meanwhile, wanted to extend their current part-time employment in the service sector at least until they had reached firmer decisions about their future. They felt assured in the knowledge that while such work meant it remained financially difficult to leave the parental home, employment offered them the opportunities to work a regular "nine-to-five" shift and the possibilities of future managerial training. This temporary lifestyle would also enable them to maintain subcultural affiliations based on a commitment to "birds, booze and a fuckin' nite oot once in a while!" (Jason). Consequently, they saw little point in saving money and were determined to spend what they earned on clothes, drink, music, football, and what Carl termed "living for the weekend." This suggests a more elastic, elongated set of youth transitions, in which the networks of kinship and family still continue to offer stability in uncertain times (Hollands, 1997; MacDonald et al., 2000). There is also evidence here of some diverse, yet culturally patterned pathways into work, alongside the bold recognition that "class does not disappear just because traditional ways of life fade away" (Beck, 1998: 99; see also Delamont, 2001).

Despite large-scale transformations in the manufacturing base, the participants exuded a self-righteous confidence in the face of the prevailing bleak economic situation. They also retained a locally specific investment in the declining regional work-based activities of mining, shipping, and steel-related industries in what is now a period of increased fragmentation and globalization. As a birthright, these symbols of industry retain a privileged place in the psychic economy of this particular subculture, though the "anatomy of labor" is now being displaced into other cultural activities, as we shall go on to find. The empty space left by de-industrialization is thereby filled by the "hereditary" promise of a white manhood that can be reiterated in other social arenas. That the subculture remained deeply nostalgic about a period they have never experienced did not lessen their sense of estrangement; indeed, their actions continue to be encased in the mythical traditions of a former era. The fictitious relationship the *Real Geordies* have with the former world of manual labor meant that they were continually recasting the past as an "imagined community" (Anderson, 1984). In the contemporary moment, the *Real Geordies* were men out of time, the unreconstructed outsiders-within whose claim to regional authenticity remained forever symbolic.

Body-reflexive Practices: Drinking and Going Out

> Perhaps that is all there is left of white working-class culture when you take the work away: football and beer. [...] It seemed to me a celebration of nothingness.
>
> (Darcus Howe, *White Tribe*, Channel 4, January 13, 2000)

Drinking culture remains firmly tied to the North East industrial heritage. Today pubs with names such as The Baltic Tavern, The Free Trade, The Ship Inn, and Offshore 44 testify to the working-class ancestry of shipping, trade and labor upon the River Tyne. Bean (1971, p. 97) has previously alluded to other pubs such as "the Hydraulic Crane, the Rifle, the Gun, the Ordanance Arms, the Forge Hammer, the Crooked Billet, the Moulders Arms, the Mechanics Arms, the Shipwrights Hotel, the Vulcan, the Blast Furnace" as further examples of industrial ties. Elsewhere, he compares the former row of drinking establishments nearby a cluster of Armstrong's engineering traders to "a chain of industrial oases" (1980, p.5). However, as most residual pubs have now either vanished or come under new ownership in the post-industrial context, the connections between drinking and work have been spatially and culturally displaced. Whereas young men's initiation into drinking culture in the region had occurred through the rites of passage derived from manual labor and the father-son rituals soon to be cemented in the workingmen's club (Coffield et al., 1986), this is no longer the case. Indeed, local drinks such as Exhibition Ale (named after the Great Exhibition in Newcastle), Newcastle Brown, and "worky-ticket," a term that derives from factory life and refers to the act of tinkering with your clocking-in and clocking-off card (hence, working-your-ticket) are a declining part of the youth drinking market. These community histories provide an interpretative backcloth against which new drinking cultures are being produced in which young women are no longer marginalized participants as discussed in recent press reports of "ladettes".[4]

The *Real Geordies* dressed in expensively tailored designer shirts. The acquisition of these garments—discussed at length informally in school—on the street allowed them to embody the veneer of "respectability." With their smart haircuts and designer gear, the group could be seen to resist popular representations of working-class masculinities as "mad, bad or dangerous." As Skeggs has shown, such cultural representations "are not straightforwardly reproduced but are resisted and transfigured in their daily enactment" (1997, p. 6). Even so, in their pursuit of high fashion, the *Real Geordies* evinced their working-class roots through the desire to belong, be legitimated, and gain acceptance. Although they despised school uniforms, they had reproduced a uniform of their own that was as smart, conservative, and functional as anything the school had to offer. The promise of exclusivity, individuality, and respectability accorded to designer clothing is, then, subsequently undermined when said items become a mainstream dimension of working-class masculinities.

On nights out, the *Real Geordies* would pass through a series of pubs usually having just one drink in each as they linked up with other members to form a chain for circuit-drinking. This hedonistic display allowed them to be seen in a number of public places and so belied the appearance that money could be a meager resource.[5] Furthermore, the circuit ritual enabled those who missed the preliminary meeting place to join the chain at another venue. Circuit-drinking remained, then, a highly regulated activity forged through familiar rituals and routine practices. The *Real Geordies* all dressed in subtle variations of a recognized style, and they knew which pubs would be frequented and in exactly which spots the others could be found; at all times, they never lost sight of whose turn it was to get the drinking round in. Moreover, they had a detailed knowledge of the price of drinks in corresponding venues and, on special week days (e.g. to mark the end of exams or a birthday celebration), were able to map out their drinking circuit to take advantage of "happy hours," "two-for-one" offers, and the like. Bottled lagers and vodka-mixers were favored at the time of the research as they allowed the "lads" to encompass a larger drinking territory than would otherwise have been possible if pints were drunk at each establishment. New places were always given a try, assessed accordingly, and subsequently incorporated or rejected from future drinking routes. Favorite "watering holes" include those with a club style atmosphere where DJs played loud house and chart music. Visiting a number of venues provided a structure for the evening, offering variety and allowing the group to have a heightened public display in the city center.

Moreover, circuit-drinking appeared to increase the potential of "funny happenings" and, as Canaan (1996) shows, allowed for greater risk-taking among young working-class men. It can also be seen as a modern-day reenactment of the earlier past-time of promenading. In this way, the subculture recuperated older forms of an industrial white masculine culture through collective rituals related to male drinking, fighting, football, and sexual conquest. As Connell explains, these actions can be understood as "body-reflexive practices" that are not biologically inherent to individuals. Rather,

> They involve social relations and symbolism; they may well involve large-scale social institutions. Particular versions of masculinity are constituted in their circuits as meaningful bodies and embodied meanings. Through body-reflexive practices, more than individual lives are formed: a social world is formed (1995, p. 64).

Drinking, swearing, and physical horseplay are more than simply the epidermal outer-skin of white masculinity. Thus, "funny stories" referring to passing out, throwing up, or acting completely out of character when under the influence of alcohol were reported—such as the time Filo insisted on urinating from the Tyne Bridge and ended up with "pissed-streaked troowsers!" or the occasion when Fat Mal ruined his best silk shirt when he fell asleep on top of his kebab and chili sauce after a heavy night out with the "lads," and so on and so forth. The *Real Geordies* appeared to derive great satisfaction from relating humorous events, sexual narratives, and tales of casual, "funny" violence (see Nayak & Kehily, 2001, for discussion). Indeed, these shared stories served to bind the group together and provided them with a sense of collective history and mutual experience.

As these "body-reflexive practices" were habitual and appeared to fashion their culturally understood life worlds, it is worth reflecting on at least one incident from the ethnography. On an unplanned night out with the *Real Geordies*, I saw how such masculine "body-reflexive practices" could enable the consolidation of a mutually understood social world and provide ammunition for further narration. Outside a chip-shop, we encountered a raucous crowd of Bigg Market "lasses" who taunted us with a colloquial rhyme, "Buy us some chips, and you can feel me greasy tits!" High spirits instigated a scene wherein Steve and Spencer were attempting to nibble chips from the cleavage of two giggling "lasses" while a boisterous food fight erupted between the others, as a set of sheepish customers looked on. As a consequence, we were barred from the chip-shop but, for the *Real Geordies*, "It wor worth it" (Duane) as, "It were a *reet* laff mon" (Cambo), and "We even got a bit of breast with wor chips!" (Steve).[6] In the absence of a regular wage, such masculine exhibitionism appeared to be of pronounced symbolic importance. It enabled the subculture to displace, and so retain the occupational meaning of "Geordie" in the dead-zone of industrial inactivity. These body-reflexive practices also provided the group with a repertoire of narratives to further augment their investments in the culture of "hard" labor. Evidently the *Real Geordies* were nostalgic about a time they had never experienced. In this respect, it is not past events themselves that are of significance, whether they are real, exaggerated, or simply fabricated. It is the emotional investments and cultural resonance achieved in embodying a white working-class masculinity.

Despite changes to the manufacturing base, the *Real Geordies* maintain "felt" investments in the traditional basis of working-class culture. These emotions are present in their nostalgic affection for the region; the emphasis on male drinking pursuits; a heavy, physical humor; the smattering of stories about fighting and sexual exploits; and the abundant parochial conservatism that colored much of their opinions on gender, sexuality, and ethnicity. The spirit of white masculine excess is very much alive in body-reflexive practices such as "gettin' mortal" (drunk) (Shaun), playing and watching football and, somewhat predictably, "shaggin"! (Carl). These techniques allow the anatomy of white male labor to be reconfigured where "Body-reflexive practices form—and are formed by— structures that have historical weight and solidity" (Connell, 1995, p. 65). This "historical solidity" can be found in routines, rituals, and working-class traditions. Indeed, the corporate branding of Newcastle as a "Party

City" is itself a material and discursive redeployment of local traditions. As Massey (1995b, p. 49) has noted, "traditions" are often themselves hard to grasp in an increasingly globalized world and may be reduced to the "commodified," "pastiche," "often romanticized," and "partially illusory" presentations." A regional example of this is the Beamish museum where industrial heritage is transformed into spectacle for modern-day consumption. Nevertheless the reenactment of "traditions" needs to be situated alongside the "risk" and uncertainty of the global economy, the fragmentation of labor markets, and the upheaval experienced by locally embedded communities.

Critically, the meaning of *Geordie* is now no longer about *production* (the colliery, shipyard, or factory) but is seemingly displaced into the arena of *consumption* (football, drinking, and going out) (Nayak, 2003a, 2003b). Lacking advanced qualifications, social mobility, and solid training experience, the task of securing stable employment would not be easy for the *Real Geordies*. The extent to which subcultural practices can retain their "magical" properties of recuperation in the adult world now remains especially problematic.

Industrial Masculinities and Structures of Feeling

In the absence of lifelong labor, the *Real Geordies* appear to be enacting the unspoken traces of a former occupational culture that is socially embedded in familial biographies and shared regional peer-group values. Thus, though the collapse of traditional apprentice schemes may have affected the *Real Geordies* most markedly in view of their familial labor histories, it had not dislodged their *investments* in an industrial lineage and the anatomy of labor.[7] In this sense, it would be wrong to assume that, just because the *Real Geordies* benefit from their gendered and ethnic status as young white men, which they undoubtedly do on occasion, this means that they necessarily occupy a "dominant hegemonic masculinity" (Connell, 1995). As Connell has shown, masculinity comprises an amalgam of configurations that are dynamic, changing, and always in flux. As peripheral working-class youth, the *Real Geordies* may enjoy power in some circumstances, but this hardly compares to a tightly marshaled, institutionally organized, and effective hegemony.

Rather, the young men's habitation of post-industrial masculinities is far more fragile and tenuous and thus bound to the hyperbolic exhibitions we have witnessed. Importantly, their masculine identities are threaded through a range of different value systems whereby they come to take up a varied currency in what is a changing gender market. This includes the divergent status that is accorded to the *Real Geordies* in school, at home, on the street, at football matches, and working on the margins of the service economy. In many ways, rather than being part of a dominant group who exercise control over their conditions of existence, they were in an economically subordinate situation, having to respond to the changes that lay ahead. As such, they come closer to what Raymond Williams (1985) describes as a "residual culture," hanging on to a disappearing past they have yet to relinquish. At the same time, it seems to me that the *Real Geordies* cannot be dismissed as powerless, "failing boys," the standard discourse that has arisen to depict young men's recent educational attainments in relation to their female counterparts. As a number of educationalists have demonstrated, the media propagation of boys as new gender victims is unhelpful and serves to obfuscate the achievements of boys as well as girls in school (Epstein, Elwood, Hey, & Maw, 1998; Foster, Kimmel, & Skelton, 2001). Furthermore, the young men I observed did not see themselves as "failures" or "crisis-ridden" and would have been offended to be depicted in this uni-dimensional, class-laden manner (see Skeggs, 2004).

Instead, the resilience of an industrial masculinity in the post-industrial moment provides an important lens through which to view the social life worlds of the *Real Geordies* and their positions within it. This is evident in work carried out in other post-industrial Northern English cities. Consider for example Sheffield— once famous for steel and coal—whose new economic transformations are neatly captured in the film *The Full Monty*. Here, former male laborers devoid of occupations are compelled to dance, strip, and perform for women in what amounts to a historic, material, and symbolic act of role reversal. Their bodies become the only remaining capital they have to sell as self-respect and dignity give way to (bare) economic necessity. Most poignantly, the nakedness of the men comes to symbolize the extent to which they have been stripped of an industrial heritage. Taylor and Jamieson's (1996) study of young men in the "city of steel" also remarks on the fond remembrance attributed to former apprenticeship schemes. It reveals how becoming a "Little Mester," that is the "master cutler," is an identity symbolically carried by contemporary generations of young men and deployed as a "protest" form of masculinity. The authors point out that though masculinity is recognized as closely tied to the concept of labor, unemployment does not entail "the sudden and total evacuation of men from the *symbolic terrain* of work, or the loss of work references in the discursive construction of hegemonic forms of masculinity" (1996, p. 166). Rather, these imaginary points of identification with manual, lifelong occupational culture are historically and culturally embedded in the performance of working-class masculinities (as witnessed in the film, *Brassed Off*). Similarly, a North East regional trainer I interviewed from the microelectronics industry disclosed a key barrier he encountered when trying to establish college courses that would lead into technical employment. "There's very much a pit mentality in-bred into young people here," he solemnly reflected, indicating the perseverance of lived cultural histories and the failure of certain retraining initiatives.

Despite evidence of an industrial hangover, there can be no escaping the fact that the *Real Geordies* are on the cusp of change, caught in the flux of transition and negotiating felt and understood pathways through it. They do not echo the industrial past entirely but adapt their responses as they see fit. This involves the creation of new drinking traditions in which women are very much a feature of the night-time economy. According to household studies undertaken in the region, there is also evidence of changing expectations of men's and women's work, at least some rearrangement of the sexual division of labor and an increasing awareness of delayed transitions as young people extend their period of stay in the familial home (Hollands, 1997; Wheelock, 1994). To this extent, Geordie identity is not being erased but is revitalized in new practices that at once draw upon, but magically reconfigure, industrial culture. Raymond Williams (1973) remarks on these complex, social class and leisure characteristics:

> ... the new generation responds in its own ways to the unique world it is inheriting, taking up many continuities, that can be traced, and reproducing many aspects of the organization, which can be separately described, yet feeling its whole life in certain ways differently, and shaping its creative response into a new structure of feeling (p. 65).

In this sense, the *Real Geordies* were managing a "structure of feeling" that intersected with their educational aspirations, cultural values, and leisure pursuits. It is evident that social class, which is rarely referred to directly, operates as a "structuring absence" (Skeggs, 1997:74) in their lives, permeating their aspirations, social activities, and broader value systems. Here, the long shadow of an industrial past that celebrated full employment, continuity, and a strict sexual division of labor cast itself darkly upon the exaggerated performances of the *Real Geordies*. The identification with a "golden past" enabled the *Real Geordies* to construe themselves as the eternal "backbone of the nation" salt-of-the-earth natives whom had failed to inherit an industrial heritage that was rightfully theirs.

Closing Remarks

This chapter on young masculinities has sought to interconnect education with labor market transitions and cultural practices. In doing so, it has shown how masculine identities are constituted through competing values and in a multiple configuration of sites. Here, it seems that local history, working-class traditions, leisure routines, and the culture of work influence the construction and performance of masculine identity. For young working-class men, a pertinent question concerns how useful it is to invest in an industrial masculinity that privileges drinking, "hardness," and a stubborn resistance to change, in what is increasingly a de-industrialized period. Certainly there is evidence to suggest that young men may accrue a "bodily capital" that has some use-value on the street, football terraces, or public house. However, shared bodily capital is rarely a substitute for labor, domestic independence, and long-term financial security. It may also militate against the new enterprise culture that prioritizes individuality, flexibility, and subservience to authority (Nayak, 2003b). With regard to the insecure times of the service sector, an investment in collective local identities, older past-times and "body-reflexive practices" can be a way of negotiating change. What was once read as resistance, then, may now come to mark the embodied formulation of a posture in retreat.

These findings also have a number of implications for educators and those working with young men. It demonstrates a need to embed school policies on gender within the local cultures and regional histories of a community. To do otherwise can only serve to imply that masculinities are asocial phenomena disconnected from the axes of time and place. The failure to account for historical context may even lead to new forms of resistance and a feminist "backlash" through the entrenchment of an old, industrial, and acutely localized white masculinity. The task for teachers is, then, to open up young men to the myriad of different, changing forms of masculine identity. This may entail rethinking what it is to be a "man" by drawing closer attention to the multiple styles of masculinity and the effects these cultural habitations have upon self and others (Frosh et al., 2002; Martino, 1995; 2001).

Exhibiting and validating a proliferation of masculine styles may at least provide young men with a greater sense of agency as they navigate the pressing structures of the social world. For all its insecurities, late-modernity does offer new ways of doing gender. For if young men are to transform their subjectivities, appropriate alternatives must be found toward which they can feel a genuine cultural affinity. Inabilities to elicit new subject positions may only serve to produce the "angry young men" feminist scholars identify (Campbell, 1993), or the displaced service sector slaves graphically depicted in *Fight Club*. Pedagogic practitioners seeking to open up debate may find it fruitful to rework the film's strap-line, thus: Lesson one: The first rule about masculinity is—there is no masculinity.

Notes

1. The term *youth transitions* is used here in a critical and reflexive manner. It does not imply a compartmentalized series of "growing" stages from youth to adulthood but the recognition of all identities as socially constituted, overlapping, and changing. The term has also been critiqued for appearing

mechanistic and, in terms of its focus upon the public world of labor markets, somewhat masculinist. However, the concept is discussed here as it remains theoretically useful for an analysis of the interplay between socio-economic structures and cultural identities. For a particularly robust defense of this terminology, see (MacDonald et al., 2000).

2. At the time of writing, a number of telephone call-center jobs that once flourished in the North East are now being outsourced to India where a highly qualified, cheap labor source exists. This illustrates the precarious nature of services and call-center work.

3. Names have been changed to protect the identities of individuals.

4. See for example Anna Ralph in the Newcastle paper *The Journal*, "Mummy returns from her big night." June 21, 2001, p.11.

5. To facilitate under-age drinking, certain bars that were renowned for younger-age drinkers were frequented. Another trick to bypass wary doormen was to enter with a group of young women, "Cos the bouncers neva turn lasses away—not in a group anyway" (Shaun).

6. Such "hyper-masculine" displays could at times present tensions in the research process (see Gough & Edwards, 1998). Though I did not wish to be seen to endorse the "laddish" behavior of the group, I was equally conscious not to appear over-patronizing, as this could result in respondents monitoring their behavior in ways that would not have been in keeping with the method of participant observation.

7. This contrasts with another local study by Coffield et al. in the mid-eighties, which declared, "young adults who never have had a job have no occupational identity at all—they are not even an unemployed shop assistant or joiner, they are simply *unemployed*" (1986, p. 81). Instead, the *Real Geordies* culturally re-imagined a manual occupational identity that they embodied in daily rituals. For more recent local accounts, see (MacDonald, 1999; MacDonald et al., 2000).

References

Anderson, B. (1984). *Imagined communities: Reflections on the origin and spread of nationalism*. London: Verso.

Ball, S. J. (1987). *The micro-politics of the school: Towards a theory of school organization*. London: Routledge.

Bates, I. (1984). *Schooling for the dole? The new vocationalism*. London: Macmillan.

Bean, D. (1971). *Tyneside: A biography*. London: Macmillan.

Bean, D. (1980). *Newcastle 900: A portrait of Newcastle upon Tyne*. Newcastle: Newcastle upon Tyne City Council.

Beck, U. (1998). *Risk society: Towards a new modernity*. London: Sage.

Campbell, B. (1993). *Goliath: Britain's dangerous places*. London: Methuen.

Canaan, J. E. (1996). "One thing leads to another": Drinking, fighting and working-class masculinities. In M. Mac an Ghaill (Ed.), *Understanding masculinities: social relations and cultural arenas* (pp. 114–125). Buckingham: Open University Press.

Chatterton, P., & Hollands, R. (2001). *Changing our 'toon': Youth nightlife and urban change in Newcastle*. Newcastle: University of Newcastle upon Tyne.

Chatterton, P., & Hollands, R. (2003). *Urban nightscapes: Youth cultures, pleasure spaces and corporate power*. London: Routledge.

Coffield, R., Borril, C., & Marshall, S. (1986). *Growing up at the margins: Young adults in the North East*. Milton Keynes: Open University Press.

Cohen, P. (1997). *Rethinking the youth question: Education, labour and cultural studies*. Basingstoke: Macmillan.

Colls, R., & Lancaster, B. (1992). *Geordies: Roots of regionalism*. Edinburgh: University Press.

Connell, R.W. (1995). *Masculinities*. Cambridge: Polity Press.

Corrigan, P. (1979). *Schooling the smashstreet kids*. Basingstoke: Macmillan.

Delamont, S. (2001). *Changing women, unchanged men? Sociological perspectives on gender in a post-industrial society*. Buckingham: Open University Press.

Epstein, D., Elwood, J., Hey, V., & Maw, J. (1998). *Failing boys?: Issues of gender and achievement*. Buckingham: Open University Press.

Foster, V., Kimmel, M., & Skelton, C. (2001). What about the boys?: An overview of the debates. In W. Martino & B. Meyenn (Eds.), *What about the boys?: Issues of masculinity in school* (pp. 1–23). Buckingham: Open University Press.

Frosh, S., Phonix, A., & Pattman, R. (2002). *Young masculinities*. Basingstoke: Palgrave.

Gough, B., & Edwards, G. (1998). The beer talking: Four lads, a carry out and the reproduction of masculinities. *The Sociological Review, 46*(3), 409–455.

Gray, R. (1981). *The aristocracy of labour in nineteenth-century Britain 1850–1914*. Basingstoke: Macmillan.

Halford, S., & Savage, M. (1997). Rethinking restructuring: embodiment, agency and identity in organizational change. In R. Lee & J. Wills (Eds.), *Geographies of economies* (pp. 108–117). London: Arnold.

Hargreaves, D. H., Hestor, S. K., & F. J. Mellor, F. J. (1975). *Deviance in classrooms*. London: Routledge & Kegan Paul.

Hollands, R. (1997). From shipyards to nightclubs: Restructuring young adults' employment, household, and consumption identities in the North-East of England. *Berkeley Journal of Sociology, 41*, 41–66.

Hudson, R. (2000). *Production, places and environment: Changing perspectives in economic geography*. Harlow: Longman.

Lancaster, B. (1992). Newcastle—capital of what? In R. Colls & B. Lancaster (Eds.), *Geordies* (pp. 53–70). Edinburgh: Edinburgh Press.

MacDonald, R. (1999). The road to nowhere: Youth, insecurity and marginal transitions. In J. Vale, J. Wheelock, & M. Hill (Eds.), *Insecure times: Living with insecurity in contemporary times* (pp. 169–183). London: Routledge.

Martino, W. (1995). Deconstructing masculinity in the English classroom: A site for reconstituting gendered subjectivity. *Gender and Education, 7*(2), 205–220.

Martino, W. (2001). "Powerful people aren't usually really kind, friendly, open people!": Boys interrogating masculinities at school. In W. Martino & B. Meyenn (Eds.), *What about the boys?: Issues of masculinity in schools* (pp. 82–95). Buckingham: Open University Press.

Massey, D. (1995a). *Spatial divisions of labour: Social structures and the geography of production*. Basingstoke: Macmillan.

Massey, D. (1995b). The conceptualisation of place. In D. Massey & P. Jess (Eds.), *A place in the world* (pp. 46–79). Milton Keynes: Open University Press.

McDowell, L. (2000). Learning to serve? Employment aspirations and attitudes of young working-class men in an era of labour market restructuring. *Gender, Place and Culture, 7*(4), 389–416.

McDowell, L. (2002). Masculine discourses and dissonances: Strutting 'lads," protest masculinity, and domestic respectability. *Environment and Planning D: Society and Space, 20,* 97–119.

Nayak, A. (2003a) *Race, place and globalization: youth cultures in a changing world.* Oxford: Berg.

Nayak, A. (2003b). Boyz to men: masculinities, schooling and labour tansitions in de-industrial times, *Educational Review 55*(2): 147–159.

Nayak, A., & Kehily, M. J. (2001). "Learning to laugh": A study of schoolboy humour in the English secondary school. In W. Martino & B. Meyenn (Eds.), *What about the boys?: Issues of masculinity in schools* (pp. 110–123). Buckingham: Open University Press.

Skeggs, B. (1997). *Formations of class and gender: Becoming respectable.* London: Sage.

Skeggs, B. (2004). *Class, self, culture.* London: Routledge.

Taylor, I., & Jamieson, R. (1996). "Proper little mesters"—nostalgia and protest masculinity in de-industrialised Sheffield. In S. Westwood & S. Williams (Eds.), *Imagining cities: scripts, signs, memory* (pp. 152–178). London: Routledge.

Thompson, E. P. (1982). *The making of the English working class.* Aylesbury: Pelican Books.

Vail, J., Wheelock, J., & Hill, M. (Eds.). (1999). *Insecure times: Living with insecurity in contemporary society.* London: Routledge.

Wheelock, J. (1994). Is Andy Capp dead? The enterprise culture and household responses to economic change. In P. Garrahan & P. Stewart (Eds.), *Urban change and renewal: The paradox of place* (pp. 81–97). Aldershot: Avebury.

Williams, R. (1973 [1961]) *The long revolution.* Harmondsworth: Penguin.

Williams, R. (1985). *The country and the city.* London: The Hogarth Press.

Willis, P. (1977). *Learning to labour: How working class kids get working class jobs.* London: Saxon House.

8 Hostile High School Hallways

Michael Kimmel

In most respects, Jamie Nabozny was a pretty typical high school kid. Born and raised in a middle-American small town of Ashland (population about 8600) on Lake Superior in the northern tip of Wisconsin, Nabozny was tall and lanky, a bit gawky, shy and quiet, a good student. And gay.

When he came out at age 11, his parents hoped it was simply a "phase" he would pass through. He was their son, after all, and they accepted him as he said he was. His classmates were not as tolerant. Beginning in seventh grade, attending first Ashland Middle School and Ashland High, school became a daily torment. Jamie was harassed, spit on, urinated on, called a "fag" by a teacher, kicked and beaten by other kids, and mock-raped while at least 20 other students looked on and laughed. Each time, he complained to school administrators; each time, his parents backed him up. And each time, the school principals and teachers shrugged off his complaints, telling Jamie that he should "expect this sort of treatment if you're gay" and that, well, "boys will be boys." (The one guidance counselor who did support him was replaced.) He was so frightened that he got sick. "Every day I had stomach aches. I lived in fear every day I got on that bus," he recalled. "I started walking to school because after a while … . I had to live every day trying to avoid being harassed." He began to come to school extremely early, so he could "get to the library before the other kids" arrived at school. "I had to use the bathrooms usually used by teachers to avoid the kids in the bathrooms." Twice, Jamie attempted suicide. Then a few other boys nearly killed him.

One morning when Nabozny arrived early to school, he went to the library to study. The library was not yet open so Nabozny sat down in the hallway. Minutes later he was met by a group of eight students led by Stephen Huntley [one of the ringleaders of the constant assaults]. Huntley began kicking Nabozny in the stomach, and continued to do so for five or ten minutes while the other students looked on laughing. [Again] Nabozny reported the incident to … the school official in charge of disciplining, [who] laughed and told Nabozny that he deserved such treatment because he is gay. Weeks later, Nabozny collapsed from internal bleeding that resulted from Huntley's beating.

(see Nabonzy v Podlesny)

Several operations and hospitalizations later, Nabozny withdrew from school, moved to Minneapolis, was diagnosed with posttraumatic stress disorder, and completed high school through a graduate equivalency diploma.

The description of Nabozny's torment does not come from Jamie Nabozny, his parents, nor from some purveyors of some mythical gay agenda. It comes from the statements of fact in the decision rendered by the U.S. Court of Appeals for the Seventh Circuit in 1996, after Nabozny successfully sued the school district and the principals of both the middle school and the high school. The district and administrators paid out close to $1 million.

Nabozny's lawsuit, coupled with a 1999 Supreme Court decision (Davis v. Monroe) opened a door for those who are the targets of bullying and harassment in school. The tide has turned on hostile hallways. School districts and administrators may be held liable if they do not intervene effectively to stop the abuse. What is amazing is not that they have to intervene, but that it took the courts until the mid-1990s to figure out that boys also might need protection from harassment and abuse.

Yes, one might say, it is terrible what happened to Jamie Nabozny. No one should have to endure such torture. Surely the school administration was criminally negligent (as found by the courts) not to intervene, as every child, gay or straight, has the right to be safe in school. There may also be, though, a voice in the back of some readers' minds that says, "But Nabozny was, gay, after all. That stuff happens to gay kids." Other readers may be remembering their own school days, as bullies have been around even before the days of slate boards and chalk being used instead of notebooks and pens. One of life's lessons is learning how to deal with them, some might think. Maybe, say the fathers, their son has to learn to fight back, to "stand up for himself." Or, maybe, say the mothers, he needs to have the inner strength to walk away.

What if, instead, I were to tell you that Jamie Nabozny is black and that all the guys who beat him up and bullied him were white? Would you have the same reaction as his school administrators, who said that he ought to expect it? Would you want to tell him to either fight back or walk away? What if I told you he was Jewish? Would you think "well, boys will be boys?" Most Americans would find such racist or anti-Semitic behavior unacceptable, an affront to their moral sensibilities. Racism and anti-Semitism are out of bounds (except, perhaps, when expressed by Ann Coulter), and most of us believe that those who openly express those sentiments should be severely punished. Why, then, is the merciless beating of a gay kid acceptable to some people? (At age 11, remember, it cannot be because he is roaming the halls as a sexual predator, coming on to countless straight guys. Perhaps it is because he appears a little kinder, gentler, or more bookish than his classmates.)

Take the case of Jesse Montgomery. Daily, Jesse was treated to verbal taunts about being "faggot, queer, homo, gay, girl, princess, fairy, freak, bitch, pansy" and more. It was "severe and unrelenting." He was regularly punched, kicked, tripped in the halls. His classmates used super-glue to glue him to his seat, threw things at him, and stole his books and notebooks. Some of the torment was directly sexual:

> One of the students grabbed his own genitals while squeezing [Jesse's] buttocks and on other occasions would stand behind [him] and grind his penis in [Jesse's] backside. The same student once threw him to the ground and pretended to rape him anally, and on another occasion sat on [Jesse's] lap and bounced while pretending to have intercourse with him (Montgomery v Indep Sch Dist no 709; see also Stodghill, 1999).

All of this occurred while other students watched and laughed. Incidentally, Jesse Montgomery is straight.

And so, finally, was another skinny white kid in Detroit: "I was harassed daily by this fat kid named Deangelo Bailey/ An eighth grader who acted obnoxious," he has told us. Bailey shoved the kid into lockers, slammed him into a urinal, and broke his nose. I suspect, though, that that victim feels like he got the last laugh. Those lines appear in the song "Brain Damage" by Eminem, who, as a boy named Marshall Mathers, was regularly the target of bullies. Deangelo Bailey sued Eminem in 2001, claiming that the song invaded his privacy and exposed him unfavorably to the public. The suit was dismissed as without factual foundation (see Sisario, 2005).

Hostile Hallways

In this chapter, I focus on different types of peer harassment in high schools—bullying, hazing, and sexual harassment. How the school and the community respond to these issues may determine—perhaps more than any specific exams or curricular innovations—the type of education (conceived broadly) that our children receive.

Many of America's high schools have become gauntlets through which students must pass every day. Bullies roam the halls, targeting the most vulnerable or isolated. Daily, as routinely as their homeroom bell, bullies beat them up, destroy their homework, shove them into lockers or into toilets, and make fun of them. It is all done in public—on playgrounds, in bathrooms and hallways, even in class. Other kids often laugh and encourage it, or they scurry to the walls, hoping to remain invisible to the bullies so that they will not become the next target. Almost never does anyone try to stop it.

Why are some students targeted? Not necessarily because they are gay, although there are increasing numbers of out gay kids in America's high schools. The average age of coming out as gay for males has dropped from 20 in 1979 to age 13 in 1998, according to a Cornell University study (Duncan, 1999; see Jones, 1999). As one might anticipate, gays and lesbians are far more often the target of hostility. A CBS poll in 1999 found that one-third of eleventh graders knew of incidents of harassment of gay or lesbian students. Almost as many (28 percent admitted to making anti-gay remarks themselves. The average high school student in Des Moines, Iowa, hears an anti-gay comment every seven minutes—and teachers intervened only about 3 percent of the time (see Carter, 1997; Fineran, 2001; Human Rights Watch, 2001, p. 39).

Anti-gay sentiments are only partly related to sexual orientation, though. They are far more deeply connected, I believe, to gender. Homosexuality can often represent gender nonconformity, so anti-gay sentiments become a shorthand method of gender policing. Tell a guy that what he is doing is "gay" and the gender police have just written him a ticket. If he persists, then they might have to lock him up.

This policing and its attendant violence occur because of what guys think being gay means: It means not being a guy. As we saw earlier, it is about gender, not necessarily sexuality. Specifically, it is the equation of homosexuality (a sexual orientation) with gender nonconformity. In a study by Human Rights watch, heterosexual students consistently reported that the targets were simply those boys who were unathletic, dressed nicely, or bookish and shy, and the girls who were athletic, assertive, or "had an attitude." Recall what Eminem said: Calling someone a faggot does not mean you think they are gay, but it does mean that you think they are not a real man. And those are fighting words (see Frosh, Phoenix, & Pattman, 2002; Human Rights Watch, 2001; Young & Sweeting, 2004).

Forget that old schoolyard adage—"sticks and stones may break my bones, but words will never hurt me." That may have been true once upon a time but not anymore. One survey found that most American boys would rather be punched in the face than called gay (see Jones, 1999).

School violence has become so utterly commonplace that many parents and administrators assume it is a false problem, a problem created by hysterical overreacting parents, some nameless forces of political correctness who want to throw a wet blanket over all naturally rambunctious male play, turning us into a nation of wimps, and the scholarly researchers who are only too happy to do their bidding. There is even a scholarly journal devoted to it, the *Journal of School Violence*, which began publishing in 2002.

The evidence of its ubiquity is quite convincing. In one study of middle and high school students in Midwestern towns, 88 percent reported having observed bullying, and 77 percent reported being a victim of bullying at some point during their school years. In another, 70 percent had been sexually harassed by their peers; 40 percent had experienced physical dating violence; 66 percent had been victimized by emotional abuse in a dating relationship; and 54 percent had been bullied. "If all the girls who have ever been sexually harassed reported the guys who did it, there would no longer be any boys in school," commented one teenage girl to the author of a study in *Seventeen* magazine (see Holt & Espelage, 2003; Hoover, Oliver, & Hazler, 1992; Stein, 2001)

These patterns emerge in elementary school, but they erupt in middle school years. A national survey of 15,686 students in grades six to ten published in the *Journal of the American Medical Association* found that 29.9 percent reported frequent involvement with bullying: 13 percent as bully, 10.9 percent as victim, and 6 percent as both (see Nansel et al., 2001). In another, one-fourth of kids in grades four to six admitted to bullying another student with some regularity in the 3 months before the survey (Limber at al, 1997). And yet another found that during one 2-week period at two Los Angeles middle schools, nearly half the 192 kids interviewed reported being bullied at least once. More than that said they had seen others targeted (see Juvonen, Graham, & Schuster, 2003). On the other side of the ledger, fewer than one in five students (19.5 percent) reported no bullying in the preceding 30 days (see Espelage, Bosworth, & Simon, 2000).

"Bullying is a problem that large numbers of kids confront on a daily basis at school; it's not just an issue for the few unfortunate ones," said Jaana Juvonen, the UCLA psychologist who co-authored the UCLA study. "We knew a small group gets picked on regularly, but we were surprised how many kids reported at least one incident. We didn't know how much bullying we would find over a few random days." (see Nishina, Juvonen, & Witkow, 2005; Nishina & Juvoven, 2005; Wolpert, 2005).

Most teachers and administrators see only the physical bullying, and most schools have rules prohibiting physical aggression. However, what about constant verbal torment or sexual harassment? A recent survey in Long Island found that only 7 percent of high school students said "physical harm" was the primary weapon of bullies; 65 percent said teasing. And this is where the "gender" of bullying appears to break down. The overwhelming majority of the physical bullying is done by boys, but there is also a significant amount of verbal bullying by girls, as recent best-sellers such as *Odd Girl Out* and *Queen Bees and Wannabes* first revealed (see Simmons, 2003; Wiseman, 2002).

The latest wrinkle in bullying is neither physical nor verbal; it is virtual. Schools are increasingly reporting cases of "cyber-bullying" in which some kids are targeted using hateful e-mail or cell phone text messages, or hateful and humiliating things are posted on cyber-bulletin boards and school chat rooms. A survey of 5,500 teens found that 72 percent said that online bullying was just as distressing as the face-to-face kind (see Lemonick, 2005)

This increasing gender parity in non-physical aggression may be deceptive. Though it is certainly the case that girls can be and frequently are as verbally aggressive as boys, it is also useful to ask who benefits from the aggression? Toward what larger social ends is the violence directed, what larger social purposes does it serve? Here the answers are equally revealing.

Boys use aggression, of course, to establish and then maintain their place in the male pecking order. Boys bullying other boys, therefore, is in the service of this larger hierarchy; the bullying makes sure that those at the top stay there and believe they are entitled to be there. Many girls, however, use verbal or relational aggression to impress those boys at the top, as if their efforts at humiliating other girls, or even re-victimizing the boys who have already been targeted, will win them the attention of the top males. Alternately, they may use aggression to police the boundaries of attractiveness that make girls subordinate to boys. In all, girls' aggression—even toward other girls—is in the service of sustaining the hierarchy, which is, itself, the expression of gender inequality.

Just because a behavior is common does not mean it is without consequences, though. For the victims of this quotidian torture, their lives become living nightmares. They lose sleep, lose status, lose friends. Some shut down, become depressed or despondent. Some self-medicate with drugs or alcohol. They feel sick more often and stay home from school. Every day, according to the *National Association of School Psychologists*, 160,000 American youths skip school fearing they will be the targets of bullies (see Boodman, 2001). Their friends fade away because they, too, are frightened off. "When I was in high school," recounts Jamie, now a 23 year-old graduate student at U. C. Berkeley,

> I was constantly harassed because people assumed I was gay. My friends were scared to be seen with me, because they would get hassled too. It was like the bullies made it appear I was contagious or something. If anyone was nice to me, or hung out with me, they'd get hassled the next day. There was only one guy who stuck with me, because he didn't care what they said. I lost all my other friends when I became a target.

The bullies, though, do not fare so well either. Though it is true that bullies often enjoy high prestige and high social standing, it is also true that their experience of entitlement leads them to overestimate the degree to which that entitlement carries over to life outside school. As a result, bullies grow up deficient in social coping and negotiating skills and are more likely to engage in substance abuse, according to William Coleman, a pediatrics professor at University of North Carolina School of Medicine. "Bullying should not be considered a normative aspect of youth development," concluded the authors of an article in the *Archives of Pediatrics and Adolescent Medicine*, "but rather a marker for more serious violent behaviors." (see Nansel et al., 2003). Bullies are four times more likely to have engaged in criminal activity before age 24, and a full 25 percent had criminal records before they turn 30 (see Juvonen et al., 2003; Lemonick, 2005).

Hazing and the Rites of Passage

If the bullies seem to pick on the marginal or unathletic kids, you might think one way to inoculate oneself against being bullied would be to go out for a sport. If they pick on the kids who are alone and helpless and don't quite "fit in," you might think one might be able to avoid that routine torment by joining a club. You would be wrong. Though joining an athletic team or an extracurricular club or organization may be somewhat palliative against being targeted for random bullying in the hallways or cafeteria, it makes you even more vulnerable to hazing.

Hazing is "any activity expected of someone joining a group that humiliates, degrades, abuses or endangers, regardless of the person's willingness to participate," according to researchers at Alfred University, who conducted the most comprehensive study of hazing ever. Hazing activities seem to be voluntary and consensual, which often leads adults and the public to dismiss them as inconsequential (see Hoover & Pollard, 2000).

Hazing is amazingly common. About 1.5 million high school students are hazed every year. In the Alfred study, 48 percent of high school students who belong to organized groups reported being subjected to hazing activities. Forty-three percent reported being subjected to humiliating activities, and 305 said that they had done something illegal as part of their initiation. About one-fifth described something dangerous or that involved substance abuse.

Hazing is ubiquitous. As one would expect, rookies on athletic teams, military recruits, and fraternity pledges have always been hazed (I return to these issues when I discuss sports and fraternities), but it is also true for the kids who join the band, debating club, or cheerleading squad. Almost every type of high school group had significantly high levels of hazing in the Alfred study. Even groups ordinarily considered "safe" used hazing; 24 percent of students involved in church groups were subjected to hazing activities. More than a third (36 percent) said they would not tell anyone about it because "there is no one to tell" or "adults won't handle it right."

Hazing may be a constant presence over the generations, but the rituals have also become more "creative," and that "creativity" is often founded on increasingly sexually humiliating events. Nowhere is this more evident than among high school athletes (see Bushweller, 2000; Nuwer, 2000). In many cases, athletes' hazing is solely physical brutality. Athletes have beaten their younger teammates with baseball bats, with socks loaded with tennis balls or pebbles, electrical cords, or belts or kicked soccer balls at their groins. In many cases, this violence is sexual. Take the case of the Mepham, Long Island high school football team. Four freshman were welcomed onto the team by being sodomized by older boys with pine cones, broom handles, and hockey sticks. Or, take the case of the high school wrestling team in Trumbull, Connecticut. Nine wrestlers were charged with felonious assault in 2000 when they bound a 15-year-old, first-year teammate with tape, rolled him up in a wrestling mat, threw the mat against the wall, and pounded. Afterward, they raped him with the handle of a plastic knife.

Coaches often look the other way, assuming that these bonding rituals heighten team spirit and bonding. If that is so, it is only through a sort of athletic Stockholm Syndrome in which the victims of torture come to identify with their torturers. Fathers, also, often defend the practice, because, "well, that's what happened when I was in high school," as one of them put it after a hazing incident was exposed in Avon, Indiana. That reasoning, alas, is a fallacy of misattribution—attributing a positive outcome (the fact that these fathers are reasonably OK guys with positive experiences) to the fact that they were beaten and hazed. Why not consider that they did all right despite their being tortured instead of because of it? As in prison, sexual humiliation and rape invokes terror and reinforces hierarchy. Art Taylor, a psychologist at the Center for the Study of Sport in Society at Northeastern University, argues that such "humiliating hazing rituals are more likely to tear people apart, destroy trust, and cause feelings of hatred." To defend such activities in the name of team building or male bonding is, at best, perverse and, at worst, criminally insane (see Bushweller, 2000).

Make no mistake: Girls haze also. Take the case of Lizzie Murtie, a 100-pound, 5-foot-1-inch high school freshman on the Essex, Vermont, gymnastics team. Fourteen years old and still collecting beanie Babies, Lizzie worshipped the older girls on the team. Then they seemed to turn against her.

Lizzie's hazing started innocently enough.[1] She had to wear a tennis outfit and stand on the street corner singing "I'm a little teapot." This might seem innocent enough. That evening, she and the other rookies went back to one of their new teammate's house for what had been advertised to their parents as a team sleepover. In the parking lot, Lizzie and the other rookies were surrounded by dozens of kids. A boy was standing off to one side of the circle. The older girls ordered the younger ones to walk over to the boy, kneel in front of him, so their mouths were directly in front of his zipper, and put their hands behind their back. Then they had to eat a banana that was stuck in his pants. (The younger girls could not see that the girls were eating fruit.)

Sworn to secrecy—the older girls said that if the younger ones told anyone they would be kicked off the team—the girls complied. However, Lizzie still felt awful.

> After it happened, I tried to block it out of my mind, but I still knew it was there … . I got really depressed. I had trouble concentrating. My grades dropped. I didn't want to be around any of my friends. I just pretty much stayed at home in my room. I felt like I couldn't trust anybody. I had looked up to them, the seniors—most of them were good students, going on to college.
>
> (see Bushweller, 2000)

It wasn't until a parent overheard a couple of the girls talking furtively about it that Lizzie, or anyone else, dared to talk about it. They did eventually talk about it, though, and the parents complained to the school board, and the offending girls ended up being required to perform 30 hours of community service. (Two girls failed to honor that commitment.) They all continued to compete and graduated with their class.

What is important for my analysis is not so much that girls can haze other girls; of course they can. Important is the fact that the hazing is so clearly about humiliating girls through subservience to boys. That the girls were ordered to perform mock fellatio—and, I am told, in some cases, real penises replace bananas—reinforces the fact that the girls are, to some degree, hazing one another in the service of some larger mission of impressing the boys.

If this remains unclear, imagine the contrasting case. A group of rookie boys are ordered to simulate cunnilingus on an older girl. Doesn't quite have the same humiliating resonance, does it? In fact, far more likely would be that the boys would also be ordered to perform mock fellatio on an older boy. It is the subservience to the boy, the "servicing" of the older boy that is the source of humiliation—whether it is done to girls or boys and whether it is done by girls or boys.

Don't Get Mad, Get Even

For some targets, the relentless torture and humiliation are simply too much to bear. A few may try to take their own lives. Close to 85 percent of all teen suicides are by boys. Some even take matters into their own hands. That is certainly the case for the overwhelming majority of boys who showed up at school one day, armed to the teeth, and opened fire on their classmates.

For the past 5 years, I have conducted a research study of all the cases of random school shootings in the United States. The Stony Brook Project on Random School Violence has examined a sample of media accounts of these events with interviews with parents, teachers, and other students at some of the communities that have experienced these tragic shootings. Our findings illustrate the issues I am raising here.

First, there are generally two types of lethal school violence. In one type, a young boy, most often a black or Latino youth, brings a loaded handgun to his urban, inner-city school. He singles out one other person—a girl who rejected him, a guy who disrespected him—and shoots directly at that person. In the other type, a young white boy (or boys) brings a small arsenal of assault weapons and rifles to school and they open fire, seemingly randomly, killing or wounding many in the melee. Often the massacre ends when the shooters turn the guns on themselves.

The first type of lethal school violence has declined precipitously in the past two decades. (This may partly be the result of the way the violence is measured: To count, it has to take place on school grounds. Given the difficulty of navigating the newly installed metal detectors in inner-city schools, potential perpetrators simply wait just off school property and open fire when they spot their target. These cases do not get reported as school violence.)

The random school shooting, however, is the only type of school violence that has increased over the past decade. That, too, is easily explainable: Before the mid-1980s, such events were simply unheard of. There were four cases documented between 1982 and 1990; there were 25 cases in the 1990s. They are also increasingly on our minds. Students report being increasingly afraid to go to school; among young people ages 12 to 24, three in ten report that violence has increased in their schools in the past year, and nearly two-fifths have worried that a classmate was potentially violent. More than half of all teens know somebody who has brought a weapon to school (although more than three-fifths of them did nothing about it), according to one study. Additionally, nearly two-thirds (63 percent) of parents believe a school shooting is somewhat or very likely to occur in their communities (see Carlson & Simmons, 2001; *USA Today*, 1999; *USA Today*, 2001).

The results of our study also reveal a striking consistency in the stories of the boys who did commit the violence: Nearly all had stories of being constantly bullied, beat up, and "gay-baited." Nearly all have stories of being mercilessly and constantly teased, picked on, and threatened. A study by the United States Secret Service found that two-thirds of the school shooters had been bullied at school and that revenge was one of their motives (see Kimmel & Mahler, 2003). The bullying they suffered was not because they were actually gay (none of them was, as far as I can tell) but because they were *different* from the other boys—shy, bookish, an honor student, artistic, musical, theatrical, non-athletic, a "geek," or weird. Theirs are stories of "cultural marginalization" based on criteria for adequate gender performance, specifically the enactment of codes of masculinity.

Students seem to understand this, even when researchers and parents do not. In a national survey of teenagers' attitudes, nearly 9 of 10 teenagers said that they believed that the school shootings were motivated by a desire "to get back at those who have hurt them" (87 percent) and that "other kids picking on them, making fun of them, or bullying them" (86 percent) were the immediate causes. Other potential causes such as violence on television, movies, computer games or videos (37 percent), boredom (18 percent), mental problems (56 percent), access to guns (56 percent), and prior physical victimization at home (61 percent) were significantly lower on the adolescents' ratings (see Gaughan, Cerio, & Myers, 2001).

In an article in the *Boston Globe* that is telling of the extent to which school violence is on the minds of students, college admissions officers commented that one of the most popular essay topics on applications for admission was the 1999 massacre at Columbine High School (discussed further). "The best essays about Columbine come from boys ... boys who are 17 years old, who are not the athletes in school, who are called nerd, who are called faggot," noted Evan Forster, the President of EssaySolutions, a company that helps high school students prepare for college entrance and complete their applications. "We've been getting great essays linking Columbine and issues of homophobia." (Langland, 2001, p A10).

Take, for example, the case of young Andy Williams, who shot several classmates in Santee, California. Andy was described as "shy" and was "constantly picked on" by others in school. Bullies stole his clothes, his money, and his food; beat him up regularly; and locked him in his locker, among other daily taunts and humiliations. One student's father baited him and called him a "queer" because he was overweight (see Green & Lieberman, 2001).

Or take Luke Woodham, a bookish and overweight 16-year-old in Pearl, Mississippi. An honor student, he was part of a little group that studied Latin and read Nietzsche. Students teased him constantly for being overweight and a nerd, taunted him as "gay" or "fag." Even his mother called him fat, stupid, and lazy. On October 1, 1997, Woodham stabbed his mother to death in her bed before he left for school. He then drove her car to school, carrying a rifle under his coat. He opened fire in the school's common area, killing two students and wounding seven others. After being subdued, he told the assistant principal, "the world has wronged me." Later, in a psychiatric interview, he said,

> I am not insane. I am angry ... . I am not spoiled or lazy; for murder is not weak and slow-witted; murder is gutsy and daring. I killed because people like me are mistreated every day. I am malicious because I am miserable.
>
> (see Chua-Eoan, 1997; Lacayo, 1998)

Fourteen-year-old Michael Carneal was a shy and frail freshman at Heath High School in Paducah, Kentucky, barely 5 feet tall, weighing 110 pounds. He wore thick glasses and played in the high school band. He felt alienated, pushed around, picked on. Boys stole his lunch and constantly teased him. He was so hypersensitive and afraid that others would see him naked that he covered the air vents in the bathroom. He was devastated when students called him a "faggot" and almost cried when the school gossip sheet labeled him as "gay." On Thanksgiving, 1997, he stole two shotguns, two semiautomatic rifles, a pistol, and 700 rounds of ammunition from a relative and, after a weekend of showing them off to his classmates, brought them to school hoping that they would bring him some instant recognition. "I just wanted the guys to think I was cool," he said. When the cool guys ignored him, he opened fire on a morning prayer circle, killing three classmates and wounding five others. Now serving a life sentence in prison, Carneal told psychiatrists weighing his sanity that "people respect me now." (see Blank, 1998).

One of America's most recent shooting seems not to conform to the pattern. On March 21, 2005, Jeff Weise, a 16-year-old Chippewa who lived on Red Lake Indian Reservation in Minnesota, opened fire in his rural reservation school, killing five students, a security guard, a teacher, and himself, all after he had also shot and killed his grandfather and his grandfather's companion. Seven students were also wounded. Despite the closeness of the Native American community, Weise was a loner who fantasized about being a Nazi and about wreaking havoc as a form of revenge (see Davey, 2005; Davey & Wilgoren, 2005).

We cannot leave this discussion without recalling Columbine High School in Littleton, Colorado. It has become the touchstone case, the case to which all observers must eventually refer. Even here, the connection between being socially marginalized, picked on and bullied propelled Eric Harris and Dylan Klebold deeper into their fantasies of a vengeful bloodbath.

Evan Todd, a 255-pound defensive lineman on the Columbine football team, an exemplar of the jock culture that Klebold and Harris found to be such an interminable torment, said of the two,

Columbine is a clean, good place, except for those rejects ... . Sure we teased them. But what do you expect with kids who come to school with weird hairdos and horns on their hats? It's not just jocks; the whole school's disgusted with them. They're a bunch of homos ... . If you want to get rid of someone, usually you tease 'em. So the whole school would call them homos.

Athletes taunted them; "nice dress," they would say. Jocks would throw rocks and bottles at them from moving cars. The school newspaper had recently published a rumor that Harris and Klebold were lovers (see Gibbs & Roche, 1999).

Both were middle-class kids. Harris's parents were a retired Army officer and a caterer, both decent, well-intentioned people. Klebold's father was a geophysicist who had recently moved into the mortgage services business, and his mother worked in job placement for the disabled. Harris had been rejected by several colleges; Klebold was due to enroll at the University of Arizona in the fall. On the surface, everything should have been fine for these two boys. The jock culture, however, was relentless. "Every time someone slammed them against a locker and threw a bottle at them, I think they'd go back to Eric or Dylan's house and plot a little more—at first as a goof, but more and more seriously over time," said one friend (see Pooley, 1999).

You probably know the rest. Harris and Klebold brought a variety of guns and explosives to their high school and proceeded to walk through the school, shooting whomever they could find. Students were terrified and tried to hide. Many students who could not hide begged for their lives. The entire school was held under siege until the police secured the building. In all, 23 students and faculty were injured, and 15 died, including one teacher and the perpetrators.

Many years later, Americans remain shocked and horrified by the tragic shooting at Columbine. In a way, it defies explanation. In another way, though, it demands it. Efforts by those who would preserve the bully culture to make it a case of psychologically unhinged but rational and conscious moral actors fall sadly short. New psychiatric analysis offers a more complex portrait of Klebold, a depressed and troubled boy, and Harris, a cold-blooded, remorseless psychopath. The effort to take the victims of relentless bullying and substitute them with an image of teenagers whose thoughts of revenge were so grandiose, who sneered with undisguised Nietzchean scorn at their classmates, reveals a psychological myopia that could only come from those who had never experienced it. (If Harris was indeed psychotic, then it begs the question of why no one in the entire school ever seems to have noticed.) The consistent Nazi associations at Columbine, Red Lake, and other cases, are revealing; Hitler was probably history's greatest example of the sad loser whose contemptuous revenge fantasies propelled him toward grandiose and violent compensations. It is, of course, the ones who are so mercilessly targeted, and seemingly without justifiable reason, who often evince airs of superiority and devise the most elaborate and grandiose plots of revenge (see Brooks, 2004a, b).

Malicious because they are miserable. Not insane, but angry. That is what these guys said. They were, in that sense, "real" guys. Real Guys do not feel sad; they get mad. They do not just get mad, either; they get even. They go out in a blaze of glory. They take others with them. Eric Harris and Dylan Klebold were not deviant nonconformists to the rules of masculinity. In fact, of all the students at Columbine High School on that sunny morning in April, 1999, it is possible that no one was more a true believer in the Guy Code than they were.

Patterns of Violence

When such a tragedy happens, our attention is immediately drawn to mainly psychological questions. What could have motivated this particular boy or pair of boys? What was going on in their lives? Their families? Did no one notice? Why did their parents not know what they were doing? Why did the other kids fail to take seriously their threats to get even with their tormentors? In virtually every case, other kids in the school knew something was up, and they knew because the perpetrators told them what they were planning. However, rarely did other kids do anything about it. Even law enforcement officials, desperate to prevent other such cases, have tried to coax other students into telling an adult what they hear. In my view, this is one of the few actual changes in the social organization of schools: The kids have listened and begun to break through the wall of silence.

There are, however, some other patterns in these tragedies that may be instructive if we are to devise positive ways to intervene. Not only are all boys not equally susceptible to resolving conflicts through lethal violence; not all schools are equally at risk for such explosions of rage. Just as most boys get through reasonably intact and healthy, so, too, are most schools unlikely to experience anything like this. Boys can be arrayed on a continuum of possible reactions to being bullied, from just shrugging it off and trying to ignore it and get on with their life, to various other compensations (alcohol, drugs, depression), to acting out (fighting, becoming a bully oneself, sexual predation toward girls), and finally to lethal violence against others or against themselves.

So, too, can schools be seen as more or less vulnerable to a random school shooting. Some schools are extremely unlikely to ever experience a school shooting; others are very vulnerable. Though almost every school is unlikely to experience a random school shooting, not all schools are equally unlikely. Of the 29 school shootings between 1982 and 2001, all but one occurred in rural or suburban schools (one in Chicago). By contrast, the Los Angeles school district has had no school shootings since 1984; in 1999, San Francisco, which has several programs to identify potentially violent students, had only two kids bring guns to school. The students themselves see this. In all four geographic regions of the country—East, South, Midwest and West—students in rural high schools rated their schools as most dangerous; in the South and West, students in suburban high schools thought their schools more dangerous than urban schools.

Second, the schools subject to random shootings all tend to be relatively racially homogenous. Not only have all but two of the shooters been white; they were students in schools with a very small percentage of minorities. Again, students' attitudes bear this out. Black students are less likely than other racial groups to believe that getting back at others could be a reason for violence, less likely than whites to see bullying as a significant problem, and less likely to believe that lack of friends could be blamed for school violence.

Geography

Perhaps it would be helpful to look at a map of the school shootings (Figure 8.1).

Even at first glance, it is evident that school shootings do not occur uniformly or evenly in the United States—which makes me skeptical of uniform cultural explanations such as violent video games, musical tastes, Internet, television, and movies. School shootings are not a national trend.

Now, here is that same map (Figure 8.2), now also revealing a deep, and increasingly familiar, division in American society: the red state/unshaded (Republican-voting), blue state/shaded(Democrat-voting) electoral divide. (In the 2004 election, only New Hampshire [red to blue] and New Mexico [blue to red] switched their color.)

What are we to make of the fact that 18 of the 29 school shootings took place in "red states" and that, of those in the "blue states," one was in suburban Oregon; one was in rural (eastern) Washington; two were in Southern California; one was in rural and another in suburban Pennsyvania; and one was in rural New Mexico? Of those 11 from "blue states," half of the counties in those states (Santee, CA: Red Hill, PA; Moses Lake, WA; and Deming, NM) voted Republican in 2000 and 2004. I am not, of course, suggesting that voting for George W. Bush in the presidential elections increases one's likelihood of a random school shooting. Red States and Blue States are proxies for a collection of attitudes and beliefs that divide America—attitudes about homosexuals, for example, about gun control, or about religion in the schools.

Public schools in red states may be situated in different social environments and have different school cultures and different gun cultures

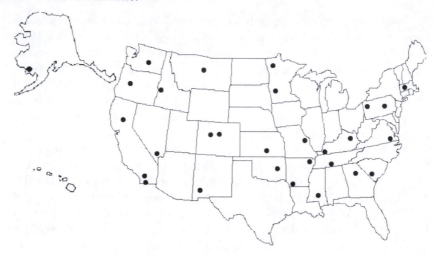

Figure 8.1 Map of random school shootings in the United States, 1974–2006.

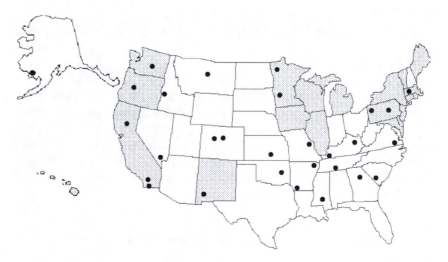

Figure 8.2 Random school shootings, 1974–2006, by "Red" states (unshaded) and "Blue" states (shaded).

than schools in blue states. And these differences may create environments in schools that are more or less conducive to school shootings. Does the school take bullying—especially homophobic bullying—seriously, or does the community shrug its metaphoric shoulders and say "Boys will be boys?" Does the school tolerate antigay statements from students or their parents? From teachers or administrators? How many families keep loaded weapons in their homes or garages?

There are also, perhaps, regional differences in the cultures of violence. Though we think of our cities as the hotbeds of crime, it turns out that southern states have long had the highest homicide rates and the highest per capita rates of violence. While Fox Butterfield has traced this historically to the immigrant cultures of Scots and Irish in colonial America, others have suggested that the South's humiliation in the Civil War was experienced as especially emasculating. In its aftermath, young white Southern boys would take a chip of wood from the family woodpile, put it on his shoulder, and dare another boy to knock it off, so that the first boy would have legitimate recourse to violence.

Race

Is there a reason it is nearly all white boys? To be sure, African-American boys face a multitude of challenges in schools, from racial stereotypes, formal and informal tracking systems, low expectations, and underachievement. They do not, however, plan and execute random and arbitrary mass shootings. This is not because they are any less committed to the Guy Code. Perhaps cultural marginalization works itself out differently for whites and minorities. Even if they are silenced or lose their voice, black boys can always tap into a collective narrative repertoire of resistance. They are told by friends to interpret homophobic bullying in racial terms, so they see their resilience as a form of resistance to racism. "White kids, they always say that stuff to us black kids," said Ellis, one of my students at Stony Brook, when I tried out this hypothesis. "Me and my friends, we don't pay them no mind because we know they're racist assholes." A black boy who is targeted by bullies may interpret his victimization in racial terms, and in so doing, his anger may be more political and less psychological.

White boys in racially homogenous schools have no other rhetoric of resistance to turn to, especially when the form of cultural ostracism is sexuality. The cultural marginalization of the boys who did commit school shootings extended to feelings that they had no other recourse: they felt they had no other friends to validate their fragile and threatened identities; they felt that school authorities and parents would be unresponsive to their plight; and they had no access to other methods of self-affirmation. Someone needed to be listening.

The "War Against Boys"[2]

Could it be that the constant pressure on boys in high schools is what really lies behind the problems that we have begun to discuss in our culture—the problems that boys are having in school? I believe so. I believe that the pressure on young guys to conform, first to the Boy Code and then to the Guy Code, is so intense and unforgiving and that the fears of failure—of being targeted, or the shame that attends being the passive bystander—is what leaves so many young guys with a knot in their stomach every time they eat in the cafeteria, go to the bathroom, walk out onto the playground, change their clothes in the locker room, or even walk between one class and the next. For so many boys, then, only by shutting down completely, becoming stoic, expressionless robots, can they navigate those public spaces. Is it any wonder that boys are having trouble in school?

The recent debate about boys in school has only partly addressed these issues. Though it is true that we have become aware that boys are having a hard time of it—and that we have not been paying very much attention to it—we do not fully understand the cause of boys' problems, and thus we cannot offer useful help.

At first glance, the evidence that boys are struggling in school is pretty overwhelming. Just look at the numbers: Boys drop out of school, are diagnosed as emotionally disturbed and commit suicide four times more often than girls; they get into fights twice as often; they murder 10 times more frequently and are 15 times more likely to be the victims of a violent crime. Boys are six times more likely to be diagnosed with attention deficit and hyperactivity disorder (see Knickerbocker, 1999). Boys score consistently below girls on tests of reading and verbal skills and have lower class rank and fewer honors than girls (Kleinfield cited in Knickerbocker).

By the time they get to college—if they do make it to college—they find they are in an ever-shrinking minority. Women are now the majority of college students, having passed men in 1982, and young American men now earn 25 percent fewer bachelor degrees than young women do. Women now outnumber men in the social and behavioral sciences by about three to one, and now they have invaded such traditionally male bastions as engineering (where they now make up 20 percent) and biology and business (virtually par; see Koerner, 1999; Lewin, 1998).

This has spurred significant anxiety among some commentators. One alarmist reporter, obviously no student of statistics, warned that if present trends continue, "the graduation line in 2068 will be all females." (Does one really need to point out that such a statement is like saying that since the black enrollment at Ole Miss was 1 in 1964, and, say, 200 in 1968 and 1,200 in 1988, that by 1994 there were no more white students there?)

To be sure, boys are in trouble, so much so that it has even caught the attention of the First Lady. Laura Bush has declared that one of her central interests in her husband's second term is to address boys' needs and boys' problems in school.

If we agree that boys are in trouble, though (and not everyone does), we do not agree on the sources of the crisis. To hear some tell it, if boys are in trouble, it is because of girls. Well, not individual girls, but the women's movement, which first drew attention to girls' problems in school two decades ago and sponsored numerous classroom reforms, including encouraging girls' involvement in science and math and campaigning to create safer schools by curtailing harassment. However, we hear, the salutary effects of paying attention to girls have been offset by the increasing problematization of boys. Some credit the rapid rise of girls' sports, which means that boys now have to share the status that comes from being a jock.

An article in the *New York Times* complained that boys had "lost out" to girl power and concluded that "the wrong sex may be getting all the attention in school" (cited in Faludi, 1998, p 46). Pop psychologist Michael Gurian claims schools "feminize" boys, forcing active, healthy and naturally rambunctious boys to conform to a regime of obedience, "pathologizing what is simply normal for boys." With testosterone surging through their little limbs, we demand that they sit still, raise their hands, and take naps. We are giving them the message, he says, that "boyhood is defective." Another writes that school is a terrible place for boys. In school, they are trapped by "The Matriarchy" and are dominated by women who cannot accept boys as they are (Zachary, 1997). "The women teachers mainly wish to control and to suppress boys." Don and Jeanne Elium's book, *Raising a Son*, ups the ante, making the hysterical claim that feminist attitudes can "create boys that are either murderous or suicidal." (cited in Epstein, Elwood, Hey, & Maw, 1998, p 7).

By far the most sustained fusillade against feminism as the cause of boys' woes comes from Christina Hoff Sommers, formerly a philosophy professor and now a resident anti-feminist pundit at the American Enterprise Institute. In her 2000 book, *The War Against Boys*, Hoff Sommers claims that "misguided feminism" has been the source of a new, anti-boy "chilly classroom climate." Schools are an "inhospitable" hostile environment for boys, where their natural propensities for rough and tumble play, competition, aggression, and rambunctious violence are cast as social problems in the making. Efforts to transform boys, to constrain or curtail them threaten time-tested and beneficial elements of masculinity and run counter to nature's plan. These differences are "natural, healthy, and, by implication, best left alone." (see Hoff Sommers, 2000, p. 75). The last four words of her book are that "boys will be boys."

Those strike me as the four most depressing words in educational policy discussions. First, because they imply such abject resignation: Boys will simply be boys, and there is nothing that anyone can do about it, so stop trying. And second, because the phrase implies such a negative image of boyhood, as if to say boys will be wild, predatory, aggressive animals and there is simply no point in trying to control them. In that sense, it is Hoff Sommers and her colleagues who are the real male bashers, who hold such a negative view of men and boys. Feminists, by contrast, believe that boys can do better, and that the future of girls—as well as boys—hangs in the balance.

The idea that feminist reforms have "thrown the gender switch," as Hoff Sommers writes, and have led to the decline of boyhood is educationally unsound and politically untenable. For one thing, it creates a false opposition between girls and boys, assuming that the educational reforms undertaken to enhance girls' educational opportunities have actually hindered boys' educational development. However, these reforms—new initiatives, classroom configurations, teacher training, increased attentiveness to students' processes, and individual learning styles—actually enable larger numbers of boys to get a better education as well as girls. Further, "gender stereotypes, particularly those related to education, hurt both girls and boys," so challenging those stereotypes and expressing less tolerance for school violence and bullying and increased attention to violence at home actually enables both girls and boys to feel safer at school (see McGee Bailey & Campbell, 1999/2000, p. 11).

For another thing, it is hard to square this woman-blaming with the collapse of school funding across the country. However, think about how such cost-slashing has affected boys—as money that might have funded after school programs, team sports, remedial programs, intervention strategies, teacher training. Across the country, sports teams, bands, orchestras, and art and music classes are disappearing, and these trends are exacerbated by the No Child Left Behind Act, which mandates widespread testing and results in channeling the paltry remaining resources toward core curriculum so that teachers can "teach to the test."

Behavioral problems among boys are increasingly "handled" not by increased teacher attention to differences among children but by storing problem students in separate classes. Cutbacks in health insurance, and especially managed care insurance, virtually demand that school psychologists (when they are there at all) diagnose problem behavior as a treatable medical condition so that drugs may be substituted for costly, "unnecessary" therapy. It is little wonder, then, that systems that could potentially identify boys who are struggling and/or violent have increasingly failed to do so. The result is often the violent, predatory outbursts I have been talking about throughout this chapter.

So What is the Answer?

Even though bullying and hazing are ubiquitous and random school shootings so rare, the issues we face are serious. Even one random school shooting is unacceptable; one life lost to suicide is one life too many. When you factor in the suicide attempts, the self-medication, the violent outburst, or the violent "inbursts" on the Internet or in video games, it is clear that we must, as a culture, address what guys think it means to be a man. Clearly, we must devise strategies to enable all sorts of boys to feel safe enough to go to school and secure enough to know that they will be valued for who they are.

Encouraging Resilience

Obviously, not all kids who are bullied or hazed decide to go out in a blaze of glory. Nor do they all self-medicate, attempt suicide, or become hostile and withdrawn. "Most kids who are bullied, they get angry about it, they get sad about it, they get depressed," commented James Garbarino, Cornell University professor who studies youthful offenders. "Very few of them take it to the point where they kill themselves or kill others, but the ones who do very often cite that experience as a very salient thing." (Okie, 2001, p. A8). In fact, most guys appear to get through the gauntlet with only a few bruises and a few scars. Yet many also carry around a wound to their hearts that will take a lifetime to heal. The stories of the guys who do not lash out are equally instructive as the stories of the guys who do. How do they survive? What are the sources of boys' resilience, that inner sense that enables them to withstand the constant torment? As the sociologist Pedro Noguera writes, "We know much less about resilience, perseverance, and the coping strategies employed by individuals whose lives are surrounded by hardships, than we do about those who succumb and become victims of their environment" (Noguera, 2008, p. 21).

Take, for example, the story of David, today a student at the University of Rhode Island. The bullying he suffered started when he was 13. "At first I tried to brush it off. But it got worse. I got beat up every day and couldn't take it. I'd fake being sick. My grades slipped." His parents tried to intervene with school officials, but the attacks continued. David's thoughts got darker.

> I felt "What did I do to deserve this?" I wanted revenge. I never sat down and planned anything—I personally couldn't pick up a gun and kill someone, it's not who I am—but I will tell you I did want to hurt them. I wanted them to feel how bad I felt.
>
> (Sullivan, 2001)

David did not hurt them, though. Perhaps David had resilience because he had what Robert Brooks, of the Harvard Medical School, calls a "charismatic adult" who makes a substantial difference in the life of the child. Most often this is one or the other parent, but it can also be a teacher, a coach, an older relative, or a religious leader, a grown-up who "sees" him, and "gets" what is happening to him. It is someone who can show him what it looks like to be a grown-up.

This does not, incidentally, have to be a man. We pay far too much heed to the mistaken belief that boys need "male role models" if they are to turn out as healthy men. There is, actually, no direct empirical evidence for this belief; we just believe it because it sounds right. Again, it mistakes form (the sex of the role model) for content (the actual quality of the relationship the boy develops with the adult). Women—mothers, teachers, and the like—can be just as important as role models for our boys. The sex of the role model matters far less than the fact that there is an adult who is fully present in the life of the boy.

Perhaps the boy can develop an alternative way to develop and feel competence. Bullying suggests that the boy is a failure at the one thing he knows he wants to be and is expected to be—a man. If there is something else that he does well—a private passion, music, art, someplace where he feels valued—he can develop a pocket of resistance.

Similarly, his friendships can make a big difference. A male friend—particularly one who is not also a target but who seems to be successful at masculinity—can validate the boy's sense of himself as masculine. "If you go to school and people make fun of you every day, and you don't have a friend, it drives you to insanity," one high school student said.

Equally important, though, may be the role of a female friend, a potential, if not actual, "girlfriend." It may be that the boys who are able to best resist the torments of incessant gay baiting and bullying are those who have some girls among their friends, and perhaps even a girlfriend—that is, girls who can also validate their sense of masculinity (which other boys do as well) and their heterosexuality (which boys alone cannot do).

School Culture

No matter how resilient our children are, no matter how many role models and charismatic adults love and support them, they still have to go to school. And it is equally true that different schools are, well, different. Some schools are far more prone to harassment, hazing, and bullying; other schools are far less prone.

This is not the problem of the occasional tease or shove, of making the rookies on the team carry the towels. It is also not simply a problem of isolating the bad apples who are bullies and either throwing them out of school or otherwise ostracizing them. It is a pattern, a system, and were it to happen on the streets or in our workplaces, someone would call the police, or at least we hope they would. In the United States, someone would surely file a lawsuit. Nor does this analysis suggest some politically correct effort to criminalize what is simply a "normal" and eternal rite of passage for boys, thus turning America into what one father called "a nation of wimps."

Still, those fears of ineffectual violence prevention programs are not completely unfounded. Many of the anti-bullying programs that are currently being promoted are too syrupy sweet, too loaded with feel-good bromides to be effective. High school kids scoff at the notion of some earnest guitar-strumming ex-hippie singing about smiling on our brother and loving one another right now. On the other hand, school environments should facilitate intellectual and emotional growth, not stifle it. "I don't feel like adolescents should have to go to school in survival mode," says Leon, from Long Beach, California. (Human Rights Watch, 2001)

Being "bully-prone" or "bully-proof" is not a simple either-or proposition. Few schools are so overwhelmed with peer harassment that all authority and decorum have evaporated, nor is any school so completely repressed in administrative lockdown that it is completely bully-proof. Maybe schools can't all be the happily dysfunctional classroom of misfits of TV's *Mr. Kotter* or *Head of the Class*, but they need not end up being cutthroat reality shows like *Survivor*. There is a continuum between these poles, and each school can be arrayed on that continuum by a set of factors. Educators and policymakers might consider the following questions:

1   What do we know? Often school climate feels differently to teachers or administrators and the students. We need good, accurate data. Anonymous student questionnaires are necessary, so kids can respond freely. Just the simple act of surveying the school sends a message to students that the administration is beginning to pay attention.

2   Is there a policy about bullying? Establishing a well-developed anti-bullying policy, using enforceable guidelines, again sends a message that adults are paying attention.

3   Does everyone know the policy? Policies are often useless unless they are well publicized. Is the policy publicized to the school, to parents?

4   Are there workshops for teachers and administrators? Are there workshops for students? Are staff members—including coaches and teachers—well trained to intervene? Do teachers know how to teach about these issues? Do they know how to effectively intervene in classroom situations? How can teachers develop a pedagogy of resilience?

Research by Shepard Kellum at Johns Hopkins reveals how classrooms, teachers, and school settings create the conditions for high or low levels of violence. Kellum watched the way aggressive first grade boys come into a class with a weak teacher, who allows high levels of chaos in the class and the formation of aggressive peer groups and bullying cliques. By sixth grade, those same boys are about 20 times more aggressive than they would have been had they walked into a first grade class that did not allow that chaos or the formation of those aggressive peer groups.

5   How well are non-classroom spaces supervised? As most bullying behaviors take place in the hallways, cafeteria, playground, locker

room, or bathrooms, these are the places where supervision may be more necessary. One school decided simply to have the teachers walk in the halls during the time between classes. If teachers stay in their classrooms, halls may become sites of harassment. Psychologist Michael Thompson reports that in the schools where adult supervision is high and visible, the boys are grateful that adults step into a potentially threatening situation. "It is as if they say 'Thank you for saving us from what we were about to do to each other.'"[3]

6   What is the likely reception to a student who reports bullying or hazing? Are they taken seriously or scoffed at by administrators as troublemakers? We often treat whistleblowers as criminals—they are "snitches" who "rat" on their "friends"—when we should treat them as heroes. Remember that in more than 80 percent of all rampage school shootings, at least one other person knew the attacker was planning something. Two or more people knew in three-fourths of all cases (Crawford, 2002, p 65).

7   Are there adequate counseling services for both bully and victim? Both of them need it.

8   How pervasive is bystander behavior? Are there any initiatives to break through bystander silence? Though bullying may take place everywhere, very few boys intervene. Additionally, the bullies depend on other boys' silence. Are boys encouraged to develop ways that they can collectively intervene?

9   It took a Supreme Court case in 1996 to force schools to own up to their responsibility in creating a school climate that is relatively free of the pervasive and cruel hazing, harassment, and bullying that has made so many students' lives a living nightmare. Whether because of the fear of lawsuits or because of a genuine interest in making schools safer—or, as in most cases, a combination of both—schools can become less "bully-prone" than they have been in the past.

Community Climate

Schools, though, cannot solve violence in isolation from the rest of the community. Often we think of schools as systems apart, but any administrator will tell you that there is a triangulated relationship among school personnel (teachers, staff, and administrators), students, and the wider community, especially parents. The parents may not be in the actual classroom, but their behaviors and attitudes shape everything that happens in the school, from the values that their children carry around in their heads to the funding and other resources that the school can draw upon to meet the educational needs of their children. Just as schools are more or less "bully-prone," so too are our communities. Parents have a particular role to play in reducing peer harassment.

Community leaders and members might ask, How well do parents listen to their children? How well have they explained the difference between telling the truth and being a tattle-tale? (Telling the truth is to help someone; tattling is to get someone else in trouble. Kids need to know this to enable them to resist being bystanders.) Are parents aware of the various warning signs that their son or daughter is a target, a perpetrator, or a bystander? Are parents prepared to intervene for their children? Can parents model and explain the difference between being assertive and being aggressive?

One issue seems especially important for fathers. As bullying and harassment have been going on for a very long time, it is a pretty sure bet that virtually every father has had to figure out how to navigate his way through these issues. Odds are that he was neither a victim nor a perpetrator—although, to be sure, some were. However, the odds are pretty good that he was a bystander. Odds are also good that he is still carrying around some shame about the fact that he did not do the right thing, that his fear got the best of him and that he betrayed his moral principles, his religious values, or his friends at some point in his life through his inaction. Fathers must begin to talk about these issues with their sons.

In a poignant story in the documentary film, *Manufacturing Consent* (1992), the linguist Noam Chomsky recalls an event from his own childhood. In first grade, he remembers, there was a fat boy who was ostracized by the other children. One day, several of them were taunting the fat boy, and one boy brought his older brother over to beat him up. Chomsky says that he thought someone ought to go over and stand by him, and so he did himself. Then he got scared and walked away, and he felt ashamed, and concluded that one should always stand by the underdog. Importantly, though, the shame of his walking away remains to this day. Telling boys such stories not only provides them a new possibility for acting differently in difficult and potentially violent situations but gives them a new, more nuanced emotional vocabulary that can be used instead of intimidation, fists, and guns.

Conclusion

A year after Jamie Nobozny filed his lawsuit, another student at the same high school found himself the target of incessant bullying and gay-baiting. He called Jamie one night and stammered a few hesitant words before he panicked and hung up. A few weeks later, the boy killed himself.[4]

High schools are not heaven; nor must they inevitably be hell. They can, though, be both haven and help, but only if we work to make them so. If we shrug our collective shoulders and say resignedly "boys will be boys," as the middle school principal told Jamie Nabozny, and as so many pundits and pop-psychologists seem to be saying, boys will never grow up to be the kind of men they are capable of becoming. If "boys will be boys" is the best we can do as a culture, we can be pretty sure that men will be boys, too.

Author's Note

This chapter represents an early and significantly modified version of a chapter in *Guyland: The perilous world where boys become men* (New York: HarperCollins, 2008). (c) 2008, by Michael Kimmel, Used by permission. All rights reserved.

Notes

1. Lizzie's story is recounted in Bushweller (2000). Available at: www.asbj. com/2000/08/0800coverstory.html
2. Some of this section is based on Kimmel (1999).
3. Michael Thompson cited in Boys to Men: Questions of Violence, *The Harvard Education Letter*, July/August 1999. Transcript available and retrieved August 2, 2005, from www.edletter.org/past/issues/1999-ja/forum.shtml.
4. See Jeff Walsh entry on Web site, "Profiles in Courage." Available and retrieved July 20, 2005, from http://www.oasisjournals.com/tags/profiles-in-courage?page=1

References

Blank, J. (1998, December). The kid no one noticed. *U.S. News and World Report*, p. 27.

Boodman, S. (2001, June 5). Teaching bullies a lesson. *Washington Post*, p. HE12.

Brooks, D. (2004a). The Columbine killers. *The New York Times*. Retrieved April 24, 2004, from http://query.nytimes.com/gst/fullpage.html?res=9B01E2DA12 3AF937A15757C0A9629C8B63

Brooks, D. (2004b). Columbine: Parents of a killer. *The New York Times*. Retrieved May 15, 2004, from http://query.nytimes.com/gst/fullpage.html?res=940DE2 D9163FF936A25756C0A9629C8B63

Bushweller, K. (2000, August). Brutal rituals, dangerous rites. *American School Board Journal*. Retrieved October 25, 2004, from www.asbj. com/2000/08/0800coverstory.html

Carlson, D., & Simmons,W. (2001). Majority of parents think a school shooting could occur in their community. *Gallup Poll Release*. Retrieved March 6, 2002, from http://www.gallup.com/poll/releases/pr010306.asp

Carter, K. (1997, March 7). Gay slurs abound. *Des Moines Register*, p. 1.

Chua-Eoan, H. (1997, October 20). Mississippi: In a dramatic turn, an alleged one-man rampage may have become a seven-pointed conspiracy. *Time*, p. 54.

Crawford, N. (2002). New ways to stop bullying. *APA Monitor*, 33(9), 64–67.

Cullen, D. (2004). The depressive and the psychopath, *Slate*. Retrieved April 20, 2004, from http://slate.msn.com/id/2099203/

Davis v. Monroe County Board of Education. (97–843) 526 U.S. 629 (1999) 120 F.3d 1390.

Davey, M. (2005, March 23). Behind the why of a rampage, loner with a taste for Nazism. *New York Times*, pp. A1, 12.

Davey, M., & Wilgoren, J. (2005, March 24). Signs of danger were missed in a troubled teenager's life. *New York Times*, pp. A1, 18.

Duncan, N. (1999). *Sexual bullying: Gender conflict and pupil culture in secondary schools*. New York: Routledge.

Epstein, D., Elwood, J., Hey, V., & Maw, J. (1998). *Failing boys*. Buckingham: Open University Press.

Espelage, D., Bosworth, K., & Simon, T. (2000). Examining the social context of bullying behaviors in early adolescence. *Journal of Counseling & Development*, 78(3), 326–333.

Faludi, S. (1998). *Stiffed*. New York: William Morrow.

Fineran, S. (2001). Sexual minority students and peer sexual harassment in high school. *Journal of School Social Work, 11*(2), 50–69.

Frosh, S., Phoenix, A., & Pattman, R. (2002). *Young masculinities*. London: Palgrave.

Gaughan, E., Cerio, J., & Myers, R. (2001). *Lethal violence in schools: A national survey. Final report*. Alfred, NY: Alfred University.

Gibbs, N., & Roche, T. (1999, December 20). The Columbine tapes: In five secret videos they recorded before the massacre, the killers reveal their hatreds—and their lust for fame. *Time*, p. 40.

Green, K., & Lieberman, B. (2001, March 10). Bullying, ridicule of Williams were routine, friends say. *San Diego Union-Tribune*, p. A1.

Hoff Sommers, C. (2000). *The war against boys*. New York: Simon and Schuster.

Holt, M., & Espelage, D. (2003). A cluster analytic investigation of victimization among high school students: Are profiles differentially associated with psychological symptoms and school belonging? *Journal of Applied School Psychology, 19*(2), 81–98.

Hoover, N., & Pollard, N. (2000). Initiation rites in American high schools: A national survey. Retrieved from Alfred University Web site: www.alfred.edu/news/html/hazing_study.html

Hoover, J. H., Oliver, R., & Hazler, R. J. (1992). Bullying: Perceptions of adolescent victims in the Midwestern USA. *School Psychology International, 13*(1), 5–16.

Human Rights Watch. (2001). Hatred in the hallways: Violence and discrimination against lesbian, gay, bisexual, and transgender students in U.S. schools. Retrieved from Human Rights Watch Web site: http://www.hrw.org/reports/pdfs/c/crd/usalbg01.pdf

Jones, R. (1999). I don't feel safe here anymore. *American School Board Journal*. Retrieved July 20, 2005, from http://www/asbj.com/199911/1199coverstory.html

Junoven, J., Graham S., & Schuster, M. (2003). Bullying among young adolescents: The strong, the weak and the troubled. *Pediatrics, 112*(6), 1231–1237.

Kimmel, M. (1999). What about the boys? What the current debates tell us—and don't tell us—about boys in school. *Michigan Feminist Studies, 14*, 1–28.

Kimmel, M., & Mahler, M. (2003). Adolescent masculinity, homophobia and violence: Random school shootings, 1982–2001. *American Behavioral Scientist*, 46(10), 1439–1458.

Knickerbocker, B. (1999). Young and male in America: It's hard being a boy. *Christian Science Monitor*. Retrieved April 29, 2004 from http://www.csmonitor.com/1999/0429/p1s3.html

Koerner, B. (1999, February 8). Where the boys aren't. *U.S. News and World Report*, p. 47–55.

Lacayo, R. (1998, April 6). Toward the root of the evil. *Time*, pp. 38–39.

Langland, C. (2001, April 15). Being scared … is not the way to go through school: College admissions essays offer a vivid look at how the Columbine massacre seared a generation. *Washington Post*, p. A-16.

Lemonick, M. (2005, April 11). The bully blight. *Time*, p. 145. Retrieved from http://www.time.com/time/magazine/article/0,9171,1047497,00.html

Lewin, T. (1998, December 6). American colleges begin to ask, where have all the men gone? *New York Times*. Retrieved from http://query.nytimes.com/gst/fullpage.html?res=940CE7DB1F3BF935A35751C1A96E958260

Limber, S. P., Cunningham, P., Florx, V., Ivey, J., Nation, M., Chai, S., et al. (1997). *Bullying among school children: Preliminary findings from a school-based intervention program*. Paper presented at the Fifth International Family Violence Research Conference, Durham, N. H. June.

McGee Bailey, S., & Campbell, P. (1999/2000). *The gender wars in education*. *WCW Research Report*. Wellesley, MA: Wellesley Centre for Research on Women.

Montgomery v. Indep Sch Dist no 709, 109 F. Supp. 2d 1081, 1089-93, D. Minn. 2000.

Nabozny v Podlesny, U.S. Court of Appeals, Seventh Circuit 92 F.3d 446, July 31, 1996.

Nansel, T.R., Overpeck, M., Pilla, R. S., Ruan, W. J., Simons-Moore, B., & Scheidt, P. (2001). Bullying behaviors among U.S. youth: Prevalence and association with psychosocial adjustment. *Journal of the American Medical Association*, 285(16), 2094–2100.

Nishina, A., & Juvonen, J. (2005). Daily reports of witnessing and experiencing peer harassment in middle school. *Child Development*, 76(2), 435–450.

Nishina, A., Juvonen, J., & Witkow, M. (2005). Sticks and stones may break my bones, but names will make me feel sick: The psychosocial, somatic and scholastic consequences of peer harassment. *Journal of Clinical Child and Adolescent Psychology*, 34(1), 37–48.

Noguera, P. (2008). *The trouble with black boys: And other reflections on race, equity, and the future of public education*. San Francisco: Jossey-Bass.

Nuwer, H. (2000). *High school hazing: When rites become wrongs*. New York: F Watts.

Okie, S. (2001, April 25). Survey: 30% of U.S. schoolchildren involved in bullying. *Washington Post*, p. A8.

Pooley, E. (1999, May 10). Portrait of a deadly bond. *Time*, p. 26–7.

Simmons, R. (2003). *Odd girl out: The hidden culture of aggression in girls*. New York & London: Harcourt.

Sisario, B. (2005, April 18). Eminem wins appeal over lawsuit. *New York Times*, p. E2. Retrieved from http://query.nytimes.com/gst/fullpage.html?res=9905E1D F1F3EF93BA25757C0A9639C8B63&partner=rssnyt&emc=rss

Stein, N. (2001). Sexual harassment meets zero tolerance: Life in K–12 schools. In W. Ayers, B. Dohrn, & R Ayers (Eds.), *Zero tolerance: Resisting the drive for punishment. A handbook for parents, students, educators and citizens.* New York: The New Press.

Sullivan, R. (2001, March 19) What makes a child resilient? *Time*, *157*(11), 35.

USA Today (1999, April 22). Fear of classmates, p. A1.

USA Today(2001, November 27). Half of teens have heard of a gun threat at school, p. 6D.

Wiseman, R. (2002). *Queen bees and wannabees.* New York: Crown.

Wolpert, S. (2005). Bullying among sixth graders a daily occurrence, UCLA study finds. Retrieved from http://www.newsroom.ucla.edu/portal/ucla/Bullying-Among-Sixth-Graders-a-6006.aspx

Young, R., & Sweeting, H. (2004). Adolescent bullying, relationships, psychological well-being and gender atypical behavior: A gender diagnosticity approach. *Sex Roles*, *50*(7-8), 565–574.

Zachary, G. P. (1997, May 2). Boys used to be boys, but do some now see boyhood as a malady. *Wall Street Journal*, pp. A1, A6.

9 Boys, Friendships, and Knowing "It Wouldn't Be Unreasonable to Assume I Am Gay"

Michael Kehler

Introduction

For some high school young men, walking through particular parts of the school can be a painful and threatening experience. Whether it is echoed in the distance or murmured under the breath of their peers, "fag," "freak," "wuss," and "gay" are searing reminders of the constant gender work required by young men to prove they are "real men" (see Pascoe, 2007). These terms are intended to signify a failure of masculinity, a failure of living up to a gendered standard of identity. Regardless of whether in fact a man demonstrates a lack of masculinity or an inadequacy in how he presents as masculine, the use of such terms publicly implies and openly denounces particular ways of being men. For high school young men who are ambiguous or outright unwilling to participate in heteronormative practices of masculinity and thus do not "fit" in with the stereotypical interests and actions of their male counterparts, the terms and references above are powerful forms of control over how boys "do boy" in schools. (see Kehler, 2004a; Mills, 2001; Mac An Ghaill, 1996; Martino, 2000, 2001) These tensions become particularly striking in situations when boys "actively shift in and out of different performances of other forms of masculinities available to them depending on their contextual reading of the space, situation at hand and the power relations operating" (Robinson, 2005, p. 23). One such situation is the same-sex friendships developed between boys in a school context (see McLeod, 2002; Renold, 2004; Walker, 1998) Building on Pease (2000), I explore what emerges as an uneasy tension for some high school young men in the development of close same-sex friendships. The focus of this chapter is on describing the close intimate relations of four young men, but I do this in relation to homophobia as a barrier within schools that currently prevents many heterosexual men from establishing male-male friendships.

The ways in which young men enact particular masculinities are increasingly complicated by the uncertainty that accompanies a shift in cultural norms and traditional gender markers that once clearly demarcated the masculine from the feminine. While admittedly the dichotomous distinctions remain a salient part of normative behavior among adolescents, the spaces in which young men renegotiate and reposition themselves as young men are less boundaried or restricted in many schools. In short, there is a growing, though not complete, acceptance of competing ways to be a man in schools. Messner (1997) suggests that "it's actually getting harder and harder for a young male to figure out how to *be* a man" (p. xiv). I argue in this chapter that a central challenge in schools that has gone largely unquestioned is the taken-for-grantedness of heterosexuality and how it is implicated in the maintenance of hegemonic masculinity through the daily interactions of adolescent youth. Kehily (2002) explains that

> school relations are organized around the assumption that heterosexuality is "the natural order of things." One effect of the naturalization of heterosexual relations is widespread homophobia, with homophobic practices often treated as routine everyday activities, particular among male peer groups (p.57).

The struggles for some nonconforming adolescent young men can in part be traced to a dominant and suffocating discourse that allows for a "business as usual" or "boys will be boys" attitude to prevail among high school young men. It is not surprising, based on the earlier work of Nayak and Kehily (1996), that schools have long been and continue to be marked by a landscape in which heterosexuality "acts as the norm within schools and the focal point around which other sexual behaviors are located" with an enduring impact that leaves "heterosexuality as natural rather than as socially conveyed through performance" (p. 224). In light of the complicated and widening range of non-traditional masculine behaviors and ways of (re)presenting oneself as young men in high school, educators need to be responsive to the ways in which heteronormativity is being routinely negotiated in the lives of young men. The response, on the part of educators, has serious implications for *all* students, those who are gay, lesbian, bi, transgender, or questioning and those who are heterosexual but are targeted by their peers as gay (for a useful analysis and elaboration, see Friend, 1998). Though cultural understandings of masculinities in schools appear to be shifting, there is a disturbing and troubling unease among young men who "fear being socially ostracized by their male peers as a result of challenging the social scripts constituting hegemonic masculinity" (Robinson, 2005, p. 30).

In this chapter, I highlight what is arguably the greatest fear for high school young men, namely the role that homophobia plays in the regulation of high school masculinities and the kind of tactics employed by young men, directed at young men, to prove that they are appropriately masculine. I do this in the context of adolescent young men developing same-sex friendships. As I mentioned in the introduction, there is considerable evidence linking the construction of masculinities in school and the perceived "feminine" of academic work as a defense against the charge of being gay (see Epstein, 1998, 2001). The driving fear that operates in many schools is the fear that men have of other men. Homophobia thus becomes the "animating condition of the dominant definition of masculinity ... the reigning definition of masculinity is a defensive effort to prevent being emasculated" (Kimmel, 1994, p. 135).

In this chapter, I discuss when and how homophobia marginalizes and de-legitimizes alternative versions of masculinity among high school young men. I examine the ways boys take up, accept, and reject certain versions of masculinity in a secondary school. Drawing on an ethnographic study (Kehler, 2000), I examine the public and visible interactions of four high school young men to provide insight into how homophobia and heterosexism are operationalized as a means of policing gender boundaries. I provide a series of events and conversations from the daily school interactions of young men to illustrate how, where, and under what circumstances high school young men employ homophobic strategies. These interactions and conversations serve as a platform for describing the tensions young men experience when they reject dominant forms of masculinity while developing male-male friendships (see also Kehler, 2004b; Robinson, 2005). Decisions, for example, to develop unusually close intimate male–male friendships and negotiate what it means to be "normal" in ways different from what is typically expected among high school young men suggest the powerful ways heterosexuality is practiced through social performances. (see Martino, 2000; Renold, 2000, 2004; Kehily, 2001).

All About the Boys, But *Which* Boys?

There is a remarkable sense of urgency to the attention currently being focused on boys, literacy, and schooling. The media have spurred on this hype with references to a "moral panic" or "crisis of masculinity" that has captured the national and international limelight. For public consumption, the argument is framed neatly and tightly as an either-or, us-them, the boys against the girls and, most important, a question of who comes out on top. "The 'boys as victims' rhetoric has a seductive but dangerous influence in its capacity to reinforce the very versions of masculinity that need to be challenged in schools" (Martino, 2001, p. 83). Though it is debated whether increased numbers of male role models and more male-centered books will improve achievement levels, what is clear is the ways that these approaches remasculinize schools by re-inscribing narrow and restrictive versions of masculinity. (see Martino, 2000; Martino & Kehler, 2006; Mills, 2004). Lingard and Douglas (1999) explain that the current debate and rush to "save the boys" from the feminizing influence of schools is problematic. There are clear divisions along ideological lines that underscore many of the current proposals to "help boys" and increase achievement levels, for example. Rather than increase equitable gender relations through schooling, Lingard and Douglas offer a cautionary note particularly with regard to hiring more male teachers, suggesting that such a move runs the risk of allowing "an influx of conservative and uncritical men" [who] could simply reinforce more traditional patterns of gender relations" (p. 58) These, and other such strategies, are quick and visible responses but with problematic messages and implications for what it means to be a boy in school (see Epstein, 2001). If the concern expressed in the mainstream media and the approaches being adopted by schools in Canada, Australia, and the United States for example, are genuinely aimed at improving achievement levels among boys, it follows that along with the aforementioned strategies, schools will need to seriously consider addressing masculinity in and of itself. The current debate, however, does very little in terms of addressing the very "significant ways in which compulsory heterosexuality impacts on the lives of boys and girls at school, not only those who identify as gay" (Epstein, 2001, p. 96). Be it in the school halls, classrooms, or parking lots, high school students routinely participate in homophobic and heterosexist practices aimed at monitoring gender relations. (see Mac An Ghaill, 1994; Nayak & Kehily, 1996; Pascoe, 2007; Redman, Epstein, Kehily, & Man An Ghaill, 2002; Robinson, 2005) As Epstein (2001) points out, "it is, in part, because of the demands made on them [boys] to be macho and, at all costs, not to appear feminized or gay" (p. 96) that many boys reject school and the kinds of academic investment required to succeed.

Attempts to rearticulate and reiterate a hegemonic masculinity through policies and practices reflect what is really at stake in the current debate. By all accounts, it is not achievement levels or performance levels at the core of the current movement to help boys but, rather, it is identity politics, it is the way of being boys and being girls that is being judged and played out in an outcomes-based arena. Largely driven by the conservative men's movement, the current agenda to help boys improve achievement levels is largely a restorative effort underwritten by men who fail to engage with the more critical and penetrating question that might problematize how and when heteronormative masculinity operate in schools at the expense of academic study and achievement. In short, there is a concerted and strategic effort put forth by a recuperativist politic to offer what Lingard and Douglas (1999) describe as a "male-repair agenda to reaffirm masculine identities" (p. 133). The "problem with the boys," as it has come to be so liberally cast about, is instead what Francis and Skelton (2005) describe as the "general brutalizing effects involved in boys' collective productions of, and struggle for, masculinity"

(p. 9). I agree with Francis and Skelton (2005), who further argue that the potential of boys and girls will be achieved only when we encourage them to "deconstruct the gender boundaries which delineate certain types of behavior and expression as only appropriate for one gender or the other"(p. 9–10). (see also Kehler and Martino, 2007). The contradictions inherent in policies and practices to remasculinize curriculum and nurture boy culture currently being adopted in schools in Canada and elsewhere is captured by McLeod (2002) who argues that current reforms are evidence of a feminist backlash in which feminism is being blamed for "destabilizing gender roles and making men more vulnerable" (p. 214).

Notions of hegemonic masculinity operate in powerful and coercive ways to control and regulate both boys and girls. Worth bearing in mind is the fact that a boy's location within diverse and different discursive contexts means that masculinity is lived and experienced differently, dependent upon the opportunities and social setting within which boys operate (see Robinson, 2005). Localized settings such as schools afford boys both different access and different opportunities to construct different masculinities. In her poignant study describing the daily interactions of students at River High, Pascoe (2007) captures the uneven terrain of gender inequality in which the ritualistic and heterosexualized public practices of some boys operate to "affirm much more than just masculinity; they affirm subjecthood and personhood through sexualized interactions in which they indicate to themselves and others that they have the ability to work their will upon the world around them" (p. 86). The notion of dominance figures prominently in the ways young men exercise and display gender practices exclusively for the purpose of denigrating the other and elevating the self among boys. Haywood and Mac An Ghaill (1997) describe the management of masculinities among boys as a process in which "relations of domination and subordination become apparent, as some groups are able to define their meaning of masculinity over others" (p. 55).

This chapter discusses some of the challenges of enacting nontraditional masculinities given what these young men understood about being boys, friendships, and at the same time being "normal." In the following study, I examine the difficulties four high school young men experience when embracing and embodying alternative representations of masculinities while resisting heteronormative masculinity. Influenced by Judith Butler's theorizing of gender, I build on her work, acknowledging "the performativity of gender and the regulatory fiction of heterosexual coherence" (1999, pp. 42–43). Her analysis usefully illustrates the active construction of powerful arrangements emerging out of gendered interactions. As Butler argues, "gendered/sexualized identities are consolidated through a heterosexual matrix of power in the effort to evade 'gender trouble'" (pp. 42–43). As such, schools are sites in which gender is actively performed and negotiated in different contexts to protect and deflect. Gender is an active performance. For many young men, we routinely ride those gender boundaries protecting ourselves by "checking the fences we have constructed on the perimeter making sure that nothing even remotely feminine might show through" (Kimmel, 1994, p. 132). Similarly, many boys actively try to deflect suspicion that they are anything less than a man. Kimmel describes the surveillance and scrutiny of peers who act as "gender police constantly threatening to unmask us as feminine, as sissies" (p. 132). A manly front is maintained by actively constructing and reconstructing a façade of masculinity that publicly affirms heterosexuality through exaggerated rules and norms of masculinity. I argue throughout this chapter that the relationship between heterosexuality and homophobia is unmistakably parasitic, in which young men attempt to prove their manhood at all costs. As such, men's fears of being suspected as gay operate in a powerful manner to sustain and maintain narrow and restrictive versions of masculinity. This chapter focuses on capturing and describing the cultural performances of masculinity while high school young men are developing in school male-male friendships.

Increasingly evident among certain high school young men is the ability to negotiate and renegotiate gendered identities in an arena and during a historical context that allows for a broader repertoire of ways for being men. Whereas practically and theoretically masculinity used to be limited by assumptions of a rigid and limiting nature, current arguments and interpretations of the school lives of young men acknowledge a greater elasticity, flexibility, and willingness expressed within and among high school masculinities (see Connell, 1995; Davison, 2000; Epstein, 2001; Martino, 2000; Mac An Ghaill, 1994; Mandel & Shakeshaft, 2000; Nayak & Kehily, 1996). This aspect of fluidly changing gender norms among men is central to better understanding the impact a "dissolution of gender norms" (see McLeod, 2002) may have on male-male relationships. Though I am not arguing that gender norms and the codes of masculinity are dissolving, I am suggesting that the shifts and the current challenges to and disruptions in how masculinities are configured in secondary schools reveal a powerful moment in the redefinition of high school masculinities.

The Study

This chapter emerges out of research conducted in a secondary school located in the midwest United States. Drawing on qualitative research methods, I conducted ethnographic research during a 7-month period in the final semester of the school term. The four young men in this study were between the ages of 17 and 18 years. After preliminary informal classroom observations and recommendations from teachers at the senior level, the four young men volunteered to participate in the study. These young men are part of a purposeful sampling then on the basis of what they demonstrated about competing forms of masculinities. In other words, they were approached to be a part of this study because of what their teachers and the author witnessed as an ability to "shift in and out of different performances of other forms of masculinities" (Robinson, 2005, p. 23). Largely grounded in feminist research methods (see Lather, 1991), this study aimed at observing, listening to, and understanding the daily and taken-for-grantedness of the school lives of four young men. I shadowed each of the participants on a rotating weekly basis. During this time, I attended classes, "chilled" in the hallways, and spent alternating weeks with each young man during the final semester (January–June) of their senior high school year. My field notes consisted of the conversations and interactions I observed during school hours. In addition to field observations, I interviewed Philip, Hunter, David and Thurston at the beginning of the study and then later at the end of the study. The initial interview explored more general information about the participants whereease the latter interview aimed at probing for deeper understandings about specific moments or events. A tape recorder was used for each of these sessions, and later the tapes were transcribed. A collection of observations gathered while shadowing these young men became a contextual prompt of sorts that then allowed these young men to explain and describe the routine interactions and conversations. The methodological complications of doing ethnographic research as a white middle-class man are taken up elsewhere (see Kehler, 2003).

This study illuminates the complexity of the lives of these high school young men by bringing to the surface a set of voices that have largely gone unheard. Though admittedly the research into student's school lives has grown considerably over the past few decades (see Mac An Ghaill, 1994; MacLeod, 1987; Pascoe, 2007; Thorne, 1993), there is a noticeable under-representation of student voices that reveal the complexities of negotiating gender identities. Admittedly this has been changing in more recent research. At the center of this study, then, are the voices and actions of Philip, Hunter, Thurston, and David, four senior high school young men who describe, explain, and routinely illustrate a kind of gender obedience to hegemonic masculinity and negotiations with heterosexualized identities. Similar to that of Frank (1996), this study aims at letting these young men speak for themselves rather than what has historically been the case in which "partial and fragmented accounts elevate certain ways of seeing and understating men and boys over others" (p. 115).

The conversations and actions of these young men demonstrate the complexity and messiness of masculinity. They reveal a sophisticated and complicated set of understandings these young men posses about what it means to be a man and, most important, what it means to be a heterosexual young man among other young men. High schools are powerful arenas in which gender identities are routinely negotiated and renegotiated (see Davison, 2004; Imms, 2000; Kehler, 2004). As these young men illustrate, there is nothing natural or biological about masculinity but, rather, it is about the careful and calculated ways young men enact or perform particular versions of masculinity in school in light of what they understand about being a man. According to Hunter, the process of being a man is carefully orchestrated where very little is left to chance. He explains, "It's like you have to come up and say the right things and do the right things in order to be cool ... . You can't just be yourself and you can't goof off in being cool" (Kehler, 2000) Whether being cool or being heterosexual, what is important in this case is the degree to which young men are able to convince their peers, and particularly other young men, that they are "real men" (see Connell, 1989; Kimmel, 1994, Martino, 2000). McLaren (1995) explains that "heterosexuality has meaning only in relation to other identities such as homosexuality ... the terms are continually and culturally negotiated within diverse historical and social arenas and in terms of competing vectors of power" (p. 112). Schools provide a single context among boys and young men where the tensions and costs for (re)negotiating heterosexualized identities are played out but are often times unnoticed and unacknowledged, routinely masked by other social dynamics. As I explain later, the costs for being anything but a real man are considerable.

Friendships and the Practices to Navigate them

In this section, I explore connections between same-sex adolescent male-male friendships and their relationship to dominant practices of masculinity and notions of heterosexuality in a secondary school setting. As mentioned earlier in this chapter, though many adolescent young men are reluctant to publicly establish and maintain male-male relationships, the importance they associate with these relationships is significant. It is understandable to some extent, then, that while young men are mindful of the norms of masculinity, some boys nonetheless transgress normative masculinity in search of intimacy, closeness, and genuine honesty among boys, qualities not always easily or openly displayed in male peer groups. The boys I describe in this chapter express similar qualities of friendships to those characterized by Way and Chu (2004), who have found these relationships to be "key relationships ... in which boys experienced the most joy, but also the most difficulty" (p. 168). In *Rethinking Masculinity*, May and Strikwerda (1992) acknowledge the tensions young men experience because of the lessons learned and the cultural taboo associated with touching between adolescent males and the frequent association linking masculinity, intimacy, sexuality, and prevailing notions of homophobia. Not dissimilar in their findings, Renold (2000), Redman et al., (2002), Haywood (1996), and Nayak and Kehily (1996) provide useful insight into the negotiation of gender identities among youth and particularly adolescent males. Building on these studies, I begin this section acknowledging the intersectionality between masculinities, heterosexuality, and homophobia. I follow from this with interview data to extend previous arguments that problematize the uneven and troubling terrain of identity politics in developing adolescent male-male friendships.

In his earlier work, Connell (1995) described the body as a significant text, "a communicative site for the construction of masculinity where true masculinity is almost always thought to proceed from men's bodies" (p.45). Nayak and Kehily (1996) similarly argue that "heterosexual masculinities are, then, naturalized through body styling" (p.221). It is the assumed natural taken-for-grantedness of heterosexualized identities that so complicates the untangling of relationships and particularly heterosexualized same-sex, male-male friendships that transgress normative rules of acceptable masculinity in schools. This study not only provides a look at the relationships four adolescent males develop with their male counterparts but the way in which friendships among young men in high school are defined by masculinizing practices. By exploring specific actions, interactions, and explanations from these young men, I offer insight into the ways friendships among boys in a secondary school are undergirded by a broader contextual understanding that links masculinity, sexuality, and homophobia.

The difficulties of developing same-sex friendships among adolescent boys and men has gained considerable interest. (see Lyman, 1987; McLeod, 2002; Redman et al., 2002; Renold, 2004; Swain, 2005; Way, 1997). Given the limits and focus of this chapter, I do not attempt to provide a comprehensive or exhaustive survey of the most current research on boy's friendships in school. Instead, my aim in this section is twofold. First, I highlight key elements emerging from a set of male-male friendships and second, I suggest the ways same-sex friendship among adolescent boys reflect back on a particularly troublesome climate in secondary schools, namely one characterized by homophobic and heterosexist underpinnings.

The influence of peer groups as a reference point contributing to how students—both boys and girls—define the self is well established. (see Davison, 2000; Gilbert & Gilbert, 1998; Imms, 2000; Willis, 1977; Wyss, 2004) As these and other studies have revealed, both femininities and masculinities are under constant surveillance and reconstruction at this time in student school lives. Importantly Wyss explains that the development and negotiation of gender identities is increasingly evident in secondary schools, where more and more students are beginning school identifying themselves as gay, lesbian, bi, transgender, or questioning youth. For adolescent young men, peer groups are central to how boys define masculinity in relation to other boys. Martino and Palotta-Chiarolli (2005), drawing on Butler, describe gender performativity among youth as a set of "self-fashioning practices" that constitute, for example, straight acting behaviors among students. "Through an ensemble of normalizing social practices and rules governing gendered conduct, students appear to have acquired a specific repertoire of skills and bodily capacities for establishing desirable form of masculinities and femininities" (Martino & Pallota-Chiarolli, p. 98). The young men in this study have navigated a set of masculine identities and, in doing so, made clear and distinct choices about acceptable norms of behavior. Part of their consideration is the importance of *really* knowing or trusting young men and being friends with their male counterparts because of the implications it can have in the broader school setting for being "outed" as anything less than a man. Anxieties such as these serve as a powerful means by which homophobia and heterosexism operate among boys to restrict and limit potential gender transgressions.

In a recent study, Pascoe (2007) acknowledges that "homophobia is indeed a central mechanism in the making of American adolescent masculinity," but she extends the connection previously made between homophobia and masculinity, suggesting this claim is too facile. Instead, Pascoe argues that this process whereby one is named "fag" or is outed, as in this study, actually contributes in significant ways to how "boys discipline themselves and each other through joking relationships" (Pascoe, p. 54). The fag discourse has a particular kind of mobility or fluidity that allows boys to invoke this language to both "connect with one another and manage the anxiety around this sort of relationship through joking about fags" (Pascoe, p. 60). Akin to other practices, such as "trying to get a girl," the following event confirms and valorizes a heterosexualizing of friendships among boys captured when Philip recalls his recent eighteenth birthday celebration. Surrounded by his male peers, he recalls,

> I felt good … . This crowd of guys circled around me and they said 'Philip, we got something for you'. And they passed me this brown paper bag and I looked inside … . You know it was like one of those things out of the movies and the guys are standing in a circle congratulating each other and like slapping each other on the back like [deepened voice] Yeahhhhh. It was just this very cool guy moment. It was just a great feeling. I felt, [pause] loved. And I mean, I know it was just a cheap porn but it was still, you know, like getting a porno on your eighteenth birthday.
>
> (Philip from Kehler, 2000)

The passing of the brown paper bag is a rite of passage (notably Philip is turning 18 years old) cloaked by secrecy and a shaming associated with the pornography but also associated with passing into an age of adulthood. The men huddled around Phillip, similar to a huddle one might find in a locker room or on a sports field, and is telling of the ritualistic masculine practices that typify how these adolescent boys come to define their masculinity in relation to other boys. In this instance, Philip does not reject the magazine and the objectification of women that it represents but rather revels in a "very cool guy moment." The masculinist tone of this scene is interrupted not at the time of the event but when Philip recalls the feelings elicited from this event. Though Philip describes the gift as a "cheap porn," he is nonetheless overwhelmed by a sense of love heightened by the boys encircling him. His attention to the emotional and physical setting is striking. In what appears to be a passage of manhood with trademarks of sporty athleticism from the locker room that engulfs Philip, he replaces a form of heterosexist male bonding among boys with an admission of a "great feeling" in which he "felt loved." His articulation of love for his male peers is curiously and puzzlingly contrasted with the intended purpose to initiate Philip into manhood. The contradiction in the rite of passage to a heterosexual manhood and a public expression of love between men is striking.

Each of the boys offers ways for understanding and explaining masculinity. Thurston locates one version of masculinity in media images. According to him, the media provide a template for many boys to know how to be boys:

> The typical male, like what they've been growing up with of what guys are supposed to be like. You see guys on t.v. who are afraid to express their feelings. So they are sort of afraid to break from that
> (from Kehler, 2000).

And on another occasion, Thurston reflects on one of his classmates describing him this way:

> He's the big stereotypical jock football player ... and I guess there must be a whole group of people like him. People who would say like, "Dude, did you see her tits?" and not even think anything about it. It's just weird and incomprehensible to me that there are people like that.

His understanding of masculinity and the ways young men express heteronormative masculinity reflects on his positioning within the school. Relatively incubated from traditional codes of masculinity, Thurston defines himself as an "alterna-teen" with interests in poetry and music that set him apart from many other boys. To some degree, Thurston sees masculinity and the forgoing version of athletic masculinity as compartmentalized by "a whole group of people like him." He sees masculinity as relatively static, captured in media images that dictate "what guys are supposed to be like" and then crystallized as a "whole group of people." His outward look to define and explain masculinity, not like that of his own embodied self, is one of a remarkably settled and unproblematic version of masculinity. He concludes his explanation of this type of masculinity saying that "I would guess they picked it up from their parents or grandparents."

Thurston struggles to explain a masculine discourse centering on the objectification of women that he frequently heard among some of his male counterparts. In an interview, he traced their behaviors and ways of being boys back to family where, as he explains, "they really treat women more as like, prizes or something other than as people" (Kehler, 2000, p. 141). For each of these boys, the various markers of masculinity were evident in daily interactions. David describes the valuing of athletic bodies and the connections made to being popular:

> Not being huge but to be bigger would be encouraged, just by what's attractive maybe. I think it is just the way guys compare one another against each other. It's like how much they can bench press … . It's different ways you can size people up.

His assessment of how boys convey masculine identities among other boys is related to the physical and athletic prowess one displays. The level of physical presence is significant. In this instance, David connects body size to what is publicly attractive and appealing. His comments are useful as a window on what boys see as important in relation to other boys. There is an obvious awareness among these boys that their masculinity is on display. It is judged on a daily basis according to "what's attractive" and the "ways you can size people up." In our ongoing interview, David, unlike many of his male peers, rejects the muscularity associated with this version of masculinity, describing it as "gross," explaining that he does "not want to look like that."

David, Philip, Thurston, and Hunter display an arguably more complicated and textured way of being a man that runs counter to these dominant images of masculinity. The more nuanced and complicated understandings of masculinity shared across these young men is framed by their friendships with other young men. In his public admission of his love for his male peers, Philip talks of an emotional commitment he holds for his friends:

> I will say without hesitation that I love each and every one of them. I mean, a lot of guys are scared to use that word. But I mean friendship, ahh; I love them, each and everyone.

(from Kehler, 2000)

According to these young men, the intimacy, closeness, and emotional bond that form in male-male friendships in school varies in terms of the quality and depth of relationship. Hunter explains:

> Like my friendship with Doug differs from Kevin, just because Kevin doesn't like to talk about certain stuff and kind of keeps stuff secret. He just kind of doesn't like to talk about mushy stuff so much and how he really feels ... . Doug and I can pretty much talk about anything.
>
> (from Kehler, 2000)

For Hunter, his friendships are marked by the ability to communicate openly and honestly without reservation. In his friendship with Kevin, Hunter detects a reluctance and level of secrecy on the part of Kevin to share how "he really feels." He acknowledges that his "best friends have always been girls," explaining that he has always "found it easier to talk to girls before, like guys." He continues, explaining differences between both the kinds of friends he has and the purposes they serve:

> So like, he would call me up and say 'Hey, can we go talk?' and he would just tell me his life. Basically I was kind of, like, his counsellor, you know, like, and his friend. Because he could tell me everything and I wasn't just like one of his other friends, like smoker friends which is like, "Yo, let's get high'.
>
> (from Kehler, 2000)

Hunter makes a distinction of being both a counselor and a friend. He also makes a clear distinction in the level of their friendship different from other friends who are "like smoker friends." Friendships among these boys are underscored by concerns of secrecy and vulnerability.

Friendships are deeply connected to masculine identities. On one hand, Hunter describes how the ability to talk openly is difficult for some boys and, at the other end of the spectrum, David reminds us of the fragility and vulnerability of feelings some boys need and want to share. He recalls a time returning home when "Josh started crying. I was just like, driving and holding Josh's hand. It's just like, something we have." Muddied by impressions of masculinity tied to sexualized identities, these boys consistently developed friendships based on an ability to be intimate, to be able to touch another young man and, according to David, "really draw from each other for a lot of strength ... [because] ... those kinds of relationships mean a lot to me where I know I am there for somebody" (Kehler, 2000, p. 88). In light of what these boys understand about masculinity, they nonetheless develop rich friendships marked by the ability to communicate, to be open, and to be honest with their male peers.

The young men in this study speak of friendships with other boys that are honest, at times physically intimate, and trustworthy. Each of the boys has a clear understanding of the rules of engagement with other boys. At the same time, they ran the risk of transgressing the rules of masculinity by accidentally misreading other boys. David explains the kind of friendship he values stating that "I like to find out what's really going on in people's lives as opposed to just 'Hey, how's it going?'" David and Hunter invest themselves in alternative masculinities most evident in how they publicly nurture and support caring relationships with other young men. They acknowledge the fact that the intimacy and closeness they have with other young men is unusual for men. David's friend, for example, describes their relationship as "uncommonly affectionate." At the same time, Hunter explains the kind of gender work other young men do to keep them from becoming vulnerable or open in relationships. He remarks that "people like Jason are sensitive but they try not to be. They try to build up a wall." This "wall" or facade of masculinity serves as a type of armour for high school young men. It is, however, not impenetrable, and perhaps that is part about which these young men are most concerned. David adds to the complexity of these relationships by suggesting that there are different sides to his friends that are revealed at different times. He explains,

> When I am around Chris, for example, he acts differently. He has more of a sensitive, caring side around me. But I noticed how a lot of guys are just interested in you know, maybe hanging with girls for maybe one night.

The conversations between these young men suggest the complicated ways they navigate between the plastic masculinities of media constructions and the intense emotional and physical yearnings high school young men actually desire. McLeod (2002) explains that "alongside traditional gender patterns there are signs of changes emerging in how young women and men negotiate friends and relationships and these, in turn, signal rearticulations of femininity and masculinity" (p. 216). As Thurston explains, the tensions emerge because "boys are afraid to express their feelings." This fear is expressed repeatedly by these young men. Hemmed in by images of normative masculinity that restrict and confine the ways men "do" masculinity in school, Haywood (1996) reminds us that one aspect of schooling made visible by its absence "is the lack of opportunities for males to talk seriously or privately about sexuality, emotions, or relationships" (p. 24). Though not a concern for Hunter, David, Thurston, or Philip, there was a shared understanding that male-male friendships were influenced by what was considered appropriate masculine behaviour. Nayak and Kehily (1996) describe a tension some boys experience who are unable to communicate openly with other boys. As they explain, "talking about personal and emotional subjects becomes problematic as it fractures the hard face of conventional masculinity" (Nayak & Kehily, p. 224). Thus, for many high school young men, "fear" operates in powerful ways to leave them feeling like David's friend Rick who, "no matter what's wrong, he would never tell you anything is wrong" or Thurston's friend John, who "won't divulge his feelings at any cost." Emotionally illiterate and physically bound by traditional masculine codes, young men negotiate the hidden and unspoken words of personal feelings in exchange for the safety of a heteronormative masculinity.

Homophobia constrains heterosexual men, thus becoming a major barrier preventing more intimate relationships. "The fear of homosexuality inhibits men from touching each other outside certain socially acceptable situations" (Garfinkel in Pease, 2000, p. 78). In their research, Anoop and Kehily (1996) similarly found that the process of "resisting dominant codes of masculinity is a precarious business within schools where being labeled 'gay' can have detrimental effects" (p. 215). Not surprisingly then, bodily transgressions from stereotypical relations of a hegemonic masculinity often prompt homophobic reactions. Philip explains that:

> There are a lot of typical guys that will say "Oh, he's gay if he's acting a certain way." That's a big thing. I don't quite understand it. I don't think it is a big deal if someone is gay. I think it is just, [pause] ignorance and comes out of society.

The public ways in which these young men embodied and enacted masculinity provoked cases of policing and surveillance from among their friends that were consistent with forms of bodily surveillance found in previous studies (see Connell, 1995, 2000; Martino, 2000, 2001; Martino & Pallota-Chiarolli, 2003; Nayak & Kehily, 1996; Renold, 2004). Philip describes a response commonly expressed by other men when he engages in practices of masculinity considered alternative to dominant constructions.

> A lot of people that I know take a hug as a homosexual gesture. There are some people that I would go to hug and they'd be like, "What the hell are you doing? Get away from me you freak."

There is an expectation for boys to greet one another in specific ways. In the foregoing instance, Philip publicly resists these norms and, in doing so, provokes a reaction from his classmates. Though similar in their intention and awareness of the norms guiding these young men, Hunter's experience with physical intimacy, such as hugging other young men, varies slightly. He remarks:

> You can always hug guys when they are having bad days. That's just a given. And I'm not like, great friends with him or anything but I saw him and I was like, what's wrong?

Hunter, like the other boys in this study, describes a kind of physical intimacy relatively uncommon among most high school adolescent boys. His obvious ability to "read people" and communicate through frank and honest discussions and through physical closeness with his peers reveals a richness in the repertoire of ways he is able to communicate with his male counterparts.

In this study, these young men were more likely to transgress codes of masculinity in places such as the car, secluded parts of school hallways, restaurants, or secluded areas of the school property and surrounding area. Common to each of these places was the relative isolation and security they promised for uninterrupted conversations between these boys. Hunter purposefully tried to be a supportive and trusting friend. He saw opportunities to "be there" and be a friend, particularly when his male peers "are having bad days." The rules of engagement appear to soften, and the masculinized boundaries between young men appear to be open to negotiation. Hunter qualifies the foregoing interaction, indicating that though the level of friendship and whether one is a "great friend" has some bearing on the kind of intimacy young men share and the extent to which there are allowances to be closer, physically and emotionally, with other young men. During an interview, he later explained that there are some "people you just don't give hugs to unless it is a total joke," but there are also "people that I can really give a hug to and like, mean it." According to David, this kind of intimacy between young men is an alternative in which

> ...being reassuring and hugging guys that way can mean so much more than what I can ever say. I am saying I am here for you and it's just like, that hug helps them feel that.
>
> (from Kehler, 2000)

The underlying tension for these young men is connected to how the interaction is contextualized and ultimately legitimized or de-legitimized by their peers. The aforementioned situation and reaction from among these young men and their peers reveal some of the ways, conditions, and spaces in which young men actively invest in non-hegemonic masculinities. It is worth noting that the broader context in which these transgressions of masculine codes are also occurring during a time, when, as Nayak and Kehily (1996) point out, "young men are the most stringent guardians of heterosexuality and may perceive being gay as 'wrong' or 'unnatural' since it violates traditional masculinity" (p. 224).

Harboring Fears and Promoting Homophobia

Same-sex friendships among high school young men are frequently predicated upon cultural understandings about masculinity and heterosexism. David, Philip, Hunter, and Thurston each describe the ways other high school young men protect themselves or create distance in the process of manufacturing certain styles of masculinity. Even though this study and others (see Mac An Ghaill, 1994; McLeod, 2002; Pease, 2000; Walker, 1998; Way, 1997) have suggested the importance of male-male friendships for high school young men, many continue to be wary of investing in these relationships largely because of a homophobic climate in many high schools.

In describing what constitutes male heterosexuality within Parnell school Mac An Ghaill (1994) reports a shifting emphases of conflicting desires, anxieties, fears, and confusions among men. Similar to the processes described earlier, Mac An Ghaill describes "sexual boundary maintenance, policing and legitimization of male heterosexual identities" (p. 90). The significance and lurking threat that homophobia plays in many schools leads "heterosexual men [to] try to avoid anything that other men might interpret as effeminate or unmanly. Men fear that any intimacy between men may sully their sexual identity" (Pease, 2000, p, 78). Consistent with past studies then (see Martino, 2000; Mills, 2001, Redman et al., 2002; Robinson, 2005), the young men in this study describe a range of fears and anxieties underscoring the kinds of possible relationships currently supported, both formally and informally, between high school young men and women.

There are a wide range of fears informing whether or not young men accept what Connell (1995) refers to as the "project of hegemonic masculinity." In the following conversation, Hunter explains that being a man and performing alternative masculinities in schools is complicated. He makes connections to suggest that for a man to be open or honestly expressive about his feelings to a young woman has implications. Though Hunter himself does not harbor such fears, he explains that boys are driven to protect themselves and remain uncommunicative because it may reveal a weakness. As Hunter explains, there are many reasons to hide one's true feelings:

> I think they are afraid from all different angles. I think they are afraid that they'll get rejected or the girl won't think they're man ... all the way to their friends making fun of them ... he is afraid, kind of whether he's saying the wrong things or just not going to accept him. And if he keeps his distance then it doesn't really matter because he's not, he doesn't have to expose himself so he doesn't have to get hurt or lose anything. But if he does then she actually knows him.

There is considerable pressure both from other young men and from young women to adhere to traditional codes of masculinity. Peer groups and particularly male-male peer groups are powerful reminders of the complex and overlapping "relations between the different kinds of masculinity: relations of alliance, dominance and subordination" (Connell, 1995, p. 37). Thurston explains that young men "feel the need to be normal ... they are just afraid because they feel they might be ostracized from some community of friends."

In addition to a common fear of being socially "outed" and thus ostracized from peers, discourses of homophobia are typically invoked by young men to affirm heterosexuality. In other words, "homophobia becomes a means of consolidating sexuality and gender through the traducing of femininity and its association with homosexuality" (Nayak & Kehily, 1996, p. 214). All things feminine are taboo. Expressions of personal feelings, close physical intimacy, and the genuine and careful listening demonstrated by these young men thus become dangerous social practices because they challenge the existing gender order in which more rigid and less forgiving constructions of heteronormative masculinity are firmly entrenched. As I mentioned, there are real fears and concerns for young men who resist dominant codes of masculinity. The most potent of these fears is the performance of heterosexuality through the display of homophobia. Kimmel (1994) describes the ways in which men incite or engage in homophobic practices in relation to other young men to "unmask us, emasculate us, reveal to us and the world that we do not measure up, that we are not real men. We are afraid to let other men see that fear. Fear makes us ashamed, because the recognition of fear in ourselves is proof to ourselves that we are not as manly as we pretend ..." (p. 131).

Homophobia is a powerful mechanism in which verbal taunts effectively punish, repress, and deny alternative displays of masculinities. Even in the absence of bodies, some high school young men take pleasure to name, locate, or marginalize young men. While sitting in Thurston's government class, for example, the teacher proceeded to describe a variety of assignments available to students. She explained that "for the artsy types you can create a mobile." In one of the following classes, a young man presented his mobile assignment. As Thurston and I sat listening, a young man leaned over, commenting, "I guess homosexuality allows for more creativity." Both prompted by the teachers' remark and articulated by the young man, creativity was linked to sexuality. In this situation, the teacher creates a context and draws on underlying assumptions about creative ability while the student articulates and names the association. As Nayak and Kehily (1996) argue, "these acts are as much about self as audience" The young man's comments become a way of naming and valorizing his own heterosexualized identity.

The foregoing instances, along with those reported elsewhere, reveal a particular and active way that young men position themselves in relation to other masculinities (see Epstein, 1998, 2001; Davison, 2004; Nilan, 2000; Pascoe, 2007; Renold, 2000). In the following situation, homophobia and heterosexism intertwine:

> On this particular day David has gone out for lunch so I wait in the music room for him to arrive. The band class has just returned from a field trip and the bulletin board has an array of trip photos. I notice David and his friend Paul in one of the pictures. The two of them are lying alongside each other with their heads propped up on pillows on what appears to be a hotel bed. I smile as I survey this and many other pictures. Under the aforementioned picture is a caption, "things that make you go mmmmm." As I stand looking at these pictures Paul, a friend of David's saddles alongside me. I remark 'that's a good picture of you two." He looks at the photo and responds, "You can say what you want, I don't mind. I look to Paul, "Pardon?" He adds, "actually David doesn't have to worry, he has a girlfriend. He doesn't have to defend himself."

That evening I received an e-mail from Paul. The text of it reads

> As far as defending that picture goes, I'm not sure to whom specifically I would have to defend it. Generally though, David and I are uncommonly affectionate, I guess I could say, in our friendship as far as typical male-male relationships go. Therefore it is possible that people who would see that picture would put two and two together, but they would not get four, if you know what I am saying. But they would think possibility that we are gay and David, having a girlfriend, would quell some suspicion. However, I don't have a girlfriend so it wouldn't be unreasonable to assume that I am gay so I would have to defend my heterosexuality.

This scenario is punctuated a week later when I notice "sick, sick, sick, faggety" scribbled under the picture of David and Paul. Gilbert and Gilbert (1998) explain that "to construct and maintain a sense of who they are, boys must draw on the available terms, categories and ways of thinking, acting and interacting which these various contexts provide, including the specific forms of masculinity associated with them" (p. 51). The photograph of these two young men becomes a textual representation and a public billboard evoking a clear and decisive response of sentiments understood by classmates. The comments, written under the picture, remained on the board for the following week. The fact that one wrote these comment speaks to an undercurrent of homophobia in the school.

In addition, it is striking to see from this exchange that Paul felt a need to "defend" and thus justify his way of being a boy with another boy.

Similar to the work of Renold (2004), these incidents reveal how homophobia gets "directed at boys who get too close to other boys and those boys who failed or chose not to access hegemonic masculine discourses/ practices" (p. 322). Boys routinely position others as gay or subordinate to affirm their own heterosexualized identities. It is interesting, too, that Paul gives me permission to say what I want about the photo. He follows up by grounding his comments in a heterosexist discourse by placing David with a girlfriend and calculating, both figuratively and metaphorically, that the relationship captured in the picture does not compute. It is also striking that Paul is compelled to help me make sense of the picture by explaining how others might interpret it. His final comment, that "it wouldn't be unreasonable to assume I am gay" is both an acknowledgement of the kind of currency a heterosexual discourse carries in school but also a reminder of the ways in which compulsory heterosexuality is routinely expressed as part of a masculine performance connected to having a girlfriend.

Concluding Remarks

This study has revealed the powerful ways four young men, differently situated in a single school setting, develop close male-male friendships. The ability, and indeed willingness, adolescent high school boys demonstrate to develop close male-male friendships is relatively under-examined. At the same time, this study illustrates some of the complex ways young men navigate within and beyond boundaries of heterosexuality. I have argued throughout this chapter that the relative absence of close intimate friendships among high school young men is reason for concern. Further, though this study points to the kinds of relationships possible among high school young men, it leaves many wondering who and where these young men are in secondary schools. In his study of college-age young men, Lyman (1987) reminds us of what may become of the relationships among young men if they continue to go unsupported or discouraged earlier on as legitimate, healthy relationships. Fearing close intimacy with other young men, Lyman reminds us of the impact this eventually has for example, in college male-male friendships that are based in emotional rules of male bonding, sexism, and misogyny. For young men unable to share and develop friendships as adolescents, we later see "male bonding in everyday life frequently tak[ing] the form of a group joking relationship by which men create a serial kind of intimacy to 'negotiate' the latent tension and aggression they feel toward each other" (p. 151).

As I mentioned in the introduction, this chapter builds on Pease (2000), who has argued that homophobia operates as a barrier preventing young men from forming close relationships. In his research, Pease spoke with adult men who were allowed to speak from their memories and to do so from a "dominant position about what it means to repress experiences of intimacy with other men" (p. 91). Pease's study was retrospective, memories of the past. In contrast, the young men described in this chapter speak from the moment, from the present, and do so in a manner rarely heard among adolescent young men. Similar to the young men Pease describes, the young men in this study either challenge or accommodate misogyny and heterosexism. These young men struggle to reject heterosexism but manage to reconfigure and renegotiate what it means to be a man among their male counterparts. Unlike past research that has claimed that boys are unable to have close friendships with boys because of the conventions of masculinity (see Kindlon & Thompson, 1999), I argue in this chapter that boys have agency in the process of negotiating masculine identities among boys. These young men "took up the project of masculinity" as Connell (1995) describes it but did so in a way that unsettles, challenges, and disrupts heteronormative masculinity. The victim discourse that prevails in past research contributes to a limited depiction of boys that has largely denied and silenced the possibility of "boys' responses to these cultural mandates, much less boys' resistance to, or at least conscious engagement with, these norms of masculinity" (Way & Chu, 2004, p. 170). As such, this study adds to an emerging cultural landscape of schools that both acknowledges the difficulties young men experience in developing close male-male friendships but also raises questions about the climate of schools that prevent and dissuade boys from developing such significant friendships at this stage in their lives.

These young men demonstrate the possibilities for forming male-male friendships and, as such, "point the way towards versions of masculinity that might be capable of tolerating difference, ambivalence and complexity around gender and sexuality" (Redman et al., 2002, p. 190). At the same time, their examples suggest a host of reasons many high school young men veer away from being close and intimate with their male peers. The chances of being mistaken as gay weighs heavily for many adolescent young men, particularly in a school context where homophobia is unchallenged or unquestioned by those in authority. To describe the young men in this study as profeminist may be a stretch. Gutterman (1994) does, however, remind us of the qualities of young men such as these who resist cultural scripts of normativity and, in doing so, they are engaged in a subversive process that allows them to "challenge the very standards of identity that afford them normative status in the culture" (p. 229). As evidenced in this study, there are young men in schools who display what Gutterman describes as a "politics of ambiguity." At a time when there is considerable attention and concern about boys and schooling, educators need to carefully consider the contextual framing of these issues in addition to underlying cultural understandings of masculinities operating in schools. I agree with Robinson (2005), who argues that "there needs to be an ongoing commitment by schools and the broader community to educational programs that focus on increasing the credibility and status of alternative forms of masculinities, including non-heterosexual masculinities" (p. 35). The unfortunate reality however, for many young men, as Lyman (1987) reminds us, is the drive to avoid establishing male-male friendships and in doing so, avoid any "admission of vulnerability, which would violate the ideals of 'strength' and 'being cool'" (p. 155).

By homogenizing adolescent boys as a coherent and homogenous group, current practices to "help the boys," "save boys," and reclaim masculinity through a recuperativist landscape do little more than further entrench a naturalized discourse of masculinity that, rather than reveal a diversity and complexity of masculinities, flattens and denies competing racial, ethnic, and sexual identities in schools.

In this chapter, I have examined the daily school interactions of four adolescent young men to better understand some of the difficulties boys experience while developing male-male friendships. The gender work many young men do among men is primarily aimed at affirming, reinforcing, and stabilizing an identity that, for all its apparent strength, is nonetheless an identity of uncertainty. Though many high school young men will not publicly admit their vulnerabilities, weaknesses, fears, and anxieties, there is a clear and unequivocal sense that they do have them and yearn to share them. Thurston reminds us of the complexity that binds but threatens to tear apart the possibilities for developing male-male relationships. In the closing minutes of our interview, I asked if there were anything he wanted to share that he thought was important. After reconfirming with me that his friend's identity would remain anonymous, he closed our interviewing by saying,

> ...Chris is a good friend of mine ... . And like, he's not afraid to share his feelings or whatever. He's constantly in the search for love, but in a non-sexual way. He's just like "I want to have somebody to hold." . . And it's provingly non-sexual by the fact that he told us that he was bisexual and that he found out when he realized he had a crush on me.
>
> (Thurston from Kehler, 2000)

The need for anonymity and safety of his friend's identity speaks to a culture of schools and the potential threats associated with non-hegemonic masculinity. Thurston also highlights the complex relationship between gender and sexualized identities that, as this study and others show, are routinely policed, regulated, and monitored from the boundaries of a highly problematic and dangerously valorized and unquestioned set of hegemonic heterosexual masculinities.

References

Anoop, N., and M Kehily (1996). Playing it straight: Masculinities, homophobias and schooling. *Journal of Gender Studies*, 5(2), 211–230.

Butler, J. (1990). *Gender trouble*. New York: Routledge.

Butler, J. (1999). *Gender trouble: Feminism and the subversion of identity*. New York: Routledge.

Coleman, W. (1990). Doing masculinity/doing theory. In J. Hearn & D. Morgan (Eds.), *Men, masculinities and social theory* (pp. 186–199). Cambridge, MA: Unwin Hyman Inc.

Connell, R. W. (1989). Cool guys, swots and wimps: The interplay of masculinity and education. *Oxford Review of Education*, 15(3), 291–303.

Connell, R. W. (1995). *Masculinities*. Berkeley: University of California Press.

Connell, R. W. (2000). *The men and the boys*. Berkeley: University of California Press.

Davison, K. (2000). Masculinities, sexualities and the student body: "Sorting" gender identities in school. In C. James (Ed.), *Experiencing difference* (pp.44–52). Halifax, NS: Fernwood.

Davison, K. (2004). Texting gender and body as a distant/ced memory: An autobiographical account of bodies, masculinities, and schooling. *Journal of Curriculum Theorizing*, 20(3), 129–149.

Epstein, D. (1998). Real boys don't work: "Underachievement," masculinity and the harassment of sissies. In D. Epstein, J. Elwood, V. Hey, & J. Maw (Eds.), *Failing boys: Issues in gender achievement* (pp. 96–108). Buckingham, UK: Open University Press.

Epstein. D. (2001). Boyz own stories: Masculinities and sexualities in schools. In W. Martino & B. Meyenn (Eds.), *What about the boys?: Issues of masculinity in schools* (pp. 96–109). Buckingham, UK: Open University Press.

Francis, B., & C. Skelton (2005). *Reassessing gender and achievement: Questioning contemporary key debates*. Abingdon: Routledge.

Frank, B. (1996). Masculinities and schooling: The making of men. In J. R. Epp & A. M. Watkinson (Eds.), *Systemic violence: How schools hurt children* (pp. 113–129). Washington, DC: The Falmer Press.

Friend, R. (1998). Heterosexism, homophobia, and the culture of schooling. In S. Books (Ed.), *Invisible children in the society and its schools*. Mahwah: N.J.: Lawrence Erlbaum Associates.

Gilbert, R., & Gilbert, P. (1998). *Masculinity goes to school*. London: Routledge.

Gutterman, D. S. (1994). Postmodernism and the interrogation of masculinity. In H. Brod & M. Kaufman (Eds.), *Theorizing masculinities* (pp. 219–238). Los Angeles: Sage Publications, Inc.

Haywood, C. (1996). "Out of the curriculum": Sex talking, talking sex. *Curriculum Studies*, 4(2), 229–249.

Haywood, C., & Mac An Ghaill, M. (1997). Schooling masculinities. In M. Mac An Ghaill (Ed.), *Understanding masculinities: Social relations and cultural arenas* (pp. 50–60). Buckingham, UK: Open University Press.

Imms, W. (2000). Multiple masculinities and the schooling of boys. *Canadian Journal of Education*, 25, 152–165.

Kehily, M. J. (2001) *Sexuality, gender and schooling: Shifting agendas in social learning.* London: Routledge.

Kehily, M. J. (2002). Bodies in school: Young men, embodiment, and heterosexual masculinities. *Men and Masculinities, 4*(2), 173–185.

Kehler, M. D. (2000). High school masculinity and gender politics: Submerged voices, emerging choices [unpublished doctoral dissertation]. East Lansing, MI: Michigan State University.

Kehler, M. D. (2003). The untold ethnographer: (Re)constructing the research self among "the boys." Paper presented at the meeting of The Canadian Sociology and Anthropology Association, Halifax, NS.

Kehler, M. D. (2004a). Masculinities and resistance: High school boys (un)doing boy. *Taboo: The Journal of Culture and Education, 8*(1), 97–113.

Kehler, M. D. (2004b). "The boys" interrupted: Images constructed, realities translated. *Education and Society, 22*(2), 83–99.

Kehler, M. D., & Martino, W. (2007). Questioning masculinities: Interrogating boys' capacities for self-problematization in schools. *Canadian Journal of Education, 30*(1), 90–112.

Kimmel, M. (1994). Masculinity as homophobia: Fear, shame, and silence in the construction of gender identity. In H. Brod & M. Kaufman (Eds.), *Theorizing masculinities* (pp. 119–141). Los Angeles: Sage Publications.

Kindlon, D., & Thompson, M. (1999). *Raising Cain: Protecting the emotional life of boys.* New York: Ballantine.

Lather, P. (1991). *Getting smart: Feminist research and pedagogy with/in the postmodern.* New York: Routledge.

Lingard, B., & Douglas, P. (1999). *Men engaging feminisms: Pro-feminism, backlashes and schooling.* Buckingham, UK: Open University

Lyman, P. (1987). The fraternal bond as a joking relationship: A case study of the role of sexist jokes in male group bonding. In M. S. Kimmel (Ed.), *Changing man: New directions in research on man and masculinity* (pp. 148–163). Newbury Park, CA: Sage.

Mac An Ghaill, M. (1994). *The making of men: Masculinities, sexualities and schooling.* Buckingham; UK: Open University Press.

Mac An Ghaill, M. (1996). Deconstructing heterosexualities within school arenas. *Curriculum Studies, 4*(2), 191–209.

MacLeod, J. (1987). *Ain't no makin' it: Leveled aspirations in a low income neighborhood.* Boulder, CO: Westview Press, Inc.

Mandle, L. & C. Shakeshaft (2000). Heterosexism in middle schools. In N. Lesko, (Ed.), *Masculinities in school* (pp. 75–103). Thousand Oaks, CA.: Sage Publications, Inc.

Martino, W. (2000). Mucking around in class, giving crap, and acting cool: Adolescent boys enacting masculinities at school. *Canadian Journal of Education, 25*(2), 102–112.

Martino, W. (2001). "Dickheads, wusses, and faggots": Addressing issues of masculinity and homophobia in the critical literacy classroom. In B. Comber & A. Simpson (Eds.), *Negotiating critical literacies in classrooms* (pp. 171–187). Thorofare, NJ: Lawrence Erlbaum Associates.

Martino, W., & Kehler, M. D. (2006). Male teachers and the "boy problem": An issue of recuperative masculinity politics. *McGill Journal of Education*, 41(2), 1–20.

Martino, W., & Pallotta-Chiarolli, M. (2003). *So what's a boy?: Addressing issues of masculinity and schooling*. Buckingham, UK: Open University Press.

May, L., & R.A. Strikwerda (1992). Male friendship and intimacy. In L. May & R.A. Strikwerda (Eds.), *Rethinking masculinity*. (pp. 95–110). Lanham, MD: Rowan & Littlefield.

McLaren, P. (1995). Moral panic, schooling and gay identity: Critical pedagogy and the politics of resistance. In G. Unks (Ed.), *The gay teen: Educational practice and theory for lesbian, gay and bisexual adolescents*. NewYork: Routledge.

McLeod, J. (2002). Working out intimacy: Young people and friendship in an age of reflexivity. *Discourse: Studies in the Cultural Politics of Education*, 23(2), 211–226.

Messner, M. (1997). *Politics of masculinities: Men in movements*. Los Angeles: Sage Publications.

Mills, M. (2001). *Challenging violence in schools: An issue of masculinities*. Buckingham, UK: Open University Press.

Mills, M. (2004). Male teachers, homophobia, misogyny and teacher education. *Teaching Education*, 15(1), 27–39.

Nayak, A., & Kehily, M. J. (1996). Playing it straight: Masculinities, homophobias and schooling. *Journal of Gender Studies*, 5(2), 211–230.

Nilan, P. (2000). "You're hopeless I swear to God": Shifting masculinities in classroom talk. *Gender and Education*, 12(1), 53–68.

Pascoe, C. J. (2007). *Dude you're a fag: Masculinity and sexuality in high school*. Berkeley: University of California Press.

Pease, B. (2000). *Recreating men: Postmodern masculinity politics*. London: Sage Publications Ltd.

Redman, P., Epstein, D., Kehily, M. J., & Mac An Ghaill, M. (2002). Boys bonding: Same-sex friendship, the unconscious and heterosexual discourse. *Discourse: Studies in the Cultural Politics of Education*, 23(2), 179–191.

Renold, E. (2000). "Coming out": Gender, (hetero)sexuality and the primary school. *Gender and Education*, 12(3), 309–326.

Renold, E. (2004). Other boys: Negotiating non-hegemonic masculinities in the primary school. *Gender and Education*, 16(2), 247–266.

Robinson, K. (2005). Reinforcing hegemonic masculinities through sexual harassment: Issues of identity, power and popularity in secondary schools. *Gender and Education*, 17(1), 19–37.

Skelton, C. (2001). *Schooling and the boys: Masculinities and primary education*. Buckingham, UK: Open University Press.

Swain, J. (2005). Sharing the same world: Boys' relations with girls during their last year of primary school. *Gender and Education*, 17(1), 75–91.

Thorne, B. (1993). *Gender play: Girls and boys in school*. Buckingham: Open University Press.

Walker, K. (1998). "I'm not friends the way she's friends": Ideological and behavioural constructions of masculinity in men's friendships. In M. Kimmel & M. Messner (Eds.), *Men's lives* (pp. 223–236). Boston: Allyn & Bacon.

Way, N. (1997). Using feminist research methods to understand the friendships of adolescent boys. *Journal of Social Sciences, 53*(4), 703–723.

Way, N., & Chu, J. Y. (Eds.) (2004). *Adolescent boys: Exploring diverse cultures of boyhood.* New York: New York University Press.

Willis, P. (1977). *Learning to labour: How working class kids get working class jobs.* London: Saxon House.

Wyss, S. (2004). "This was my hell": The violence experienced by gender non-conforming youth in US high schools. *International Journal of Qualitative Studies in Education, 17*(5), 709–730.

10 Tomboys and "Female Masculinity"

(Dis)Embodying Hegemonic Masculinity, Queering Gender Identities and Relations

Emma Renold

Introduction

In dialogue with previous chapters, this chapter contributes and develops a range of themes from interrupting public discourses that homogenize and normalize school-based masculinities by providing a more nuanced analysis of the impact and effect of masculinities on boys (and, I would argue, girls' lives) to critiquing the discourses that essentialize gender and sexual difference by engaging with poststructuralist and queer theories of gender identities and relations. Regarding the latter, this chapter directly responds to and addresses Judith Halberstam's (1998) observation in "Female Masculinity" that studies of masculinities are confined to boys and boyhood rather than focusing specifically upon what it means for girls to "do boy." Directly confronting and disrupting the notion that "masculinity" can be desired and displayed only by male bodies, this chapter explores girls' appropriation of hegemonic masculinity and the seduction of contemporary tomboyism within an increasingly sexualized girlhood (Mitchell and Reid-Walsh, 2005). In so doing, I problematize school-based programs that encourage the pursuit of hegemonic constructions of masculinity (see Mills, 2001). Moreover, by exploring ways in which even non-dominant gender experimentations can subvert and reinforce dominant and normative gender configurations, I suggest there is nothing straightforward about the promotion of diversity and difference when it comes to gender. It pivots awkwardly and problematically upon a complex configuration of context-specific and embodied power relations.

Drawing upon ethnographic data from two U.K. school-based projects (Renold 2005; Renold and Allan 2006) exploring girls' and boys' (age 10 and 11) constructions of masculinities, femininities, and sexualities, the chapter focuses upon a small number of upper primary school girls' embodiment of hegemonic masculinity and their infiltration into a range of "masculinized" activities in their negotiation and resistance to heterosexualized femininities. The chapter thus critically explores what it means to subject not only the concept of hegemonic masculinity but the subject position "tomboy" (usually branded as "sexist" and "misogynistic") to a queer analytic framework and how a queer analysis radically shakes up popular understandings of contemporary gender relations and identity-work and the implications this has for policy and practice in, for example, school-based gender-equity programs.

Queering "Gender": "Female Masculinity" and the "Heterosexual Matrix"

> The regulation of gender has always been part of the work of heterosexist normativity.
>
> (Butler 2004, p. 186)

> [Female masculinity] is not about subverting male power or taking up a position against male power, but refusing to engage and turning a blind eye to conventional masculinities.
>
> (Halberstam 1998, p. 9)

The impact of social constructionist perspectives over the last 30 years or so have contributed significantly to understandings of how sexuality and gender are shaped and reshaped by the societies and cultures within which we live. Though policy discourse on gender and gender relations are steeped in sex-role socialization theories (see Martino and Berill 2003), feminist accounts have long since troubled the relationship between (biological) sex and (social) gender by arguing how the category sex (e.g., male/female) is the product of "gender" (rather than the other way around), thus laying the blame for gender inequalities at the door of society rather than biology. Perhaps less widely communicated in public discourse are contemporary socio-historical accounts that literally trace the *making* of sex (Lacquer, 1990) and (hetero/homo)sexuality (Foucault 1978; Katz 1996; Weeks 1981, 1986). These have been pivotal in disrupting essentialist truths and dualisms about the "nature" of sex, gender and sexuality as something fixed, natural, stable, and coherent. Indeed, the performativity of gender identities as outlined by Butler (1990) is grounded in disrupting the naturalness of sex/gender and is key in theorizing girls' engagement with hegemonic masculinity or what Halberstam has conceptualized as "female masculinity"[1] (Halberstam 1998). The notion that gender is not something one is or has but rather an effect of ongoing performances that create the illusion of a coherent and convincing gender identity is central in understanding the ways in which girls can appropriate a range of masculinities and disrupting the widely held notion that "masculinity" can only be desired and displayed by male bodies and confined to boys and boyhood. Indeed, it is difficult to conceptualize the viability of the subject position "tomboy" without acknowledging the performative nature of "gender" and in particular how gender categories (e.g., male and female) do not preexist *behind* the "performances" of gender but come into being *through* their performances. In many ways tomboyism (e.g., girls' appropriation of "hegemonic masculinity") provides compelling evidence of the illusory nature of gender (in which the origin is as performative as the copy) with many girls-as-tomboys expressing "masculinity" better than their young male contemporaries.

The analytic framework for this chapter draws extensively on branches of "queer theory." In so doing, I hope to offer a powerful critique to the essentialist discourse of "gender difference" and foreground the ways in which gender is always already bound up with sexuality from early childhood onward. Though there is much debate over what constitutes "queer theory" (see Hostetler and Herdt, 1998), the radical shakeup of the relationship and interdependency of gender and sexuality has provided some complex (and challenging) theoretical accounts of the gendering of sexuality and the sexualization of gender (see Butler, 1990, 1993; Sedgwick, 1990). Proponents of queer theory have provided the conceptual space from which to expose and contest the hegemony of heterosexuality and the politics and practice of heteronormative and heterosexist social worlds. And it is the social world of the school, the enduring heteronormative discourses circulating in girls' constructions of their sex-gender-sexual identities and the de-coupling and troubling of sex (boys) and gender (masculinity), that this chapter is concerned with.

Central to my analysis of the extent to which girls can "queer" and radically shakeup normative gender/sexuality discourses is my appropriation of Judith Butler's hegemonic heterosexual matrix, which foregrounds the ways in which children's identity categories as "girls" and "boys" are inextricably tied to dominant notions of heterosexuality:

> I use the term *heterosexual matrix* ... to designate that grid of cultural intelligibility through which bodies, genders, and desires are naturalized ... a hegemonic discursive/epistemological model of gender intelligibility that assumes that for bodies to cohere and make sense there must be a stable sex expressed through a stable gender (masculine expresses male, feminine expresses female) that is oppositionally and hierarchically defined through the compulsory practice of heterosexuality.
>
> (Butler 1990, p. 151)

For Butler then, the "real" expressions of masculinity and femininity (what she defines as "intelligible genders") are embedded and hierarchically structured within a presupposed heterosexuality. In other words, to be a "real" boy or girl would involve desiring or growing up to desire the opposite sex. Disrupting the linear story that there is first a sexed subject that expresses itself through gender and then through sexuality is crucial to theorize the ways in which girls' appropriation of stereotypically "masculine" discourses and practices have the potential to disrupt the power of the "heterosexual imaginary" (see Ingraham, 1996). Indeed, paying attention to how the binaries of sex (male/female), sexuality (hetero/homo), and gender (masculinity/femininity) interact with the social generational binary of child (innocent)/adolescent (sexual) is crucial, although often a neglected dimension in analyses of queer subject positions (which tend to focus upon adults and teenagers), such as "female masculinity." Following Halberstam (1998), I am interested in critically exploring the notion of female masculinity as a queer subject position that has the potential to "successfully challenge hegemonic models of gender conformity" and explore the ways in which it represents an alternative or counter-discourse to normative masculinities and femininities (within middle childhood at least). At the same time, however, I also intend to foreground the relational nature of the ways in which gender identities get constructed through social interaction and thus pay attention to the social costs and consequences of tomboys' investment in "dominant masculinities" (e.g., the tomboys' take-up of the "sissy" discourse in their denigration of normative sexualized femininities) and the potential challenge the "tomboy" subject position raises for school-based gender equity/reform programs and policies that encourage disinvestment in hegemonic masculine discourses and practices.

Methods and Methodology

The analysis presented in this chapter draws upon qualitative data from two U.K. school-based projects (Renold 2005; Renold and Allan 2006). The first is a doctoral project in which I conducted a year-long ethnographic study exploring the construction of children's gender and sexual identities in their final year (year 6) of primary school (Renold 1999, 2005). This research took place during the academic year 1995-1996 in two contrasting primary schools situated in a small semi-rural town in the East of England: Tipton Primary (white, working- and middle-class catchment) and Hirstwood Primary (white, predominantly middle-class catchment). Alongside ongoing participant observation, one of the main methods employed to "get close" to children's social worlds was through unstructured (child-led) exploratory group interviews. These interviews often took off in some quite unexpected directions, including discussions and disclosures on more sensitive areas such as bullying, homophobia, sexual harassment, boyfriends and girlfriends, and talk about schoolwork, play, friendships, music, popular culture, fashion, and appearance.

Over the course of the year, each child (59 in total) participated in at least six group interviews (82 group interviews in total). This longitudinal element enabled an exploration of how, individually and collectively, children's ideas, experiences, and the group dynamic shifted and changed over time. Although children were free to talk about whatever they wanted, I would sometimes direct the focus of the discussion from a prior observation (e.g., gendering of playground space) or a key "critical" moment (e.g., latest "romantic" breakup). There were a number of occasions when some groups would raise the same "critical" incident that offered multiple and contrasting perspectives (from boys' monopolization of playground space to specific incidents of heterosexual harassment). As Frosh et al. (2002) found in their U.K. study of young masculinities, the group interviews became and were enthusiastically taken up as another key social site for "performing" and "doing identity." Though this research project has been published elsewhere (see Renold, 2005), the data and analysis are re-presented and integrated with the following research project to offer fresh insights into the role of tomboyism and appropriation of masculinities in contemporary girlhood.

The second project that this chapter draws upon is from a pilot study exploring girls' and boys' perceptions and experiences of how they feel about and perform "academic success" in year 5 (9- and 10-year-olds). This research was carried out over a 6-week period in June–July 2002, in three year 5 classes by Alexandra Allan and myself in three schools in a city in South Wales (United Kingdom): Riverbank Primary (multi-ethnic, working-class catchment); Dockland Primary (multi-ethnic working-class catchment); and Allbright Primary (predominantly white, middle-class catchment).[2] We adopted a multi-method approach integrating friendship group interviews, participant observations, and pupil diaries. Though the interviews predominantly explored children's views about school and schoolwork and specifically the gendering of children's dispositions to school and schoolwork, a significant part of the interview involved encouraging children to talk about gender relations and gender identity–work more widely. It is girls' and boys' talk about gender relations and specifically their constructions of school-based masculinities, femininities, and sexualities that this chapter will draw upon, primarily to illuminate the analysis of the more in-depth and longitudinal ethnographic research of children's gender and sexual relations in the doctoral research project.

Girls "Doing Boy": Ditching (Hyper)Femininity, Doing (Hegemonic) Masculinity

Over the last two decades, many ethnographic studies exploring school-based gender relations and identity work in middle childhood have come across girls who define themselves as tomboys or describe tomboy-associated behaviors (see Best, 1983; Clarke, 1989; Davies, 1989, 1993; Ellis, 1993; Francis, 1998; Paechter and Clark, 2007; Thorne, 1993).

Although tomboyism defies any singular definition, there is general agreement in much of the literature that tomboyism is a subject position available only to "girls" and usually involves a preference for stereotypically masculine activities and (sometimes) appearances and a general rejection of conventional feminine pursuits and identity-work (Carr, 1998). Central to tomboyism, then, are the power relations involved in girls' appropriation of hegemonic masculinity and rejection of stereotypical "femininity" that is often theorized as a bid for social power:

> ...to oppose stereotypical or normalized feminine positioning is to reject the disempowerment that come with it. For extreme tomboy, rejection of the feminine goes along with the identification with boys, with the adoption of a form of hegemonic masculinity and a claiming of a share of male power through acting as an honorary boy.
>
> (Paechter 2004, p. 9).

> Implicit in the concept of "tomboy" is a devaluing of traditional notions of femininity, a railing against the perceived limitations of being female.
>
> (Reay, 2001, p. 162)

When girls in the pilot project raised the topic of tomboys and tomboyism in discussions of diverse and different femininities, they drew our attention to the diversity of tomboyism and tomboyism as a continuum:

> A girl who likes boy things and wears the clothes
> They ALWAYS wear trousers
> A girl that looks like a boy ... no, more acts like one. That's it.
> Where you like boys' stuff more than girls' stuff.
> Kathy is a tomboy. She hates make-up and she hates Barbie.

A persistent theme in the girls' accounts were girls who were "not girlie," who "act like boys" and "dress like boys" but who did not necessarily hang out or "play with" the boys, as Aaisha and Sadie stress below:

> *Sally:* I'm wearing tomboy things today and trainers.
> *Claire:* Yeah, but that don't mean you're a tomboy.
> *Aaisha:* It's what you wear and if you play football (with the boys).
> (Riverbank Primary)

> *Sadie:* Rachel and Rowan say they are tomboys and they are sort of but I think they don't really play football and play with other boys ... dinosaur games and everything.
>
> (Allbright Primary)

Many of the girls (and boys) seemed to be differentiating between "real" tomboys and "pseudo-tomboys" or what might better be differentiated as "tomboyism." "Pseudo-" tomboys were those girls who mobilized the tomboy subject position and participated in some of the associated behaviors as and when it suited them. As Ellen suggests, just "playing sports" does not "make you a tomboy."

> *Ellen:* Yeah I like boys' things (...) like I am a member of the baseball team, cos I got in. I like playing football, rugby, I like playing all sorts of sports but it doesn't make you a tomboy or anything.
>
> (Dockside Primary)

Thus, doing "masculinity" for these girls is something they can exclusively invest in and claim as their primary gender identity (i.e., a one-way cross-gender identification (see Erica's story below) or something more fluid—a mobile enterprise where girls try on and take up dominant masculinities *and* femininities (i.e., they do not maintain an outright aversion to girlhood).

"I'm Definitely a Tomboy": "Tomboy" as a Discrete Subject Position

Described by Reay (2001) as "traitors to girlhood," the subject position "tomboy" is almost the antithesis to "girlie" femininities, rejecting all things stereotypically feminine and embracing all things stereotypically masculine. As many other studies note, tomboys are a distinctive and rare phenomenon. In both the doctoral research project and the more recent pilot project, there were two girls, Sadie (Allbright Primary) and Erica (Hirstwood Primary), both white and middle class, who, for a number of years, had exclusively invested in and publicly celebrated their exclusive "tomboy" status. Rejecting conventional feminine appearance (Erica: "I'm a girl without all the make-up") and sexualized femininity (Erica: "I hate all that boyfriend talk"), a strong component of "being a tomboy" was the disassociation of their "girlie" peers' preoccupation with fashion and romance, as Sadie explains below:

> *Sadie:* I am a tomboy and I'm popular with the boys usually and I'm not that popular with the girls though I do play with the girls sometimes (...) I've always been a tomboy, since I was about five (...) the reason I am a tomboy is cos all the boys things are sporty (...) I prefer sports and boys play football and I play with them (...) and I like boys' clothes and everything, I like BBs, boys fashionable skate clothes and things.

Adrian: Sadie is definitely a tomboy. She doesn't like (girlie) fashion, she doesn't care what she wears ... she'd go out in a vest. She don't care."

(Allbright Primary)

Like Jodie (age 7) in Reay's research, Zoe (age 8) in Francis's research and Maddison (age 6) in Blaise's (2005) research, Erica's lower junior years were spent self-identifying as a boy and successfully persuading other boys to include her as an honorary boy (she told me how she used to be known as "Eric"). Not only did she spend all her playground time being "with the boys" and developing male friendships but, during most of her primary school years, she was accepted and respected as "one of the boys"—symbolized by her unwavering acceptance into boys' own footballing culture at playtimes and her official place on the school's "A" team. Erica's and Sadie's exclusive identification as "tomboys" and frequent positioning by other children as "one of the boys" also seemed to exclude them from being routinely positioned by other girls and boys in the local boyfriend/girlfriend circuit. Crucially, their tomboy status also seemed to deflect sexualized comments and harassment from the boys, about which many of the girls complained (see Renold 2002, Renold and Ringrose, 2008). This last point is returned to and explored in detail later in the chapter.

"I'm Not a Girlie": Top-girls and Tomboyism

In both the doctoral and pilot project, there were individual girls and groups of girls who could be described as engaging in tomboyism, insofar as they fulfilled criteria outlined earlier, but did not self-identify as "tomboys." Though there were many girls in the pilot project who, like Alice in Reay's research or Maddison in Blaise's research, shifted between gendered subject positions (e.g., "girlie" one day, "girl with attitude" or "tomboy" the next). There were a group of girls in the doctoral project who consistently constructed their gender and sexual identities by socially and culturally distancing themselves from heterosexualized "girlie" hyper-femininities. Labeled by a group of boys as the "top-girls," they were an all-white predominantly non–working-class group of girls in a predominantly working-class environment. Like Erica and Sadie, they engaged in a vociferous and powerful (possibly class-based) critique of heteroseuxalised girlie femininities but did so while retaining rather than ditching girlhood altogether. They frequently (in group interviews) critiqued the notion that girls' bodies are solely commodities for the attraction of boys and men, as illustrated in the extract below where Harriet and her friends talk about the school disco:

Harriet: Yeah, they all wear like mini-skirts to discos, but I don't want to, I'm wearing my shorts-dungarees to the discos (laughs) ... and they're all wearing these mini-skirts. [...]
Amanda: I'm just wearing my check T-shirt/ and shorts.
Harriet: Yeah.
ER: So
Amanda: They wear, they wear like mini-skirts to impress the boys.
ER: Do you think so?
Amanda: Yeah and we, I'm just going in something that is comfortable, not so that boys'll go out with me.
[...]
Harriet: She (Kisrty) likes to impress the boys, but me and Amanda aren't, don't really care.
[...]
Amanda: Some people like something that's comfy and then some people think 'oh I've got to look like tarty/
Harriet: Yeah going around and getting all the boys around you.
ER: So you don't feel like that at all?
Harriet: No, if boys like you then they like you for the way you are not coz of how you look or how fashionable you are.
ER: What about you Amanda, do you feel the same or not?
Amanda Yeah the same because you can't, I mean the boys can't fancy you like just coz you've got good clothes on/
Harriet: Yeah, they fancy you just .. they should go out with the clothes not you (laughs).

(Tipton Primary)

From their perspective, girlie femininities were, as Halberstam (1998) argues, "bad for your health" as the following extract critiquing the anxiety ridden talk of girls' obsessions with body-size and dieting illustrates:

Hayley: (referring to super-models) I wouldn't do that, I wouldn't want to look like that coz they're so skinny and I wouldn't want to be anorexic or anything/
Jo: No, coz a lot of people go anorexic just to look like the models.
ER: So you're quite wary of that are you?
All: Yeah.
Harriet: I don't care what they/ look like, I look like I wanna look like.
Jo: I don't care what they look like.

Like Erica, they favored "comfy" over "tarty," they interchanged high heels for trainers, tight-fitting T-shirts and cropped tops for baggy T-shirts and wore trousers or cycling shorts under their skirts rather than mini-skirts and baseball caps (turned backward). Adopting a sporty fashion that emphasized their active girlhood symbolized their flight from femininity. Just like the teenage girls in Fine and MacPherson's research (1994, p. 239), these girls were adamant to distance themselves from producing femininities that aligned them with "being Barbie" and "reinforcing guys all the time." Though they differed from Erica, who wanted nothing to do with boys as boyfriends, they did sporadically engage in the local boyfriend/girlfriend culture and discourses of romance, albeit on their own terms. They would, however, strongly differentiate themselves from Reay's "spice girls," who were active participants in the boyfriend/girlfriend culture, "flirting, letter writing, falling in and out of love and talk of broken hearts." Rather, they were "girls with attitude" but channeled their disruptions and assertiveness specifically in challenging existing gendered and sexualized discursive practices and inequities: initially through infiltrating boys' footballing culture at playtimes and then other gendered inequities in the classroom.

However, as Bronwyn Davies (1993) notes, they were finding access to boy-ish things increasingly being undermined by the policing of heterosexual boundaries. Although, little by little, they were actively positioning themselves as "more than girlfriends" (although drawing on their heterosexual capital as ex-girlfriends) and countering some of the heterosexist discourses for wanting to play football (e.g., often charged with status of "wannabe girlfriends" in desire to hang out with the boys). In contrast to Reay's (2001) "spice girls," who were lauded as "little cows" and "bitches" for countering sexism and being assertive, the "top-girls" version of what could loosely be described as a liberal feminist resistance was, in the main, supported by their class teacher (although not by all the boys!). Though other individual girls did, from time to time, draw upon similar discourses of equity and anti-sexism, their impact was minimal by comparison. Collectivity was a key strength. Indeed, the "top-girls" were an exclusive, high-status and tightly-knit friendship group. However, like the "tomboys," their "girl-power" seemed only possible by taking up and drawing upon masculinist discourses (e.g., raiding boy-culture to empower and rally against hetero/sexism) and a number of Othering practices (e.g., gendered bullying and teasing), which denigrated non-hegemonic masculinities and other femininities that did not mirror their own. Nevertheless, girls' infiltration and assimilation of "masculine" discourses and practices did support and enable them to overturn many day-to-day gender and sexual inequities (see Renold and Ringrose, 2008, for further theorizations of the "top-girl" and "tomboy" subject position as both resisting, and regulatory of, heteronormative discourses).

Girls-as-tomboys: Appropriating Hegemonic Masculinity, Challenging Heteronormativity

Given the ways in which young contemporary femininities can raid and embrace boy-culture (from football to fashion), the persistence and generational renewal of the tomboy subject position accessed by young girls today is, perhaps, surprising. Indeed, the branding and commercialization of multiple femininities is big business in the consumer cultures of young girlhood (Russell and Tyler, 2002). Girls have access now to a range of sartorial femininities that extend way beyond the clichéd pink and fluffy representations of "girly" culture to be found in stores such as "Girl Heaven" (see Russell and Tyler 2002) or toys such as Barbie. Representations of powerful and risk-taking female protagonists and super-heroes can be found in a number of children's cartoons and multiple femininities abound in contemporary doll-culture (see Inness, 2004).[3] However, though there appears to be an increasing number of girls shifting between and taking up and trying on a range of femininities, some of which are highly critical of hyper-femininity within girlie culture (e.g., the "top-girls") and some of whom are less so (e.g., Reay's "spice girls"), being a "tomboy" and crossing the symbolic gender divide by wanting to be "one of the boys" rather than "with the boys" continues to thrive as stories by Sophia (early 2000s), Jodie (late 1990s), and Erica (mid-1990s) testify. Perhaps it is thus not the case, as Thorne (1993, p. 115) speculates in her discussion of "tomboy lore" that the lessening grip of gender stereotyping renders the tomboy subject position redundant: "The terms 'lady' and 'tomboy' are linked, and the undermining of one leads the other to falter" (Thorne 1993, p. 115). Rather, I suggest that its persistent presence alongside other femininities is maintained by the increasing pressures of young heterosexualized femininities. Contrary to the representation of multiple femininities and the popularized post-feminist discourse that "girls can do anything" (Harris, 2004), accessing such liberatory discourses still necessitates the projection of a coherent and recognizable heterosexual identity.

As I illustrate throughout "Girls, Boys and Junior Sexualities" (Renold 2005), in girls' own social and cultural worlds, pressures of compulsory heterosexuality loom large in body projects, identity work, and peer relations. Even the "top-girls" infiltration into and out of boy-culture and their collective alliance to an all-female peer group positioned them, unambiguously, as girls within girlhood. Though they were having some success in being able to call upon critical frameworks that enabled them to disassociate themselves from, resist and, to some extent, challenge dominant notions of the (hetero)erotic girl, it took more than a year for the girls to successfully counter, if only momentarily, some of the sexist and heterosexist discourses in which they were positioned as "potential girlfriends" for wanting to play football. Though working within existing symbolic systems by taking and subverting male dominance for themselves helped them to collectively challenge and transform gendered discriminatory practices and maintain a version of femininity and feminism across playground and classroom cultures, their desire to be friends with the boys was fraught with (hetero)sexual tension. Even when a "heterosexual relationship" was not sought after or desired ("I don't want to be boyfriends or girlfriends or anything"), the girls admitted that it almost inevitably happens ("you still do"):

> *Harriet:* Like Adrian, we get on with. We don't fancy him of course. He doesn't fancy us. But we get on with him like a friend, coz boys aren't just for boyfriends and girls aren't just for girlfriends ... you can have close friends that are boys ... .
> The other people on the table, all I do is talk to them, I don't want to be boyfriends or girlfriends or anything.
> Mandy/Sophie: Yeah.
> Harriet: Like Pete, her boyfriend (Mandy), I just to talk to him, it's not ... he's just like a friend, not boyfriend or girlfriend ... coz you need some boys to talk to sometimes not just all girls all the time but you don't want to get in a ... like a relationship with them ... BUT YOU STILL DO (shrugs her shoulders).
> Mandy/Sophie: Yeah, yeah.

They all reported struggling to strike up and maintain boy-girl friendships, free from sexual innuendo. Indeed, when Harriet reflects upon her relationship with boys further, she ends up positioning herself as a boy:

> Harriet: Well some boys are like ... say like Aaron he's like "oh I hate you" and stuff, but these boys they like try and be kind to you and like ... they like treat you like a boy and stuff, well not a boy, but they treat you like friends like we are. It's sometimes better to have a boy's opinion than a girls' if you want to find out something or

Harriet's account illuminates and symbolizes the lack of discursive space to describe platonic cross-gender interactions. She struggles to express her relationship with boys that are "kind" to her without positioning herself as a boy. By momentarily positioning herself as a boy she can eliminate any heteronormative discourse that may inscribe her interactions as hetero/sexual.

Harriet's account also exposes the ways in which the heterosexual matrix underscores most boys' and girls' gender identities and social interactions. Though research is increasingly recognizing the homosexualization of boys who embrace femininity, (Boldt, 1996, Renold , 2004; McInnes, 2004), little critical attention is paid to the compulsory heterosexualization of girls beyond a generational hurried erotics discourse of "growing up too quickly," which does little to foreground or challenge the heterosexualization of femininities. Moreover, I would argue that "being a tomboy" is perhaps one of the few remaining legitimate subjects of girlhood that can directly deflect the male heterosexual gaze and subvert or queer (heterosexualized) girlie culture. Erica (year 6) and Sadie (year 5), for example, exclusively positioned themselves and were positioned by others as "tomboys" (as "one of the boys," as "honorary boys"). Their longitudinal performative "masculinity" and queering of gender and sexual norms (e.g., tomboy as "drag") seemed to shield them from a number of heterosexualizing processes within their local peer culture, from sexual harassment and innuendo to coercive romantic positionings within an increasingly compulsory boyfriend/girlfriend culture.

Tomboys and Female Masculinity: Sexist, Misogynistic, or Queer?

Examining the costs and consequences of girls' engagement and investment with tomboyism for gender relations and contemporary representations of masculinities and femininities have led many authors to brand the tomboy subject position as inherently "sexist" (Thorne, 1993) or "misogynistic" (Reay, 2001). They argue that crossing the gender divide entrenches and valorizes a particular version of masculinity—a hegemonic (heterosexual) masculinity—and that, in doing so, reinforces and perpetuates rather than reworks and destabilizes "gender stereotypes" or "normative gender positionings." Though I fully sympathize with and support the difficulty of theorizing whether girls' infiltration and assimilation of masculinized discourses and practices transgress or consolidate normative gender regimes, it seems to me that solely scrutinizing tomboyism's relation to the transformation of normative gender discourses neglects the ways in which sexuality and the intersection between sexuality and gender operate to produce a more complex interpretation. When sexuality is foregrounded, it is usually with reference to the demise of tomboyism in adolescence— because of the conflation of female masculinity and non-heterosexuality (see Thorne, 1993; Carr, 1998). What I hope I have gone some way to illustrate in this chapter is not only the multiple interpretation of girls' appropriation of tomboyism and thus the increasing purchase that "masculinity" has upon girls and girlhood but the seduction of tomboyism (and "masculinity") within an all-pervasive heterosexual matrix. Like Butler (2004), I want to draw attention to the analysis (and thus understanding) that can be lost from neglecting to explore the ways in which girls appropriate "masculinity" and, within this, the complex ways in which gender and sexuality operate together: "To insist upon a radical separation of gender and sexuality is to miss the opportunity to analyze that particular operation of homophobic power" (Butler, 2004, p. 186). Though a gendered analysis will explore the tomboy discourse in relation to the celebration and seduction of masculinity (e.g., "boys are better") or the devaluing and ditching of femininity (e.g., "girls are crap"), a queer analytic framework will also bring into focus the ways in which tomboyism has the potential to offer girls within an increasingly heterosexualized girlhood an escape route from compulsory heterosexuality and the male heterosexual gaze (the policing agents of which can be girls and boys; see Renold, 2005).[4] However, just as I want to emphasize the radical possibilities of girls' exclusive investment in the tomboy subject position and the subversive potential of tomboyism in their outright rejection or critical interrogation of heterosexualized "girlie" culture, I simultaneously need to make visible and thus not downplay the ways in which the term *girl* continues to be used as a term of abuse in the policing of normative (hetero)masculinities (and "tomboy" subject positionings). Moreover, the continued existence of the tomboy subject position perhaps illustrates not only an enduring misogynistic culture but the ways in which heterosexism and heteronormativity operate to regulate all children's childhoods (these debates and the theorizing of the tomboy subject position are explored further in Renold, 2006; Renold and Ringrose, 2008; and Renold, 2008).

Conclusions

One of the central aims of this chapter was to directly address and confront what it means to include girls' appropriation of masculinities within studies on school-based masculinities. Theoretically, such a focus necessitates conceptualizing gender (i.e., the ways in which children live out social/cultural category "girl" and "boy") as (dis)embodied (i.e., by no means fixed to a "sexed" body), as relational (i.e., the ways in which the tomboy discourse is constructed in opposition to "girly" femininities), as sexuality (e.g., the ways in which taking up the "tomboy" subject position within middle childhood can radically disrupt often compulsory heterosexualized femininities within girlhood), and as power (how tomboyism valorizes hegemonic masculinity and thus subordinates normative femininities and non-hegemonic masculinities). Substantively and in relation to education policy and practice, viewing gender in this way throws up a number of challenges for gender equity programs, particularly those that focus exclusively on the problem with "boys" and the problematization of hegemonic masculinity per se.

There has been a considerable focus on the coercive and damaging forces of "hegemonic" (heterosexual) masculinities and the pressures experienced by boys to "do boy" in particular ways (see Frosh et al., 2001; Mac and Ghaill, 2004, 2002; Mills, 2001; Renold, 2001; Salisbury and Jackson, 1996; Skelton, 2001)—usually through displays of "hardness," "having a laugh," sporting prowess, non-studious behavior, popular fashion, and "any interest in past times and subjects constructed as masculine" (Francis, 1998, p. 337). Many of these authors reach the conclusion and often recommend that traditional macho cultures need to be challenged and changed by encouraging boys to develop "softer" non-hegemonic masculinities. Such recommendations, however, do not sit easily alongside the widely held knowledge that to "do boy" in non-hegemonic ways often involves inhabiting a marginalized and often painful position within a system of gender relations that carries a host of derogatory labels for any boy who dares to deviate from a normative masculinity (see Willis, 1977; Kessler et al., 1985; Connell, 1989; Abraham, 1989; Best, 1983; Thorne, 1993; Eder, Evans, & Parker, 1995; Gilbert and Gilbert, 1998; Connolly, 1998, 2004; Skelton, 2001). However, in a previous article (Renold, 2004) in which I attempted to explore and theorize the extent to which it is possible to live out the category boy in non-hegemonic ways and the possibilities of desiring, investing, and inhabiting alternative masculinities that are not necessarily subordinate or oppressive, a central finding was that though it was possible for some boys to construct and inhabit non-hegemonic masculinities, the need to define and project themselves as "boys" (as "male") was strong and involved disassociating themselves from, and traducing all things, feminine and female. The ways in which the boys were "doing gender" and reinforcing yet simultaneously subverting hegemonic gender and sexual relations has strong parallels with the ways in which the tomboy subject position is both radical (as a queer space to disrupt heteronormative gender and sexual discourses and practices) and conventional (in its reinforcing of rigid and constraining gender and sexual norms). My point here is that any policies, practices, and programs of change (e.g., gender equity programs) that do not focus upon gender *relations*, that is boys and girls, masculinities and femininities, and the power relations at play in their construction (e.g., the impact of investing in non-hegemonic masculinities upon other girls and boys), will struggle to attend to the complex ways in which gender and indeed sexuality operate to regulate the social and cultural worlds of contemporary school-girls and school-boys (see Renold and Ringrose, forthcoming)

Thus, doing gender/sexuality otherwise, in non-normative ways (e.g., boys doing "soft" masculinities, girls doing tomboy) may involve appropriating normative notions of masculinity and femininity that serve to reinforce and/or radically subvert traditional masculinities and femininities. Consequently, encouraging and promoting diversity and difference when it comes to gender identities and relations is a complex and problematic task that will involve some careful consideration of the impact upon both girls and boys of the social and emotional costs and consequences of what it means to do gender/sexuality in normative and non-normative ways.

Notes

1. For a full and critical interrogation of applying Halberstam's concept of 'female masculinity' to explore girls' embodiment and discursive appropriation of hegemonic masculinity, see Paechter (2006).
2. My thanks go to Cardiff University for the award of a research grant to fund this pilot study (Cardiff Young Research Initiative, 2002).
3. See, for example, U.S. imported children's programmes such as "Dora the Explorer" and superhero "Violet"in the recent Disney animation film, 'The Incredibles." Even the gender of "CBeebies" cartoon "Super-baby" is female.
4. I stress the term *girls* because of the ways in which the self-identified tomboys in both studies (Renold, 2005; Renold and Allan, 2006) all stressed the ways in which they were "girls" doing "masculinity" (e.g., "I'm still a girl" or "it doesn't make you a boy"). Retaining their core gender identity was important to them.

References

Abraham, J. (1989) Gender differences and anti-school boys, *Sociological Review*, 37(1), 65–88.

Best, R. (1983). *We've all got scars: What girls and boys learn in elementary school*. Bloomington: Indiana University Press.

Blaise, M. (2005). A feminist poststructuralist study of children "doing" gender in an urban kindergarten classroom. *Early Childhood Research Quarterly*, 20, 85–108.

Boldt, G. (1996). Sexist and heterosexist responses to gender bending in an elementary classroom. *Curriculum Enquiry*, 26(2), 113–131.

Butler, J. (1990). *Gender trouble: Feminism and the subversion of identity*. London: Routledge.

Butler, J. (1993). *Bodies that matter: On the discursive limits of sex*. London: Routledge.

Butler, J. (2004). *Undoing gender*. New York: Routledge.

Carr, C. (1998). Tomboy resistance and conformity: Agency in social and psychological gender theory. *Gender and Society*, 12(5), 528–553.

Clarke, M. (1989). *The great divide: Gender in the primary school*. Melbourne: Curriculum Development Centre.

Connell, R. W. (1989) Cool guys, swots and wimps: the interplay of masculinity and education, *Oxford Review of Education* 15(3), 291–303.

Connell, R. W. (1995). *Masculinities: Knowledge, power and social change*. Cambridge: Polity Press.

Connolly, P. (1998) *Racisms, gendered identities and young children: Social relations in a multi-ethnic, inner-city primary school*. London: Routledge.

Connolly, P. (2004). *Boys and schooling in the early years*. London: RoutledgeFalmer.

Davies, B. (1989). *Frogs, tails and feminist tales: Pre-school children and gender*. Sydney: Allen and Unwin.

Davies, B. (1993). *Shards of glass: Children reading and writing beyond gendered identities*. St Leonards, NSW: Allen & Unwin.

Eder, D., Evans, C. C., & Parker, S. (1995). *School talk: Gender and adolescent school culture*. New Brunswick, NJ: Rutgers University Press.

Ellis, J. (1993) If I were a Boy ... : Constructing knowledge about gender issues, *Curriculum Enquiry*, 23(4), 367–393

Fine, M., and Macpherson, P. (1994). Over dinner: Feminism and adolescent bodies. In H. L. Radtke and J. S. Henderikus (Eds.), *Power/gender: Social relations in theory and practice*. London: Sage Publications Ltd.

Foucault, M. (1978). *The will to knowledge: The history of sexuality Vol. 1.* (trans. R. Hurley). Harmondsworth: Penguin.

Francis, B. (1998). *Power plays: Primary school children's constructions of gender, power and adult work*. Stoke-on-Trent: Trentham Books.

Frosh, S., Phoenix, A. and Pattman, R. (2002) *Young masculinities*. Basingstoke: Palgrave.

Gilbert, R., & Gilbert, P. (1998). *Masculinity goes to school*. Sydney: Allen and Unwin.

Halberstam, J. (1998). *Female masculinity*. Durham: NC: Duke University Press.

Harris, A. (2004). *Future girl*. London: Routledge.

Hatcher, R. (1995). Boyfriends, girlfriends: Gender and "race" in children's cultures. *International Play Journal*, *3*, 187–197.

Hostetler, A., & Herdt, G. H. (1998). Culture, sexual lifeways and developmental subjectivities: Rethinking sexual taxonomies. *Social Research*, *65*(2), 249–290.

Ingraham, C. (1996) The heterosexual imaginary: Feminist sociology and theories of gender. In R. Henessy and C. Ingraham (Eds.) *Materialist feminism*. London: Routledge.

Inness, S.A. (2004). It's a girl thing: Tough female action figures in the toy store. In S. A. Inness (Ed.), *Action chicks: New images of tough women in popular culture* (pp. 75–95). New York: Palgrave.

Katz, J. (1996). *The invention of heterosexuality*. New York: Plume.

Kessler, S., Ashenden, D. J., Connell, R. W., & Dowsett, G. W. (1985). Gender relations in secondary schooling. *Sociology of Education*, *58*, 34–48.

Lacquer, T. (1990) *Making sex, body and gender from the Greeks to Freud*, London: Harvard Univeristy Press.

Mac an Ghaill, M. (2004). *The making of men: Masculinities, sexualities and schooling*, Open University Press: Buckingham.

Martino, W. and Berill, D. (2003) Boys, schooling and masculinities: Interrogating the 'Right' way to educate boys, *Educational Review*, 55(2), 99–117

McInnes, D. (2004). Melancholy and the productive negotiations of power in sissy boy experience. In M. L. Rasmussen, E. Rofes, & S. Talburt (Eds.), *Youth and sexualities: Pleasure, subversion and insubordination in and out of schools*. Basingstoke: Palgrave.

Mills, M. (2001). *Challenging violence in schools: An issue of masculinities*. Buckingham: Open University Press.

Mitchell, C. and Reid-Walsh, J. (2005) *Seven going on seventeen: Tween studies in the culture of girlhood*. New York: Peter Lang.

Paechter, C. (2006). Masculine femininities/feminine masculinities: Power, identities and gender. *Gender and Education*, 18(3), 253–263.

Paechter, C. and Clark, S. (2007) "Who are tomboys and how do we recognize them?" *Women's Studies International Forum* 30(4), 342–54.

Reay, D. (2001). Spice girls, nice girls, girlies and tomboys: Gender discourses, girls' cultures and femininities in the primary classroom. *Gender and Education, 13*(2), 153–166.

Renold, E. (1999) Presumed innocence: An ethnographic exploration into the construction of sexual and gender identities in the primary school [unpublished doctoral dissertation]. University of Wales, Cardiff.

Renold, E. (2002). Presumed innocence: (Hetero)sexual, homophobic and heterosexist harassment amongst children in the primary school. *Childhood, 9*(4), 415–433.

Renold, E. (2004). Other boys: Negotiating non-hegemonic masculinities in the primary school. *Gender and Education, 16*(2), 247–267.

Renold, E. (2005). *Girls, boys and junior sexualities.* London: Routledge Falmer.

Renold, E. (2006). They won't let us play ... unless you're going out with one of them: Girls, boys and butler's "heterosexual matrix" in the primary years. *British Journal of Sociology, 27*(4), 491–511.

Renold, E. (2008). Queering masculinity: Re-theorising contemporary tomboyism in the schizoid space of innocent/heterosexualized young femininities, *International Journal of Girlhood Studies,* 1(2): 129–151

Renold, E., & Allan, A. (2006). Bright and beautiful: High-achieving girls, ambivalent femininities and the feminisation of success. *Discourse: Studies in the Cultural Politics of Education, 27*(4), 457–475.

Renold, E., & Ringrose, J. (2008). Regulation and rupture: Mapping tween and teenage girls' "resistance" to the heterosexual matrix. *Feminist Theory: An International Interdisciplinary Journal, 9*(3), 335–360.

Renold, E., & Ringrose, J. (in press 2009). Phallic girls?: Girls' negotiations of phallogocentric power. In N. Rodriguez, & J. Landreau (Eds.), *Queer masculinities: A critical reader in education.* Amsterdam: Springer Press.

Russell, R., & Tyler, M. (2002). Thank heaven for little girls: Girl heaven and the commercial context of feminine childhood. *Sociology, 36*(3), 619–637.

Salisbury, J., & Jackson, D. (1996). *Challenging macho values: Practical ways of working with adolescent boys.* London: The Falmer Press.

Sedgwick, E. K. (1990). *Epistemology of the closet.* Berkeley: University of California Press.

Skelton, C. (2001). *Schooling the boys: Masculinities and primary education.* Buckingham, UK: Open University Press.

Thorne, B. (1993). *Gender play: Boys and girls in school.* Buckingham, UK: Open University Press.

Weeks, J. (1981). *Sex, politics and society: The regulation of sexuality since 1800.* Harlow: Longman.

Weeks, J. (1986). *Sexuality.* London: Routledge.

Willis, P. (1977). *Learning to labour: How working class kids get working class jobs.* Farnborough: Saxon House.

11 What Can He Want?

Male Teachers, Young Children, and Teaching Desire

James R. King

Introduction

There is a recurrent discourse that polices men's entrance to and work within the field of early education. In a study of men who did choose to cross this gender-based teaching border (King, 1997), I found that that male classroom teachers in grades K to 3 did so with the realization that their teaching, their talk, their very persons would be subjected to constant surveillance. Their cause for the monitoring (and self-monitoring that it engendered) was the entropy that was bound up in the imagined sexual potential of these male teachers. After all, in the cultural imagination, early education is often considered or hoped to be an asexual content of women's care work. What *could* a man want? This chapter will argue that the cohesive link in the suspicion surrounding men's teaching is the underlying trope of desire, desire that can be revealed in all teaching.

The Arguments and their Formatting

There are several potentials for ambiguity in the title chosen for this chapter. The first half, "What can he want?" is a play on Loraine Code's (1991) *What can she know?* Code's analysis revealed the patriarchal delimitation of what counts as knowledge and women's responses to it. In my response to the title's question about men's desire and in recognition of the gender-based reversal that is required, one is tempted to respond "Everything!" Within such a promiscuity of unbridled need, this chapter offers an alternative look at the consequences of men's pervasive desire in classrooms that are, by intention, by design, and by practice desire-free zones, when desire is read as sexual desire. However, for all of men's acquisitive use of the culture, desire is the masculine discourse that cannot break its own code of silence. In fact, rather than considering *the what* of men's desire, it is at least productive to first examine *the can*. Can he desire? Is he allowed? Is he able? In contrast to the pervasive assumption of the activity of men's desire is the suppressed inability to articulate it. Desire, broadly conceived, may be taken up and enacted by teaching males when they teach, but with what result? These questions, considered from a post-patriarchal stance (non-phallic, non-penetrative), comprise the first arguments in the chapter.

The second half of the title offers several other occasions for multiple meanings. From a frame of identity construction, the notions of male and male teachers are ripe for interrogation when gender is deconstructed as a social achievement. The meaning intended by the use of "teacher" is subject to various interpretations, from child advocate to "in loco parentis," often in a single conversation. "Maleness" in this arena of talk may range from sympathetic paternalism (e.g., the "need" for more male teachers) to accusations of sexual improprieties (e.g., "those male teachers just want to get at kids," where "get at" is a euphemism for sexual contacts, where "contact" is a euphemism for sexually informed touching, where "sexually informed ... ."). Similarly, what we mean by "children" is under constant negotiation, depending on the circumstances of the talk that brings them to life. "Children" or, ubiquitously, "the child," means something different when we talk about innocence or when we talk about discipline. When men, and teachers, and children are brought together and their respective desires are acknowledged, much confusion, much regulation, and much panic ensue. Why is this so?

It is also the case that this chapter does not address actual teachers, actual classrooms, or actual men when it analyses *what can he want*. Rather, the focus here is on the language and thinking practices that we all systematically use to conjure up a male, a teacher, or a male-teacher when we want to use them to make a point, to have an example, or to teach a lesson. These are never real people but constructions that serve the speakers' purposes. So, the point of this chapter is to look at the underlying reasoning that is behind the use of the pointed labels or to make an example of someone (something) or the teaching of lessons at others' expenses, and to examine some alternative ways of thinking about the nexus of caring and abuse that we have created in our talk about our children and their teachers.

Thinking About Men Who Choose to Teach

How is it that this seemingly innocuous, and perhaps productive, situation of men teaching young children should raise such clamor and chaos in our daily lives? Perhaps individuals reading this chapter will not have encountered this proposed nexus of potential problems. If this is the case, imagine yourself as the anxious parent of a 6-year-old boy or girl. Imagine standing together on the threshold of this first grade classroom. As the parent, you will have considered that your youngster, in the first extended out-of-home experience, is about to spend nine months in the daily care of this teacher. The teacher is male. He is perhaps a "father-figure," a needed influence, or a friend. However, what do you worry about? In this chapter I am examining one possible interpretation of the male teacher and the male teacher body.

Our collective ideas about what should, what could, and what should not happen between your child and this teacher in this classroom are influenced by the experiences that you had as a student and what we have all come to know from our engagements with popular culture. This cultural ecology is a rich field of data. In this chapter, I will reframe the talk, the writing, and the gossip that has been collected around this problematic relationship between male teachers, young children, and their respective and interactive desires. My purpose in writing them together is to first examine the assumptions that fuel negative popular opinion about males who desire teaching. Viewing male teachers as potential pedophiles effectively dissuades men from early education. I re-view the objectification of children as victims that is necessary to bully their teachers. My goal is to re-place the option of productive male adults who work with children *because* of their desire, not in spite of it.

When men are framed by others with their imagined sexual potential with children, their every action is interpreted by others as sexual. When children are framed by their potential as victims, they are endlessly objectified, and their caregivers' anxieties are made limitless. What education loses in accepting these assumptions without interrogation is a chance to understand the transactions of nonsexual desires that I believe *are* productive for both teachers and their students.

Desire in Teaching: What's Not to Want?

What are the characteristics that are found in your memorable teachers from elementary school? In retrospect, how much of what we remember about our best (and worst) teachers were behaviors or characteristics that were actually there? And how much of what we remember has more to do with each of us and how we experienced our lives at that time, for that school year? In other words, to what degree is our "remembered teacher" a function of *our* desire as a student at that time? How did our desires as students construct the teacher of our fantasies, the teacher we wanted him or her to be? Since that time, how has our recurring desire for "that" teacher revised him or her to suit our needs now? Desire works in reciprocal and subtle ways. It can be an unspoken, even an unacknowledged transaction between teachers and their students. Much of this theorizing on the workings of learning desire has been undertaken by feminists writing with/in Lacanian sensibilities (Felman, 1997) and outside patriarchal approaches to knowledge and teachers (Pagano, 1990). The current focus on teachers in their classrooms with students will necessarily limit the discussion to instances of desire situated in and recovered from writing about intentional learning contexts. The conflation of desire and power that is used to characterize these social spaces is a definitional tension that echoes through the layers of classrooms' social contexts. We all want something. When we are in charge, we may be more likely to get it. However, getting it may be less satisfying than wanting it.

In a patriarchal culture, masculinity may be (problematically) seen as the embodiment of desire, in contrast to its object. Similarly, traditional teaching may be understood as a patriarchal project. In classrooms beyond the elementary grades, the focus is often on content acquisition, knowledge transmission, and teachers are knowledgeable authorities, with ostensibly little occasion for desire. Yet, these are the very pedagogies that Felman (1997) argues are subtextually driven by desire. In the primary grades, the products and the goal are the students as they are shaped into learners (citizens). Men who bring desire into the classroom in (and adhered to) their bodies make us aware of what (all) teaching entails. An imagined moral conflict ensues. Men's axiomatic, inherent, embodied desire exists in tension with assumptions about pristine early-grades teaching. This definitional conflict requires some elaboration. First, early-grades teaching. Then, learning desire in classrooms is deconstructed.

Teaching that is Centered on Children and Teachers' Desires in Doing So

Much teaching within the early grades is intentionally child-centered. According to Walkerdine (1990), teachers vacate their own agenda to make way for the emerging child. The chaos and irrationality that is seen as characteristic of the world outside of the classroom is held at bay by committed teachers so that the children may develop their individual identities in a contained, rational environment. Yet, teachers' centering on the child, at the expense of their own personhood, is seen as irrational by Walkerdine, and teachers are construed as the "containers of irrationality" (p. 54). Such analysis also reinstates a benign, antiseptic teacher with no desire of his or her own, a construction that has troubled many writers (King, 1997; McWilliam, 1995). Viewing early-grades teaching in such a way certainly offers challenges to males, who may not be accustomed to "giving way" (psychologically or otherwise) to anyone, let alone a young child. However, before addressing men's "lack of fit" for a job of moving over, it is important to consider alterative analyses of the intent to teach as they reveal more active, though unstated, teacher agendas that include their desire.

Felman (1997) argues that such fantasies of teaching as *devotion* and as a *burden of service* can be understood as latent metaphors that distort or cover up the underlying, prototypic white, heterosexual power relations between students and teachers and teachers and the community. "… [T]he one who knows is the white teacher, and the other (blacks, girls, and women or children as ignorant) is understood as impoverished in his or her marked ignorance." (p. 88). More directly, she argues "… fantasies of devotion (from students) screen (teachers') hostility and hide it from (their) consciousness" (p. 86, my elaborations). Making application to early education is somewhat problematized by the almost exclusive staffing by women. Felman explains the psychodynamics that underlie authoritarian pedagogies, but these are presumably based on patriarchal relationships between knowledge and knower, teacher and learner. However, it is also important to point out that patriarchal teaching is also regularly accomplished by most female teachers, who choose to focus on knowledge, accuracy, and authority in teaching the other. In contrast, early-grades, or primary teaching, is seen as more child-centered. Though knowing is important, it is part of a relationship between teachers and students (Noddings, 1992). Further, Walkerdine's critiques suggest that the difference may be a matter of focus. Paradoxically, teachers of young children may be seen as creating the ultimate "other," as they wait for the personhood of the emerging child. This rebirthing is also drenched in desire, which is manifested in teachers' waiting for the students whom they want.

A second reversal obtains when one considers, as I do here, males' participation in "non-male" teaching spaces, the early grades. It is apparent that primary teaching is a female workspace. Elsewhere, I have argued that it can also be a decidedly non-feminist context (King, 1997). However, the important point is that even when we understand teaching as a call to service (Nias, 1989), there remains the intentionality of the act that necessitates desire at some level. Felman's argument that teaching is the enactment of teachers' desire also instantiates teaching as proto-male, at least to the extent that female teachers are understood to devalue women as other. Part of the problem here is that teaching is not a monolithic activity. In fact, early education is one context that can be contrasted with more traditional forms of pedagogy (information delivery). Perhaps realizing the internal conflicts that rest in the deployment of teaching desire, Felman offers "… in one way or another, every pedagogy stems from its confrontation with the impossibility of teaching" (p. 20). She uses the metaphor of the therapeutic discourse as a teaching analog. In therapy, the analyst reflects the patient's thoughts with the expectation that the knowledge will be resisted by the patient. Yet, the feedback is essential because the "knowledge which is inaccessible to itself because it cannot tolerate knowing what it knows (subliminally)" (p. 28, my elaboration). From this perspective, the analyst (and the teacher) offer knowledge back to the patient (or student) with the patient/student as the "true other." In more traditional teaching, certainly in content-driven instruction, the teachers' questions and feedback are both addressed to content that is external to the student (in books, in lecture, from the teacher).

In contrast to teaching that is premised on content mastery is teaching that is about the interpersonal relationship that subtends the teacher's production and projection of their personal desires. This is the case for both male and female teachers, but the characteristic of authority-based teaching is perhaps more likely to be attributed to male teachers because the association of the masculine and desire. Second, in early elementary classrooms, where the interpersonal *is* teaching, teachers, who are construed as asexual, can have agendas of desire and passion, but these attachments are to the learning of the child or the project of the emergent child, and not the actual, corporeal child. Primary teachers may be passionate but only about the learning of their students (King, 1997).

In more child- and learner-centered pedagogies, the response that a teacher desires (the answer) may not be in the text but may well reside within the student (a feeling, a process, a reaction). Formulating such answers is a reflexive, internal process that generates answers that cannot be anticipated by the teacher. According to Felman, who references Lacan, facilitating a teaching/learning interaction that is not predetermined necessitates the true other who gives the answer that is not expected. Knowledge from the other is a surprise, based on a "return of difference" (p. 28). From this dynamic perspective, knowledge may be construed as a structural dynamic, and "the person in whom I presume knowledge to exist, thereby acquires my love" (p. 29). Upon this premise, Felman argues that knowledge (from a reflexive construction) and love are inextricably linked. Yet, teachers' production of these Precious Others is a short-lived theoretical fantasy. Their demise is part of the transaction, for in the devotion fantasies of teachers, a "conflict may derive from the fact that the other (the fantasized student who does the work of adoring) is negated" (p. 86).

In a trope similar to that of Feldman, Todd (1997) suggests that "desire is that which ceaselessly circulates through the unsaid of classroom life (manifesting itself in expectations, hopes, visions, and fears)" (p. 239). It is more likely in early education that producing the child is an interactive enterprise. For example, as her teacher, my articulated hopes for Sally may well become the grist of lunchroom musings. Combined with the communitarian knowledge about Sally and her family, a group of teachers may even hope with me. In this way, according to Todd's (1997) premise, we all love Sally. In particular, the notions of equity, democracy, and social justice for the lives of children whom we teach drape our classrooms with our desire. In our intentions that "things could (should) be better," slogans are punched from Ellison machines, bulletin boards are mounted, and our desires are produced, set in motion, and often derailed in our attempts to make things better for students. Noddings's (1992) invocation to care for students as a form of pedagogy is based on this unspoken desire. Our care, regard, and love for our students is thus instantiated through

Lacanian deconstruction of the unspoken, through more direct discourses, and through what Todd calls "another kind of textuality as well; a body discourse where gesture informs any teaching and learning experience" (p. 239).

The ambiguity connoted from gesture necessitates my elaboration. Here is one location where men's caring has been made problematic. What are teachers allowed to do with their teacher bodies, for/to another's body, to indicate care? When teachers' gestures comprise a semiotic array, how does doing X (e.g., a pat on the back) or not doing X (e.g., withholding an intended pat on the back) configure in a reading of teachers' desire? What if the teacher is male? What if my imagined student, Sally, is Sam, and I am a gay male who teaches him? My indignant response is "no different." However, others are prepared to assume otherwise.

The notion of the "return of difference" holds much promise for the study of desire in classrooms. In post-structural accounts of teaching, it is the construction of and manipulation of difference (once constructed) that has the power to teach. Additionally, the power to construct the difference is held by the teacher. Following Lacan, and the interpretation offered by Felman, Todd (1997) suggests that, through classroom interaction based on teachers' desires, difference is observed and located within the students and that teachers re-present that constructed difference, a discursive creation, back to the students to *teach* about difference. Therefore, difference is not simply a matter of naming ambient variance that "occurs" in our classrooms. Rather, citing classroom difference is a teacher construction that creates an occasion for students' learning, an occasion for the enactment of teachers' desire.

Wanting Something Different in Teachers and Students

It is not always the students who are constructed as different. Teachers can also be marginalized by perceived difference. Men who chose to teach with women are at risk for their differences (King, 1997). Male or female, the ability to write classroom difference resides within the authority of teachers. If this discursive practice of teachers is borne of their desire, the relative social positioning of teachers will certainly impact their reliance on creating difference from and solidarity with students. It is here that my internal relationship with who "I" am as the teacher becomes more salient. Creating "the difference" from a position of "being different" is a different act. A male teacher who is teaching in a "female" context may perceive himself as not fitting in or as fitting in better than normal. In a group of primary males with whom I studied (King, 1997), some men separated from their female colleagues and blamed them in ways that I determined to be misogynistic for the problems that they (the men) faced as teachers in primary education. In one of these classrooms, even the students taught by one of the primary male separatists dismissed the other students in the school and the other teachers as "not original (individual), not up to (our/his) standards."

The primary males in the study who did "fit in" did so by teaching in "women's ways" through relationships, by caring, and with purposeful attention to "the child." These proto-female males also discursively established themselves as "better" at women's ways of teaching than their female colleagues. Though largely valuing the traditional "maternalistic" approaches to early education, these men established their own roles by competing with the women. From their perspectives, they had won a contest that no one else may even have seen.

In addition to gender identification differences, these men also expressed difference in terms of their sexual orientations and others' perceptions and attributions of their sexual orientations. Gay men in the study were concerned that their designated difference (either self-designated, or in others' suppositions) marked their performances as male teachers. It is a convoluted, nested set of arguments. First, teaching is women's work because women are "naturally" inclined to care for (teach) children. However, men can do this work. Second, men who do this work must be suspect for entering an occupation with lower pay and prestige. Third, it is also the case that men are masculine and therefore suspect because of their potential (or necessity) for sex. Fourth, a gay man, who is assumed to be "not masculine" may teach with "women's ways" and talk in ways consistent with women's discourse (Tannen, 1994). Perhaps, then, these men who are "gay" may comfortably, productively fill this work niche. However, finally, because men are not to be alone around children (in childcare and early teaching work), the "gay male" is constructed as the one who wants sex with his young students, and the spotlight is moved from men and their privilege. Furthermore, the sweatshop of women's compulsory care that is early elementary education is left intact. The substance of the tactic is inaccurate, amoral, and unethical. It is also highly effective in dissuading men, gay and straight, from teaching young children. In effect, the tactic has it both ways: a recuperative call for men into early education and a simultaneous threat that keeps them out.

Kelly (1997) also argues for the effect of the languaging practices, specifically literacy, in the production of classroom desire. Desire is constituted by language, and language therefore mediates desire. The meanings that we make of ourselves as teachers and as students are those that are available to us in the linguistic repertoire that we control. Though teachers project desire onto their students through teaching practices, students reactively construct their own desire based on their language and that modeled by the teacher. More important, as a discursive construction, it is through the regulatory use of language that desires are made manageable, acceptable, and pleasing to the teacher. However, desire is also the manifestation of discontent. The want is based on a lack and schooling appropriates this paradox for educational purposes.

> The social acts pedagogically in that it proffers the illusion of satisfaction while banking on inevitable absence and dissatisfaction. Without the condition of dissatisfaction, change (that things could be better) has no grounds in which to sow, for its seeds thrive in the ground of discontent. Discontent is contemporaneous with language. Desire, the manifestation of discontent, is, then, what links the unconscious into language.
>
> (Kelly, 1997, p. 33, my elaboration)

In my first read of Kelly's discussion of desire and its discontents, my frame of reference was the students and teachers' tacit manipulation of "the social" to produce a condition for learning. The projection of teachers' desire for their students' learning also sets up the same conditions. Our desire thrives in its discontent. Our students who don't "get it" make our continuing desire a likely expectation. This realization from Kelly regarding our desire and our language to express it becomes even more problematic when Pagano's (1990) gender-based analysis is included:

> Men and women are (not) in the same position to know the same things since their relationship(s) to language ... are different. Since education has everything to do with finding our positions in language, education must treat men and women differently within the range of common interest (that) defines the educational project (p. 68).

The arguments for re-instituting conscious deployment of teachers' desires as part of their teaching practice come from feminist standpoints but ones that are distinctly post-structural. What can it mean, then, for a male to adopt these interrogations regarding desire and apply them to his work in classrooms? A quick answer that appropriates the feminist reasoning is "Nothing different than what anyone else (female) would do." That is, biological gender shouldn't matter in these moves toward more present, self-actualized teaching. Yet, "masculinity," "males," and "being a guy" comprise a set of free-floating signifiers that all bond with the teaching behaviors and perhaps change the valance of the behaviors. So, though I may approach my teaching with youngsters in what I see as a gender-neutral way, others will take up my teaching actions and assign them different interpretations based on the fact that a male performed them. These intentions and strategies necessitate a discussion of being male in teaching, of being perceived as male in teaching, and pretending to be male while teaching.

On Being Male, On Being a Teacher, or "The Man Teacher"

Though calls for "men teachers" in the early grades continue to be heard, they may be muted and shaded by cautions, conditions, and expectations for what kind of man schools want. "The call" and its various instantiations are yet another instance of unarticulated educational desire. Exactly what is it that schooling wants in a man for young children? What kind of man? To do what kind of tasks? Some years ago, Siefert (1988) engaged with the complexities that are entailed in desiring men for teaching. On one hand, "the call" may have intended to solicit caring, child-centered males who would presumably be more capable of the nurturing that some see as isomorphic with primary teaching. Or the call may have been to recruit a squad of replacements for necessary, but missing-in-action fathers. In either case, these calls were made on behalf of "the children." Seifert has considered the dilemmas of the men who would cross this gender boundary into what is arguably a low-paying, low-autonomy, and low-prestige job. However, the presence of men in a previously all-female work niche and/or role tends to shift the perceived worth and resulting pay for the work (Reskin, 1991). Therefore, "bringing in the men" can be a productive strategy for enhancing the careers of women who teach (or nurse). However, for the men who teach in elementary, being there for both the children and the women can be complex and burdensome when they are under such intense scrutiny for their suitability.

Men's desire to teach young children is often wrongly construed as pedophilic (Sargent, 2001). Elsewhere I have argued that such tactics are the policing mechanisms of a patriarchal economy that depends on the relatively inexpensive work of women (teachers; King, 1997). However, despite the inaccuracy of the claim, the duplicitous motivation, and the unethical strategy of these sexual accusations, men continue to be bullied by this opportunistic rhetoric. In a productive reversal of the general reasoning, Silin (1997) argues that teachers do in fact have pederastic relationships with their students. Teachers are understood as occupying all-knowing, phallic subject positions and children, as students, are constructed as innocent receptacles, waiting to be filled with knowledge. Silin calls this educational pederasty, which is an analog for teachers' patriarchal control of knowledge. Yet, in the early grades, it is largely women who perform this phallic instruction in service of patriarchy. What happens when a man executes the same kind of teaching alongside the women? What happens if he teaches differently than his female colleagues? And a final question: What is my agenda in constructing this rhetorical position of "those poor boys" who want to be teachers? The next section in the chapter argues that, as teachers, these boys-to-men are responsible for developing a meta-awareness of what their desire entails.

Masculinity and the Construction of New Men and Boys

Some speculate that men's entrance into this work niche, a niche that is based on women's ways of teaching, will disrupt the political, emotional, and economic context of early-grades teaching. To better understand the gendered significance of men's participation in early-grades teaching, it is helpful to consider more recent accounts of masculinity for their applications to men who teach in primary grades. From my perspective, the discourses that follow create new stances for understanding masculinity, or new masculinities. Gardiner (2002) offers several points of consensus between feminism and feminist-inflected masculinity studies. The first common ground is that masculinity *is* a gender and, therefore, like feminism, has been influenced by historical, political, and cultural processes. It is reasonable to assume that power within the masculine is both distributive and unequal with its members. Second, masculinity is not *one* thing. Though heterosexist, patriarchal masculinity projects its own unity and impermeability, the various instantiations of "being male" are anything but. Consider the current marketing of the metro-sexual. The grooming, clothing, and objectification remain a hard sell for heterosexual males. Third, it is the reciprocity of feminism and masculinity studies that is the most salient point of common ground. One can readily understand masculinity studies as a consequence of feminism. In addition, feminism was/is written in relief, as not-masculine. Both feminist and masculinity scholars write into the other, albeit sometimes from different standpoints, and of course, not with equal footing and certainly without symmetry. After all, masculinity studies could be (and have been) criticized for gender reification rather than praised for critiquing the patriarchal enterprise. Masculinity must be studied, if only, but not only, to denaturalize it.

At the school level, there are several attempts to study boys, and their masculinities in what Weaver-Hightower (2003) summarizes as the "boy turn" in research on gender in education. The boy turn results from several social factors, most notably feminism and its backlash (p. 476). Weaver-Hightower dichotomizes the texts of the boy turn between theory-based and school-based inquiries. The summary leads readers to "pro-feminism" for a review of the issues. Lingard and Douglas (1999) also argue for a stance that they label as "pro-feminism." It is a position that acknowledges men's unique set of experiences without privileging it. It also allows for critique, for examination from feminist perspectives. In distinguishing pro-feminism from other approaches to masculinity studies, Lingard and Douglas offer a brief typology of purposeful inquiry into the masculine. Men's rights, which emerged from the men's liberation movement of the 1970s, concerns itself with fathers' rights, divorce reform, men's health, and other pro-male and not (intentionally) anti-feminist issues. Masculine therapy, also from the earlier men's rights movement, deals with the inner lives of men as they confront their own sexism and more frequently the sense of loss for the new male. This latter position has given rise to the more separatist, conservative and reclamationist, mythopoetic men's movement (Bly, 1991; Keen, 1991). Another approach identified by Lingard and Douglas is labeled conservative, or the Christian men's movement. The conflation of athleticism (stadium sites, coaches as speakers) and Christianity reifies a particular, heterosexist masculine ideal. Finally, pro-feminism argues for an alignment with feminism, a current focus on issues of power related to gender, and criticism of the masculine as a form of oppression while simultaneously considering its privileged status.

Buchbinder's (1998) approach to masculinity is somewhat different. Rather than forming a typology, he relegates *all* masculinity to acts of performance. The stakes of a convincing performance are the individual male's need to perform masculinity as flawlessly as possible, lest he suffer the withdrawal of power available (notionally, anyway) to all men in the culture, and the consequence of the displeasure, and possibly the ridicule, from any other man. From this perspective, all men are potentially equally at risk for infraction, and consequently are wedded to the surveillance of self and others. It is an uncomfortable marriage. Buchbinder's theorizing brings to mind the (not-so-) secret society. "We all know that patriarchy is unethical, but we won't tell. And, in order to keep the 'privilege' inherent in being male, we agree to a set of practices that make us impervious. Solidarity." However, who is pulling the strings? Everyone. These hegemonies are reenacted in every culture enclave. School is one such place.

Masculinity Development in School Contexts

In terms of schooling, a pro-feminist approach would support the current work directed toward equalizing girls' opportunity structure in schools. It would also argue for more inquiry directed at boys' failure to achieve academically and at their complicit involvement in the predictable academic falloff. Not being able to "need" generally, and specifically at school, young boys may more likely "gut it out," join a social group that may actively discourage school achievement to bolster the achievement of "the masculine." Though girls are not yet over the achievement hump, at least their plight has received some equity-inspired attention in the literature. Boys and young men continue to fail infamously. Lingard and Douglas (1999) point out the need for the "remasculinization of schooling" (p. 55). However, theirs is an importantly different call than that sounded by the sexist alarmists of the early 1970's (e.g., Sugg, 1978). Whereas the claim in the early seventies was about the "feminization of schools," Lingard and Douglas (1999) suggest

In confronting the problems that boys experience in schooling within the gender equity framework, the important issue is not how boys are disadvantaged as distinct from girls, but how can we address the problems that both boys and girls face in learning how to balance their roles in the private and public spheres of life (p. 56).

However, what of young men in schools? How is it that schools culture the men who will become teachers? Critical sociological work on the production of masculinities, particularly in schools, has added much to the discussion on masculinities in schools.

Though recognizing the diversity within a group called "boys," several commonalities can be drawn from the perspective of a critical sociology of schooling masculinities. Gilbert and Gilbert (1998) argue that the range of acceptable masculinities at school is surprisingly narrow. At first, the argument seems untenable. After all, if patriarchy has established hegemonic males as the top of the gender food chain, shouldn't the larvae be eating royal jelly? (Whoops, cross-dressing in my metaphors!) Apparently not, argue the Gilberts. In fact, the phrase "boys will be boys" is deconstructed to reveal the narrowness that the positioning as "boys" entails.

Narrow and stereotypic versions of masculinity clearly influence boys' lives, affecting how they take up school curriculum options, how they can read and make sense of "men's studies," how they participate as learners in the school environment, and how they can imagine lives as men outside of the school (p. 24).

Interview findings presented by Martino (2001) also confirm the small set of opportunity structures that are sanctioned for "the masculine." Boys cannot talk about emotions. They must devalue what is happening at school, presumably not a stretch for most. Meyenn and Parker (2001) add that indeed boys can be (are acknowledged definitionally as capable of being) bad in schools. In contrast, Letts (2001) offers that math and science are, for some boys, a crucible for forging masculinity. Letts also takes the phrase "boys will be boys" to task, but with a different rhetorical strategy than that used by Gilbert and Gilbert (1998). Boys, that is, individuals in the group "boys," are diverse. A single boy in that group "will be boys," connoting the diversity of gender and social roles that each boy can (and does) inhabit. Yet, from the heavy surveillance directed toward the performances of masculinity, one cautiously chooses only the straight *and* narrow. Chapman (2001), like Letts (2001), suggests that maths are a boy's own language, but the ready agreement that maths are for, and supportive of, boys is contraindicated by the general pattern that boys purposefully under-perform academically to fit in with others who are academically self-sabotaging to be perceived as more "masculine." So even if a particular boy has an affinity for this subject area, and perhaps some acumen, the social may trump the cognitive. When boys have found that social group, and are with their "mates," Gard (2001) reminds us that the boys will enact violence in both discourse and "play." Of course, the whole enterprise of socially producing, and subsequently deconstructing, "violence" is ripe for interrogation (cf. Jones, 2002). These complementary studies from *What about the boys?* (Martino and Meyenn, 2001) offer a confirmatory gaze at masculinity that reinstates its problematic status within schools. Though several authors in this forward-looking collection of essays and research reports offer "productive pedagogies," it is to a more trenchant criticism that I now turn.

Newkirk's (2002) *Misreading masculinity: Boys, literacy and popular culture* mines the interstices of texts, teaching, and boys. Why is it that so many times what our boys choose as a topic or focus is simply not okay for the classroom? "Gross-out" texts and gory violence are not usually allowed into school literacy practices. Indeed, Weaver-Hightower (2003) fixates the "boy turn" on studies of boys' literacy. "... [Literacy is] a field that is often cited as subject area of disadvantage for boys." He further points out, from a pro-feminist stance, that "[h]igher literacy scores have not translated into superior social or economic status for girls ...". However, rather than blaming girls, or pathologizing and rescuing boys in a post-Columbine panic, Newkirk urges us to rethink the school practices that tacitly endorse inactive, text-mediated learning in preference to embodied, active learning. Who would *want* to write when would-be-writers are forbidden to write about anything that is interesting to them. Newkirk points out that schools' needs for control and their fears of violence, eroticism, and anything having to do with real bodies make literacy a very narrow experience for boys (and girls, for that matter). It is not my intent to essentialize boys as exclusively focused on the foregoing forbidden topics. It *is* my intent to highlight the fact that "things young male" are more likely to be suppressed in the name of "school literacy." These fundamental criticisms of school-based literacy practices lead Newkirk to offer productive, thoughtful directions for teachers and schools reflective work on what Lingard and Douglas call the "re-masculinization" of schooling. It is also important to point out that this is not the same approach as providing textual reification for patriarchal masculinity (Brozo, 2002). New masculinities go beyond what Lingard and Douglas describe as masculine therapy approach "dominated by co-counseling, twelve-step and recovery groups" and influenced largely by Jungian mythopoetic movements (Bly, 1991; Keen, 1991). It seems curious to encourage young men, as Brozo does, to recover from something that they haven't yet mastered. However, maybe obeisance is the point. In any case, Newkirk's approach is to critique the literacy practices in schools that marginalize masculinity, a root cause if there ever was one. In doing so, Newkirk does not give masculinity carte blanche, like it receives from the mythopoetic reclamation of patriarchal excess. (See Buchbinder, 1998, pp. 30–47, for a thoughtful critique of the mythopoetic project in masculinity studies).

Skelton (2001) provides a cohesive tie between the world of adult males and the young men whom they teach. Arguing from a classification of masculinity studies similar to that of Lingard and Douglas (1999), Skelton takes the next step and connects the different ideologies about masculinity to pedagogies related to the chosen perspectives in masculinity. For conservative masculinity (men's rights, spiritual groups), teaching might entail a "return to traditional forms of educational organization" (pp. 47–48). For critics of hegemonic masculinities, such as pro-feminist teachers, the instructional implications are less clear. However, following poststructual identity formation, boys (as well as girls) would be seen adopting multiple subject positions and not be forced into expected roles. The social construction of masculine gender would be in relation to practices such as achievement, relation to "things female," language use, and the like. Skelton also sagely observes that since elementary teaching is construed as women's work (see also King, 1997), most of the information about the men who work there is exactly not about their masculinity. In what ways can we retrofit these male bodies as exemplars of "the masculine?" What are the relationships between the "marginal males" and the children whom they teach?

Child as Object and Agent in Masculinity Discussions

What adults make of children and childhood is an important consideration in how we understand the male teachers who work with them. In a vision of teaching that foregrounds the desire of teachers, the objects of desire are important factors in this equation. Cannella (2001) has suggested a set of three intersecting accounts of childhood that relate to adults' habits of objectifying children. The first is a childhood that is natural and universal. This account is enacted whenever we discuss "the child" or talk about "children" and "kids" in unexamined ways. Given a single unifying account, it is possible, and perhaps even compelling, to monitor children for their compliance to this constructed ideal. In the process, actual children are lost in the comparison. A second frame for children and childhood is that of innocence and neediness. Adults are compelled to attend to this need that they perceive from children. Innocence is possible, however, only through the adults' selective withholding and sharing of knowledge, information that has undergone some kind of scrutiny. In keeping with making only partial knowledge available is the responsibility for adult surveillance to maintain innocence as the absence of corrupting knowledge. Teachers thereby protect children's innocence by functioning as gatekeepers. Cannella's third frame for childhood and children is one of opposition. Children and adults live in separate, parallel universes. More powerful adults are able to intervene in the alternate reality, should it become a threat to the adult sense of order. Similar to Cannella, Woodrow and Brennan (2001) offer three analogous alternatives based on popular culture images used to represent children. They offer innocence, monster, and embryo adult. The monster category contains the child in need of rules and discipline, not unlike the surveillance scheme offered by Cannella. The embryo adult may be seen as a reversal on the theme of separate realities, whereby with careful regulation, the Other is transfigured into Same.

Texts and images about our children and their lives (as distinct from adults' lives) form fairly stable, if variable, discourses. In this use, discourse is an organized set of understandings and ways of communicating that define a community (Gee, 1999). A group of adults who collectively and consistently believe that young humans are innocents is more likely to have a cohesive and confirmatory verbal exchange than a mixed-beliefs group, whereas a "child-as-monster" adult and a "child-as-innocent" adult may more likely to have a talk about their difference. The point here is that we each have beliefs and several different discourse structures on childhood and children. These same beliefs also impact teachers and the ways that we structure and recognize the "learning" that satisfies our latent desires.

One seemingly unproblematic lens into childhood is that of a developmental learner. Yet, Mayall (2002) has suggested that the scholarization of childhood may make the life of a child isomorphic with that of a student. Therefore, the agendas that are important to schools, such as achievement, test performances, and behavior (in classrooms) become important to home life as well. The amount of child activity that is required in classrooms and work that is sent home at end of the school day may well qualify schooling to be "the work of the child." In this way, Mayall comes to regard children as agents in their own process of schooling (p. 21). In many ways, then, these agents of schoolwork can be seen taking the job home nightly. Yet, like any other minority, children's options for their own activity (type and level) in classrooms are limited. From these vantage points, the teacher has considerable social and political influence over children's lives as workers, both in the immediate classroom and in controlling activity and behaviors at home. In effect, teachers' performances as "in loco parentis" have shifted to the parents' performance as "el loco maestro." It is important, therefore, to understand the relationships we assume teachers have with children.

Again in the field of literacy, how teachers understand children impacts how they teach reading. In one ethnographic study of three female first grade teachers' gender and literacy beliefs, Boggs (1999) revealed the learning limits that obtained when the teachers mutually constructed literacy and gender. One of the teachers in the study related to her class from a restrictive gender lens (e.g., girls and boys are each allowed only certain gender-based behaviors). Interestingly, the narrowing of gender behaviors also narrowed the literate opportunities, especially for the boys. For example, boys were cajoled to behave like the girls at the reading table. In contrast, the teacher who was not observed relating to her class through gender ultimately provided broader literacy opportunities in her class. More specifically, Bembry (2004) reported that the teacher who she observed conflated reading disability with gender (male) and race (black).

Like school objects, children are also present in the culture as images and present in the imaginations as stories (about children). The emphasis on images of children in the public gaze allows adults to assert their control of children. This is not unlike pornographic claims on women's bodies as objects of desire. The emphasis on behaviors and scores of children in schools allows the public, through children's teachers as agent, to assert control over "students." As such, the representations, whether visual, graphic, or rhetorical, are never about the child in image, or text, or talk but about the adults who produce and consume childhood through these various representations. It is a complex use of children and childhood. A discussion of the work of Kincaid (1992, 1998) is a productive start in understanding how the sexual and gendered commodifications of children influences teaching behavior.

The modern child was constructed out of Victorian sensibility and morality, as a space free of adult corruptions, and consequently, innocent, empty, and vacuous (Kincaid, 1992). On one hand, innocence was and is an attribute valued for its civilizing tendency, a productive agenda in the second half of the nineteenth century. On the other hand, innocence became a consumer product, a prize. In fact, we are trained to adore it and to despoil it. Innocence is the irresistible void. According to Kincaid, we have enthusiastically sexualized the child while systematically denying we are doing any such thing. Kincaid (1998) makes a case that our understandings of children and their nascent sexuality have much to do with adults, our projected desires, and the dynamics of consumer culture. Kincaid asks us to take a hard look at the way that we loudly proclaim and defend the innocence of childhood and simultaneously, obviously, sexualize it for our own purposes. His first line of argument is the incessant, over-rich information flow on child sex panics. This abundance of information is directly tied to its marketability. That is, if we didn't crave the titillation of child sex, the safe "tsk tsk" over a cup of coffee, narratives of child sex would not be present in the newspaper that we serve as a context for the coffee. Kincaid considers the preponderance of sexy, childhood stories of sexual abuse and incest on Oprah, Dr. Phil, Morrie, and other daytime talk shows. He examines our limitless thirst for more. A second ubiquitous example is provided in Kincaid's treatment of the eroticization of children (especially young girls) in advertising and beauty pageants. He claims, rightly I think, that we can't continue to have it both ways.

In agreement, Pringle (1995) argues that the "burgeoning child abuse industry has largely been promoted by, and to the career benefit of, men professionals in the fields of health (psychiatry and paediatrics) and social work (child protection and mental health)" (p. 26). After reading Kincaid for several years and considering the cautions about "no touch policies" from Johnson (1997) and criticisms of sex panics from Silin (1995, 1997), I am realizing that, in ceaseless circulation of stories about male teachers and the pedophilic sex they are assumed to desire, teachers and children are both being used. This is not to argue against protecting children from real harm at the hands of abusive adults. Rather, my critical reaction is to the circulation of sexy stories about the imagined sex lives of children and their teachers. The worst implication is that discourse fixated on imagined sex is distracted from the more immediate needs in teaching young children: resourcing, sexist devaluing of child care work, and the systematic disregard for the daily well-being of far too many children. Second, deflecting our gaze toward the imagined, exotic pedophile as the perpetrator of sexual abuse ignores the peril that real children face in their own homes at the hands of their own family members and their families' "friends." Finally, here is where we do our homework. As tedious as it appears, we must know our own intentions toward children when we, any of us, desire a life teaching them. Only when we understand what we want can we offer what might be helpful to our students.

References

Bembry, C. (2004). *Literacy experiences of African-American second grade males: responses to their teacher's reading instruction*. A paper for the McNair Project. Tampa: University of South Florida.

Bly, R. (1991). *Iron John: A book about men*. Shaftesbury: Element.

Boggs, M. (1999). Reading boys: a post-structural inquiry into first-grade literacy and masculinity during the language arts block [unpublished doctoral dissertation]. Tampa: University of South Florida.

Brozo, W. (2002). *To be a boy, to be a reader*. Newark, DE: International Reading Association.

Buchbinder, D. (1998). *Performance anxieties: re-producing masculinity*. St. Leonards, NSW: Allen & Unwin.

Cannella, G. (2001). Natural born curriculum: popular culture and the representation of childhood. In J. Jipson & R. Johnson (Eds.), *Resistance and representation: rethinking childhood education* (pp. 15–22). New York: Peter Lang.

Chapman, A. (2001). Maths talk is boys' talk: constructing masculinity in school mathematics. In W. Martino & B. Meyenn (Eds.), *What about the boys?: issues of masculinity in schools* (pp. 169–185). Philadelphia: Open University Press.

Code, L. (1991). *What can she know?: feminist theory and the construction of knowledge.* Ithaca, NY: Cornell University Press.

Felman, S. (1997). Psychoanalysis and education: teaching terminable and interminable. In S. Todd (Ed.), *Learning desire: perspectives on pedagogy, culture and the unsaid* (pp. 17–43). New York: Routledge.

Gard, M. (2001). I like smashing people, and I like getting smashed myself: addressing issues of masculinity in physical education and sport. In W. Martino & B. Meyenn (Eds.), *What about the boys?: issues of masculinity in schools* (pp. 169–185). Philadelphia: Open University Press.

Gardiner, J. (2002). Introduction. In J. Gardiner (Ed.), *Masculinity studies and feminist theory: new directions* (pp. 1–29). New York: Columbia University Press.

Gee, J. (1999). *An introduction to discourse theory and method.* New York: Routledge.

Gilbert, R., & Gilbert, P. (1998). *Masculinity goes to school.* New York: Routledge.

Johnson, R. (1997). The no touch policy. In J. Tobin (Ed.), *Making a place for pleasure in early childhood education* (pp. 101–118). New Haven, CT: Yale University Press.

Jones, G. (2002). *Killing monsters: why children need fantasy, superheroes, and make-believe violence.* New York: Basic Books.

Keen, S. (1991). *Fire in the belly: on being a man.* New York: Bantam.

Kelly, U. (1997). *Schooling desire.* New York: Routledge.

Kincaid, J. (1998). *Erotic innocence: the culture of child molesting.* Durham, NC: Duke University Press

Kincaid, J. (1992). *Child loving: the erotic child and Victorian culture.* New York: Routledge.

King, J. (1997). *Uncommon caring: learning from men who teach young children.* New York: Teachers College Press.

Letts, W. (2001). Boys will be boys (if they pay attention in science class). In W. Martino & B. Meyenn (Eds.), *What about the boys?: issues of masculinity in schools* (pp. 186–198). Philadelphia: Open University Press.

Lingard, B., & Douglas, P. (1999). *Men engaging feminisms: pro-feminism, backlashes, and schooling.* Philadelphia: Open University Press.

Martino, W. (2001). "Powerful people aren't usually kind, friendly, open people!" Boys interrogating masculinities at school. In W. Martino & B. Meyenn (Eds.), *What about the boys?: issues of masculinity in schools* (pp. 82–95). Philadelphia: Open University Press.

Martino, W. & Meyenn, B. (Eds.) (2001) *What about the boys?: issues of masculinity in schools.* Philadelphia: Open University Press.

Mayall, B. (2002). *Towards a sociology for childhood: thinking from children's lives.* Philadelphia: Open University Press.

McWilliam, E. (1995). *In broken images: feminist tales for a different teacher education.* New York: Teachers College Press.

Meyenn, B., & Parker, J. (2001). Naughty boys at school: perspectives on boys and discipline. In W. Martino & B. Meyenn (Eds.), *What about the boys?:*

issues of masculinity in schools (pp. 169–185). Philadelphia: Open University Press.

Newkirk, T. (2002). *Misreading masculinity: boys, literacy, and popular culture.* Portsmouth, NH: Heinemann.

Nias, J. (1989). *Primary teachers talking: a study of teaching as work.* New York: Routledge.

Noddings, N. (1992). *The challenge to care in schools.* New York: Teachers College Press.

Pagano, J. (1990). *Exiles and communities: teaching in the patriarchal wilderness.* Albany, NY: SUNY Press.

Pringle, K. (1995). *Men, masculinities, and social welfare.* London: UCL Press.

Reskin, B. (1991). Bring the men back in. In J. Lorber & S. Farrell (Eds.), *The social construction of gender* (pp. 141–161). Beverly Hills, CA: Sage.

Sargent, P. (2001). *Real men or real teachers.* Harriman, TN: Men's Studies Press.

Seifert, K. (1988). Men in early childhood education. In B. Spodek, O. Sarancho, & D. Peters (Eds.), *Professionalism and the early childhood practitioner* (pp. 105–116). New York: Teachers College Press.

Silin, J. (1995). *Sex, death and the education of children: our passion for ignorance in the age of AIDS.* New York: Teachers College Press.

Silin, J. (1997). The pervert in the classroom. In J. Tobin (Ed.), *Making a place for pleasure in early childhood education* (pp. 214–234). New Haven, CT: Yale University Press.

Skelton, C. (2001). *Schooling the boys: masculinities and primary education.* Philadelphia: Open University Press.

Sugg, R. (1978). *Mother teacher: the feminization of American education.* Charlottesville: University of Virginia Press.

Tannen, D. (1994). *Gender and discourse.* New York: Oxford University Press.

Todd, S. (1997). Looking at pedagogy in 3-D: rethinking difference, disparity and desire. In S. Todd (Ed.), *Learning desire: perspectives on pedagogy, culture, and the unsaid* (pp. 237–260). New York: Routledge.

Walkerdine, V. (1990). *School girl fictions.* London: Verso.

Weaver-Hightower, M. (2003). The "boy turn" in research on gender and education. *Review of Educational Research, 73,* 471–498.

Woodrow, C., & Brennan, M. (2001). Interrupting dominant images: critical and ethical issues. In J. Jipson & R. Johnson (Eds.), *Resistance and representation: rethinking childhood education* (pp. 23–44). New York: Peter Lang.

12 Beyond Male Role Models

Interrogating the Role of Male Teachers in Boys' Education

Wayne Martino

Introduction

Educational stakeholders (including teacher unions, teacher training agencies, ministries and boards of education) and the popular media have resorted to invoking the male role model within a context of moral concern about the underachieving boy (see Carrington & McPhee, 2008; Carrington, Tymms, & Morrell, 2005; Martino & Kehler, 2006; Martino, 2004; Mills, Martino, & Lingard, 2004; House of Representatives Standing Committee, 2002; Education Queensland, 2002; Ontario College of Teachers, 2004; National Education Association, 2003). This has led to the male teacher emerging as central to a project of re-masculinization of elementary schooling that is designed to rehabilitate boys' damaged or failing masculinities (see Lingard & Douglas, 1999; Carrington, 2002; Skelton 2002; Martino & Kehler, 2007). Hence, my aim in this chapter is to expose the limits of such a recuperative masculinity politics by providing a more informed research-based knowledge about the role of male teachers in terms of their capacity to positively influence boys' achievement in schools. I draw on both a recent male teacher recruiting document produced here in Ontario by a consortium of educational stakeholders and a preliminary study into male elementary teachers' perceptions and experiences as teachers. In so doing, I raise important questions about the need for policy makers and educational stakeholders to engage with a broader research-based knowledge about the troubled connection between dominant constructions of masculinity and the gendered construction of elementary school teaching (see Blount, 2005; Coulter & Harper, 2005; Grummet, 1988; Johnston, McKeown, & McEwen, 1999; Martino, 2008; Noddings, 2001; Pepperell & Smedley, 1998; Thornton & Bricheno, 2006).

This is particularly important given that recent policy initiatives surrounding the male teacher debate and the call for more male role models in Australia, North America, and the United Kingdom continue to be driven by a neo-liberal agenda that supports a recuperative masculinity politics (see Carrington, 2002; Lingard & Douglas, 1999; NEA, 2003). Such a politics is downplayed or masked, however, through invoking affirmative action policies that cast both male teachers and boys as victims of the increasing feminization of elementary schooling. *Narrowing the Gender Gap: Attracting Men to Teaching*, produced by a consortium of interest groups and stake holders in Ontario (Ontario College of Teachers, 2004) and the *Male Teachers' Strategy*, produced by Education Queensland in Australia, which represents a strategic plan for the attraction, recruitment and retention of male teachers in the public school system, are examples of such recuperative masculinity politics masquerading as affirmative action policy-making initiatives (see Goward, 2004). In engaging with dominant narratives about role models and the desire for a more gender-balanced workforce, these policy/public documents fail to engage with important issues about the status historically of teaching as woman's work (see Martino, 2008). This is further exacerbated by a failure to address the dynamics of gender politics and, more specifically, relations of masculinity as they are played out and negotiated in male teachers' lives and how these, in turn impact on relations with boys in schools (see Martino & Frank, 2006; Roulsten & Mills, 2000). For example, Foster and Newman (2005) claim that

> The range of competing masculinities that is representative of the complexities of men's experiences in the world 'outside' remains scarcely acknowledged inside the primary school, either by the men themselves or by their female colleagues (p. 342).

This chapter, therefore, is based on a commitment and indeed argues for a more informed policy discussion by educational stakeholders that engages with a broader research-based literature that addresses the significance of male teachers' masculinities within the context of doing women's work (see Carrington, 2002; Francis & Skelton, 2001; King, 1998; Williams, 1993). This involves addressing important issues pertaining to perceived barriers to recruiting male elementary school teachers without resorting to the familiar narratives of invoking male role models as a defeminizing strategy for recuperating hegemonic masculinity that will supposedly result in addressing boys' underachievement and disaffection with schooling (see McCready, 2008).

Addressing Key Assumptions About Male Teacher Recruitment

In the existing literature on teachers as "role models," there are a number of assumptions underlying the current demand for more male teachers to be employed, which may be identified in terms of the following:

- *"Increased numbers of male teachers are needed to address 'the boy problem' because they more attuned to boys' learning needs."* It has been argued that elementary schools are "feminizing institutions," dominated by women teachers, that encourage girls to the detriment of boys (see Mills et al,, 2004; Martino & Kehler, 2006, for a critique of the role of the male teacher vis-à-vis the boy-friendly curriculum; see also Skelton, 2002, 2003). However, Mahony, Hextall, & Menter, (2004) provide evidence that illuminates the extent to which schools are actually becoming more masculinized. For example, in the U.K. context, they argue that the new performance management policy represents "a further move towards masculinization of teaching already evident in the introduction of more didactic teaching styles, reconfigured management-oriented roles of headteachers and policies to recruit more men" (p. 132). Within a policy context committed supposedly to raising standards and ensuring that the education system realizes its full potential, teachers are required to meet *threshold standards* as a basis for establishing a trajectory of career progression and promotion that, Mahony et al. argue, support male teachers. In fact, according to these authors, relative to their numbers, men occupy a disproportionate number of head teacher posts (p 133). Arnot and Miles (2005) attribute this policy shift toward performativity in the school context to a New Labor politics, which has promoted an increased feminization of teaching while simultaneously supporting the re-masculinization of schooling, outlined along the lines elaborated by Mahony et al. (2004). In addition, Arnot & Miles argue that such a policy shift—from a focus on "egalitarianism" to that of "performativity"—has also led to defining underachievement as "a boy problem" while ignoring or failing to address "the production of hierarchical masculinities and laddishness" (p. 173; see Epstein, Elwood, Hey, & Maw, 1998; Martino & Meyenn, 2001; Martino & Pallotta-Chiarolli, 2003; 2005; Jackson, 2002). Elsewhere, boys' underachievement has been attributed explicitly to the feminization of schooling, with the call for more male teachers who are central to implementing a *boy-friendly curriculum* that caters for boys' learning styles (see Martino, 2004; Mitchell, 2004; Ontario Ministry of Education, 2004).
- *"Male teachers are essentially different from female teachers, and as a result teach in different ways."* Because male teachers are considered to be essentially different from their female counterparts, the increasing feminization of elementary schooling is attributed to the problem of boys' underachievement (see Martino & Kehler, 2006; Roulsten & Mills, 2000; Skelton, 2002; Titus, 2004; and Weaver-Hightower, 2003, for a critique of such positions). This often translates into perceptions about the capacity for male teachers to better control

and motivate boys in school (see Johnston et al., 1999; Pepperell & Smedley, 1998). However, there appears to be no evidence that simply increasing the representation of male teachers in elementary schools leads to better educational or social outcomes for boys, or girls for that matter (see Lahelma, 2000; Lingard, Martino, Mills, & Bahr, 2002). Carrington et al. (2005), in fact, question the empirical basis for such claims and provide evidence to the contrary, drawing on their research with 8,978 children, 11 years old, from English elementary schools. They conclude, on the basis of their research findings, that "there was no indication that male teachers were particularly effective with boys, or female teachers with girls" (p 11). They also add that "there was no indication that effective results were associated with male or female teachers, with particularly high ability children" (p 11). In light of their study, Carrington et al. raise important concerns about current recruitment policies that position the male teacher as central to reducing the so-called gender gap in achievement and attitude, which they assert is 'somewhat misplaced' (p 13) (see also Carrington & McPhee, 2008). In addition, other research by Thornton & Brichenco (2002) suggests that there is a correlation between greater numbers of male teachers and poorer discipline in schools. Moreover, these researchers did not discover that higher numbers of male teachers translated into better school achievement levels for boys. Similarly, in the United States, Ehrenberg, Goldhaber, and Brewer (1995) did not find that matching teachers and children by gender and ethnicity impacted on attainment.

- *"Increasing the number of male teachers will provide boys with 'role models' who are better equipped to address their alienation and disaffection with schooling."* Research has exposed the naivety behind such claims or positions, which assume that simply being male is a basis for some sort of positive identification for boys with male teachers that results in increased motivation and willingness to engage in learning (see Carrington et al., 2007; Marsh, Martin, & Cheng, 2008). For example, research has found the exact opposite to be the case, with such forms of identification resulting in problematic forms of male bonding at the basis of which is a desire to reinforce hegemonic heterosexual masculinities (Connolly, 1995; Martino & Frank, 2006; Skelton, 2001). Some research also suggests that such forms of male bonding may be actually detracting or impacting negatively on boys' achievement in schools (Francis & Skelton, 2001, 2005; Francis, 2000; Martino & Pallotta-Chiarolli, 2003; Skelton, 2001, 2002; Warrington & Younger, 2000).

"Narrowing the Gender Gap: Attracting Men to Teaching"

The Ontario College of Teachers (2004), along with a consortium of other stakeholders here in Ontario, produced a document that is committed to narrowing the gender gap in teaching. It represents an exemplary instance of mobilizing a recuperative masculinity politics that is built on many of the problematic assumptions outlined earlier. The document, for example, identifies the problem in terms of "persistent low numbers of males applying to the province's faculties of education." This has contributed, it claims, to the "disparity between the proportions of male and female teachers" in elementary schools, which has "accelerated" to the extent that is has become "a professional and public concern" (p. 2). Such a platform of moral concern forms the basis from which to launch an investigation into the problem of the lack of male role models in schools. This is achieved by providing a review of the literature that is followed by presentation of focus group research conducted with a "cross-section of male high school students, early and second career teachers, senior administrators and education stakeholders" (p. 2). An on-line survey was also conducted targeting male university students. The results of the research are reported and reveal the following:

1   Male high school teachers were not attracted to teaching because of the perception of low salaries and low status and lack of male teacher role models.
2   Male teachers considered initial salaries to be too low and stated that there was need for more male visibility in promoting teaching.
3   Senior administrators identified teacher status and starting salaries as issues impacting on male teacher recruitment and advocated more vigorous marketing and mentoring programs.

Though the series of recommendations offered in this document speak to addressing these concerns, in addition it calls for the Ontario Ministry of Education to support research to determine whether there is a "correlation between achievement of boys and the presence of male teachers in Ontario classrooms" (p. 3). This is in spite of the fact that the document appears to already authorize such a position in the following section, entitled, "Concerning the Gender Gap." Here, reference is made to media reports in which the Education Minister at the time, Gerard Kennedy, is stated as suggesting that male teacher shortage has contributed to boys' underachievement in schools:

> According to media reports in April, 2004, Education Minister Gerard Kennedy, suggested that the male teacher shortage contributed to the poor academic performance levels of boys and young men in

Ontario Classrooms: "We have a problem with boys; male students are struggling in a number of areas," Kennedy told the London Free Press. There is some reasonable research that's suggesting that the lack of male role models in teaching positions can be an influencer here (p. 5).

The Ontario College of Teachers (2004) appears to lend support for such claims while failing to consider the literature outlined in the previous section of this chapter, which provides an empirical basis for arguing the contrary. The point is that literature exists that calls into question the validity of such claims, but it is not cited in this report, which appears to be motivated by a recuperative masculinity politics that is fueled by concerns about the increasing feminization of schooling and its impact on boys' achievement. The report invokes a discourse of the male teacher as "a dying breed" and, hence, positions male teachers as victims of a culture that fails to acknowledge and value men as teachers (p 5). This is related to the sense that it is "somehow inappropriate for male teachers to be in contact with young children" (p. 5). Though this is attributed to the cultural perception that men are less nurturing than women, no attempt is made to draw on the literature, which raises important questions about the status of doing women's work and its historical legacy (see Blount, 2005; Grumet, 1988; Martino, 2008; Williams, 1993). Moreover, the literature that deals with the problematic effects of hegemonic masculinity and its role in negating the feminized attributes of emotionality and caring is glaringly absent from any discussion about the culture that legitimates and recuperates such a gender system in the first place and is built on diametrically opposed binaries for determining legitimate masculinity (see King, 1998; Roulsten & Mills, 2000; Skelton, 2001, 2002, 2003).

The literature review documented by the Ontario College of Teachers includes support for the position that "male role models do matter" (p. 9). Sources such as the report from the Parliamentary Inquiry into Boys Education and the Male Teachers' Strategy produced by Education Queensland in Australia are quoted to validate such claims. This is particularly illuminating, given the significant critique that has been documented regarding the Australian government's role in its support for boys' education, which has been attributed to a neo-liberal and neo-conservative politics that is committed to supporting the assumptions outlined in the previous section, despite the evidence-based research that it has commissioned and published (see Alloway, Freebody, Gilbert, & Muspratt, 2002; Lingard et al., 2002; see also Mills et al, 2004 for a critique of the Male Teachers' Strategy and Mills, Martino, & Lingard, 2007, for a detailed critique of the Parliamentary Inquiry report). Such interventions surrounding the call for more male role models are often driven by common sense understandings about socialization that fail to address the limits imposed by systems of hierarchical masculinity and how boys/male teachers are positioned and take up positions within such unequal power relations.

For the most part, the section that deals with reporting on the research conducted by this consortium of stakeholders fails to contextualize the themes generated by participating subjects in response to the broader research literature. For example, the perception of elementary school teaching as *feminine* or a caregiving profession is never taken up in a way that engages with the research based literature about "uncommon caring" and the homophobic policing of masculinities for male teachers (Drudy, Martin, Woods, & O'Flynn, 2005; King, 1998, 2004; Martino & Frank, 2006; Thornton & Bricheno, 2006). It also fails to engage with other research literature surrounding high school students' perception of and attitudes towards teaching as a potential career choice. For example, Drudy et al. (2005) found that one of the reasons male school leavers in Ireland gave for either choosing or avoiding teaching as a potential career choice was related to their perception of the gender-appropriateness of the profession. For instance, they claim that "the socialization of males and females and the formation of gender identities have been demonstrated to be important factors in the way that men and women orient themselves" (p. 85). Thus, the decision for males to become teachers would appear to go against the dominant socializing influences governing what it means to be appropriately masculine. In fact, Drudy et al. claim that males who actually chose teaching as a career were much less influenced by factors such as pay and prestige and were "much more oriented towards caring and altruistic factors than were males in general" (p. 92).

Though higher pay, job security and the opportunity to act as a male role model emerged as factors that high school students identified as potentially attracting them to the profession in the Ontario of College Teachers' study, in research by Drudy et al., low pay was offered as the fourth frequently offered explanation for the declining numbers of male teachers. The proportion offering low pay as a reason for the declining numbers of teachers was just 8 percent. However, 40.9 percent of male school leavers ranked job conditions as the main reason for choosing elementary teaching with "satisfaction of showing children how to do things" and "teaching as a worthwhile calling" falling far behind, with only 14.3 percent nominating these as top-ranked reasons (p. 101). The female school leavers tended to rank "satisfaction of showing children how to do things" much more highly than the boys (36.5 %), which revealed that gender did appear to be influencing their perceptions of teaching as a profession. Overall, this study found that "boys seemed to be less oriented towards children or less willing to admit an interest in children" but that this did not seem to be related to fears about "false child abuse allegations" documented in the popular press (p. 104). Such studies, not referred to in the Ontario College of Teachers' report, raise important questions about the nature and perception of elementary school teaching as women's work and its impact in terms of potentially conflicting with many males' sense of what is considered to be appropriately masculine. This is accentuated in other studies that document the experiences of male students training to be elementary school teachers who talk about receiving negative reactions from their peers for choosing to study what one male teacher candidate termed "a Mickey Mouse woman's course" (Johnston et al., 1999, p. 60; Thornton & Bricheno, 2006).

This relates specifically to the restrictions imposed by dominant perceptions of masculinity, which are not addressed by what Carrington et al. (2005) identify as "role model recruitment drives" (p. 2; see also Carrington & Skelton, 2003). In short, what the policy makers and stakeholders fail to address within the context of the male teacher debate is the troubled connection between dominant constructions of masculinity and the gendered construction of teaching (see Carrington, 2002). In addition to this, the failure to address the moral panic about pedophilia as a barrier to male recruitment never seems to get addressed by policy makers/stakeholders in terms that speak to the role that homophobia and heterosexism play in the policing of acceptable masculinity as it is embodied by the male elementary school teacher (see Mills, 2004). For example, the Ontario College of Teachers (2004) documents the fear that drives many male elementary school teachers' concerns about how to relate to children and which pertain to potential accusations of sexual misconduct. This is framed within the discursive context of positioning male teachers as victims as opposed to addressing or raising questions about the nature of hegemonic heterosexual masculinities and the limits that they impose on male teachers.

Thus, it is not surprising that not one of the recommendations stipulated by the Ontario College of Teachers' recruitment drive document actually points to the significance of addressing and interrogating hegemonic masculinity and the sort of limits it imposes, with the view to promoting and legitimating less oppressive forms of masculinity. In its failure to cite research-based literature that documents the troubled connections between dominant constructions of masculinity and the gendered construction of teaching, such educational stakeholders actually contribute to recuperating rather than interrogating the limits of normative masculinity.

The Voices of Male Elementary School Teachers

In this section, I draw on interviews with a male elementary school teacher, Ben, age 40, who teaches at an inner-city school in Toronto, and a senior administrative officer, Doug, age 45, a former elementary school teacher who is currently employed by one of the teacher unions in Canada. Both expressed interest in talking to me about their experiences and perceptions as male elementary school teachers. Both were contacted through friends and agreed to be interviewed. The aim of this preliminary research was to examine male teachers' self-perceptions and experiences of being a male teacher.[1] The study was based on the premise, articulated by Coffey & Delamont (2000), that

> By listening to and making sense of teachers' experiences and accounts we are better placed to understand those everyday teaching realities. The work of teaching is not only about managing the classroom and delivering the curriculum, it is also about managing and negotiating biographies, identities and selves (p. 74).

Given the concerns and issues raised about hegemonic masculinity in the research literature on male teachers, I thought that talking to male teachers was one way of providing a deeper understanding of the restrictions that dominant perceptions of masculinity impose (see Carrington, 2002; Francis & Skelton, 2001). Questions such as the following were used as a guide in the interview situation: Why did you choose to become a teacher? Can you talk about your experiences in the classroom? Are there any issues that impact on male teachers specifically? In presenting the perspectives of these male elementary school teachers, my aim is to raise important questions about male teachers' perceptions of masculinity in a way that points to the discursive limits imposed by the male role model debate as it has been articulated by the popular media and educational stakeholders in Ontario (see Mitchell, 2004; Ontario College of Teachers, 2004).

Ben works in a culturally diverse school with a large Tamil and South Asian population in inner-city Toronto. There are also many students from Chinese and African backgrounds at the school. Ben mentions that he has only one white student in his year 4 class. The dynamics of gender and masculinity are identified early on by Ben in terms of how he situates (or rather locates) himself within the professional context of doing women's work (see Williams, 1993). He identifies elementary schools as "female institutions" in the way that they are "shaped and the way that they are run," but does not see this as problematic or in terms of a deficit requiring the re-masculinization of schooling. In fact, it is this very aspect of elementary schooling that attracts or is attractive to men who are either gay or don't feel the need to assert traditional masculinity. "They tend to be more comfortable here," he claims.

> I think that there is a reasonably small proportion of men who would find the dynamics of elementary schools comfortable. I'm wondering exactly what I mean when I say that, as to what those feminine dynamics are. Well, my partner for example works in a very male workplace and there is this edge of sort of aggression and competition and strategy and maneuvering which tends to take place very much in his workplace which I notice very little in elementary schools. There just tends to be a milder, more caring, more conciliatory style of interaction among staff, partly because it's mainly female.

Elementary schools are constructed as gendered spaces wherein teaching and the culture of the workplace are defined in terms of the feminized capacity for nurturing and caring (see Noddings, 2001). But, as King (1998) argues, historically this social construction of the elementary school teacher "has been loaded with features that surround the constructs of female and mother" (p 9; see also Sugg, 1978). This is highlighted by Ben, who, however, is able to embrace such a culture without succumbing apparently to the stigma attached to the devaluation of the feminine:

> I think elementary schools are quite feminine. I mean if we're looking at what's traditionally been defined as masculine values and feminine values, you see much more of the feminine values manifest in an elementary school.

Ben links this to the dislocation of masculinity for some boys who have been taught to reject such values or rather who have been socialized at home to adopt a more traditional masculinity. This leads him to account for some boys' behavioral problems, which he perceives to be a manifestation of resistance to female teachers' exercise of power and authority in elementary classrooms and schools (see Robinson, 2000):

> I think one of the things that happens because of that is that your behavioral problems in elementary schools tend to be almost all boys because they are boys who very often are socialized in one way at home toward a much more traditionally masculine way of behavior and then they bump against the very feminized institution or schooling system where all the authority usually comes from women, and it's difficult for them to adjust. I'm not saying that that's the case with all behavioral boys, but I think sometimes that conflict of the gender of power and the gender of spaces does affect student behavior.

Here Ben refers to the threat posed by female teachers for boys with their gendered expectations regarding male authority. However, rather than resorting to simplistic accounts that recuperate the male teacher as a role model and disciplinarian for problem boys, he draws attention to the dynamics of masculinity for boys who respond defensively to female authority in elementary schools. He attributes this to a system of institutionalized patriarchy in which boys learn to associate a certain form of power and authority with males rather than females.

Ben also talks about his perception of the concentration of males teaching upper levels or the higher grades of elementary school (see Carrington, 2002; Skelton, 2003). For example, he indicates that there are more males teaching at the intermediate level (grades 7 and 8):

> My guess is that it has to do with it being a more parental and even maternal role the younger that you get with kids. It's not just about cognitive development and imparting information and developing ideas, it's much more about helping kids to get along, providing in Grade 1 the whole wiping the noses, doing up the coats sort of thing. I think that a lot of men are not generally interested in that more parental role with younger kids.

Ben explains that it is the emphasis on parenting, and by implication mothering, that may explain why many males choose not to embrace teaching younger children (see Grummet, 1988; King, 1998). He adds that being a gay male, however, sets him apart from these men. For example, he indicates that his motivation or desire for teaching younger children may in fact be linked to the realization that he will not have any children of his own:

> And perhaps not surprisingly, among the elementary school teachers, at least that I'm aware of, who are male, a goodly percentage are gay. I actually must reflect that that's probably part of the motivation for me as well. Not having plans to have children of my own, there is a certain parental function which is played out in interacting with younger children on a daily basis.

As a consequence, he embraces what he perceives to be the emphasis on the parenting and maternal function of teaching younger children in elementary schools—wiping their noses and helping them with their coats—as opposed to positioning himself as just a teacher who imparts knowledge and who is harbinger of masculinity to prepubescent youth. This raises important questions about issues of sexual orientation and how they impact on male teachers' self-perceptions and perception of doing women's work (see King, 1998, 2004; Silin, 1997).

However, though Ben is clearly defying such a gender regime grounded in the bifurcation gender identity categories and practices, the other male teacher's account of being an elementary school teacher serves to solidify and reinscribe essentialist notions of gender development and identity as they pertain to both teacher and student. Doug (age 45), who is currently employed by a teachers' union in Canada, talks at length about his own desire—which he sees as representative of many male elementary school teachers, in general—for embracing what Ben identifies as the educative versus parenting function of teaching. These are understood in terms of discourses that rely on bifurcating gender through pitting women's work—with all that this entails with regards to solidifying the "mothering" or maternal function of teaching younger children—against what is considered to be more natural for men in terms of their capacity (or rather predisposition) for being more rational in their approach to dealing with children. This is understood in terms of males' preference for the intellectual challenge of problem-solving methods and approaches to teaching. This, for Doug, is what he perceives to be the domain of the upper levels of elementary schooling which is captured in his comments here:

> There is something I think intriguing myself personally in dealing with the student who is capable of beginning to make logical connections at a more sophisticated level. Solving problems with them is more collaborative, it's not you providing the solution or you're making solution happen, but you're allowing them to mature. You can have a dialogue with them. There's something exciting about seeing a mind that's beginning to take on more adult orientations in terms of the way they look at the world and the questions and conflicts that they're debating within themselves. So I think that that is intrinsically a reward, at least it was for me in the intermediate classroom.

Such comments are made within the overall context of differentiating his desire and compatibility for teaching at the intermediate level with his wife's preference for teaching kindergarten children. He prefaces this following comment with a statement about male teachers' "natural affinity" in terms of how this translates into the grade assignments allocated to male teachers at the intermediate levels:

> I could definitely say it had more to do with the comfort level, the motivators of the individual. As I said, my wife is a teacher and she certainly is very comfortable, very happy teaching kindergarten and yet her experience at the intermediate level would be what led her to not look forward to those opportunities and certainly she would do

her best to avoid them on the long term basis. And certainly I can say that I would equally not prefer primary teaching assignment for any length of time.

This relies on a limited notion or understanding of choice. There is a sense that a female's preference for teaching younger children and a male teacher's preference for teaching older children are merely the result of a natural predisposition or inclination. Such an essentialist discourse leads Doug to adopt a position that inscribes men as disadvantaged, particularly with regard to the discriminatory requirements governing admission to Teacher Education Faculties in Canada. He claims that admission and application requirements stipulated for these programs have an "inherent bias" that works against males:

> Well I think it's a bit of a self-perpetuating myth in that if you have fewer males in the profession they're perceived as not being a male profession and it sort of feeds upon itself to some degree and it's beginning to perhaps accelerate. Maybe it was going to reach that. I've certainly taught a number of students who had never had a male teacher until they reached grade 7. So if those students have internalised that, it may be something that's going to inevitably come back when they're making career choices. That's one of the things we're trying to look at in terms of the decision making. There's many other areas, by no means thinking it's an issue but certainly one that was suggested, the way in which admissions are accepted to the faculties of Education may have an inherent bias. We have some hint of that in the research we've done with students in that male teenagers don't perceive themselves as having many experiences interacting with younger children on the one hand. On the other hand when we asked them a slightly different question they can identify where they do and yet clearly part of the decision for an admission to a faculty of education is based upon an application form that asks for those type of experiences. So if you don't consciously recognize that you've had those experiences you may feel that you won't be successful, you may not then apply. So there has been some suggestion of that but at this point have no conclusion, it's simply that the question has been asked and certainly some of the work we've done, teenage males seem to have some difficulty identifying specifically where they had interactions with younger children that may lead them to a non teaching career.

Men here emerge as victims of a process that denies males access to a profession on the basis of their lack of personal experience of working with younger children. The problem of attracting and recruiting male teachers is also simplistically reduced to the failure of having visible male role models in elementary school classrooms. The male role model discourse is invoked within a context that positions male teachers as harbingers of masculinity to a profession and to boys who risk being feminized. This is made clear in the following comment in which Doug positions male teachers as providing important rites of passage for prepubescent boys:

> I mean I've had the experience, sort of it's a common experience of grade 6 teachers that over one weekend in February the children went away and suddenly came back as pre adolescent, hormone raging students and it was very marked, very apparent and it was an experience I think certainly other teachers who have taught grade 6 have had. So they are reaching at a point where a number of things happening within their physiology that are making them look at the world differently, react differently. So that's part of the experience of an intermediate teacher is to deal with that pre pubescent issue, it certainly is very striking.

This leads him to resort to essentialist accounts of gender to explain why female teachers tend to have problems disciplining boys, which leads them to seek support and help from the male intermediate teachers, who are better able to deal with boys' behavioral problems.

> I think if you interviewed female teachers as to their perception of their male colleagues I think it would be interesting. My guess is that they would readily identify that males gravitate to the intermediate, that that's done for reasons similar to the ones I've described, very much when there is a crisis in the school particularly if it's e a disciplinary issue at a lower grade that the intermediate teacher will get called upon to go down and lend support. I would suggest that's done based usually on gender, it has really very little to do with anything else.

The point is that to rely on essentialist frameworks for explaining differences between males and females leads to a justification of the status quo and, hence, a reinstatement of traditional or hegemonic masculinities. Such frameworks rely on an implicit sexism and misogyny that is veiled by a common-sense discourse about what comes natural to men and women and boys and girls in terms of their inclinations, preferences, ways of thinking, and behaving.

Both these interviews highlight the extent to which particular constructions of masculinity inform male teachers' positions vis-à-vis their perception of elementary school teaching. Particular explanatory frameworks inform male teachers' understanding about the profession and nature of teaching in elementary schools. Just documenting these teachers' perspectives provides some insight into the dynamics of masculinity and sexuality in terms that require a more sophisticated analysis than that provided by the popular media and educational stakeholders advocating male role models as a means by which to address the problem of boys' underachievement and disaffection with schooling (see Carrington & McPhee, 2008).

Conclusion

In this chapter, my aim has been to raise some questions about the limits imposed by those advocating more male role models in elementary schools as a means by which to address the problem of boys' underachievement. By drawing on research-based literature that is not referred to in many male teacher recruitment-driving policy initiatives, the focus has been on identifying the gaps and silences in such texts and the assumptions informing the construction of both male teachers and boys as victims of the increasing feminization of elementary schooling. What is denied is a more sophisticated research-based knowledge about the influence of hegemonic heterosexual masculinities and the limits they impose on both boys' and men's lives in schools (see Francis & Skelton, 2001; Martino & Frank, 2006). This was also exemplified by the inclusion of two male elementary school teachers' voices as a basis for examining their perceptions of elementary school teaching and their understanding of the dynamics of masculinity vis-à-vis men doing women's work. On the basis of the literature reviewed and research documented in this chapter, caution is advocated regarding the claims made about the capacity of male teachers as role models to positively influence boys' achievement in schools. Despite the truth status that is ascribed to such claims by educational stakeholders and policy makers concerned about male teacher shortage, it is important to emphasize that there is no empirical basis for linking the influence of male role models to increased achievement for boys in schools. In this capacity, this chapter highlights the need for a more informed evidence-based approach to addressing the boy problem in schools and the role that male teachers might play in addressing issues of gender justice.

Note

1. This chapter is based on a research project funded by the Social Sciences and Humanities Research Council of Canada entitled, "The influence of male elementary school teachers as role models" (410-2006-115381).

References

Alloway, N., Freebody, P., Gilbert, P., & Muspratt, S. (2002). *Boys, literacy and schooling: Expanding the repertoires of practice.* Melbourne: Curriculum Corporation.

Arnot, M., & Miles, P. (2005). A reconstruction of the gender agenda: The contradictory gender dimensions in New Labour's educational and economic policy. *Oxford Review of Education, 31*(1), 173–189.

Blount, J. (2005). *Fit to teach: Same-sex desire, gender, and school work in the twentieth century.* Albany: State University of New York Press.

Carrington, B. (2002). A quintessentially feminine domain? Student teachers' constructions of primary teaching as a career. *Educational Studies, 28*(3), 287–303.

Carrington, B., & McPhee, A. (2008). Boys' underachievement and the feminization of teaching. *Journal of Education for Teaching, 34*(2), 109–120.

Carrington, B., & Skelton, C. (2003). Re-thinking "role-models": Equal opportunities in teacher recruitment in England and Wales. *Journal of Educational Policy, 18*(3), 253–265.

Carrington, B., Tymms, P., & Merrell, C. (2005). Role models, school improvement and the gender gap—do men bring out the best in boys and women and the best in girls? Paper presented to EARLI 2005 Conference, University of Nicosia.

Carrington, B., Francis, B., Hutchings, M., Skelton, C., Reade, B., & Hall, I (2007). Does the gender of the teacher really matter? Seven to eight-year-olds' accounts of their interactions with their teachers. *Educational Studies, 33*(4), 397–413.

Coffey, A., & Delamont, S. (2000). *Feminism and the classroom teacher: Research, praxis and pedagogy.* London & New York: RoutledgeFalmer.

Connolly, P. (1995). Boys will be boys? Racism, sexuality and the construction of masculine identities among infant boys. In J. Holland & M. Blair (Eds.), *Equality and difference: Debates and issues in feminist research and pedagogy* (pp. 169–196). Clevedon: Multilingual Matters.

Coulter, R., & Harper, H. (2005). *History is hers: Women teachers in twentieth century Ontario.* Calgary, Alberta: Detselig Enterprises Ltd.

Drudy, S., Martin, M., Woods, M., & O'Flynn, J. (2005). *Men and the classroom: Gender imbalance in teaching.* London & NY: Routledge.

Education Queensland. (2002). *Male teachers' strategy 2002–2005.* Brisbane: Education Queensland.

Ehrenberg, R. G., Goldhaber, D. D., & Brewer, D. J. (1995). Do teachers' race, gender, and ethnicity matter? Evidence from the National Education Longitudinal Study of 1988. *Industrial and Labor Relations Review, 48*, 547–561.

Epstein, D., Elwood, J., Hey, V., & Maw, J. (Eds.). (1998). *Failing boys?: Issues in gender and achievement.* Buckingham: Open University Press.

Foster, T., & Newman, E. (2005). Just a knock back? Identity bruising on the route to becoming a male primary school teacher. *Teachers and Teaching: Theory and Practice, 11*(4), 341–358.

Francis, B. (2000). *Boys, girls and achievement: Addressing the classroom issues.* London: RoutledgeFalmer.

Francis, B., & Skelton, C. (2001). Men teachers and the construction of heterosexual masculinity in the classroom. *Sex Education, 1*(1), 9–21.

Francis, B., & Skelton, C. (2005). *Reassessing gender and achievement: Questioning contemporary key debates.* Abingdon, UK: Routledge.

Goward, P. (2004, March 11). Better pay would lure more men into schools. *The Australian*, p.15.

Grumet, M. (1988). *Bitter milk: Women and teaching.* Amherst: University of Massachusetts Press.

House of Representatives Standing Committee on Education and Training. (2002). *Boys' education: Getting it right.* Canberra: Commonwealth Government of Australia.

Jackson, C. (2002). Laddishness as a self-worth protection strategy. *Gender and Education, 14*(1), 37–51.

Johnston, J., McKeown, E., & McEwen, A. (1999). Choosing primary teaching as a career: The perspectives of males and females in training. *Journal of Education for Teaching, 25*(1), 55–64.

King, J. (1998). *Uncommon caring: Learning from men who teach young children.* New York and London: Teachers' College Press.

King, J. (2004). The (im)possibility of gay teachers for young children. *Theory into Practice, 43*(2), 122–127.

Lahelma, E. (2000). Lack of male teachers: A problem for students or teachers? *Pedagogy, Culture and Society, 8*(2), 173–186.

Lingard, B., & Douglas, P. (1999). *Men engaging feminisms: Profeminism, backlashes and schooling.* Buckingham: Open University Press.

Lingard, B., Martino, W., Mills, M., & Bahr, M. (2002). *Addressing the educational needs of boys.* Canberra: Department of Education, Science and Training. Retrieved from http://www.dest.gov.au/sectors/school_education/publications_resources/profiles/addressing_educational_needs_of_boys.htm

Mahony, P., Hextall, I., & Menter, I. (2004). Threshold assessment and performance management: Modernizing or masculinizing teaching in England. *Gender and Education, 16*(2), 132–149.

Marsh, H., Martin, A., & Cheng, J. (2008). A multilevel perspective on gender in classroom motivation and climate: Potential benefits of male teachers for boys. *Journal of Educational Psychology, 100*(1), 78–95.

Martino, W. (2004). The boy problem: Boys, schooling and masculinities. In R. Transit (Ed.), *Disciplining the child via the discourse of the professions* (pp. 19–34). Springfield, IL: Charles C Thomas.

Martino, W. (2008). Male teachers as role models: Addressing issues of masculinity, pedagogy and the re-masculinization of schooling. *Curriculum Inquiry, 38*(2), 189–223.

Martino, W., & Frank, B. W. (2006). The tyranny of surveillance: Male teachers and the policing of masculinities in a single sex school. *Gender & Education, 18*(1), 17–33.

Martino, W., & Kehler, M. (2006). Male teachers and the 'boy problem: An issue of recuperative masculinity politics. *McGill Journal of Education, 41*(2), 113–131.

Martino, W., & Kehler, M. (2007). Gender-based literacy reform: A question of challenging or recuperating gender binaries. *Canadian Journal of Education, 30*(2), 406–431.

Martino, W. & Meyenn, B. (eds), 2001. *What about the boys?: Issues of masculinity and schooling*, Buckingham: Open University Press.

Martino, W., & Pallotta-Chiarolli, M. (2003). *So what's a boy?: Addressing issues of masculinity and schooling*. Buckingham: Open University Press.

Martino, W., & Pallotta-Chiarolli, M. (2005). *Being normal is the only way to be: Boys and adolescent perspectives on gender and school*. Sydney: UNSW Press.

McCreedy, L. (2008). Perspectives on the troubles of the Black and Latino Male School Intervention Study (BLMSIS). Paper presented at the AERA, Annual Meeting, New York, March 24–28.

Mills, M. (2004). Male teachers, homophobia, misogyny and teacher education. *Teaching Education, 15*(1), 27–39.

Mills, M., Martino, W., & Lingard, B. (2004). Issues in the male teacher debate: Masculinities, misogyny and homophobia. *British Journal of the Sociology of Education, 25*(3), 355–369.

Mills, M., Martino, W., & Lingard, B. (2007). Getting boys' education "right": The Australian government's Parliamentary Inquiry Report as an exemplary instance of recuperative masculinity politics. *British Journal of the Sociology of Education, 28*(1), 5–21.

Mitchell, A. (2004, January 17). Goodbye Mr. Chips. *Globe and Mail*, p. F1.

National Education Association. (2003, October). *The guy teacher*. Retrieved December 2, 2006, from http://www.nea.org/neatoday/0310/cover.html

Noddings, N. (2001). The care tradition: Beyond add women and stir. *Theory into Practice, 40*(1), 29–35.

Ontario College of Teachers. (2004). *Narrowing the gender gap: Attracting men to teaching*. Retrieved July 1, 2006, from http://www.oct.ca/publications/documents.aspx?lang=en-CA

Ontario Ministry of Education. (2004). *Me read? No way!* Toronto: Queens Printer for Ontario.

Pepperell, S., & Smedley, S. (1998). Calls for more men in primary teaching: Problematizing issues. *International Journal of Inclusive Education, 2*(4), 341–357.

Robinson, K. (2000). Great tits, miss!: The silencing of male students' sexual harassment of female teachers in secondary schools: A focus on gendered authority. *Discourse, 21*(1), 75–90.

Roulston, K., & Mills, M. (2000). Male teachers in feminised teaching areas: Marching to the men's movement drums. *Oxford Review of Education, 26*(1), 221–237.

Silin, J. (1997). The pervert in the classroom. In J. Tobin (Ed.), *Making a place for pleasure in early childhood education* (pp. 214–234). New Haven & London, CT: Yale University Press.

Skelton, C. (2001). *Schooling the boys: Masculinities and primary education*. Buckingham: Open University Press.

Skelton, C. (2002). The feminisation of schooling or re-masculinising primary education? *International Studies in Sociology of Education, 12*(1), 77–96.

Skelton, C. (2003). Male primary teachers and perceptions of masculinity. *Education Review*, 55(2), 195–210.

Sugg, R. (1978). *Motherteacher: The feminization of American education.* Charlottesville: University Press of Virginia.

Thornton, M., & Bricheno, P. (2006). *Missing men in education.* Stoke-on-Trent: Trentham.

Thornton, M., & Brichenco, P. (2002). Staff gender balance in primary schools. Paper presented at BERA 2002, University of Exeter, September 12–14.

Titus, J. (2004). Boy trouble: Rhetorical framing of boys' underachievement. *Discourse*, 25(2), 145–169.

Warrington, M., & Younger, M. (2000). The other side of the gender gap. *Gender and Education*, 12(4), 493–507.

Weaver-Hightower, M. (2003). The "boy turn" in research on gender and education. *Review of Educational Research*, 73(4), 471–498.

Williams, C. (1993). *Doing "women's work": Men in nontraditional occupations.* Newbury Park, London & New Delhi: Sage.

Index